HANDBOOKS

TAHOE

ANN MARIE BROWN

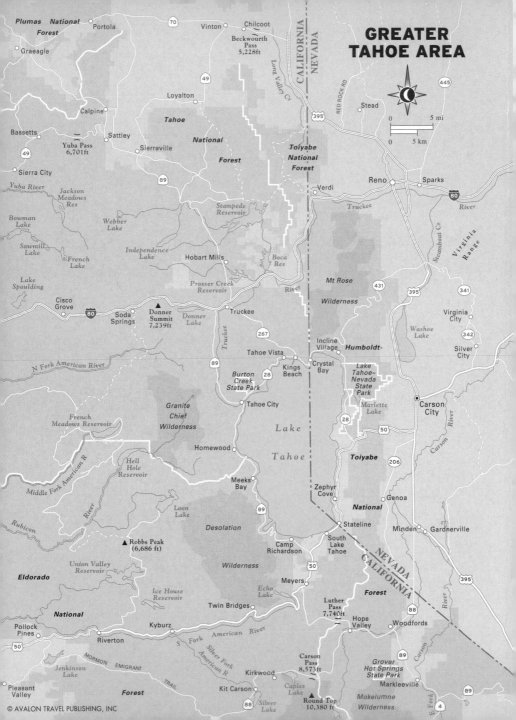

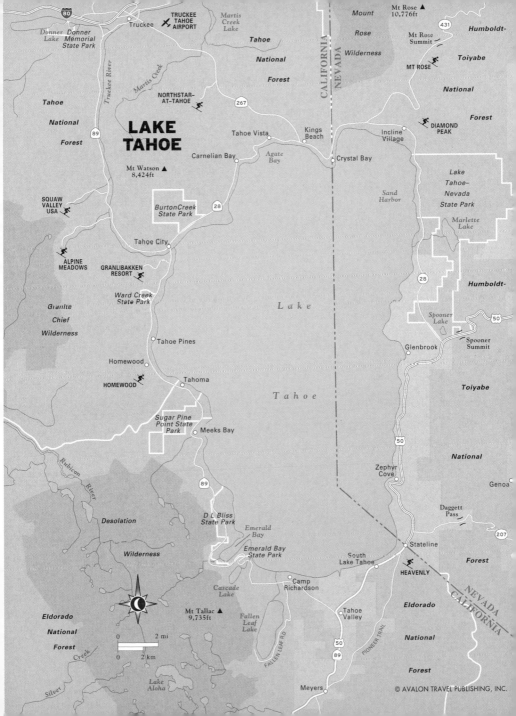

DISCOVER TAHOE

To most visitors, the Tahoe region is clearly defined by its 22-mile-long, azure-blue lake – "a noble sheet of blue water lifted six thousand three hundred feet above the level of the sea, and walled in by a rim of snow-clad mountain peaks," to quote the oft-quoted words of Mark Twain. The 10th deepest lake in the world – 1,645 feet at its deepest point – and third deepest in North America, Lake Tahoe is also blessed with remarkable water clarity and a boulder-lined, sandy shoreline that makes it one of the most photogenic lakes in the West. By any measure, Lake Tahoe can be counted among the notable treasures of North America's landscape.

Bordered by three federally designated wilderness areas – Desolation, Granite Chief, and Mount Rose – plus much of Tahoe National Forest, and numerous state parks, the Tahoe basin is a veritable playground for outdoors enthusiasts. It's also a major tourist destination, with more than 250,000 visitors per day pouring in on summer holidays. Besides ogling the world-famous lake, most

Lake Tahoe as seen from the Rubicon Trail

summer visitors come to hike, mountain bike, golf, or enjoy the wide variety of water sports. If you ever wanted to try rock climbing, fly-fishing, horseback riding, sailing, ballooning, or backcountry skiing, Tahoe is the place to do it. Commercial services for outdoor-oriented visitors abound, offering every kind of equipment rental imaginable as well as expert guiding and tour services.

In summer, getting out on the water tops most travelers' itin-eraries. Sign up for a boat cruise on the lake where, from the upper deck of a stern-wheeler paddleboat, visitors can cruise Mississippi River-style in the Tahoe sunshine, or peer into the lake's crystal-clear depths aboard a glass-bottom sailboat. Adventurous travelers can pilot their own watercraft – everything from a fast ride on a Jet Ski or Waverunner to a mellow paddle in a colorful kayak. For a whitewater adventure, raft a wild ride on the Lower Truckee or East Fork Carson Rivers, or opt for a much gentler float down the Upper Truckee River in an inflatable raft or inner tube. Fly-fishers can cast

The trusty steeds at Zephyr Cove Stables can handle even the most precious load.
© ANN MARIE BROWN

for rainbow trout in dozens of streams and watercourses, while boat anglers can troll the depths of Donner Lake, Fallen Leaf Lake, or even Lake Tahoe itself, in search of a trophy mackinaw.

Hikers and backpackers have hundreds of miles of trails to choose from, ranging from easy strolls along Lake Tahoe's shoreline to strenuous multiday treks in the wilderness. The 165-mile Tahoe Rim Trail makes a full circuit around the lake, tracing the mountain rim at elevations ranging from 6,300 to 10,333 feet. The Desolation Wilderness is one of the most heavily visited wilderness areas in the United States. The region's popularity is warranted; Desolation's stark granite landscape and multiple dozens of alpine lakes are some of the most scenic in the entire Sierra Nevada.

Mountain bikers consider the Tahoe area a mecca, with hundreds of miles of dirt trails to ride, including the famous Flume Trail. Casual cyclists on both fat and skinny tires enjoy the substantial network of paved, level bike paths that line the north, west, and south shores of the lake. The paths incorporate a variety of sightseeing destinations, including swimming beaches, picnic areas, and historic sites, so families can easily fill an entire day using only a bike for transportation.

Wild tiger lilies grow near streams and wet areas.

Although a greater number of visitors pour into Tahoe in the summer months than in winter, it is Tahoe's world-class ski resorts that have made the lake an internationally recognized destination. More than a dozen alpine ski resorts are located near the lake including Squaw Valley USA, the largest ski resort in California, which rose to fame after hosting the 1960 Winter Olympic Games. And with a wide range of "non-vertical" activities available in Tahoe's snowy wonderland – from ice-skating to dogsled rides to snowmobile tours to sipping hot chocolate beside a roaring fire – even those who don't ski or snowboard can enjoy the lake in winter.

Year-round, travelers arrive in droves to play the odds at high-rise casinos on the Nevada side of the lake, where gambling is legal. These big South Shore casinos attract thousands of visitors who come to Tahoe for its indoor recreation opportunities, including big-name entertainment, elegant restaurants, and ample nightlife. Fourteen golf courses around the lake provide more "civilized" outdoor fun, from low-priced public courses to exclusive private clubs.

With all this activity, tourism is a billion-dollar industry. More than 1,000 motels, hotels, and resorts vie for visitor dollars, along with

a verdant meadow below the summit of Ralston Peak

an even greater number of restaurants and other tourism-related businesses. Unfortunately, this commercialism extracts a toll: traffic jams and packed parking lots are common around the lake; pollution threatens Lake Tahoe's famous water clarity; and much of Tahoe's 72-mile shoreline is paved over and lined with private property.

The great naturalist John Muir fought unsuccessfully for the preservation of Lake Tahoe as a national park. Fortunately, the efforts of Muir and other preservationists have not fallen on deaf ears. Although Lake Tahoe never gained the benefit of federal protection, the Tahoe basin is managed by a passel of planning agencies that recognize the importance of Tahoe's environmental health – not just for biological reasons, but also as key to the region's economic prosperity. Meanwhile, visitors can enjoy the wide-ranging abundance Lake Tahoe offers, including a surprising amount of urban amenities set within the frame of its compelling mountain scenery. Tahoe is one of few places on earth where, if you choose to, you can hike to a pristine wilderness area, shop for a dinner dress, dine at a trendy bistro, and gamble the night away, all in a single day at the lake.

Colorful aspen groves attract photographers and nature lovers to Tahoe each autumn.
© ANN MARIE BROWN

Contents

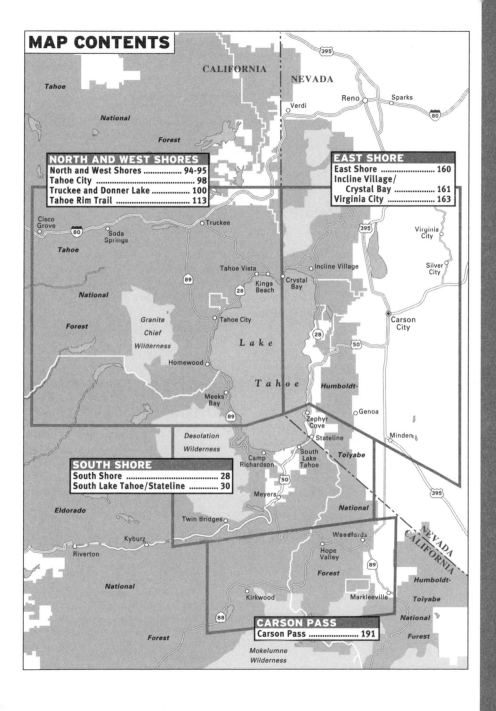

MAP CONTENTS

CALIFORNIA

NEVADA

Tahoe

National

Forest

Reno   Sparks

Verdi

80

Cisco
Grove   80
         Soda
         Springs

Tahoe

Truckee

395

Virginia
City

Silver
City

National

Tahoe Vista

89

28

Kings
Beach

Crystal
Bay

Incline Village

Forest

Granite
Chief

Wilderness

Tahoe City

Homewood

L a k e

Carson
City

28

50

T a h o e

Humboldt-

Meeks
Bay

89

Desolation

Wilderness

Zephyr
Cove

Stateline

Genoa

Minden

Toiyabe

Camp
Richardson

South
Lake
Tahoe

Eldorado

Meyers
50

National

395

Twin Bridges

Kyburz

Riverton

National

Woodfords

Hope
Valley

89

NEVADA
CALIFORNIA

Forest

Humboldt-

Kirkwood

Markleeville

Toiyabe

88

Forest

National

Mokelumne
Wilderness

The Lay of the Land

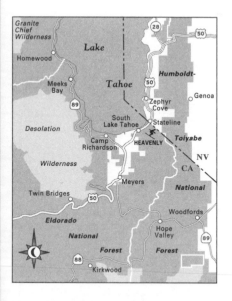

SOUTH SHORE

Perched on either side of the California–Nevada border, the twin cities of **South Lake Tahoe** and **Stateline** are comprised of a mix of high-rise casino resorts, upscale restaurants, fast-food joints, low-budget motels, luxury condos, and quaint cabins. The main attraction is **Heavenly Ski Resort** and its high-speed **gondola.** The atmosphere is decidedly urban, with traffic jams common and a constant parade of cars on Highway 50, the main drag. Restaurants and shops are within easy walking distance, and shuttles and buses run constantly. In summer, myriad activities are located within blocks of the downtown areas, including golfing, swimming, boating, and sightseeing cruises on the lake. Or escape the throngs and head out to nearby trailheads for adventures in Tahoe's spectacular scenery.

NORTH AND WEST SHORES

Tahoe City, the biggest town on the North Shore, offers plenty of lodgings, shops, restaurants, and recreation activities—but is more laid-back than the South Shore's cities. The most famous sight is the aptly named Fanny Bridge. The West Shore is even more sedate, with small hamlets offering a few restaurants, quaint lodgings, and lake-related activities. Along the west side of the lake are two state parks: Sugar Pine Point and D. L. Bliss and miles of Tahoe National Forest lands. Here, hikers, bikers, and cross-country skiers enjoy miles of trails. To the west of Tahoe City lies **Truckee** and **Donner Summit,** an area with the best snow conditions around the lake and multiple major ski resorts, including famous **Squaw Valley, Alpine Meadows,** and **Northstar-at-Tahoe.**

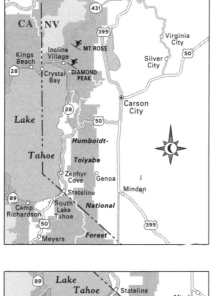

EAST SHORE

The East Shore on the Nevada side still has an abundance of shoreline protected as parkland and open to the public. A 20-mile stretch from Incline Village south to **Zephyr Cove** is almost entirely undeveloped, with little besides forests and occasional vistas of Tahoe's boulder-strewn shoreline. This is where beach-lovers have the best chance at claiming a private cove, and hikers and mountain bikers can enjoy some of the best lake views. Businesses and services are located north at the twin towns of **Crystal Bay** and **Incline Village.** A handful of casinos and two first-rate golf courses are found here, and just a few miles away are two alpine ski resorts—**Diamond Peak and Mount Rose.** Further east and less than an hour away, you can relive the Wild West with a visit to **Virginia City.**

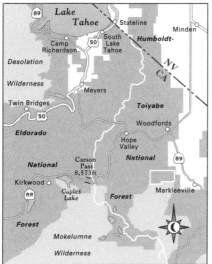

CARSON PASS

The heart of Carson Pass is less than an hour from bustling South Lake Tahoe, but psychologically it's a world away. "Developed" is a relative term here; there is little in the way of visitor services except for a few scattered cabin resorts. Those who choose to explore here find high peaks, alpine lakes, fields of wildflowers, and dramatic Sierra scenery. Most of this land is encompassed in Alpine County, one of the least populated counties. The biggest town, **Markleeville,** has a population of only a few hundred people. Its numbers are boosted substantially by the visitors who flock here in summer for hiking, mountain biking, and some of the best fishing anywhere in the Sierra, and in winter for downhill and cross-country skiing.

Planning Your Trip

Since Tahoe is a year-round destination, travelers should plan their visits according to how they want to spend their time. Snow can fall as early as mid-October, and the spring melt can hold off till mid-June. The most dependable months for skiing and winter sports are usually December–March. Summer is a too-brief season that lasts only about three months (mid-June–early October), and in that time thousands of recreationists take to Tahoe's roads, trails, and lakeshore.

For the best experience, it is wise to plan a visit outside of summer and winter weekends, especially holiday weekends. The lovely autumn off-season (September and October) is one of the least crowded and most pleasant periods at the lake, when Tahoe's abundant aspen groves put on their annual autumn color show. After Labor Day, rates at most Tahoe lodgings drop considerably, and they remain low until the ski season starts, usually at the end of November or in early December.

WHEN TO GO

Which season is best at Lake Tahoe? Each month of the year has its own myriad charms. With more than 300 days of sunshine per year on average, visitors can enjoy many pleasant days around the lake year-round. The **summer** months, June–August, are ideal for outdoor recreation and lazing around the lake. The Tahoe region is blessed with typical Sierra summer weather: warm, clear days with temperatures in the 70s and low 80s (Fahrenheit), and cool nights with temperatures in the 40s and 50s.

Autumn is also a fine time to visit Lake Tahoe. Much of the region is graced with groves of deciduous aspen trees, which put on a splendid show of color every fall. Temperatures are generally cooler in September and October as the hours of daylight shorten. Still, the entire region, including the peaks, trails, and passes of the high country, often remains open and accessible until late October or early November, when the first snowfall arrives.

For many Tahoe regulars, **winter** is the main event. Starting as early as mid-November and often lasting into April, the season of snow beckons skiers, snowboarders, and winter-sports aficionados from all over the globe. Because the timing of snowfall and snowmelt vary greatly from year to year, always phone ahead for condition updates before planning your trip.

The quietest season in Lake Tahoe is **spring**. Lowest visitation levels are recorded March 1–May 15, when most people's thoughts have turned away from skiing, even though there is often plenty of snow until late April. In the spring months, snow levels are still too high to allow for hiking, mountain biking, and other trail-related sports, although this can be a good time for backcountry skiing and snowshoeing.

WHAT TO TAKE

If you're visiting Lake Tahoe for the first time, you may be surprised to find that this mountainous region is by no means remote or cut off from the trappings and comforts of civilization. In fact, Tahoe has all the amenities of most small cities. Within a few miles of any spot around the lake's perimeter, you'll find major chain grocery stores, restaurants of both the upscale and hole-in-the-wall variety (and everything in between), lodgings of all types, gas stations, post offices, and even coffeehouses and tanning salons. This greatly relieves the pressure of packing for your trip to Tahoe. If you choose to, you can leave almost everything at home except for the clothes on your back. Anything you need, you can buy, particularly in the big towns of Tahoe City, South Lake Tahoe, and Stateline.

In the summer months, a few personal items you might want to pack are **hiking boots** or sturdy shoes for walking, and a small **day pack** or fanny pack. Even nonhikers are often inspired to take a walk on one of Lake Tahoe's myriad trails. Sturdy shoes or hiking boots are far more comfortable, and a lot safer, than the casual sightseeing shoes you might wear around town. A small day pack or fanny pack is useful for holding a bottle of water, a snack, and your camera.

It's also wise to bring a variety of **clothing for layering.** Weather changes constantly in the Sierra Nevada Mountains; it's smart to pack rain gear, jackets, and clothes for both warm and cool weather—even though you may spend your entire vacation in nothing but shorts and a T-shirt.

The general rule of thumb for summer trips to Lake Tahoe: Bring warm clothes for eve-nings (especially if you're camping) and layers for daytime. Always carry lightweight rain gear with you, as summer afternoon thunderstorms are common. Spring and fall are cooler, so pack warmer layers.

For winter trips to the lake, always carry **snow chains** for your car tires, even if you have a four-wheel-drive vehicle. Although most of Tahoe's roads and highways are kept plowed in winter, chains are often required. It is far less expensive to buy chains for your car at a big-box store in a large city (Wal-Mart–type stores carry chains, as well as auto supply stores) than it is to buy or rent them at Lake Tahoe.

Explore Tahoe

THE BEST OF LAKE TAHOE

It's a travesty to imagine having only a short time to spend at Lake Tahoe, but if a brief stay is all your travel plans allow, you'll have to pack in as much as you can. If you only have a couple of days to spend at the lake, here are a few not-to-be-missed highlights.

Be sure to take a **boat excursion** on the lake. The best way to gain a sense of Tahoe's mind-boggling size is to get out on a boat in the middle of it. Your choices for mode of travel are wide ranging; passenger service is available on huge stern-wheeler paddleboats, sailboats, yachts, and speedboats. For a more intimate cruising experience, your best bet is to choose one of the smaller-capacity vessels, like the 30-passenger sailboat *Woodwind* or the 76-foot classic yacht *Safari Rose* on the South Shore, or the 35-foot sailboat *Avalanche* on the North Shore. If you decide to take one of the big paddleboat cruises, the best choice on the South Shore is a history cruise on the *Tahoe Queen,* during which an actor portrays Mark Twain. On the North Shore, the *Tahoe Gal* offers a wonderful sunset dinner cruise.

If you are willing to get up before sunrise, you could begin a day at Lake Tahoe in dramatic style, by taking a scenic one-hour **hot-air balloon flight** over the lake. The views from 2,500 feet above the lake's surface are unforgettable. But for those who prefer to sleep in a little later, there are less ambitious ways to get up high and get a good look at your surroundings. The **Heavenly Gondola** whisks sightseers up an incline of almost 2,800 feet in a mere 12 minutes, while passengers enjoy nonstop panoramic views. On the uphill trip, be sure to disembark at the observation platform perched at 9,123 feet in elevation. On the North Shore, the cable car at Squaw Valley effectively provides the same experience, but the best lake views are at Heavenly.

If you don't mind spending a few hours behind the wheel, consider taking a drive around all or part of the lakeshore. To make a complete circumnavigation by car, the entire route is 72 miles and requires about three hours without stops. This popular drive is what the Tahoe tourist bureaus call **"The Most Beautiful Drive in America,"** but as anyone who has ever been to Yosemite or Yellowstone knows, this is a bit of an exaggeration. Still, the lakeshore drive is a highly scenic introduction to the Tahoe basin. Where you start from is irrelevant, but plan on five to six hours instead of three so you have time for a few side trips. And drive in a clockwise direction so you are always on the lake side of the highway.

Along the way, be sure to stop at the drive-up viewpoints at **Inspiration Point** above Emerald Bay on the South Shore and **Memorial Point** south of Incline Village. If you'd like to go for a short hike, consider taking the one-mile trail to **Vikingsholm** at Emerald Bay, or the similar-length path to **Stateline Lookout** on the North Shore. Those who would rather spend their precious time picnicking should pack along some goodies and make a beeline for the beachside picnic areas at **Sand Harbor** or **Cave Rock** on the East Shore, the West Shore's **Ehrman Mansion** at **Sugar Pine Point State Park**, or **Pope, Kiva,** or **Baldwin Beaches** on the South Shore. **Nevada Beach**, on the Nevada side of South Shore, is another great choice for picnicking or beach going.

If you are staying on the South Shore and want to see some of the sights mentioned above without driving a car, take advantage of the **Nifty Fifty Trolley,** which offers narrated tours on open-sided buses, replicas of 19th-century streetcars. Or go for a bike ride on the South Shore's paved **Pope-Baldwin Bike Path.** Bike rentals are easy to come by and the trail passes by several interesting sites, including the **Tallac Historic Site** and the **Stream Profile Chamber,** and a few of the South Shore's loveliest beaches.

The quintessential way to end any day at Lake Tahoe is by savoring a **lake-view dinner.** On the South Shore, several wonderful restaurants provide breathtaking views as well as outstanding cuisine, including Blue Water Bistro, Edgewood Restaurant, The Summit, 19 Kitchen, and The Beacon. The North and West Shores also serve up great blue-water views and delicious food. Try to get a table at Chambers Landing, Sunnyside, Christy Hill, Wolfdale's, or Gar Woods Grill, for cuisine and a view you will long remember. If you still have energy left after dinner, head over to one of the casinos in Stateline or Crystal Bay to catch an evening show.

THE NONSKIER'S WINTER WONDERLAND

Your partner is addicted to skiing and snowboarding, and will spend his/her vacation pushing the envelope on double black diamond runs, terrain parks, and half-pipes. You, on the other hand, can never quite figure out how to gracefully dismount the chairlift, and usually end your day at the resort's first-aid station. Three words of advice: Give it up. There is plenty of other fun stuff to do in the snow at Lake Tahoe, and none of it will lead to you being strapped to a sled pulled by the ski patrol.

DAY 1
Go **snowshoeing.** No experience is required; snowshoeing is as easy as walking, and rentals are a real bargain compared to skiing equipment. Beginners can snowshoe along the lakeshore at Camp Richardson and the Tallac Historic Site, around the meadow at Squaw Valley, or on easy trails at Spooner Lake. More experienced snowshoers can set off into the backcountry on a multitude of trails.

DAY 2
Now that you're feeling more confident in the snow, try **cross-country skiing.** Even those who shun the downhill slopes can

have a great time cross-country skiing on beginner-level, flat trails. It's a fun way for nonskiers to play in the snow without risking breaking a leg. Most people can learn the basics of cross-country skiing in about 30 minutes. Great places for beginners to get started with a lesson and rental package are Spooner Lake on the East Shore, Royal Gorge or Northstar-at-Tahoe near Truckee, Tahoe Cross-Country near Tahoe City, or Kirkwood Cross-Country at Carson Pass. You'll be kicking and gliding like a pro in only a couple of hours.

DAY 3

If you are feeling a bit tired from the last two days of snow play, let Trigger or Rover and their friends do the work of pulling you through the snow. **Horse-drawn sleigh rides** are available in Squaw Valley on the North Shore, and Camp Richardson and Stateline on the South Shore. **Dogsled tours** led by eager, panting huskies are available at the Resort at Squaw Creek and Sugar Bowl on the North Shore and Kirkwood in Carson Pass.

DAY 4

Go **ice-skating** in the morning and **tubing** in the afternoon. Ice-skating rinks are found at several locations around the lake; the best outdoor rinks are at Squaw Valley's High Camp and Northstar-at-Tahoe.

If you'd rather skate indoors where the weather is more predictable, the South Lake Tahoe Ice Arena is a popular regulation-size rink. For an afternoon of tubing or sledding, head to Hansen's Resort in South Lake Tahoe or North Tahoe Regional Park in Tahoe Vista. Almost all of Lake Tahoe's alpine ski resorts offer tubing or sledding, too, but they charge the big bucks for it.

DAY 5

Do a little winter **sightseeing.** In the morning, ride the scenic cable car at Squaw Valley USA or the gondola at Heavenly. In the afternoon, take a sightseeing cruise aboard the *Tahoe Queen* or MS *Dixie II* stern-wheeler paddleboats. If it's too cold on the upper deck, you can always enjoy the view from down below in one of the heated, enclosed cabins.

DAY 6

Go **snowmobiling.** Hey, since there is horsepower involved, your adrenaline-addicted snowboarding spouse might even be willing to join you. No experience is required, and proper clothing (snowsuits, snow boots, and helmet) is often included in the tour fee. Snowmobiling tours are offered on the North Shore along the high ridges of Tahoe National Forest, or on the South Shore above Zephyr Cove.

THE PEAK-BAGGER

You've come to Lake Tahoe with a purpose. You have one week of vacation time and you want to hike all of the Tahoe basin's highest summits—a worthwhile mission, to be sure. Okay, lace up your boots, fill your pack with plenty of snacks and water, and let's get climbing.

DAY 1

Start with a warm-up peak, so you can get used to the high-elevation air around the lake. The lofty 9,235-foot summit of **Ralston Peak** is no slacker in the view department, but it can be reached with a "cheat" that will make your first day a breeze (compared to the rest of the week, anyway). Instead of hiking from the Ralston Peak Trailhead off Highway 50, take the boat taxi across Echo Lakes and follow the Pacific Crest Trail for 2.3 miles to the Ralston Trail, then head up to the summit. This 8.6-mile round-trip has a mere 1,800-foot elevation gain, and Ralston's summit view is a stunner: Nearly a dozen lakes of the Desolation Wilderness are in sight, as well as mighty Pyramid Peak and Mount Tallac.

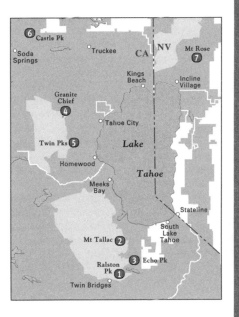

DAY 2

So much for your easy day. Today, while you are still fresh, it's time to tackle **Mount Tallac.** This mighty 9,735-foot summit that towers over the southwest shore may not be the tallest mountain around the lake, but it scores the highest marks for its summit view. Getting there is a bit of a buttkicker, especially since the first two miles of the hike are deceptively easy. From the 2.1-mile mark at Cathedral Lake, the trail gains 2,100 feet in only 2.6 miles – a grade that gives pause to even the fittest of hikers. The entire hike is 9.4 miles roundtrip with a 3,400-foot elevation gain. But there's a reason that hundreds of hikers make this trip every summer weekend: The summit view is remarkable, taking in Lake Tahoe, Emerald Bay, Fallen Leaf Lake, the lake-filled basins of Desolation Wilderness, and distinctive Ralston and Pyramid peaks. Unless the wind is fierce on top, you won't want to give up your summit perch any time soon.

DAY 3

Since you are still on the south side of the lake, and to rest up a bit from your day at Tallac, head for the summit of **Echo Peak** above Upper Angora Lake. The trail to the lake is one of the easiest hikes in existence around Lake Tahoe. Make sure you enjoy a glass of lemonade at the Angora Lakes Resort before beginning the attack on Echo Peak, elevation 8,588 feet, which is more than 1,200 feet higher, but accessible in about a mile. You'll long remember the merciless grade on this short stretch, but you'll also remember the visual reward – a 360-degree panorama that includes the Echo Lakes, Fallen Leaf Lake, Lake Tahoe, and numerous other lakes and peaks in the Desolation Wilderness.

DAY 4

Enough with the easy stuff. Today is the day to bag **Granite Chief** and getting there is no picnic. Follow the Granite Chief Trail from Squaw Valley and then the Pacific Crest Trail south, and you'll make it to the summit in 5.5 miles with a 2,800-foot elevation gain (11 miles round-trip). And no, you can't cheat and take the Squaw Valley cable car to the ridge. Granite Chief's summit, elevation 9,086 feet, offers a head-swiveling vista of neighboring peaks – Tinker Knob, Castle Peak, Needle Peak, Twin Peaks, and the jagged Crystal Range in Desolation Wilderness. Yes, you can see Lake Tahoe, also.

DAY 5

With luck, your peak-bagging vacation just happens to coincide with the summer wildflower bloom, because your next hike passes through acres of flower fields. Start at the West Shore's Twin Peaks Trailhead for the Tahoe Rim Trail and follow an initially mellow course along Ward Creek, which becomes increasingly steep as you go. After six miles one-way and a 2,400-foot elevation gain, you'll be standing on the eastern summit of **Twin Peaks,** elevation 8,878 feet. Easily identifiable landmarks include Granite Chief, Tinker Knob, Mount Rose, Freel Peak, and Mount Tallac, amid a host of lesser known peaks and precipices. Heck, while you're up here, you might as well bag the western summit of Twin Peaks, too.

DAY 6

Castle Peak beckons, and you must answer the call. You can hike to this summit via a shorter path (5.4 miles round-trip) on a dirt road from the north side of I-80 near Boreal Ridge, or a longer route (9.4 miles round-trip) from the south side of I-80. Take your pick. The elevation gain is about 2,100 feet. The throat of an ancient volcano, the multiturreted summit of 9,103-foot Castle Peak provides a horizon-expanding view, reaching as far as the Diablo Range 100 miles to the west and equally as far to the north. No matter which way you go, the trail is relatively easy until you reach Castle Pass; from there the last 1.2 miles to the top are memorably steep. The eastern turret of the "castle" is the highest summit.

DAY 7

Hope you have some cool temperatures today, because you are heading for the volcanic summit of 10,778-foot **Mount Rose** and much of the route is treeless, waterless, and exposed. The 10-mile round-trip has a meager 2,300-foot elevation gain, which sounds quite manageable until you realize that the vast majority of that gain occurs in the final 2.6 miles to the summit. The final half mile is the most challenging, partly because of the high-elevation air and partly because of the exposed volcanic terrain. But on clear days, the summit view spreads so far and wide that it is easy to pick out Mount Lassen, nearly 100 miles to the north.

When you have finished your hike, drive back down the Mount Rose Highway to the Big Water Grille above Incline Village. Enjoy a few drinks at the bar and pat yourself on the back for being such a fine mountaineer.

SUMMERTIME FAMILY FUN

Lake Tahoe has something to offer for everyone, including the under-12 set and yes, even the most jaded teenagers. If you're on summer vacation with your kids, here are some suggested activities that every member of the family can enjoy.

DAYS 1-2

Start your visit on the South Shore, with a stay at one of Stateline's casino resorts. Stateline is a good place to gently break your kids into the idea of being away from their handheld video games; if they start to experience electronic stimuli withdrawal, you can always take them to the casinos' game arcades. While on the South Shore, plan to spend at least one full day enjoying one or more of the many water sports Lake Tahoe has to offer. Teenagers can rent and pilot their own personal watercraft or go for a parasailing ride. One parent and one child can paddle a double kayak together, or share in the fun of pedaling a paddleboat (it's propelled with your feet, like a bike).

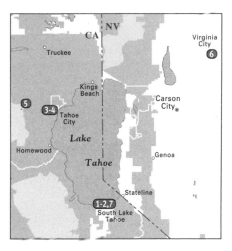

Everyone is sure to enjoy a boat cruise on the lake, but be sure to pick one that is age appropriate for the kids in your clan. Families with young ones should sign up for the *Tahoe Queen's* Family Fun Cruise, which has "Tahoe Tessie" on board to entertain the little ones. If your kids are older, go for a cruise on one of the ***Woodwind*** sailboats instead, or take a ride on the blazing fast *Tahoe Thunder*.

When it's time for dinner, forego the refined California cuisine and head for the kid-friendly Burger Lounge or Hard Rock Cafe. For something that may be more appealing to the adults, too, try The Beacon at Camp Richardson Resort or Shoreline Cafe. After your meal, head over to the **Tahoe Amusement Park** and let the kids take a ride on the carousel or tilt-a-whirl in the long daylight hours of summer. Or, if you want to expose them to a little

natural history, head over to **Fallen Leaf Lake Campground** for the evening ranger program, which is usually an informative talk about local wildlife or other aspects of Tahoe's natural history.

DAYS 3-4

It's time to leave the urban side of Lake Tahoe behind and experience some of the area's natural outdoor adventures. From the South Shore, drive north on Highway 89, following the line of the West Shore to Tahoe City. To break up the drive, stop at **Inspiration Point** to ogle the view of Emerald Bay, then continue to **Sugar Pine Point State Park.** Take a walk on one of the short interpretive trails that start at the nature center at **Ehrman Mansion,** or take a free tour of the historic mansion itself. The kids can stick their toes in the water at the mansion's calm stretch of beach.

Back in the car, head for the Tahoe City Y, where you can rent a raft and float lazily down the **Truckee River** to River Ranch Lodge. Jump out of the boat and go for a swim anywhere you wish, or pull up along the riverbank and have a picnic. At the end of the float, a bus will bring you back to your starting point, and from there you can rent bikes and pedal the five-mile **Truckee River Recreation Trail** – following roughly the same route you just traveled in a raft, but this time on a paved bike path that parallels the river. After an affordable family dinner at the Bridgetender Tavern or Rosie's Cafe in Tahoe City, take the kids over to **Commons Beach,** where a playground area includes a miniboulder for junior "rock climbers" ages six and older, plus swings and other playground equipment for kids of all ages. Older kids can enjoy a dip in the lake.

DAY 5

Spend a day at **Squaw Valley USA.** The resort offers a multitude of activities that appeal to kids, including ice-skating and swimming at High Camp Bath and Tennis Club, horseback riding (guided trail rides of various lengths and pony rides for the little ones), a ropes course (basically a huge jungle gym), two rock climbing walls, and the Skyjump Bungee Trampoline, where kids can do somersaults and flips while hanging tethered in midair. If you'd like to include something educational, drive the kids over to nearby Truckee, where they can enjoy the hands-on exhibits at the **Sierra Nevada Children's Museum.** Have an early dinner at the ever-popular Truckee Diner or O. B.'s

Pub, and then – if you time it right – you can show up at **Donner Memorial State Park** just in time for their evening campfire program. The kids will enjoy hearing a park ranger tell the stories of the emigrants who traveled over Donner Pass in the 1800s.

DAY 6

Time to head for the Nevada side of the lake. Drive east around the North Shore, with a brief side trip to Tahoe Meadows on the Mount Rose Highway for a quick walk among the wildflowers. Then continue east to **Virginia City,** site of the 1860s Comstock gold- and silver-mining boom. The under-12 set will certainly want to take a ride on the Virginia and Truckee Railroad and tour the underground mine in the Ponderosa Saloon; the whole family will enjoy strolling along the wooden sidewalks and imagining what this town was like in its heyday. Have dinner in Virginia City (the kids will want to order sarsaparillas) and then drive back to Lake Tahoe as the sun sinks in the west.

DAY 7

Hard to believe, but your week with the kids in Tahoe is almost over. Head back down to the South Shore for your final day. A great way to end your trip is with a ride on the **Heavenly gondola** to its spectacular observation platform high above the lake. Picnic tables are located at the overlook, so pack along some sandwiches and have lunch at 9,123 feet. This is the time to pop the question to your kids: "So, what was your favorite part of your vacation at Tahoe?" To which they will surely answer: "All of it."

THE ADRENALINE JUNKIE

You spend all week in an office cubicle shuffling papers and answering emails. In an average day, the biggest risk you take is driving in rush-hour traffic while simultaneously talking on your cell phone. It's time for your Tahoe vacation and you want to experience some genuine thrills. You came to the right place. Fuel up with a few shots of espresso and let's get started.

DAY 1

Get on your mountain bike (or rent one, if yours is at home) and pedal the world-famous **Flume Trail** on Tahoe's East Shore. Since it's your first day of vacation, you probably don't want to go crazy and ride the entire bloodcurdling 24-mile loop, so instead arrange a shuttle pickup with the Spooner Lake Outdoor Company and ride the trail point-to-point, an adrenaline-inducing 13 miles. Along the way, watch out for the 1,600-foot near-vertical drop-offs.

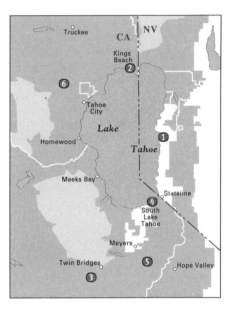

DAY 2

Since you spent so much time ogling the lake from the Flume Trail yesterday, today's the day to get out on the water. Have you ever wondered what it feels like to fly 2,000 feet in the air, being dragged on a towrope behind a fast-moving boat? Ever wonder what would happen if the driver let go of the rope? You'll find out when you go for a boat-launched **hang-gliding** ride courtesy of Adventure Ambassadors at Tahoe Vista Recreation Area. Luckily, you don't have to go solo on this one – you'll fly tandem with a certified instructor – but it's still plenty exciting.

DAY 3

Today is the day to feel nothing but air under your feet, and experience the absolute thrill of hanging on to a rock wall with only your fingers and toes (okay, you'll be roped in, but the psychological effect is similar). Sign up with the Tahoe Adventure Company or Alpine Skills International for one of their beginning **rock climbing** classes on Lover's Leap, a chunk of granite that rises 600 feet straight up from the American River. You'll be performing all kinds of vertical acrobatics in the time it takes to say "on belay."

DAY 4

Another day on the lake. Start by getting up at the crack of dawn to go for a 5 A.M. **hot-air balloon** flight. Your one-hour ride will take you as high as 2,500 feet above the lake's surface, providing dizzying views of the Tahoe basin. You may find yourself wondering just how much control the pilot *really* has. If floating along in the atmosphere proves too tame for you, after the postflight champagne toast head over to Timber Cove Marina to feel some g-forces aboard the *Tahoe Thunder.* This is the fastest tour speedboat on the lake, boasting over 800 horsepower. You'll come away with a new understanding of the word "fast."

DAY 5

Time to get back on the mountain bike. If you love the feel of gravity-induced speed, you'll love **Mr. Toad's Wild Ride,** i.e. the Saxon Creek Trail. This is the South Shore's most famous (or infamous) ride, which features an extremely technical, obstacle-ridden downhill stretch suitable for advanced riders only. Be sure to bring along your first-aid kit.

DAY 6

Head over to the Truckee River for a day of **rafting,** and not the leisurely, floating kind that everyone does on the stretch from Tahoe City to River Ranch. Instead, sign up for a guided trip on the Lower Truckee River, which offers Class II and III rapids almost all summer long. Compared to what you've been doing all week, this white water will probably seem fairly mild, but maybe that will help to ease the transition back to your boring, no-thrills office job. Sorry, but it had to happen some time. Vacation's over, but here's the good news: It's time to start planning for next year.

SOUTH SHORE

Far and away the most populated stretch of Lake Tahoe shoreline is the South Shore, with most of the development centered around the twin cities of South Lake Tahoe (in California) and Stateline (in Nevada). Consisting mainly of a haphazard, unplanned strip of commercial enterprises, the cities of the South Shore are suffering from a mild case of urban blight. If you are expecting to see a quaint mountain village perched along the shores of the lake, you won't find it here.

Fortunately an effort at self-improvement is being made. In the last decade, the construction of two new "village" complexes, comprised of lodgings, restaurants, and shops—one at Ski Run Boulevard and the other between Heavenly Village Way and Stateline Avenue—has forced the removal of many old and unsightly motels, fast-food restaurants, and gas stations. Since they encourage walking, not driving, these new village centers are much kinder to Lake Tahoe's natural environment, and they have added a certain metropolitan flair to the downtown area of the South Shore.

Despite all the buildings and a constant parade of automobile traffic, there is still a wealth of scenic beauty to be found here. Even busy Highway 50 has occasional spots where drivers are treated to views of Lake Tahoe's mesmerizing blue waters. And just a short drive from town lies the southern stretch of Desolation Wilderness, one of the most stunning glacier-sculpted landscapes in the Sierra Nevada. Hikers and backpackers can spend weeks exploring its miles of trails, visiting dozens of alpine lakes, and climbing a banquet of peaks

© ANN MARIE BROWN

SOUTH SHORE

HIGHLIGHTS

☾ Woodwind and Woodwind II cruises: Among many possible choices, two of the best Tahoe cruising excursions available are on the 30- and 50-passenger *Woodwind* sailboats, which have glass-bottom viewing windows that allow guests to peer beneath the surface of the lake (page 29).

☾ Heavenly Gondola: No matter what time of year, don't miss taking a scenic gondola ride at Heavenly Ski Resort. On the uphill leg, be sure to disembark at the overlook platform and check out the view from 9,123 feet in elevation (page 31).

☾ Inspiration Point at Emerald Bay: The blue-green expanse of Emerald Bay, with magical Fannette Island poking up from the lake's surface, is one of the most photographed sights in the United States. The drive-up overlook at Inspiration Point is one of the best spots to get a good look and a few snapshots (page 34).

☾ Eagle Lake: You'll need to get a very early start to beat the crowds on the trail to Eagle Lake, but this short and lovely hike is worth the effort. The hike takes in the sight and sound of cascading Eagle Creek, the granite shores of a picturesque glacial cirque lake in the Desolation Wilderness, and fine views of distant Emerald Bay (page 43).

☾ Pope-Baldwin Bike Path: You don't have to be Lance Armstrong, or even especially athletic, to ride this level, paved bike trail, which travels past some of the South Shore's greatest sights, including Baldwin Beach, the Tallac Historic Site, and the Stream Profile Chamber (page 52).

☾ Kayaking: Sign up for a tour with Kayak Tahoe and you'll paddle your own boat through the sparkling waters of Emerald Bay or along the boulder-strewn beaches of the East Shore in the company of a knowledgeable guide. Confident beginners can forego the tour, simply rent a kayak, and set out on their own (page 54).

☾ Ballooning: This memorable excursion with Lake Tahoe Balloons includes an early-morning boat cruise on the lake, launch of the hot-air balloon from the boat deck, a view-filled flight through the skies above Lake Tahoe, and a champagne toast after landing (page 60).

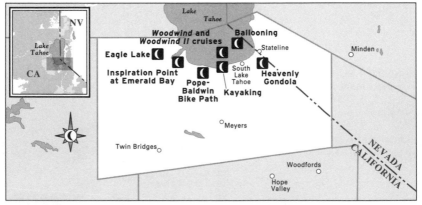

LOOK FOR ☾ TO FIND RECOMMENDED SIGHTS, ACTIVITIES, DINING, AND LODGING.

and precipices. Outside the wilderness area, a host of other outdoor activities are possible in the grand Tahoe scenery—mountain biking, boating, golfing, fishing, horseback riding, and rock climbing, to name a few—as well as a multitude of winter sports.

For the less ambitious, much can be seen right from your car windows. Heading west and north from the cities of the South Shore, travelers enjoy a scenic ride up Highway 89/Emerald Bay Road to Emerald Bay itself, one of the most photographed places in the United States. Along the way, pristine stretches of Tahoe shoreline await your blanket and picnic basket. There are historic sites to be toured, boat cruises to take, and outdoor arts and festivals to enjoy. Quite simply, there is such an abundance of fun things to do in the South Shore region that it's impossible not to enjoy a vacation here.

PLANNING YOUR TIME

Many visitors spend a week or more in and around the South Shore, both in the winter and summer seasons. Even if you aren't a casino-and-nightlife kind of person, the South Shore offers enough activities to keep anyone busy for several days, no matter what their interests, and no matter what the season. Just visiting a few of the South Shore's sightseeing highlights will require a minimum of two days. Be sure to plan enough time to ride the **Heavenly gondola,** take a boat cruise on the *Tahoe Queen* or the *Woodwind,* and drive or ride public transportation up to scenic **Inspiration Point at Emerald Bay.** History buffs will want to allow a few days just to visit the numerous museums and historic sites in the area, including **Vikingsholm Castle** and **Tallac Historic Site.** Outdoor recreationists will be hard-pressed to squeeze in enough hiking, biking, boating, fishing, or snow-related sports before their vacation ends—no matter how much time they have allotted. At a minimum, even the most casual adventurer should take the short hike to **Eagle Lake,** go for a spin on the paved **Pope-Baldwin Bike Path,** and spend a few hours out on the lake in a rental kayak.

TOUR BOATS AND CRUISES
Tahoe Queen and MS *Dixie II*

One of the most popular activities at Lake Tahoe is cruising around the lake in a Mark Twain–style stern-wheeler paddleboat. On the South Shore, the *Tahoe Queen* operates out of Ski Run Marina and the MS *Dixie II* departs from Zephyr Cove Marina. Both boats are operated year-round by Lake Tahoe Cruises (800/23-TAHOE or 530/541-3364, www.laketahoecruises.com). The vessels are large enough to hold a few hundred people, but even so, the tours are so popular that they sometimes sell out.

The MS *Dixie II* offers daily cruises year-round, including a champagne brunch cruise, a Glenbrook-area history cruise that includes breakfast, a sunset dinner/dance cruise, and an Emerald Bay sightseeing cruise. The video *Sunken Treasures of Lake Tahoe* plays below deck during the daytime cruises, but few passengers bother to watch it—most head above deck to enjoy the fresh air, sunshine, and lake views. In winter, guests can choose to relax on the enclosed, lower decks, or head out onto the open third deck for snapping pictures and

The American flag flies above the rotating paddlewheel of the MS *Dixie II*.

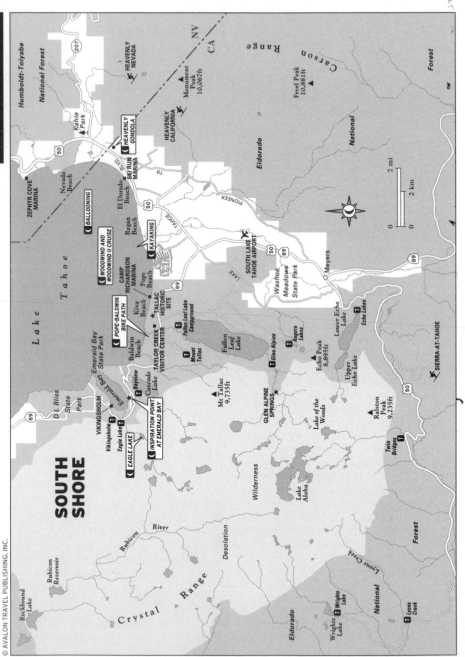

soaking up the winter sun. Rates are $26–30 for adults and $9–12 for children under 12, except for dinner cruises, which are $44–55 adults and $18–31 children.

The *Tahoe Queen*, a similar type of paddleboat that offers a similar array of cruises, also features a glass bottom that permits riders to peer into the clear Tahoe depths. The *Tahoe Queen* features a few cruises that are more interesting than the standard tours, including the Family Fun Cruise, with a costumed "Tahoe Tessie" on board to entertain the kids; and Mark Twain's Tales of Tahoe Cruise, with actor McAvoy Layne portraying the ghost of Mark Twain, who describes his adventures at Lake Tahoe in 1861 ($29 adults; $9 children 11 and under). The *Tahoe Queen* also runs a skier/boarder shuttle from the South Shore to the North Shore's Squaw Valley ski resort in winter (see *Downhill Skiing and Snowboarding*).

◖ Woodwind and Woodwind II

If you'd rather not set sail with a couple of hundred strangers, more intimate cruises are available. The sailboats *Woodwind* and *Woodwind II* offer lake excursions for 20–30 passengers at a time, complete with billowing white sails, sturdy masts, tinkling halyards, full bar service, and glass-bottom viewing windows that allow passengers to look beneath Tahoe's surface. The on-board crew does all the work of sailing; guests relax on the deck or down below in enclosed cabins and enjoy the ride. The *Woodwind* is a 40-foot trimaran that sails from Camp Richardson to Emerald Bay, passing near the Tallac Historic Site, Vikingsholm Castle, Fannette Island, and the bald eagle nesting site at Eagle Point. The *Woodwind II* is a 55-foot catamaran that sails from Zephyr Cove along the lake's East Shore, passing Cave Rock and then heading out into the center of the 1,600-foot-deep lake for a 360-degree Tahoe panorama. Cruises on both boats are available during the day and at sunset; the cost is $26–36 for adults, $12 for children (888/867-6394, www.sailwoodwind.com).

An elegant addition to the Woodwind fleet is the 76-foot classic yacht *Safari Rose*

($95 adults; $55 children 12 and under). This teak-paneled, plushly upholstered vessel offers a half-day sightseeing cruise to Lake Tahoe's West Shore, including a walking tour of the historic Ehrman Mansion at Sugar Pine Point State Park; a half-day "Round-the-Lake" Tour which visits both the West and East Shores; and special summer evening tours such as the Monday Martini Cruise and Wednesday Wine Tasting Cruise. Lunch is included on the daytime cruises; cocktails are served in the evening.

Tahoe
For more than half a decade the wooden cruiser *Tahoe* (888/867-6394, www.tahoeboatcruises.com, $95 adults, $55 children 12 and under, buffet lunch included) has been carrying visitors across the waters of Lake Tahoe. This meticulously restored 40-foot yacht sails up to 16 passengers to the East Shore and Thunderbird Lodge, where they can take a guided walking tour of this architectural oddity.

Tahoe Star
Harrah's and Harveys casinos offer a cruise on Bill Harrah's 54-foot yacht, the *Tahoe Star* (775/588-6611, www.harrahs.com, $50 per person). The 90-minute cruise costs $40 per person and departs daily in summer at 2 P.M. For something more lascivious, the *Tahoe Star* also skims the water twice at night—7 P.M. and 9 P.M.—with the scantily clad "Skipper Girls" on board. Passengers must be 21 or older for the evening cruises.

Tahoe Thunder
For some people, the only speed that holds their interest is "fast." The *Tahoe Thunder* (530/544-5387 or 530/544-2942, www.tahoethunder.com, $50 adults, $25 children 12 and under) can brag of supplying the fastest Coast Guard–inspected public speedboat ride on the lake. Operating out of Timber Cove Marina, the *Tahoe Thunder* is a 33-foot catamaran with horsepower that tops 800. Don't forget your jacket for the chilling breeze brought on by high g-forces.

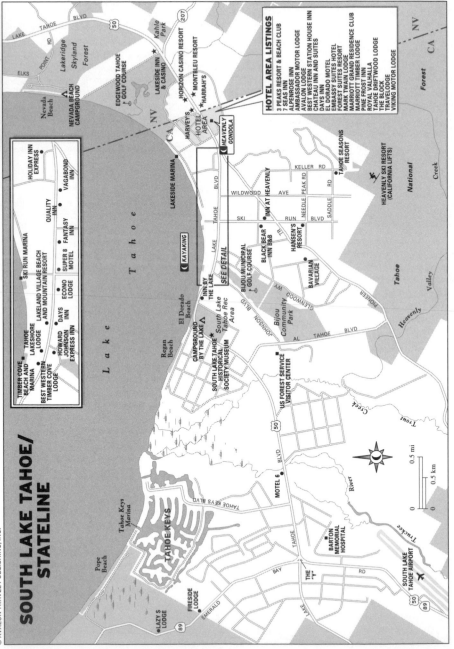

SOUTH LAKE TAHOE/ STATELINE

© AVALON TRAVEL PUBLISHING, INC.

HOTEL AREA LISTINGS

3 PEAKS RESORT & BEACH CLUB
7 SEAS INN
ALPENROSE INN
AMBASSADOR MOTOR LODGE
AVALON LODGE
BEST WESTERN STATION HOUSE INN
CHATEAU INN AND SUITES
DAYS INN
EL DORADO MOTEL
EMBASSY SUITES HOTEL
FOREST SUITES RESORT
MARK TWAIN LODGE
MARRIOTT GRAND RESIDENCE CLUB
MARRIOTT TIMBER LODGE
PINE FRIST INN
ROYAL VALHALLA
TAHOE DRIFTWOOD LODGE
THE BLOCK
TRAVELODGE
VIKING MOTOR LODGE

HOLIDAY INN EXPRESS
VAGABOND INN
QUALITY INN
FANTASY INN
SKI RUN MARINA
SUPER 8 MOTEL
LAKELAND VILLAGE BEACH AND MOUNTAIN RESORT
ECONO LODGE
DAYS INN
TAHOE LAKESHORE LODGE
HOWARD JOHNSON EXPRESS INN
TIMBER COVE BEACH AND MARINA
BEST WESTERN TIMBER COVE LODGE

KAYAKING

INN BY THE LAKE
SEE DETAIL
EL Dorado Beach
Regan Beach
CAMPGROUND BY THE LAKE
South Lake Tahoe Rec Area
SOUTH LAKE TAHOE HISTORICAL SOCIETY MUSEUM

Nevada Beach
NEVADA BEACH CAMPGROUND

Lake Tahoe

EDGEWOOD TAHOE GOLF COURSE
LAKESIDE INN & CASINO
HORIZON CASINO RESORT
MONTBLEU RESORT
HARRAH'S
HARVEY'S
HOTEL AREA
HEAVENLY GONDOLA

LAKESIDE MARINA
LAKESIDE MARINA

Kahle Park

Lakeridge
Skyland Forest

ELKS
POINT RD
LAKE TAHOE BLVD

KELLER RD
WILDWOOD AVE
PEAK RD
NEEDLE
SADDLE
INN AT HEAVENLY
SKI RUN BLVD
TAHOE SEASONS RESORT
HEAVENLY SKI RESORT (CALIFORNIA LIFTS)

National Forest

BLACK BEAR INN B&B
HANSEN'S RESORT
BAVARIAN VILLAGE

BIJOU MUNICIPAL GOLF COURSE
Bijou Community Park
GLENWOOD WY
JOHNSON BLVD
AL TAHOE BLVD
PIONEER
Tahoe Valley

US FOREST SERVICE VISITOR CENTER

Trout Creek

MOTEL 6

Upper Truckee River

BARTON MEMORIAL HOSPITAL

TAHOE KEYS

Tahoe Keys Marina

Pope Beach

LAZY S LODGE
FIRESIDE LODGE
EMERALD

TAHOE KEYS BLVD

THE "Y"
BAY
RD
SOUTH LAKE TAHOE AIRPORT

0.5 mi
0.5 km
0

Sights

KAHLE PARK

Just a few blocks past the Stateline casinos at Kahle Drive and Highway 50 lies a beautiful preserved area that is popular with joggers, dog walkers, and nature lovers. Kahle Park (775/586-7271), which lies on the Nevada side of the state line, features a one-mile interpretive trail that focuses on Tahoe's human and natural history. Named for the Washoe Indian word for the rock-grinding tools the tribe used to prepare food, Lam Watah Trail visits a meadow that was the traditional site of a Washoe spring encampment. Signs explain the importance of Tahoe's meadows and wetlands as a filtering system for the lake. The trail winds its way to the lakeshore at Nevada Beach, one of the largest stretches of coarse white sand in all of Tahoe.

🚠 HEAVENLY GONDOLA

Spring, summer, fall, or winter, take a ride on the Heavenly Ski Resort Gondola (1001 Heavenly Village Way, 775/586-7000, www .skiheavenly.com, 9 A.M.–4 P.M. daily in winter, 9 A.M.–5 P.M. daily in summer). The lower terminal for the eight-passenger tram cars is in downtown Stateline at Heavenly Village; the upper end is 2.4 miles up the mountain. The gondola whisks sightseers up an incline of almost 2,800 feet in a mere 12 minutes, providing nonstop panoramic views. On the uphill trip, be sure to disembark at the 14,000-square-foot observation platform perched amid the granite at 9,123 feet in elevation (the gondola doesn't stop there on the way back downhill). The 360-degree views include the Carson Valley and surrounding desert to the east, the Desolation Wilderness to the west, and the entire expanse of Lake Tahoe laid out from south to north. Then hop back on the gondola for the final stint to the top, where you can ski in winter, hike in summer, or simply turn around and ride back down, enjoying the lake views all over again. Sightseeing tickets vary in price by season; plan on paying $24–30 for adults,

© ANN MARIE BROWN

Skiers and nonskiers alike will enjoy a scenic gondola ride at Heavenly Ski Resort.

$22–28 for seniors over 65 and teens 13–18, and $16–20 for children ages 5–12. Children four and under are free. The easiest parking for the gondola is at the city-owned garage on Bellamy Court, off Heavenly Village Way ($1.50 per 30 minutes).

SOUTH LAKE TAHOE HISTORICAL SOCIETY MUSEUM

At this small but surprising museum (3058 Hwy. 50, South Lake Tahoe, 530/541-5458, 11 A.M.–4 P.M. Tues.–Sat., $1 admission) located next to the Chamber of Commerce, visitors can see the lake through the eyes of its early explorers and residents. Housing the region's most comprehensive collection of early photographs, pioneer tools, farm implements, and Washoe Indian baskets, the museum showcases an entirely different way of life at the lake than what we know today.

Exhibits document eclectic bits and pieces of Tahoe history, from the Pony Express to the gold- and silver-mining era, from the invention of snow sports to the beginning of the casino industry. Several displays of photographs and memorabilia highlight Tahoe's early tourist resorts (the Tahoe Tavern, the Tallac Hotel, and Fallen Leaf Lake Lodge). An entire section is devoted to the Lake Valley Railroad and the massive steamships that transported passengers around the lake in the late 19th century, before the development of highways and widespread use of the automobile. A highlight is the model of the historic vessel SS *Tahoe,* which was the largest of the steamers that plied Lake Tahoe's waters, measuring nearly 170 feet in length and with a carrying capacity of 200 passengers. Eventually the ship was scuttled near Glenbrook Bay because maintaining her was no longer economical.

On the grounds behind the museum is the Tahoe Basin's oldest still-standing building, Osgood's Toll House, circa 1859, and a 1930s-era log cabin.

TALLAC HISTORIC SITE

Located near the U.S. Forest Service's visitors center is the Tallac Historic Site (2.7 miles north of the Y on Hwy. 89/Emerald Bay Rd., 530/541-5227 or 530/573-2694, www.tahoe-heritage.org, dawn–dusk June–Sept., free admission, guided tours $5 mid-June–mid-Sept.), a 150-acre chunk of lakeshore property that is home to a cluster of late 1800s and early 1900s summer homes and mansions—a total of 28 buildings in all. The impressive structures were built by prominent San Francisco families with money acquired in banking, railroad-building, and land speculation.

Three grand homes from Tahoe's "Era of Opulence," still housing some of their original furnishings, can be seen at Tallac—the Baldwin, Pope, and Heller estates. All three estates are on the National Register of Historic Places. The **Baldwin Estate,** built in 1921, is now home to the **Tallac Museum,** which features an impressive display of Washoe Indian

exhibits. The neighboring **Pope Estate,** built in 1894 by George Tallant and later owned by the Lloyd Tevis and George Pope families, is the interpretive center for the Tallac site. The building can be visited on docent-led tours in the summer months. On summer weekends living-history programs often take place, featuring costumed docents playing the roles of real people from Tallac's history.

Those interested in gardening shouldn't miss the Pope Estate's arboretum, a tranquil spot with a pond, small waterfall, and a collection of plants and trees from around the world put together by Mrs. William Tevis, the daughter of a California governor, in the early 20th century. (The Tevis family purchased the Pope Estate from its original owners.)

The **Heller Estate,** constructed in 1923, is also known as **Valhalla** and is the home of the annual Valhalla Arts and Music Festival, a series of concerts and dramatic performances held throughout summer. (For program information and tickets, phone 530/541-4975 or 888/632-5859 or go to www.valhalla-tallac .com.) Arts and crafts are sold at two small twin cabins on the estate. Valhalla includes a grand hall with a 40-foot-high fireplace, and can be rented for weddings and events.

A few archaeological remains of the **Tallac Resort** can also be seen at the Tallac Historic Site. The opulent resort, which owner/entrepreneur Elias "Lucky" Baldwin called the "Greatest Casino in America," had its heyday in the 1890s, when the wealthy would come from all over California and Nevada to dine, dance, and gamble in elegance on the shores of Lake Tahoe. In addition to the casino, the Tallac Resort included two large and lavish hotels with a ballroom and tennis courts. Guests at the resort would enjoy orchestra concerts, steamer rides across the lake, croquet, and other organized activities. Visitors today can see the remains of the casino foundation and walk the resort's rock-lined promenade.

Present-day Tallac visitors can also stop in at the boathouse on the grounds of the Pope Estate, where an organization called Tahoe

Classic Yacht (530/544-2307, www.tahoeclassicyacht.org) runs a small maritime museum highlighting the history of watercraft on Lake Tahoe. Under restoration at the boathouse as of 2006 is the *Quich Cha Kiddin,* a 38-foot cruiser built in 1921.

The Tallac site enjoys an incredibly scenic location on Lake Tahoe's shore, so don't miss the chance to stroll along the beach, or walk out on the pier behind the boathouse. And take note of the trees on the Tallac grounds. Because they were protected by the wealthy Tallac landowners during the great logging era of the late 1800s, they are some of the finest examples of old-growth conifers remaining in the Tahoe basin.

TAYLOR CREEK VISITOR CENTER

Managed by the U.S. Forest Service, the Taylor Creek Visitor Center (three miles north of the South Lake Tahoe Y on Hwy. 89/Emerald Bay Rd., 530/573-2674, 8 A.M.–5:30 P.M. daily mid-June–Sept., weekends only early June and Oct.) provides in-depth information on the natural ecology of the Lake Tahoe basin. Maps and guides are for sale and interpretive programs are held regularly in summer. Visitors could easily spend most of a day here attending free lectures and nature walks. The Taylor Creek Visitor Center is the starting point for four short interpretive trails: Rainbow Trail, Smokey's Trail, Lake of the Sky Trail, and Forest Tree Trail, as well as a trail that leads to the neighboring Tallac Historic Site. The wheelchair-accessible Rainbow Trail travels to the center's main attraction: the **Stream Profile Chamber,** an underground structure that allow visitors to walk alongside the depths of Taylor Creek. Through large glass windows, you can peer into the water to watch rainbow trout, kokanee salmon, and other fishy creatures going about their business. Autumn is the most interesting season here, when the colorful kokanee swim up Taylor Creek to spawn and die. The visitor center holds a Kokanee Salmon Festival each year during the first weekend in October.

GLEN ALPINE SPRINGS

A pleasant one-mile walk along a cascading stream from near the western edge of Fallen Leaf Lake will bring you to the Glen Alpine Springs Historic Site, where one of the first resorts in the Lake Tahoe Basin was located. Glen Alpine became popular in the 1860s when naturally carbonated spring water was discovered on the land. A resort with tent cabins and a dining hall was constructed around the spring. Resort guests would take part in a host of outdoor activities like fishing and hiking, while enjoying the supposed health benefits of the spring water. Through the years, the resort changed hands several times and became progressively more developed and less rustic. A handful of buildings still stand from the resort's zenith in the 1890s, including a few designed by the famous architect Bernard Maybeck, the genius behind the San Francisco Palace of Fine Art. On-site docents staff an interpretive center (530/573-2405, 10:30 A.M.–3:30 P.M. daily mid-June–mid-Sept.). Guided tours of the grounds and buildings are offered on weekends at 1 P.M. Be sure to wear sturdy walking shoes for the rocky dirt and gravel road/trail; the entire hike is two miles round-trip but mostly level. The Glen Alpine Trailhead is located at the end of Fallen Leaf Lake Road, 5.4 miles west of Highway 89.

BALDWIN BEACH

Summer visitors can enjoy the U.S. Forest Service's Baldwin Beach (dawn–dusk June–Sept.), a stunning stretch of coarse white sand on the shores of South Tahoe. Bring your kayaks, rubber rafts, or inner tubes; launching is easy here. A natural lagoon where Tallac Creek empties into Lake Tahoe on the northwest end of the beach is a popular swimming area for families with young children, because the water is shallow and surprisingly warm. Nearby, two other beaches—Pope and Kiva—are also managed by the Forest Service. Parking fee is $5 per car. Pope, Kiva, and Baldwin beaches are 2, 2.5, and 4 miles north of the South Lake Tahoe Y, respectively, on Highway 89/Emerald Bay Road.

SOUTH SHORE

[INSPIRATION POINT AT EMERALD BAY

Lake Tahoe's Emerald Bay, with its blue-green water and single, dramatic island, is one of the most photographed spots in the United States. Get your own snapshot at well-named Inspiration Point, perched hundreds of feet above Emerald Bay's three-mile-long cove. From this drive-up overlook, it is easy to imagine the glacial forces that carved out this remarkable scene. As the glaciers moved through, Emerald Bay very nearly became a separate lake, like nearby Fallen Leaf and Cascade Lakes, except that the terminal moraine at its mouth was never completed. So the beautiful bay remains an "add-on" to Lake Tahoe, connected to the main body of the lake on only one edge. Interpretive signs at the overlook relay some impressive figures about the lake, including the fact that if Lake Tahoe was drained, its massive volume of water would cover the entire state of California to a depth of more than a foot. The Inspiration Point parking lot is directly across Highway 89/Emerald Bay Road

from the entrance to Bayview Campground; 7.5 miles north of the South Lake Tahoe Y on Highway 89/Emerald Bay Road.

VIKINGSHOLM CASTLE

The curious can take a one-mile walk downhill (and uphill on the way back!) to see Vikingsholm Castle at Emerald Bay State Park (530/525-7232 or 530/541-6498, www.sierraspf.org or www.parks.ca.gov, 11 A.M.–4 P.M. daily Memorial Day–Sept. 30, tours $5 adults, $3 children 6–17, free for children 5 and under), a Scandinavian-style mansion built in 1929 on some of Tahoe's most beautiful shoreline. Lora Josephine Knight, a wealthy Chicago widow, purchased this land at the edge of Emerald Bay and had her dream home constructed out of native stone and timber, without disturbing any of the property's existing trees. A short distance offshore, Ms. Knight had a stone teahouse built on the highest point on Fannette Island, the only island in Lake Tahoe. Guests would be shuttled by boat to the island and servants would help them up the steep pathway to

At Inspiration Point, travelers get a bird's-eye view of Emerald Bay, one of the West's most photographed spots.

© ANN MARIE BROWN

the teahouse, where they would sip Earl Gray and make polite conversation.

Considered to be one of the finest examples of Scandinavian architecture in North America, the 38-room Vikingsholm Castle is both beautiful and strange. Modeled in the style of a Norse fortress of about A.D. 800, the structure is capped with turrets and towers. Design motifs include hand-hewn beams carved with dragon heads and decorated with hand-painted flowers. Inside, the castle is furnished with authentic Scandinavian antiques as well as precisely crafted museum replicas. Part of the roof is sod, which is kept thoroughly watered so that it stays green all summer and can support wild-

flowers. A short distance behind the castle is the lower cascade of Eagle Falls.

Whatever you think about the building itself, its setting is spectacular. It's well worth the down-and-then-up walk just to enjoy the beautiful stretch of Emerald Bay shoreline that Lora Knight so dearly loved. (She spent 16 summers here until her death in 1945.) The hike does have a 500-foot elevation gain on the return uphill, so wear sturdy shoes and try to avoid the heat of midday. A $6 parking fee is charged at the Vikingsholm/Harvey West parking lot, which is located 8.5 miles north of the South Lake Tahoe Y on Highway 89/Emerald Bay Road.

Recreation

HIKING

One of the most popular activities on the South Shore is going for a hike, as the spectacular Sierra scenery quite naturally inspires the urge to explore. Before you set out on the trail, make sure you are prepared with a few essentials, such as bottled water (or some sort of water-filtering device), food, and a trail map. Because many of Tahoe's trails have rocky, uneven surfaces, hiking boots are highly recommended. Sunscreen and/or a sun hat are musts at this high elevation, and you don't want to be without mosquito repellent if the bugs are biting. And keep in mind that weather in the Sierra can change dramatically in a short period of time, so it's always wise to carry a lightweight rain poncho or jacket, and additional clothing for layering.

For more information on the trails described below, contact the Lake Tahoe Basin Management Unit (35 College Dr., South Lake Tahoe, 530/573-2600, www.r5.fs.fed.us/ltbmu) or the Pacific Ranger District of Eldorado National Forest (7887 Hwy. 50, Pollock Pines, 530/647-5415, www.r5.fs.fed.us/eldorado).

The following hikes are listed from south to north along the Highway 89/Emerald Bay

Road corridor, and from east to west along the Highway 50/Lake Tahoe Boulevard corridor.

Angora Lakes

- Distance: 1.2 miles round-trip
- Duration: 1 hour
- Rating: Easy
- Elevation change: 250 feet
- Trailhead: Angora Lakes
- Directions: From the Y-junction of Hwy. 50 and Hwy. 89 in South Lake Tahoe, drive 3 miles northwest on Hwy. 89 to Fallen Leaf Lake Rd. on the left (1 mile past Camp Richardson). Turn left and drive 2 miles to Tahoe Mountain Rd. Turn left and drive 0.4 mile, then turn right on Forest Service Rd. 12N14, which alternates as paved and unpaved. Drive 2.8 miles, passing the Angora Fire Lookout, to the parking lot at the road's end. The trailhead is on the left side of the upper parking lot.

Angora Lakes is especially popular with children's day camps and groups, so you may feel like an outsider on this trail if you aren't accompanied by someone under the age of 10. But this easy walk is a winner, and requires so little effort that it can be done by almost anyone. The drive to the trailhead on a partially paved, partially dirt road offers scenic beauty of its own, especially as it climbs the ridge by the Angora Fire Lookout. At the upper parking lot at the road's end, you'll find the trail (a dirt road) on the left side.

In a mere 0.3 mile of walking through a pine-and-fir forest dotted with many rounded granite boulders, the road/trail reaches the first lake, Lower Angora, named after the angora goats that were grazed in this area in the 1870s. A few private houses are perched on the lake's far side. In another few minutes of walking you arrive at Upper Angora Lake and Angora Lakes Resort, which was constructed in 1920 by the Hildinger family and has eight picturesque little cabins for rent. Members of the same family still run the resort today, but the cabins are so popular that getting a reservation is almost impossible. At 7,280 feet in elevation, Upper Angora Lake is set in a perfect bowl-shaped glacial cirque. Some people paddle around the lake in rubber rafts, and by midsummer, swimmers usually find the water warm enough to take a dip. Hikers can take advantage of the lake's small beach, fish from shore for trout, or rent rowboats for a few bucks an hour. No matter what else you choose to do at Upper Angora Lake, most everybody who visits here makes a stop at the refreshment stand to buy a big glass of lemonade. Given the sun-exposed hike, that lemonade stand is a gold mine.

Option: Energetic types who want to turn this easy walk into more of an adventure can ascend to the summit of Echo Peak, elevation 8,588 feet, from Upper Angora Lake. From the resort, head to the left around the lake and you'll see a use trail that ascends the ridge leading up to the peak. In fact, you'll probably see several use trails, all marked with rock cairns. Choose one and begin a grunt of a climb, gaining more than 1,200 feet in a little over a mile. Most people make it from the upper lake to the summit in under an hour, with some serious huffing and puffing. Echo Peak's view makes it all worthwhile. It's a 360-degree panorama that includes the Echo Lakes, Fallen Leaf Lake, Lake Tahoe, and numerous other lakes and peaks in the Desolation Wilderness to the west.

Fallen Leaf Lake's Moraine Trail

- Distance: 2.5 miles round-trip
- Duration: 1.5 hours
- Rating: Easy
- Elevation change: 50 feet
- Trailhead: Fallen Leaf Lake Campground
- Directions: From the Y-junction of Hwy. 50 and Hwy. 89 in South Lake Tahoe, drive 3 miles northwest on Hwy. 89 to Fallen Leaf Lake Rd. on the left (1 mile past Camp Richardson). Turn left and drive 0.6 mile to the campground entrance on the right. The trail begins by campsite #75.

Picturesque Fallen Leaf Lake, measuring three miles long, is the second-largest alpine lake in the Tahoe Basin. Much of the lakeshore is bounded by private property, so access to the lake is fairly limited. However, the short and easy Moraine Trail leads from near the entrance to Fallen Leaf Lake Campground to the lake's northwest edge. The narrow, sandy path meanders for 0.25 mile through groves of quaking aspen, then heads to the right when it reaches the lakeshore and crosses Fallen Leaf Lake's dam. On the far side, it skirts the edge of the west shore to Sawmill Cove, an ideal spot for swimming or picnicking. This is a remarkably easy walk, and a great place for a casual stroll with your dog. If possible, try to visit here in October, when you can see the aspens put on their fall color show. In winter, this trail is a popular beginner-level cross-country skiing route.

Grass, Susie, Heather, and Aloha Lakes

- Distance: 5.4–12.4 miles round-trip
- Duration: 3–7 hours
- Rating: Moderate
- Elevation change: 500–1,400 feet
- Trailhead: Glen Alpine

© ANN MARIE BROWN

Backpackers heft their burdens alongside Heather Lake in the Desolation Wilderness

- Directions: From the Y-Junction of Hwy. 50 and Hwy. 89 in South Lake Tahoe, drive 3 miles northwest on Hwy. 89 to Fallen Leaf Lake Rd. on the left (1 mile past Camp Richardson). Turn left and drive 5.4 miles to the end of the road and the Glen Alpine Trailhead. Dayhikers are required to fill out a self-serve wilderness permit at the trailhead.

To complete this entire lake-filled trip, the mileage may be long, but the trail's grade is so gentle that the hike is much easier than you'd expect. This trail visits three lakes directly and travels near a fourth, so you can tailor your hiking distance to whatever your mood, abilities, and schedule allow. The trailhead is at Glen Alpine at the end of Fallen Leaf Lake Road. After an easy walk up the gravel and dirt road, which travels one mile to the site of the historic Glen Alpine Springs Resort (an interpretive center and various displays are found here), the path narrows to a single-track trail and continues for another 0.7 mile to the Desolation Wilderness boundary and a left turnoff for Grass Lake. Hikers wanting a short, easy

hike can turn left here and walk one mile to the edge of Grass Lake, 2.7 miles from the trailhead. Swimming is the primary activity at this pretty, popular lake.

Those seeking more scenery and a longer day on the trail should skip the Grass Lake turnoff and instead continue another 1.6 miles to the next junction. There, bear left for Susie Lake, then left again 0.5 mile later. At 4.2 miles from your start you'll reach Susie Lake's scenic shoreline, which has an abundance of established backpacking sites tucked amid groves of whitebark pines and hemlocks. Many people make large, island-dotted Susie Lake their turnaround point for an 8.4-mile day, but it's a pity not to continue for another mile to even more dramatic Heather Lake, a treeless, granite-bound beauty. The additional ascent is minimal and much of the walk is a lovely stroll around Susie's southwestern shore. Where the trail reaches Heather Lake, it skirts along its northern edge on a steep, rocky slope. Just beyond the lake's northwest shore, where a scarce few trees create shade and shelter for camping or picnicking, is the pass leading to

A HIKER'S CHECKLIST

Aside from the shoes on your feet, it doesn't take much equipment to go day hiking. While backpackers must concern themselves with tents, sleeping pads, pots and pans, and the like, day hikers have an easier time of it. Still, too many day hikers set out carrying too little and get into trouble as a result. Here's a list of essentials every well-equipped day hiker should carry:

1. Food and water. Water is even more important than food, although it's unwise to get caught without a picnic, or at least some edible supplies for emergencies. If you don't want to carry the weight of a couple of water bottles, at least carry a purifier or filtering device so you can obtain water from streams, rivers, or lakes. Never, ever drink water from a natural source without purifying it. The microscopic organism *Giardia lamblia* may be found in Sierra water sources and can cause a litany of terrible gastrointestinal problems. Only purifying or boiling water from natural sources will eliminate *Giardia*.

The new water-bottle-style purifiers, such as those made by Exstream or Bota, are almost as light as an empty plastic bottle and eliminate the need to carry both a filter and a bottle. You simply dip the bottle in the stream, screw on the top (which has a filter inside it), and squeeze the bottle to drink. The water is filtered on its way out of the squeeze top.

What you carry for food is up to you. Some people go gourmet and carry the complete inventory of a fancy grocery store. If you don't want to bother with much weight, stick with high-energy snacks like nutrition bars, nuts, dried fruit, turkey or beef jerky, and crackers. The best rule is to bring more than you think you can eat. You can always carry it back out with you, or give it to somebody on the trail who needs it. If you are hiking in a group, each of you should carry your own food and water just in case someone gets too far ahead or behind.

2. A good trail map. Never count on trail signs to get you where you want to go. A variety of maps are for sale at Tahoe's visitors centers and outdoor stores. Suggested hiking maps include those published by Tom Harrison Maps (Lake Tahoe Recreation Map or Desolation Wilderness Trail Map) or the Lake Tahoe Trail Map by Adventure Maps.

3. Extra clothing. On Tahoe's trails, conditions can change at any time. Not only can the weather suddenly turn windy, cloudy, or rainy (it can even snow!), but your own body conditions also change: You'll perspire as you hike up a sunny hill and then get chilled at the top of a windy ridge or when you head into shade. Because of this, cotton fabrics don't function well in the outdoors. Once cotton gets wet, it stays wet. Generally, polyester-blend fabrics dry faster. Some high-tech fabrics will actually wick moisture away from your skin. Invest in a few items of clothing made from these fabrics and you'll be more comfortable when you hike.

Always carry a lightweight jacket with you, preferably one that is waterproof and windresistant. If your jacket isn't waterproof, pack along one of the $2, single-use rain ponchos that come in a package the size of a deck of cards (available at outdoors stores or drugstores). If you can't part with two bucks, carry an extra-large garbage bag. In cooler temperatures, or when heading to a mountain summit even on a hot day, carry gloves and a hat as well.

4. Flashlight. Always carry a couple of these, just in case your hike takes a little longer than you planned. Miniflashlights are available everywhere, weigh almost nothing, and can save the day. A popular variety are the tiny "squeeze" LED flashlights, about the size and shape of a quarter, which you can clip on to any key ring. Some turn on and off with a small switch, so you don't have to squeeze them for extended periods. (The Photon Micro-Light is a popular brand.) Whatever kind of flashlight you carry, make sure the batteries work before you set out on the trail. Take along an extra set of batteries and an extra bulb, or simply an extra flashlight or two. You never know when the darn things will run out of juice.

© ANN MARIE BROWN

A few yards below the summit of Mount Tallac, hikers admire sweeping views of the Desolation Wilderness.

5. Sunglasses and sunscreen. You know the dangers of the sun, and the higher the elevation, the more dangerous it is. Wear sunglasses to protect your eyes and sunscreen with a high SPF on any exposed skin. Put on your sunscreen 30 minutes before you go outdoors so it has time to take effect. Many hikers also protect their faces with a lightweight, wide-brimmed hat. Don't forget to protect your lips, too, by wearing a lip balm with a high SPF.

6. Insect repellent. Several kinds of insect repellent now come with sunscreen, so you can combine items 5 and 6 and put on one lotion instead of two. Many types of insect repellent have an active ingredient called DEET, which is extremely effective but also potentially toxic. Children should not use repellent with high levels of DEET, although it seems to be safe for adults. Other types of repellent are made from natural substances, such as lemon oil. What works best? Everybody has an opinion. In a

wet meadow in the middle of a major mosquito hatch, nothing works except covering your entire body in mosquito netting. For typical summer days outside of a hatch period, find a repellent you like and carry it with you.

7. First-aid kit. Nothing major is required here unless you're fully trained in first aid, but a few supplies for blister repairs, an elastic bandage, an antibiotic ointment, and an anti-inflammatory medicine such as ibuprofen can be valuable tools in minor and major emergencies. If anyone in your party is allergic to bee stings or anything else in the outdoors, carry their medication.

8. Swiss Army-style pocketknife. Carry one with several blades, a can opener, scissors, and tweezers.

9. Compass. Know how to use it. If you don't know how, take a class or get someone to show you.

10. Emergency supplies. Ask yourself, "What would I need if I had to spend the night outside?" Aside from food, water, and other items previously listed, here are some basic emergency supplies that will get you through an unplanned night in the wilderness:

- *A lightweight space blanket.* Get a blanket or sleeping bag made of foil-like Mylar film designed to reflect radiating body heat. These can also make a great emergency shelter, and weigh and cost almost nothing.

- *A couple of packs of matches and a candle.* Keep these in a waterproof container (or zipper-style bag), just in case you ever need to build a fire in a serious emergency.

- *A whistle.* If you ever need help, you can blow a whistle for a lot longer than you can shout.

- *A small signal mirror.* It could be just what you need to get found if you ever get lost.

11. Fun stuff. These items aren't necessary, but they can make your trip a lot more fun: a wildflower and/or bird identification book, a small pair of binoculars, a fishing license and lightweight fishing equipment, and an extra pair of socks (these can feel like heaven halfway through a long hike).

Lake Aloha. If you still have the energy, walk onward for one more mile to the northern shore of Aloha, 6.2 miles from your start at Glen Alpine. Lake Aloha is a huge, shallow lake peppered with hundreds of tiny islands—a surreal but beautiful sight to behold. It was created when several small lakes were dammed to form one massive basin.

Gilmore and Half Moon Lakes

- Distance: 12.4 miles round-trip
- Duration: 6–7 hours
- Rating: Moderate
- Elevation change: 1,750 feet
- Trailhead: Echo Lakes
- Directions: From the Y-junction of Hwy. 50 and Hwy. 89 in South Lake Tahoe, drive 3 miles northwest on Hwy. 89 to Fallen Leaf Lake Rd. on the left (1 mile past Camp Richardson). Turn left and drive 5.4 miles to the end of the road and the Glen Alpine Trailhead. Dayhikers are required to fill out a self-serve wilderness permit at the trailhead.

This hike follows the path less traveled to three scenic lakes in the Desolation Wilderness. The route is the same as the trail to Susie, Heather, and Aloha Lakes for the first 3.3 miles, but then heads right to join the Pacific Crest Trail heading north to Gilmore Lake, one mile farther. It's a pleasant hike all the way, gaining only 1,750 feet over 4.3 miles. Snuggled at the base of Mount Tallac's southwest slope, Gilmore Lake is a nearly circular body of water that is forested on its southern shore and backed by a steep talus slope to the north. It is visited mostly by hikers heading from Fallen Leaf Lake to Mount Tallac, and backpackers making their way on the Pacific Crest Trail over Dicks Pass. After enjoying a rest and perhaps a swim at Gilmore, simply retrace your steps 0.7 mile on the Pacific Crest Trail, then turn right on the trail to Half Moon Lake. A brief, easy climb followed by a mostly level walk brings you around the North Shore of the lake. Crescent-shaped Half Moon Lake and its tiny neighbor, Alta Morris Lake, are contained in a huge glacial cirque that rates among the most beautiful spots in all of Desolation Wilderness, yet the lakes are not heavily visited. They are just far enough off the main trail (1.9 miles) that many hikers heading for other destinations won't bother to make the detour. That leaves you with a chance of solitude at the gorgeous lakes, which are set at the base of Dick's Peak (9,974 feet) and Jack's Peak (9,856 feet).

Mount Tallac

- Distance: 9.4 miles round-trip
- Duration: 5–6 hours
- Rating: Strenuous
- Elevation change: 3,400 feet
- Trailhead: Mount Tallac
- Directions: From the Y-junction of Hwy. 50 and Hwy. 89 in South Lake Tahoe, drive 3.5 miles northwest on Hwy. 89 to the left turnoff for the Mount Tallac Trailhead and Camp Shelly (across Hwy. 89 from the Baldwin Beach entrance). Turn left and drive 0.4 mile, then turn left and drive 0.6 mile to the signed trailhead. Day hikers are required to fill out a self-serve wilderness permit at the trailhead.

There are two popular trails that lead to Mount Tallac (pronounced "tull-ACK," with the accent on the second syllable), but the route that offers the most views almost all the way to the top is the one from the Mount Tallac Trailhead. This a butt-kicker of a hike, with 3,400 feet of elevation gain from the bottom to the top, and two-thirds of it crammed into the last 2.6 miles. (The other route begins at the Glen Alpine Trailhead at Fallen Leaf Lake, is about one mile longer, and has slightly less elevation gain.) Regardless of its difficulty, this is one of the most popular hikes near South Lake Tahoe, and also one of the most rewarding. The best way to avoid the heaviest crowds is to hike the trail on a weekday, preferably after Labor Day but before late October, when the 9,735-foot summit often sees its first snow.

The trail starts out deceptively easy, following

an almost level course along a lateral moraine for 1.5 miles to tiny Floating Island Lake. The grass-edged lake once had a 20-foot-wide mat of soil and grass floating around its surface, earning its name, but the "floating island" has been absent for some years. A half mile farther is rocky but small Cathedral Lake, a relatively nondescript body of water, but a good place to rest up before the ensuing climb. And climb you will from here on out. At Cathedral Lake, you've completed 2.1 miles of the hike (almost halfway) but you've gained only 1,200 feet. You've got more than 2,100 feet left to gain over the next 2.6 miles—a punishing climb with almost no shade along the way. Fortunately, a nearly constant banquet of views awaits, with all of South Lake Tahoe spread out before you. The trail winds around to the less-steep southwest side of Mount Tallac, and a quarter mile below the summit, it joins the "other" trail coming up from Gilmore Lake. The last few hundred feet seem to take forever, but finally you ascend the pile of jumbled rocks that mark the top. It's hard to decide which direction to face. To the east, of course, is Lake Tahoe, Emerald Bay, and Fallen Leaf Lake. To the west and south are the lake-laden basins of Desolation Wilderness, and distinctive Ralston and Pyramid peaks. Unless the wind is fierce on top, you won't want to give up this summit vista any time soon.

If you can arrange a car shuttle, a great way to hike Tallac is to go uphill from the Tallac Trailhead as described here, then come back down the west side of the mountain, passing by Gilmore Lake on the way to the Glen Alpine Trailhead at Fallen Leaf Lake. This provides the maximum amount of scenery in a hike of about 11 miles. Some people start at the Glen Alpine Trailhead and make a semiloop by heading up Tallac's west side to the summit, then descending on the east side and taking a cutoff trail from Cathedral Lake to the Stanford High Sierra Camp at Fallen Leaf Lake. But since there is no parking at the Stanford camp unless you are a paying guest, hikers then have to walk back for a couple of miles along the road to the Glen Alpine Trailhead. A car

shuttle from the Tallac Trailhead to the Glen Alpine Trailhead is a much better way to go.

Cascade Falls

- Distance: 1.5 miles round-trip
- Duration: 1 hour
- Rating: Easy
- Elevation change: 200 feet
- Trailhead: Bayview
- Directions: From the Y-junction of Hwy. 50 and Hwy. 89 in South Lake Tahoe, drive 7.5 miles northwest on Hwy. 89 to Bayview Campground on the left. Turn left and drive to the trailhead parking area at the camp's far end. If the lot is full, park in the dirt parking area along Hwy. 89, outside the camp entrance. Take the trail to the left from the trailhead signboard (no wilderness permit is required for Cascade Falls hikers).

The hike to Cascade Falls is one of the best easy hikes near South Lake Tahoe, but good timing is imperative. The waterfall is at its best

© ANN MARIE BROWN

Cascade Falls tumbles gracefully down the cliffs to the western edge of Cascade Lake.

only in the early summer months, and dwindles to a meager dribble by August. In its peak season (May, June, and July), Cascade Falls is a wide stream of white water that plummets 200 feet over fractured granite into Cascade Lake's southwest end. At full flow, as it billows and scatters in the wind creating a misty cloud of spray, it is easy to see why the waterfall was once known as White Cloud Falls.

The hike to Cascade Falls is remarkably level, following a hillside ridge high above azure blue Cascade Lake, elevation 6,464 feet. The route meanders in and out of Jeffrey-pine forest, alternately providing shade and open views. After a mere five minutes of walking, you're rewarded with a tremendous vista of the lake, which is separated from Lake Tahoe by a thin strip of land—the handiwork of glaciers. Soon the path follows an exposed granite ledge that drops off steeply to more dramatic views. The trail peters out near the edge of Cascade Creek, so how far you go is up to you. The best views of the waterfall are not right at the water's edge but about a quarter mile back on the trail. Upstream of the falls are some lovely aquamarine pools, surrounded by large shelves of granite that might inspire a picnic. In July, bright pink penstemon blooms in profusion among the rocky crevices of this trail.

Upper Velma, Fontanillis, and Dicks Lakes Loop

- Distance: 10.5 miles round-trip
- Duration: 5–6 hours
- Rating: Strenuous
- Elevation change: 2,700 feet
- Trailhead: Bayview
- Directions: From the Y-junction of Hwy. 50 and Hwy. 89 in South Lake Tahoe, drive 7.5 miles northwest on Hwy. 89 to Bayview Campground on the left. Turn left and drive to the trailhead parking area at the camp's far end. If the lot is full, park in the dirt parking area along Hwy. 89, outside the camp entrance. Day hikers are required to fill out a self-serve wilderness permit at the trailhead.

The marshiest of the three Velma Lakes, Upper Velma Lake is shallow and tranquil.

© ANN MARIE BROWN

The Bayview Trailhead offers easy access from Highway 89 at Emerald Bay to the spectacular Desolation Wilderness, but it comes with the price of a steep climb. From the trailhead at Bayview Campground, hikers begin with an 850-foot ascent over a slope blanketed with white firs to Granite Lake at 1.2 miles out. Along the way, there are occasional overlook points where the trail breaks out of the trees to provide expansive views of Emerald Bay, Cascade Lake, and Lake Tahoe. Given the heart-pumping climb, it's not surprising that many dog-walkers and exercise seekers just make small but scenic Granite Lake their destination and turnaround point. Those who seek more adventure and are willing to pay for it can continue the climb for another 0.9 mile and 800 feet of gain to the base of Maggie's Peaks. There the grade mellows out for a while before the trail descends to a junction with a path on the right coming in from Eagle Lake. Continue straight (left) and you'll reach the start of this lake-filled loop, now 3.7 miles from the trailhead. Most people go right first, heading

for Upper and Middle Velma Lakes, which are located a short distance off the main trail. Shallow and marshy Upper Velma may not be worth the extra walk, but granite-backed Middle Velma certainly is. Continuing on the loop, you'll skirt along the shoreline of Fontanillis Lake, a remarkably long and narrow body of water named for its plentiful brook trout, and then reach Dicks Lake, the most scenic of the lot. Oval-shaped Dicks Lake is set in a dramatic glacial cirque, with Dicks Peak rising behind it. The final leg of the loop beyond Dicks Lake is a fascinating stroll over a series of low, glacially carved ridges and basins dotted with small ponds. For a genuine taste of the Desolation Wilderness landscape, you can't do much better than this hike.

◖ Eagle Lake

- Distance: 2 miles round-trip
- Duration: 1.5 hours
- Rating: Easy/moderate
- Elevation change: 500 feet
- Trailhead: Eagle Lake
- Directions: From the Y-junction of Hwy. 50 and Hwy. 89 in South Lake Tahoe, drive 8.5 miles northwest on Hwy. 89 to the Eagle Falls/Eagle Lake parking lot on the left. A $3 parking fee is charged unless you park outside the lot alongside the highway. Day hikers are required to fill out a self-serve wilderness permit at the trailhead.

On summer days, it can be difficult finding a parking spot at the trailhead for Eagle Lake. The reason, simply, is because you get so much bang for your buck on this relatively easy, one-mile hike. Yes, the trail has a climb of 500 feet, and yes, it is rocky in places, but given enough time, even a three-year-old could make it to Eagle Lake. The lake is tucked into a beautiful glacial cirque in the Desolation Wilderness, and to get there, the trail crosses the cascading waters of Eagle Creek on a sturdy footbridge above Upper Eagle Falls. Many people just hike in the first 0.25 mile to the waterfall and then call it a day. If you do so, be sure

© ANN MARIE BROWN

A one-mile hike leads to Eagle Lake, a popular spot for picnicking and fishing.

to walk the short and informative interpretive loop that takes off from the footbridge; it provides lovely high views of Emerald Bay with little additional effort. The main trail parallels Eagle Creek much of the rest of the way to the lake. In addition to the up-close beauty of this white-fir and Jeffrey-pine forest, the path offers splendid views of Emerald Bay; just turn around and take a look. Eagle Lake is a beauty, with a granite backdrop and a mix of rocky and forested shoreline that invites long picnics and leisurely swims. For many visitors, Eagle Lake is their first taste of Desolation Wilderness, and it's compelling enough to get anyone hooked for life.

The only way to have a hope for solitude on this trail is to hike it very early in the morning—say 7 A.M.—or wait until an autumn weekday when most of the vacation crowds have dispersed.

Middle Velma Lake

• Distance: 10 miles round-trip
• Duration: 5–6 hours
• Rating: Strenuous
• Elevation change: 2,100 feet
• Trailhead: Eagle Lake
• Directions: From the Y-junction of Hwy. 50 and Hwy. 89 in South Lake Tahoe, drive 8.5 miles northwest on Hwy. 89 to the Eagle Falls/Eagle Lake parking lot on the left. A $3 parking fee is charged unless you park outside the lot alongside the highway. Day hikers are required to fill out a self-serve wilderness permit at the trailhead.

The hike to Middle Velma Lake follows the same path as the trail to Eagle Lake, and the same rules apply: Parking can be difficult on summer days and the crowds can be quite dense along the trail, even though Middle Velma Lake requires a much longer and more strenuous trek. Nonetheless, so many people get inspired by the scenery at Eagle Lake that they decide to continue along the trail to see more, and Middle Velma is the next destination. The junction for Velma Lakes is just 100 yards before the shore

of Eagle Lake. At this junction, you gratefully leave a percentage of the crowds behind, and ascend the hillside to a spectacular view of Eagle Lake and Lake Tahoe from up high. The ascent continues for the next 1.7 miles, with only occasional breaks for level walking. At 2.7 miles from the trailhead, a trail comes in on the left from the Bayview Trailhead; you continue straight for Middle Velma Lake. The grade becomes much easier and in less than a mile you reach a major fork—left for Dicks Lake and Dicks Pass; right for Middle Velma Lake. Head right and enjoy a long downhill stretch, followed by a few right turns in quick succession, all signed for Middle Velma. Five miles from your start you are on the shores of this lovely lake, which is dotted with rocky islands and popular with backpackers because of its hemlock-shaded shoreline. Anglers generally do well here. So do swimmers and picnickers.

Vikingsholm and Lower Eagle Falls

• Distance: 2.5 miles round-trip
• Duration: 1.5 hours
• Rating: Easy/moderate
• Elevation change: 500 feet
• Trailhead: Vikingsholm
• Directions: From the Y-junction of Hwy. 50 and Hwy. 89 in South Lake Tahoe, drive 8.7 miles northwest on Hwy. 89 to the Vikingsholm parking lot on the right, just past the Eagle Falls/Eagle Lake parking lot on the left. A $6 parking fee is charged.

The busiest trail near the South Shore is the short hike to Vikingsholm, a Scandinavian-style mansion built in the 1920s on some of Lake Tahoe's most beautiful shoreline. The mansion belonged to Lora J. Knight, a wealthy Chicago widow who dreamed of building a home on glacier-carved Emerald Bay in the style of an ancient Viking castle. A short distance offshore, Knight also built a teahouse on Fannette Island, the only island in Lake Tahoe. The uniqueness of this property and its location attract a huge number of curiosity seekers on every summer day, so solitude-lovers should take this walk as early in the morning as possible, and preferably on a weekday. The path is a dirt road, not a trail, and leads downhill from Highway 89 to the lakeshore. Even from the parking area the views of Emerald Bay are spectacular; many people go no farther than the stone overlook constructed on granite slabs a few yards from the parking lot. But if you follow the dirt road, you'll enjoy an easy downhill stroll past sprays of summer wildflowers to the Vikingsholm grounds. For five bucks, guided tours of the castle are available. Many hikers are content just to wander along the picnic-table-dotted shoreline, or follow the trail behind Vikingsholm for another 0.25 mile to the base of Lower Eagle Falls, a refreshing cascade of white water in early summer. Near the castle the Vikingsholm Trail joins the Rubicon Trail, so those seeking a longer walk can follow Rubicon Trail south and then east for 1.6 miles to Emerald Bay State Park's Eagle Point Campground, or north for 4.5 miles to D. L. Bliss State Park (see *Rubicon Trail*). The vast majority of people just turn around at Vikingsholm and head back uphill, and many are unpleasantly surprised by the 500-foot elevation gain that awaits—especially since the trail is hot and shadeless at midday.

Rubicon Trail

- Distance: 5.5 miles one-way
- Duration: 2.5 hours
- Rating: Moderate
- Elevation change: 500 feet
- Trailhead: Vikingsholm
- Directions: From the Y-junction of Hwy. 50 and Hwy. 89 in South Lake Tahoe, drive 8.7 miles northwest on Hwy. 89 to the Vikingsholm parking lot on the right, just past the Eagle Falls/Eagle Lake parking lot on the left. A $6 parking fee is charged.

The Rubicon Trail is Tahoe's premier lakeshore hike. If you want to get the maximum dose of Lake Tahoe eye candy, with postcard-perfect views of rocky inlets, sandy coves, and boats bobbing in the water, this is your trail. Since the hike is 5.5 miles one-way and be-

gins and ends at large trailheads at two state parks—Emerald Bay and D. L. Bliss—many hikers do this walk as a one-way trip by leaving one car at either trailhead, or coordinating with the Tahoe Trolley's schedule (800/736-6365, www.laketahoetransit.com) for bus shuttle service. Most prefer to start at the Vikingsholm trailhead by Emerald Bay and hike northward to the trail's end at D. L. Bliss, as there is less elevation gain traveling in this direction. Campers at Emerald Bay State Park's Eagle Point Campground are fortunate to have the option of hiking the Rubicon Trail right from camp. They get to explore an extra 1.6 miles of the Rubicon Trail, curving around the edge of Emerald Bay from the campground to Vikingsholm Castle—a stretch that is not seen by most Rubicon hikers because of the lack of day-use parking at the campground. And of course, the ambitious can hike the trail in both directions instead of just one-way.

No matter how you do it, the path stays close to the lakeshore, although often high above it, and has a very relaxed grade. Highlights along the trail include Rubicon Point, Emerald Point, and Vikingsholm Castle, but really, the entire path is a highlight. Don't miss taking the short side trail that curves around the shoreline at Emerald Point, where the 1920s-era Emerald Bay Resort once stood, and allow some extra time so you can take the short tour of Vikingsholm Castle ($5 fee). Those who hike the 1.6-mile trail segment from Eagle Point Campground to Vikingsholm have an excellent chance of spotting bald eagles. For many years a pair has built a nest in a snag right next to the trail; lucky hikers can stand below and watch the mother eagle feeding her babies (don't forget binoculars).

Not surprisingly, the trail is extremely crowded, especially in the peak season, so you might want to plan this trip for after Labor Day. The most jammed-up section occurs as you near the end of the trail by Rubicon Point, where the drop-offs into the lake are so steep that the trail is lined with chain-link fencing, and the path is so narrow that only one person can pass through at a time. Still, even on the busiest days, everybody is in high spirits as they enjoy this eye-popping, film-burning, lakeside scenery.

Lower and Upper Echo Lakes
- Distance: 2.7–5.4 miles round-trip
- Duration: 2–3 hours
- Rating: Easy
- Elevation change: 200 feet
- Trailhead: Echo Lakes
- Directions: From the Y-junction of Hwy. 50 and Hwy. 89 in South Lake Tahoe, drive 9.8 miles southwest on Hwy. 50 to the Echo Lakes/Berkeley Camp turnoff on the right, at Johnson Pass Rd. Turn right and drive 0.6 mile to Echo Lakes Rd. Turn left and drive 1 mile to the Echo Lakes parking lot, above the resort.

Many hikers use the twin Echo Lakes as their entry point to the Desolation Wilderness, with dozens of lakes accessible via short day hikes or longer backpacking trips. But those who just want a shorter, simpler trip will also enjoy a visit to Echo Lakes, where a small resort provides boat taxi service across the two beautiful alpine lakes. The boat service (one-way fares are $7 adults, $5 children, $3 dogs) allows casual hikers to choose from a 5.4-mile round-trip hike out-and-back along the north shore of the lakes, or a shorter one-way walk of 2.7 miles combined with a scenic boat ride. The trail, which travels through stands of Jeffrey pines and white firs and offers nearly nonstop lake views, is nearly level and manageable even for nonhikers. Both the upper and lower lake's shorelines are dotted with quaint private cabins, inspiring envy in all who visit here.

Tamarack, Ralston, and Cagwin Lakes
- Distance: 3.5–9 miles round-trip
- Duration: 2–5 hours
- Rating: Moderate
- Elevation change: 400 feet
- Trailhead: Echo Lakes

- Directions: From the Y-junction of Hwy. 50 and Hwy. 89 in South Lake Tahoe, drive 9.8 miles southwest on Hwy. 50 to the Echo Lakes/Berkeley Camp turnoff on the right, at Johnson Pass Rd. Turn right and drive 0.6 mile to Echo Lakes Rd. Turn left and drive 1 mile to the Echo Lakes parking lot, above the resort. Day hikers are required to fill out a self-serve wilderness permit.

Whether or not you utilize the Echo Lakes boat taxi will determine the exact distance and difficulty of this lovely hike. Taking the boat in both directions makes this an easy, 3.5-mile trip, but done entirely on foot, the hike is 9 miles. A one-way boat ride puts the mileage at 6.2. Take your pick; one-way fares are $7 adults, $5 children, $3 dogs; round-trip fares are double. However you do it, this hike leads to three distinctly different lakes in the Desolation Wilderness. Deep, dark Tamarack Lake is marked by a tree-covered island and forested shoreline with an abundance of backpacking campsites. Ralston Lake sits in a glacially carved bowl with the steep walls of 9,235-foot Ralston Peak rising straight up from its shore. Tiny, peaceful Cagwin Lake is surrounded by forest and the least dramatic of the three. The lakes are accessible via a nearly level walk on the Pacific Crest Trail, gaining less than 400 feet over 1.1 miles from the boat dock at Upper Echo Lake's west end. Turn left at the trail marker for Tamarack Lake and you'll be on its shoreline in a few minutes; the other two lakes lie less than a half mile beyond. The ease of this trail combined with the spectacular scenery means you are sure to have company at the lakes, but there's enough shoreline so that everybody can find their own private picnic or fishing spot.

Lake of the Woods and Ropi Lake
- Distance: 9.6 miles round-trip
- Duration: 5–6 hours
- Rating: Moderate/strenuous
- Elevation change: 1,800 feet
- Trailhead: Echo Lakes

• Directions: From the Y-junction of Hwy. 50 and Hwy. 89 in South Lake Tahoe, drive 9.8 miles southwest on Hwy. 50 to the Echo Lakes/Berkeley Camp turnoff on the right, at Johnson Pass Rd. Turn right and drive 0.6 mile to Echo Lakes Rd. Turn left and drive 1 mile to the Echo Lakes parking lot, above the resort. Take the boat taxi across Echo Lakes ($14 fee for adult round-trip) and begin your hike at the west end of Upper Echo Lake. Day hikers are required to fill out a self-serve wilderness permit at the boat drop-off point.

As with the above hike to Tamarack, Ralston, and Cagwin Lakes, the length of this trip is made much easier by utilizing the boat taxi service at Echo Lakes, which is both a time and energy saver, and quite enjoyable besides. From the boat dock at the western end of Echo Lakes, follow the gently graded Pacific Crest Trail (PCT) for 2.3 miles, gaining only 800 feet, but on a granite-lined trail that is exposed to the sun most of the day and can be hot. A left turn off the PCT near Haypress Meadows leads you to a junction with the Ralston Peak Trail (see listing in this chapter). Take the trail signed for Lake of the Woods that leads west and downhill. It makes a steep descent over 0.5 mile, losing 350 feet and depositing you on the northeast shore of Lake of the Woods, one of the larger natural lakes in this basin and a popular backpacking, swimming, and picnicking spot. Many hikers make this their destination, or follow the popular trail that leads right (west) to Lake Aloha in less than a mile, another worthwhile destination. (Giant Lake Aloha was formed when dozens of smaller lakes were dammed, forming one huge, shallow body of water dotted with hundreds of small islands.) For this trip, head left (south) instead, following the path along the eastern edge of Lake of the Woods for 0.6 mile, then heading downhill, across Lake of the Woods' outlet stream and west to Ropi Lake. You'll lose another 500 feet in elevation along the way. Peppered with multiple dead snags, Ropi Lake is desolate but beautiful, and has many good

campsites on its shores. For the ambitious, it is an easy cross-country stroll from Ropi Lake to neighboring Osma and Toem Lakes (west) or Pitt and Avalanche Lakes (south). Avalanche Lake is perched above the upper cascades of spectacular Horsetail Falls, the big waterfall that is easily seen from U.S. Highway 50 near Strawberry.

Ralston Peak

• Distance: 8.2 or 8.6 miles round-trip
• Duration: 4–6 hours
• Rating: Moderate/strenuous
• Elevation change: 2,800 or 1,800 feet
• Trailhead: Echo Lakes or Ralston Peak
• Directions: From the Y-junction of Hwy. 50 and Hwy. 89 in South Lake Tahoe, drive 9.8 miles southwest on Hwy. 50 to the Echo Lakes/Berkeley Camp turnoff on the right, at Johnson Pass Rd. Turn right and drive 0.6 mile to Echo Lakes Rd. Turn left and drive 1 mile to the Echo Lakes parking lot, above the resort. Take the boat taxi across Echo Lakes ($14 adult round-trip) and begin your hike at the west end of Upper Echo Lake. Day hikers are required to fill out a self-serve wilderness permit at the boat drop-off point.

For the Ralston Peak trailhead off Highway 50, from the Y-junction of Highways 50 and 89 in South Lake Tahoe, drive 14 miles southwest on Highway 50 to the turnoff for Camp Sacramento. Turn right (north) and park in the parking lot signed for Ralston Trail. Day hikers are required to fill out a self-serve wilderness permit at the trailhead.

There are two common routes to Ralston Peak: the easier route, which utilizes the boat taxi at Echo Lakes for an 8.6-miles round-trip with an 1,800-foot elevation gain; or the harder route, which begins at the Ralston Peak Trailhead off Highway 50 for an 8.2-miles round-trip with a 2,800-foot elevation gain. Solitude seekers will enjoy the harder route since it gets less foot traffic. Pure pleasure seekers will enjoy the easier route, which passes near lovely Tamarack Lake on a remarkably mellow grade to

© ANN MARIE BROWN

From the 9,235-foot summit of Ralston Peak, hikers look down on nearly a dozen lakes.

Ralston's lofty 9,235-foot summit. Either path offers the same reward at the end: one of the best views possible in the Desolation Wilderness, with nearly a dozen lakes in sight, Pyramid Peak holding court to the west, and Mount Tallac towering directly north. The Ralston Trail from Highway 50 begins with multiple switchbacks up a densely forested slope, and even after it breaks free of the trees it continues on a relentlessly steep ascent to the summit. The route from Echo Lakes follows the easy grade of the Pacific Crest Trail for the first 2.3 miles (be sure to take the 100-yard spur off the main trail to see Tamarack Lake), gaining only 800 feet in elevation. It's a walk in the park, except that there is little shade and the exposed granite can be hot. Then, after two left turns near Haypress Meadows, the grade steepens. The final half mile of trail to the summit can be a bit hard to discern (watch for trail cairns to aid you), but just keep heading uphill and you'll get there. When you do, you'll have a big smile on your face. Ralston's summit view is one you will long remember.

Horsetail Falls/ Pyramid Creek Loop

- Distance: 1.5 miles round-trip
- Duration: 1 hour
- Rating: Easy/moderate
- Elevation change: 100 feet
- Trailhead: Twin Bridges
- Directions: From the Y-junction of Hwy. 50 and Hwy. 89 in South Lake Tahoe, drive 15 miles southwest on Hwy. 50 to Twin Bridges. Turn right into the parking lot signed for Pyramid Creek ($3 parking fee).

You'll know why they call it Horsetail Falls the minute you first see it while cruising along Highway 50. Straight and narrow at the top and fanning out to a wide inverted V at the bottom, Horsetail Falls swishes hundreds of feet down Pyramid Creek's glacier-carved canyon. Its powerful stream is reinforced by four lakes: Toem, Ropi, Pitt, and Avalanche. The sight of this dramatic waterfall inspires thousands of highway drivers every day to stop and take a closer look, especially in the heavy snowmelt period from May to July. Few of them hike very far on the trail, as it soon becomes apparent that the waterfall is a long way from the parking lot. Most just pick a spot along the rushing cascades of Pyramid Creek and enjoy the wet and wonderful scenery, especially near a lacy cataract known as The Cascades. Technically the main trail doesn't go to Horsetail Falls at all. Instead, it follows a course known as the Pyramid Creek Loop, which is marked by small brown hiker signs nailed to trees. Much of the path traverses exposed slabs of granite, the handiwork of glaciers, and the open landscape provides good long-distance views of the falls.

Experienced hikers have the option of heading off the 1.5-mile Pyramid Creek Loop to the Desolation Wilderness boundary, where they must fill out a self-serve wilderness permit. From there, it is possible to make your way to the lower cascade of Horsetail Falls, although it is a trail-less route all the way and not advisable for the unprepared. If you choose to attempt the trip, use extra caution. Accidents happen in this area every year because of the slick rock and fast moving water.

Twin and Island Lakes

- Distance: 6.6 miles round-trip
- Duration: 3–4 hours
- Rating: Moderate
- Elevation change: 1,200 feet
- Trailhead: Wrights Lake/Twin Lake
- Directions: From the Y-junction of Hwy. 50 and Hwy. 89 in South Lake Tahoe, drive 17 miles southwest on Hwy. 50 to the signed Wrights Lake turnoff on the right (4.5 miles east of Kyburz). Drive 8 miles north on Wrights Lake Road to Wrights Lake Campground. Bear right at the information center and continue 1.2 miles to the road's end at the Twin Lakes Trailhead. Day hikers are required to fill out a self-serve wilderness permit at the trailhead.

Sculpted by glacial ice more than 1,000 feet deep during the last ice age, the granitic Crystal Range is one of the gems of Tahoe's Desolation Wilderness. The Crystal Basin Recreation Area provides convenient access to this rugged landscape of glaciated basins and saw-toothed peaks. Of a host of trail choices, the 3.3-mile day hike to Twin and Island Lakes offers the best payoffs in the least mileage: spectacular wildflower displays, excellent swimming opportunities in four rock-bound lakes, and miles of solid granite beneath your feet as you walk. Not surprisingly, this is the most popular day-hiking trail in the Crystal Basin.

The path's first stretch meanders past a lush, flower-filled meadow, overflowing with lupine and tiger lilies. A gentle climb through a red-fir and lodgepole-pine forest leads to a major junction just beyond the wilderness boundary, 1.3 miles out. Bear left and ascend more vigorously for 0.75 mile on exposed granite slabs. At the top of the ridge, another wildflower garden awaits, this one bursting with fireweed, paintbrush, and ranger buttons. Vistas of stark, jagged peaks to the northeast produce

an inspiring backdrop. At 2.4 miles you enter Twin Lakes' dramatic granite basin, where the receding glaciers polished each rock to a glowing sheen. The outlet stream from Upper Twin Lake cascades into the shimmering depths of Lower Twin Lake, forming a boisterous waterfall. If you can tear yourself away from the lake's inviting picnic spots, cross its old stone dam and continue along the northwest shore to well-named Boomerang Lake, shaped like an L, at 3 miles. Its tantalizing waters suggest a swim. Near the lakeshore you'll find the tiny, white, bell-shaped flowers of cassiope. Another 0.25 mile of climbing leads you to the shallow glacial valley that contains enchanting Island Lake, dotted with a multitude of rocky islands. From this high point, views of the Crystal Basin's granite ringed cirque are the best of the trip.

Grouse, Hemlock, and Smith Lakes

- Distance: 6.8 miles round-trip
- Duration: 3–5 hours
- Rating: Strenuous
- Elevation change: 1,750 feet
- Trailhead: Wrights Lake/Twin Lake
- Directions: From the Y junction of Hwy. 50 and Hwy. 89 in South Lake Tahoe, drive 17 miles southwest on Hwy. 50 to the signed Wrights Lake turnoff on the right (4.5 miles east of Kyburz). Drive 8 miles north on Wrights Lake Road to Wrights Lake Campground. Bear right at the information center and continue 1.2 miles to the road's end at the Twin Lakes Trailhead. Day hikers are required to fill out a self-serve wilderness permit at the trailhead.

The trail to Grouse, Hemlock, and Smith Lakes consists of an almost relentless climb, but the reward is a series of alpine lakes that get more scenic the higher you go. The trail follows the same wildflower-filled course as the path to Twin and Island Lakes for the first 1.3 miles to just past the wilderness boundary. Here, at a major junction, bear right. Small and pretty Grouse Lake is a one-mile, heart-pumping climb away. Be sure to check out the views looking back toward Wrights Lake and Icehouse Reservoir as you ascend. Grouse Lake is a popular backpacking spot, with designated sites marked by wooden posts. Continue onward and upward for another 0.5 mile to small and stark Hemlock Lake, which is bounded by a forbidding granite slope on one side and a grove of scrawny hemlock trees on the other. This is a classic Desolation Wilderness lake, a perfect circle of sparkling blue surrounded by light-colored granite. You might be tempted to stop here, but Smith Lake lies another 0.5 mile beyond, way up high near tree line at 8,700 feet, and it's a stunner. Don't forget your bathing suit for this trip; at least one of these lakes is sure to lure you in.

Gertrude and Tyler Lakes

- Distance: 8.4 miles round-trip
- Duration: 4–6 hours
- Rating: Moderate/strenuous
- Elevation change: 1,350 feet
- Trailhead: Wrights Lake/Twin Lake
- Directions: From the Y-junction of Hwy. 50 and Hwy. 89 in South Lake Tahoe, drive 17 miles southwest on Hwy. 50 to the signed Wrights Lake turnoff on the right (4.5 miles east of Kyburz). Drive 8 miles north on Wrights Lake Rd. to Wrights Lake Campground. Bear right at the information center and continue 1.2 miles to the road's end at the Twin Lakes Trailhead. Day hikers are required to fill out a self-serve wilderness permit at the trailhead.

There's a whole lot of hiking to be done in the Wrights Lake region of the Crystal Basin Recreation Area—so much that it can seem like too many trails to choose from. The trip to Gertrude and Tyler Lakes stands out because it offers great scenery, smaller crowds, and a chance to practice your cross-country skills on the way to Tyler Lake. A clearly defined trail leads to pretty Gertrude Lake, but Tyler Lake, slightly higher and lovelier, awaits

only those who forge their own way. Start at the Twin Lakes Trailhead by taking the trail heading toward Rockbound Pass (not the main Twin Lakes Trail). You'll enjoy a remarkably easy grade until you reach a sign for Tyler Lake at 1.6 miles. There, bear right and prepare to work a lot harder for the rest of this trip. One memorable half-mile stretch goes almost straight uphill. The worst doesn't last long, thankfully, and the views of the spectacular peaks of the Crystal Range will spur you onward. Keep watch at 3.2 miles for an easy-to-miss spur trail on the left, 100 yards long, which leads to the grave of William Tyler, a rancher who died here in a blizzard in the 1920s. A half mile beyond this spur is Gertrude Lake at 8,000 feet in elevation. But hold on; before you head to Gertrude Lake, watch for the nearly invisible right fork just beyond the grave spur trail; this is an informal use trail to Tyler Lake. Occasional rock cairns signal the way. Even if you miss the use trail, you should be able to find Tyler Lake simply by heading cross-country 0.5 mile to the southeast of Gertrude Lake. Of the two lakes, Tyler is more beautiful, set in a granite basin with a few sparse whitebark pines on its shore. Since many hikers don't even bother trying to find it, you have a better chance at solitude here than at almost any of the lakes in the Crystal Basin.

Sylvia and Lyons Lakes

- Distance: 9.8 miles round-trip
- Duration: 5–6 hours
- Rating: Moderate/strenuous
- Elevation change: 1,700 feet
- Trailhead: Lyons Creek
- Directions: From the Y-junction of Hwy. 50 and Hwy. 89 in South Lake Tahoe, drive 17 miles southwest on Hwy. 50 to the signed Wrights Lake turnoff on the right (4.5 miles east of Kyburz). Drive 4 miles north on Wrights Lake Rd. to the signed turnoff for Lyons Creek Trail. Turn right and drive 0.5 mile to the trailhead. Day hikers are required to fill out a self-serve wilderness permit at the trailhead.

The entire Crystal Basin Recreation Area is well known for summer wildflowers, but the trail with the most rewards in the flower department is the Lyons Creek Trail to Sylvia and Lyons Lakes. Although the trail is no secret, it has the advantage of being a few miles away from busy Wrights Lake Campground and its multiple trailheads into the Desolation Wilderness, so this trail sees somewhat less traffic than others in the area. Even after the peak of the wildflower season ends, the path's final destination at Lyons Lake is always rewarding. The trail's grade is gentle almost all the way except for the final half mile to Lyons Lake. The path keeps to the south side of Lyons Creek for four miles, passing through a succession of woods and meadows, and offering occasional views of Pyramid Peak. After finally crossing the creek at 4.2 miles, the trail reaches a junction. Lyons Lake is to the left and steeply uphill; Sylvia Lake is 0.4 mile to the right on a mostly level course. If you are tiring out, you might skip the side trip to Sylvia Lake, which doesn't compare in size or beauty to Lyons Lake. Sylvia Lake is small and forested around its edges, and is often a breeding ground for mosquitoes. Lyons Lake is the prize on this trail, and a demanding 0.5-mile climb, gaining 400 feet, will get you there. After some huffing and puffing, you arrive at Lyons Lake's rock dam and gape in surprise at the visual impact of its commanding granite amphitheater. Make sure you come well prepared with a picnic, a book, and a towel. You won't want to leave this spot any time soon.

BIKING

Many consider Lake Tahoe to be a mecca of sorts for mountain biking in the Sierra Nevada. Bikes are allowed, even welcomed, on an abundance of trails, including large sections of the Tahoe Rim Trail. Much of the reason for this is because of the concentrated efforts of the **Tahoe Area Mountain Bicycling Association** (530/583-1197, www.tambaonline.com), a group of riders who work hard to keep trails open and maintained, and provide information on riding responsibly on Tahoe's trails.

Among the biking community, the South Lake region is well known for its abundance of rocks and hills. Combined with the heart-pumping, high-elevation air, these obstacles make the trails here well suited to riders seeking a challenge. But that's not to say there aren't opportunities for the more casual rider, both on dirt and on pavement. South Lake Tahoe is laced with paved bike paths, as well as places to rent bikes of all shapes and sizes, including beach cruisers and bikes towing kid trailers. For people who want to ride around downtown South Lake Tahoe, the **South Lake Tahoe Bike Path** starts at El Dorado Beach on Highway 50 and runs five miles west through town, connecting to other bike trails and bike lanes. Most of the ride has an urban feel to it, but a few scenic bridges cross over Trout Creek and the Upper Truckee River.

Last but not least, for those who want a leg up on the mountain, **Heavenly Ski Resort** (530/586-7000 or 800/243-2836, www.skiheavenly.com) allows mountain bikers to bring their machines on the gondola so they can start their ride at the top of the hill, not the bottom. Check with Heavenly to see which trails are currently open to bikes.

Rentals

Anderson's Bike Rental (645 Hwy. 89, South Lake Tahoe, 530/541-0500) is located less than a half mile from the start of the Pope-Baldwin Bike Path. Rentals are also available just up the road at Camp Richardson Outdoor Sports (1900 Jameson Beach Rd., South Lake Tahoe, 530/542 6584).

If you need to rent a mountain bike, contact Shore Line Bike Rentals and Sales (775/588-8777 or 530/544-1621). With three locations in the Heavenly and casino area of South Lake Tahoe, they will gladly set you up with a bike and a free map of the Power Line Trail. Two other places to rent bikes and get information are Lakeview Sports (3131 Hwy. 50, South Lake Tahoe, 530/544-0183) or Tahoe Bike Shop (2277 Hwy. 50, South Lake Tahoe, 530/544-8060).

SOUTH SHORE

(Pope-Baldwin Bike Path

The bike path travels only 3.4 miles one-way, but it passes by some of South Lake Tahoe's greatest attractions. This is a trail for meandering and sightseeing; be sure to bring a bike lock so you can take advantage of all the things to do along the way.

Don't miss getting off your bike to take a look at the underwater world at the Forest Service's Stream Profile Chamber at Taylor Creek. Autumn is the most fascinating time of year, when the kokanee salmon turn bright red and swim up the creek to spawn. You'll also want to step inside a few of the historic buildings at Tallac Historic Site, and if you pack along a picnic and a towel in a small knapsack, you can spend a few hours along the lakeshore at Pope or Baldwin Beaches. In between these highlights are pleasant stretches of trail for casual pedaling through the pines. The bike path begins just south of Camp Richardson along Highway 89. Rent bikes at Anderson's

Bicyclists along the Pope-Baldwin Bike Path stop to admire spawning kokanee salmon in Taylor Creek.

Bike Rental or at Camp Richardson Outdoor Sports just up the road.

Fallen Leaf Lake Road

This is another easy paved ride, although it isn't technically a bike path. This narrow, paved road winds 5.5 miles from Highway 89 along the edge of Fallen Leaf Lake and past dozens of charming cottages. It then continues beyond the lake to the Glen Alpine Trailhead for the Desolation Wilderness. Although cars travel on this road, they rarely drive as fast as you can ride, due to the narrowness of the road. Start the trip by parking near the entrance to Fallen Leaf Lake Campground, or you can access Fallen Leaf Lake Road from the Pope-Baldwin Bike Path.

Angora Ridge Lookout and Angora Lakes

More challenging, but still manageable for reasonably fit cyclists, is the 12-mile ride to Angora Ridge Lookout and Angora Lakes. Best suited for mountain bikes, the ride starts near Fallen Leaf Lake Campground, then follows Fallen Leaf Lake Road for two miles to Tahoe Mountain Road. A left here is followed by a right turn 0.4 mile later on to dirt Forest Road 1214, Angora Ridge Road. The road climbs to the top of Angora Ridge, elevation 7,290 feet. Views are good from the road, but walk a few feet to the fire lookout to get the best perspective on Fallen Leaf Lake, 1,000 feet below. From the lookout, the road descends slightly to the parking lot for Angora Lakes. The last mile to the lakes is on a car-free dirt trail, but the route is shared with a lot of hikers and dog-walkers. You'll ride uphill to Lower Angora Lake, which has a few private homes on its edges, then proceed on level ground to more beautiful Upper Angora Lake, home to Angora Lakes Resort and its handful of picturesque cabins. (You must lock up your bike at the bike rack before entering the resort area.)

Powerline Trail

Mountain bikers of all abilities can handle the first few miles of Powerline Trail, a dirt road/

MOUNTAIN BIKE ETIQUETTE

Mountain bikes are great. They take you off the pavement and into the woods, to places of natural beauty. Riding a mountain bike is great exercise and the simple joy of it can make you feel like a kid again.

On the other hand, mountain bikes cause a lot of controversy. In the past 20 years, mountain bikers have shown up on Tahoe trails that were once the exclusive domain of hikers and horseback riders. Some say the peace and quiet has been shattered. Some say that trail surfaces are being ruined by the weight and force of mountain bikes. Some say that mountain bikes are too fast and clumsy to share the trail with other types of users.

Much of the debate can be resolved if bikers follow a few simple rules, and if nonbikers practice a little tolerance. The following are a list of suggestions for low-impact, "soft cycling." Follow them and you'll help to give mountain biking the good name it deserves:

1. Ride only on trails where bikes are permitted. Obey all signs, speed limits, and trail closures, and stay off private property. Tahoe has such a great abundance of wonderful trails for mountain biking, there is no reason to ride where bikes aren't permitted, such as in the wilderness areas or on the Pacific Crest Trail. Some sections of the Tahoe Rim Trail are open to bikes on even days of the month but closed on odd days, and some sections are not open at all. It is your responsibility to know if you are on a "legal" trail or not.

2. Yield to equestrians. Horses can be badly spooked by bicyclists, so give them plenty of room. If horses are approaching you, stop alongside the trail until they pass. If you are riding with friends, the group of you should move to one side of the trail. (If your group is spread out on both sides of the trail, the horse may feel "surrounded.") If horses are traveling in your direction and you need to pass them, call out politely to the rider and ask permission. If the horse and rider moves off the trail, and the rider tells you it's okay, then pass.

3. Yield to hikers. Bikers travel much faster than hikers. Understand that you have the potential to scare the daylights out of hikers as you speed downhill around a curve and overtake them from behind, or race at them head-on. Make sure you give other trail users plenty of room, and keep your speed down as you near them. If you see a hiker on the trail, slow down to a crawl, and give them plenty of room.

4. Be as friendly and polite as possible. Potential ill will can easily be eliminated by a friendly greeting as you pass: "Hello, what a beautiful day today...." Always say thank you to other trail users for allowing you to pass.

5. Avoid riding on wet trails. Bike tires leave ruts in wet soil that accelerate erosion. This makes bikers very unpopular with land managers and other trail users.

6. On narrow trails, riders going downhill should always yield to riders going uphill. Get out of the uphill rider's way so he or she can keep momentum on the climb.

7. Never, ever skid. Learn to use both breaks properly so that you never skid with your back wheel, which ruins the trail. Eighty percent of your braking power comes from the front brake, so don't forget to use it.

8. Stay in the center of the trail. All riders love single-track, and the only way to keep trails narrow is to stop making them wider. If obstacles are in your way, like tree branches or snow patches, don't be lazy and ride around them. Hurdle them, ride through them, or walk your bike over them, but stay in the middle of the trail.

trail that begins off Oneidas Street in South Lake Tahoe. Drive south of the Y on Highway 89, turn east on Pioneer Trail and follow it to Oneidas Street. Turn right and drive to the Powerline Trailhead on the north (left) side of the road. The road/trail, which is also an off-highway vehicle route and runs more or less parallel to Pioneer Trail, starts with a gentle series of ups and downs as it follows underneath its namesake power lines. Where the trail crosses a creek and leaves the power lines behind, the more serious climbing begins. After a few switchbacks, the road reaches a T-junction. Bear right, then a quarter mile later, go left to get back on Powerline Trail, which is now single-track. This narrower path crosses Cold Creek and ascends behind the homes of Montgomery Estates to deliver you to Ski Run Boulevard by Heavenly Ski Resort. You can ride back on Ski Run to Pioneer Trail to your starting point on Oneidas Street for a 14-mile loop.

Corral Trail Loop

Another short, fun ride from Oneidas Street is the five-mile Corral Trail Loop, which starts just past the Trout Creek bridge on Oneidas (about two miles from Pioneer Trail). Follow the single-track Corral Trail up a short climb, then downhill through a rocky, technical stretch. Eventually the trail smoothes out and offers some twisting, fast turns and small jumps. After about two miles the trail junctions with Powerline Trail. Go left to head back to Oneidas, then left on the road for a paved climb back uphill to your car. If you'd rather get the climbing out of the way at the start of your ride, park near the Powerline Trailhead and begin the loop from there.

Mr. Toad's Wild Ride

Experienced mountain bikers favor Mr. Toad's Wild Ride, otherwise known as the Saxon Creek Trail. The East Shore has its famous Flume Trail; the South Shore has this much more treacherous point-to-point ride, which features an extremely technical, obstacle-ridden downhill stretch suitable for advanced riders only. The north end of the trail is at Forest Service Road 12N01A, on the south side of Oneidas Street. The south end of the trail is at the Big Meadow Trailhead for the Tahoe Rim Trail, 5.3 miles south of Meyers on Highway 89. Most riders start at the Big Meadow Trailhead and follow the Tahoe Rim Trail east and then north for 4.5 miles to Tucker Flat, elevation 8,830 feet. The route is single-track almost all the way and climbs through forest to a ridge, then makes a short descent to Tucker Flat and a junction of trails. If this first part

proved to be too technical for you, turn around now; things are about to get much scarier. Turn left on Saxon Creek Trail and begin a highly technical downhill stretch, with lots of large rocks and big drop-offs. The trail follows the drainage of Saxon Creek and the descent is fast and furious. Finally the obstacles peter out and the ride gets smoother with lots of fast, banked turns. Saxon Creek Trail eventually meets up with Forest Service Road 12N01A, which delivers you to Oneidas Street, where your car shuttle should be waiting for you. Hope they brought some extra bandages.

BOATING AND WATER SPORTS

In winter at Lake Tahoe, it's all about the slopes. In summer, it's all about the lake—finding ways to get in it, on it, and around it. Whether you want just want to look at the lake while enjoying an easygoing cruise, swim in the lake and then relax on its golden beaches, or race around the lake on a speedboat or personal watercraft, there are literally hundreds of ways to enjoy Lake Tahoe's mighty blue expanse.

🅒 Kayaking

Whether you are a brand-new beginner or longtime expert, the waters of Lake Tahoe can provide hours of pleasure as you tool around its shimmering surface in a colorful, lightweight kayak. Much of the beauty of the experience lies in the fact that you are self-propelled, gliding along the lake without the noise and distraction of an engine. Traveling in this quiet fashion, and at a relatively slow pace, you are almost guaranteed to see wildlife. A family of ducks or a gaggle of geese may swim by your boat; an eagle or an osprey may soar overhead. Since most kayakers paddle close to the shoreline, deer and other land animals are also commonly seen.

A company called **Kayak Tahoe** (in Timber Cove Marina behind the Best Western Timber Cove Lodge, South Lake Tahoe, 530/544-2011, www.kayaktahoe.com) leads kayak tours, rents kayaks to do-it-yourselfers, and operates a kayaking school. No experience is necessary for rentals or tours; beginners are outfitted with a sit-on-top kayak and with only a few minutes of instruction can set out on their own. Rental rates are $38 per half day for single kayaks and $55 for doubles; kayaks can also be rented for one or two hours, or all day. Reservations are required for guided tours along Tahoe's East Shore or Emerald Bay ($65–80 for a six-hour tour) or evening sunset or moonlight tours ($30–35 for a two-hour tour).

Sit-on-top kayaks can also be rented at most of the South Shore's marinas, including Camp Richardson, Zephyr Cove, Ski Run, Lakeside, Round Hill, Timber Cove, and Tahoe Keys. Those who have brought their own kayaks to Lake Tahoe can put in at almost any public beach or marina they can drive to. The most popular area for kayaking on the South Shore is the sparkling waters of **Emerald Bay.** Most boaters launch from Baldwin Beach and paddle about two miles to Emerald Point, then steer around the point and into Emerald Bay. It's another 1.5 miles from Emerald Point to the back of the bay, where Vikingsholm Castle is located. Kayakers can stop for a rest on the beach, take a guided tour of the castle ($5), or pay a visit to Fannette Island, where the owner of Vikingsholm held tea parties. A **boat-in campground** (530/541-3030 or 530/525-7277, www.parks.ca.gov, $22) is located on the shores of Emerald Bay State Park for those who want to turn this into a two-day adventure.

Kayakers with bigger ambitions should check out the Lake Tahoe Water Trail map (530/542-5651, www.laketahoewatertrail.org), which shows available boat launches, campsites, lodging, dining, and more for all 72 miles of lake shoreline.

Sailing

If the idea of plying Tahoe's waters by using only a combination of the wind and your own skill appeals to you, check out **Sailing Ventures** in Tahoe Keys Marina (775/691-8200, www.sailingventures.com or www.sailtahoe.com,), which offers the South Shore's only professional sail training. Rates are $175

for two people for a two-hour demonstration class or $350 per person for a more extensive two-day class. If you already know how to sail, sailboats can be rented in Tahoe Keys Marina or Ski Run Marina at **Tahoe Sports** (530/544-8888 or 530/544-0200, www.tahoesports .com). Rates are $100 per hour, $300 for a half-day, or $550 per day.

Water Sports Outfitters and Marinas

Literally dozens of water-sports companies are located around the South Shore, ready and willing to rent you a jet ski, Sea Doo, Waverunner, hydro bike, or powerboat for racing around the lake. **Action Watersports** (3411 Hwy. 50, South Lake Tahoe, 530/544-0183, www.action-watersports.com), located at Timber Cove Marina behind the Best Western Timber Cove Lodge, rents all of the above and also offers parasailing rides. For the uninitiated, this is an activity in which one or two participants soar high above the lake, attached to a parachute being pulled by a boat. Potential parasailing passengers, be forewarned: Everyone on shore will stare at you while you "fly," so this is a poor activity for those prone to shyness. Action Watersports has two other locations: one at Camp Richardson Marina (530/542-6570) and another at Lakeside Marina (530/541-9800).

Tahoe Sports (www.tahoesports.com) in Ski Run Marina (530/544-0200) and Tahoe Keys Marina (530/544-8888) rents powerboats, jet skis, and other water toys by the hour or the day. They also operate Lakeview Sports (530/544-0183) near El Dorado Beach in downtown South Lake Tahoe. In addition to a full array of rentals, they lead guided jet ski tours to Emerald Bay. Their parasailing operation out of Ski Run Marina soars the highest of any company on the lake—more than 1,200 feet above the water.

Closer to the casinos, **Lakeside Marina** (Park Ave. and Lakeshore Dr., Stateline, 530/541-9800) has Waverunner and Sea Doo rentals. And on the Nevada side of South Shore, **H2O Sports** (775/588-4155,

SOUTH SHORE

© ANN MARIE BROWN

Almost every type of watercraft is available for rent on the South Shore.

www.rhpbeach.com) operates out of Round Hill Pines Beach, two miles northeast of Stateline. They rent Sea Doos, kayaks, paddle boats, and sea cycles, and offer parasailing rides. At nearby **Zephyr Cove Resort** (775/589-4908, www.zephyrcove.com), you can rent just about anything with horsepower—powerboats, wave runners, ski boats—and yes, they have parasailing, too.

If you don't know how to water-ski or wakeboard, or would like to improve your skills, Lake Tahoe is a great place to learn. Try **Don Borges Water Ski School** at Round Hill Pines Beach, two miles northeast of Stateline (530/541-1351, www.rhpbeach.com) or **Lake View Sports** at El Dorado Boat Launch (3131 Hwy. 50, South Lake Tahoe, 530/544-0183).

If you brought your own boat or personal watercraft to Lake Tahoe and just need to find a boat ramp on the South Shore where you can put it in the water, you can do so at South Lake Tahoe Recreation Area (530/542-6055), Tahoe Keys Marina (530/541-2155), Timber Cove Marina (530/544-2942), Lakeside Marina (530/541-6626), or Camp Richardson Marina (530/542-6570).

SWIMMING

If it's a pristine Tahoe beach you desire, you have a handful of good choices on the South Shore. Three of the most scenic are **Baldwin, Kiva,** and **Pope Beaches,** all managed by the U.S. Forest Service, with restrooms and picnic facilities on site. The beaches are located between two and four miles north of the South Lake Tahoe Y on Highway 89. A parking fee of $5 is charged at Baldwin and Pope beaches, but you can avoid the fee by riding your bike or walking instead of driving. The paved Pope-Baldwin Bike Path runs right through all three beach parking lots. There is no fee at Kiva Beach, but swimmers beware: There are lots of rocks in the water near the shoreline. On the positive side, views of Mount Tallac are divine, and dogs are allowed at Kiva Beach (but not at Pope and Baldwin). The neighboring **Camp Richardson Resort** also has a pay beach, but it is so crowded on summer days that it can be difficult to find a spot to lay down your towel.

SOUTH SHORE

Closer to downtown South Lake are two no-fee beaches. **El Dorado Beach** is located between Rufus Allen Boulevard and Lakeview Avenue and is visible from Highway 50. Restrooms, a boat launch, and picnic facilities are provided. A grassy strip overlooking the lake makes a nice spot for a picnic. A couple of blocks way is **Regan Beach** (Lakeview Ave. and Sacramento Ave.), which has a food concession, restrooms, picnic facilities, and playground, but almost no sand. It's more like a neighborhood park than a beach, but you can swim here. For parents with little ones, the grass might be easier to manage than sand anyway.

Also in the downtown area, just behind the Best Western Timber Cove Lodge is **Timber Cove Beach,** a great choice for families because of shallow water and the presence of a snack bar, kayak rentals, and a pier and restaurant.

Two miles northeast of Stateline, spectacular **Nevada Beach** is located at Elk Point Road, off Highway 50. The beach is nearly a mile long and much wider than most Tahoe beaches. It's a wonderful place to spend a day, but note that it is often windy here by mid-afternoon, when the windsurfers and kiteboarders take over from the sunbathers and casual swimmers. Restrooms and picnic facilities are available, along with an accompanying $5 parking fee. If you don't mind a short hike, you can forgo the fee by parking at Kahle Park (Kahle Dr. and Hwy. 50) and walking the one-mile trail to Nevada Beach.

Also on the Nevada side of South Shore, the private **Zephyr Cove Resort** (800/238-2463, www.zephyrcove.com) has a lovely strip of sand, as well as a restaurant, restrooms, beach volleyball, and the marina for the MS *Dixie II* and *Woodwind II* cruises. The parking fee is $7. The same exorbitant rate is charged at nearby **Round Hill Pines Beach** (775/588-3055, www.rhpbeach.com), which provides a similar array of beach and boating activities.

If you are willing to hike, **Emerald Bay Beach** by Vikingsholm Castle is a wonderful white-sand beach with picnic tables. Accessing

Families enjoy the white sands and shallow waters at Zephyr Cove.

© A'N MARIE BROWN

the beach requires a two-mile round-trip hike with a 500-foot elevation gain on the return trip, and you still have to pay a parking fee at the Vikingsholm trailhead: $6.

Finally, when you think about swimming or beach-going, don't forget there's another lake around here besides Tahoe. **Fallen Leaf Lake,** south of Camp Richardson, has a lovely stretch of shoreline and a swimming beach on its northwest end, accessible by a short walk from Fallen Leaf Campground. Your dog is allowed to join you, too.

FISHING

Lake Tahoe is famous for its huge mackinaw trout, but the trophy fish don't just jump on to your line. Because of the lake's massive size and depth, the best fishing is always done by boat and in the company of an experienced guide who knows the lake. Although mackinaw can be fished year-round, the bite is best in spring and early summer, when the fish move from the deepest parts of the lake into shallower water. The average size of a mackinaw is three to five pounds, but fish as large as 10 pounds are fairly common. Occasionally a 20–30 pounder will be caught; the lake record was more than 37 pounds.

The lake also offers an excellent kokanee salmon fishery, with most action occurring around midsummer. Kokanee, or landlocked salmon, are considerably smaller than mackinaw, but are strong fighters and provide exciting fishing. The lake record kokanee was four pounds, 15 ounces. Brown and rainbow trout are also commonly caught in Lake Tahoe. The lake is open for fishing year-round, except for within 300 feet of its tributaries October 1–June 30.

Dozens of South Lake Tahoe guide services can take you out on the lake and greatly increase your chances of catching fish. Most services have a 90 percent or better catch rate. Bait, tackle, and beverages are usually provided, and your fish will be cleaned and bagged for you. One of the biggest and best guide services is **Tahoe Sport Fishing Company** (900 Ski Run Blvd., South Lake Tahoe, 530/541-5448 or 800/696-7797, www.tahoesportfishing. com), with a fleet of seven boats available for private charter. They operate year-round out of Ski Run Marina and Zephyr Cove and offer four- or five-hour trips in the morning or afternoon ($85–95 per person), or all-day trips ($135). Fishing gear, bait, and tackle are provided, as well as snacks and drinks, and foul-weather gear if needed. If you catch fish, your guides will not only clean and bag it for you, they will even arrange to have it delivered to your favorite South Shore restaurant so it can be served to you at dinner.

There are too many other excellent **guide services** to list, but a few that come well recommended are Mile High Fishing Charters at the Tahoe Keys Marina (530/541-5312 or 866/752-3473, www.fishtahoe.com), O'Malley's Fishing Charters at Zephyr Cove Marina (775/588-4102, www.tahoefishingcharters.com), Eagle Point Fishing Charters at Tahoe Keys Marina (530/577-6834), and Don Sheetz Fishing Charters (530/541-5566 or 877/270-0742).

Nearby **Fallen Leaf Lake** also offers good boat fishing for mackinaw and rainbow trout. Shoreline anglers generally have better luck at this lake, too (try using worms, spinners, or lures). Access the lake by walking a quarter mile from Fallen Leaf Lake Campground. Fishing within 250 feet of the dam is illegal. Captain Aaron Fox with Backwater Charters (530/544-1977 or 530/307-8906, call for rates) will take you out on Fallen Leaf Lake in his boat for guided fishing.

If you are a fly fisher hoping for some inside knowledge about the streams and rivers in the Tahoe area, pay a visit to **Tahoe Fly Fishing Outfitters** (2705 Hwy. 50, South Lake Tahoe, 530/541-8208 or 877/541-8208, www.tahoeflyfishing.com). In addition to their full-service fly shop, they offer guided trips and fly-fishing instruction, and complete equipment rentals (everything from waders to fly rods). The store sells a huge selection of hand-tied flies, many made by local experts. Guide rates are $125 for two hours, $195 for four hours, or $295 for all-day. Beginners might want to sign up for the popular Introduction to Fly Fishing class, taught outside at a stream ($50 per person).

Anglers who want to get access to the high mountain lakes and streams of Desolation Wilderness without having to walk should contact Cascade Stables (see *Horseback Riding*) for information on fishing-oriented pack trips.

And finally, if you just want your four-year-old to catch his or her first fish, head over to the **Tahoe Trout Farm** (1023 Blue Lake Ave., South Lake Tahoe, 530/541-1491), a stocked pond for children 15 and under. No license is required and no limits apply; they charge by the fish. Bait and tackle are provided.

HORSEBACK RIDING

Feeling aerobically challenged? Let Trigger do the walking for you. A variety of guided two-hour and four-hour trail rides are offered by the trusty steeds at **Camp Richardson Corral** (Emerald Bay Rd. at Fallen Leaf Lake Rd., South Lake Tahoe, 530/541-3113 or 877/541-3113). The Breakfast Ride (8–10 A.M.) is one of the most popular choices. Guests enjoy a crisp morning horseback ride followed by a cholesterol-laden breakfast of bacon and eggs, hotcakes, and cowboy coffee. The horses eat hay, of course. The evening Steak Ride (4:30–7 P.M.) is also popular. Riders follow trails through the forest and across Taylor Creek and back, returning to a hearty western steak barbecue. Children must be six years or older to ride; no experience is necessary. Camp Richardson also offers overnight horseback trips to several high mountain lakes; reservations are required.

Cascade Stables (2199 Cascade Rd., South Lake Tahoe, 530/541-2055) has a similar list of rides: hourly, all-day, breakfast and dinner rides, and longer pack trips. One- and two-hour rides, suitable for beginners, skirt the edge of Cascade Lake or head to a scenic overlook of Lake Tahoe. The steak-and-potatoes dinner ride includes a hearty meal cooked over an open fire. More experienced riders can sign up for all-day trips that explore the sparkling lakes and streams of the Desolation Wilderness.

A few miles to the east of South Lake Tahoe, **Zephyr Cove Stables** (775/588-5664, www.zephyrcovestables.com) provides equestrian services on the Nevada side of South Shore. Breakfast, lunch, and dinner rides are available, or one- to two-hour rides without meals.

At all locations, riders should expect to pay about $30 per hour for a regular ride, or $40–65 for a ride that includes a meal.

ROCK CLIMBING

One look at the South Lake Tahoe shoreline and the verdict is clear: This place rocks. Experts and beginners alike will find plenty of bouldering and climbing opportunities around the South Shore. A popular beginner area is located in **Eagle Creek Canyon** near Emerald Bay, a quarter mile up the Eagle Lake Trail near the bridge over the creek. A 75-foot-tall cliff erroneously named **90-Foot Wall** can be climbed year-round. Various climbs and routes are possible, giving beginners and intermediates ample practice opportunities. Bolt anchors are positioned on top of the cliff, making toproping easy. Another popular top-roping site

is **Pie Shop,** named after a bakery that used to be near the rock's base. Pie Shop is located off Sawmill Road (one mile south of the South Lake Tahoe Airport).

A famous climbing area to the west of the South Shore is **Lover's Leap,** located off Highway 50 by Strawberry. This distinctive chunk of granite that rises 600 feet from the American River Canyon floor was made famous by climbing legend Royal Robbins in the 1960s. Single- and multiple-pitch routes are available, offering variety for climbers of all levels. About 30 separate boulder problems also present good challenges. Farther west on Highway 50, the Echo Lake and Kyburz areas offer more climbing opportunities, including the steep knobs of Phantom Spires near the Wrights Lake road turnoff, and the smooth, solid cracks of Sugarloaf near Kyburz, where the hardest climb in the world was established by Tony Yaniro in 1978.

Generally the best months for climbing around the South Shore are May, June, September, and October. July and August are often too hot, except for shaded climbing areas like Eagle Lake Cliff. Winter is obviously too cold. For **climbing instruction** and/or **guide service,** contact the Tahoe Adventure Company (530/913-9212 or 866/830-6125, www.tahoeadventurecompany.com). Although the company is based on the North Shore, they offer classes at several South Shore locations, including Lover's Leap, Phantom Spires, and Sugarloaf. A five-hour beginner's lesson costs about $150. Several other reputable companies offer guiding service and classes on the South Shore: Lover's Leap Guides (530/318-2939, www.loversleap.net), Alpine Skills International (530/582-9170, www.alpineskills.com), and Epic Adventures (408/261-0464, www.climbepic.com).

To purchase rock-climbing equipment on the South Shore, go to Sports Ltd. (1032 Hwy. 89, South Lake Tahoe, 530/544-2284).

GOLF

Golfers looking for a bargain should head to **Bijou Municipal Golf Course** (3464 Fairway Ave., South Lake Tahoe, 530/542-6097, www.recreationintahoe.com), run by the City of South Lake Tahoe Parks and Recreation Department. This nine-hole, par-32 course offers fine views of Freel Peak and Heavenly Ski Area and is the perfect place to hit a few balls without breaking the bank. Green fees are only $12–18, and tee times are on a first-come, first-served basis, so you can golf at the spur of the moment.

Or, for a longer day on the greens, make a reservation at the 18-hole **Lake Tahoe Golf Course** (2500 Emerald Bay Rd., South Lake Tahoe, 530/577-0788, www.laketahoegc.com). This par-72 course, designed by Billy Bell Jr., boasts spacious fairways backed by snow-capped mountains. The Upper Truckee River comes into play on 13 holes. Breakfast and lunch are served, plus cocktails on the mountain-view sundeck. Private and group lessons are offered at the full-service pro shop. Green fees are $41–74.

Another of South Lake Tahoe's scenic courses is **Tahoe Paradise** (3021 Hwy. 50, South Lake Tahoe, 530/577-2121, www.tahoe-paradisegc.com), an 18-hole beauty nestled among the sugar pines just four miles south of the South Lake Tahoe Y. This par-66 executive course costs only $29–57 to play, but be prepared for narrow, tree-lined fairways. If you aren't a straight shooter, play somewhere else.

Just across the Nevada state line in the casino area is **Edgewood Tahoe Golf Course** (180 Lake Pkwy., Stateline, 775/588-3566 or 888/881-8659, www.edgewood-tahoe.com). This 18-hole, par-72 course, built by architect George Fazio and his nephew Tom Fazio in 1969, is a favorite of well-to-do golfers and celebrities. Green fees are $200, which keeps out the riffraff. Bordering Lake Tahoe, the course is remarkably scenic, and has been lauded by *Golf Digest Magazine* as one of America's top 100 courses. You've probably seen photographs of its 18th hole, which has so much water around it, it's almost an island. Even if you don't play golf, tag along with someone who does and go have a meal in the fabulous lakeview Edgewood Restaurant.

(BALLOONING

South Shore visitors longing to go up, up, and away can do just that with **Lake Tahoe Balloons** (530/544-1221 or 800/872-9294, www.laketahoeballoons.com, $225). The company launches their balloons not from land but from the surface of the lake, via the *Tahoe Flyer,* the world's only certified balloon launch and recovery boat. Balloon rides are usually offered in the early-morning hours only (5–7 A.M. launch time, May–Oct.), when the wind is relatively calm. The staff at Lake Tahoe Balloons will pick you up at your South Lake Tahoe hotel and drive you to the marina. A continental breakfast is served on board the boat as it cruises to the designated launch site on the lake. Passengers watch as the balloon is inflated, then board its basket for a one-hour flight. During the flight, passengers will fly as high as 2,500 feet above the water's surface, enjoying a bird's-eye view of the entire Tahoe basin, and experiencing the odd (and somewhat daunting) sensation of being propelled only by blasts of hot air, the skill of the balloon pilot, and the whim of the wind. After the flight, passengers are treated to a traditional postflight champagne toast. The entire adventure takes about four hours.

WINTER SPORTS
Downhill Skiing and Snowboarding

Boasting the largest concentration of ski areas in North America, Lake Tahoe offers skiers and snowboarders plenty of terrain, plenty of variety, and most years, plenty of snow. Thanksgiving is the traditional opening day for downhill (alpine) skiing and snowboarding around Lake Tahoe, but this varies according to the whims of Mother Nature. The ski season usually lasts into early April. At Tahoe's lake level (6,200 feet), about 125 inches of snow fall each year, but the higher elevations receive as much as 500 inches. At most Tahoe ski resorts, snow bases are usually between 100 and 200 inches December–March.

If you want to ski on the South Shore, you have two close-by choices: Heavenly Valley Ski

© ANN MARIE BROWN

Even the smallest of tykes can learn to ski from Heavenly's patient instructors.

Resort and Sierra-at-Tahoe. **Heavenly Valley Ski Resort** (3860 Saddle Rd., South Lake Tahoe, 530/586-7000 or 800/243-2836, www .skiheavenly.com) holds numerous Tahoe records, including the fact that it has the highest summit elevation of any resort around the lake (10,040 feet). With 4,800 skiable acres, there is ample slope space for all. In fact, Heavenly has more skiable acreage than any other Tahoe ski area, with 34 lifts serving 86 runs, the longest of which is a prodigious 5.5 miles. The resort's greatest vertical drop is 3,500 feet, considered to be the longest on the West Coast. All in all, megaresort Heavenly can brag of a lot of "mosts" and "bests." That means this isn't the best place for beginners to try out their first pair of skis, but it's tons of fun for intermediate and advanced skiers and riders. One-third of the mountain is for expert skiers; the other two-thirds is beginner- and intermediate-level terrain. Snowboarding is permitted on all slopes.

Since the resort typically sees 360 inches of snow per season, and they have plenty of snow-making equipment, there's usually plenty of white stuff, too—but never as much as there is at some of Tahoe's other resorts, where the annual snowfall can exceed 450–500 inches. If Heavenly has one shortcoming, it's that the season often ends a bit early.

Heavenly was purchased by Vail Resorts Inc. in the spring of 2002 and a blizzard of success has fallen upon it ever since. The resort has been posting record seasons and was rated one of the Top 20 Ski Resorts in North America by *Ski Magazine*. Part of the reason for Heavenly's good fortune is the location of its $23 million **gondola**, which was completed in 2001 and sits smack in the middle of downtown at Highway 50 and Heavenly Village Way. Skiers and riders can walk to the gondola from hundreds of lodgings options on both sides of the California and Nevada state line. Traveling 2.4 miles in about 12 minutes, Heavenly's gondola is California's longest, and its 138 cabins carrying eight passengers apiece give it the most uphill carrying capacity of any gondola in the state. Even nonskiers enjoy riding the gondola; the lake views are sublime. On the uphill ride, skiers and nonskiers alike can disembark about two-thirds of the way up and take in the vista from a 14,000-square-foot observation deck. At the top of the gondola is a lodge and restaurant, as well as Heavenly's Adventure Peak snow park.

Like most large Tahoe resorts, it isn't cheap to ski or ride here. Heavenly alters its ticket prices based on the peak periods of the ski season, with the highest prices usually occurring during the last two weeks of December and between mid-February and the end of March. Pre-Thanksgiving and April tickets are usually the cheapest. For all-day tickets, adults can expect to pay $62–73, teenagers $52–60, and children 12 and under $30–38. Seniors 65 and older pay $50–58. To save a few bucks, purchase multiple-day tickets at least seven days in advance at Heavenly's website.

To the west on Highway 50, 12 miles from South Lake Tahoe, lies **Sierra-at-Tahoe** (1111 Sierra-at-Tahoe Rd., Twin Bridges, 530/659-7453, www.sierraattahoe.com). With a high elevation of 8,852 feet, Sierra-at-Tahoe ski area has several things going for it. For skiers and riders traveling from Sacramento or the San Francisco Bay Area, Sierra-at-Tahoe is within easy reach, shaving nearly 30 minutes off the trip to South Lake Tahoe. Owned by the same corporation as Northstar-at-Tahoe near Truckee, the resort has 2,100 mostly wind-protected acres and 46 runs, so there's no shortage of terrain. There's no snowmaking equipment, either, since the average annual snowfall is a whopping 480 inches, one of the greatest around Tahoe. Lastly, the summit is graced by the **Grandview Bar and Grill,** where an ordinary pizza or a hamburger achieve new culinary heights. Maybe it's due to the dizzying view of Lake Tahoe from the restaurant, but *Snow Country Magazine* listed Sierra-at-Tahoe as the best resort in California for on-mountain food. A total of seven restaurants and bars are located on the mountain, and a Pizza Utility Vehicle, or PUV, cruises the parking lot. This giant golf-cart-on-steroids will deliver fresh-baked pizza right to your car window.

Snowboarders are fond of Sierra-at-Tahoe because of its six terrain parks and two radical half-pipes, including a 17-foot-wall gem that was ranked as one of the top 10 half-pipes in North America by *Transworld Snowboarding*. Expert skiers who like to have a few obstacles in their path enjoy the amount of tree skiing possible on the slopes. And parents of wee ones will appreciate the fact that the resort has licensed day care for children aged 18 months to five years. Ski and snowboard lessons and learning programs are a priority at Sierra-at-Tahoe. With their "Learn to Ski Guarantee," beginners are promised they will be able to ski or snowboard from the top of the mountain after three lessons, or the fourth lesson is free. With all this, it is no surprise that Sierra-at-Tahoe has a well-earned reputation as a family-friendly resort.

Adult all-day tickets are $59, youths aged 13–22 are $49, and children age 12 and under are $14. Seniors aged 65–69 are $34, seniors 70 and over are $17. All prices are a few bucks higher on holidays.

Finally, skiers and boarders who would like to head to the North Shore's slopes but don't want to drive in the snow can take advantage of the *Tahoe Queen's* **North Shore Ski Shuttle** (reservations: 775/589-4906 or 800/238-2463, www.laketahoecruises.com). Departing from various South Lake Tahoe lodgings at about 7 A.M., the trip consists of a bus ride to **Squaw Valley USA,** or **Northstar-at-Tahoe,** a day of skiing, an then a floating return trip across the lake on the *Tahoe Queen,* with food and drinks available for purchase and a live band. Cost is $39, or $99 including lift tickets at Squaw.

Dozens, perhaps even hundreds, of rental shops in town can supply you with skiing and boarding equipment before you reach the slopes. **Heavenly Sports** has three locations, including 988 Stateline Avenue, South Lake Tahoe, 530/544-1921. **Powder House Lake Tahoe** also has three locations in South Lake, including one that is 100 feet from the Heavenly gondola (530/542-6222). **House of Ski** (209 Kingsbury Grade, Stateline, 775/588-5935 or 800/475-4432, www.houseofski.com) has been renting ski equipment on the South Shore since 1979.

Cross-Country Skiing

The South Shore alpine ski resorts don't particularly cater to cross-country (Nordic) skiers. Heavenly's Adventure Peak area offers a meager four kilometers of trail for cross-country skiers— a token offering at best. Instead, the cross-country skiing hot spots of the South Shore are better suited to do-it-yourselfers—people who have their own equipment and know where to go. One of the most popular areas is **Echo Lake Sno-Park,** on the north side of Highway 50, one mile west of Echo Summit (along the road to Echo Lakes). There is parking for about 60 cars, but you must purchase a Sno-Park permit ($5/day or $25/year, purchasable on site; 530/644-6048). From the Sno-Park, you can ski up to the twin Echo Lakes, then follow the trail along their north shores and beyond as far as you please. It's 3.5 miles to the far end of Upper Echo Lake, 6 miles to Lake Margery, and 7 miles to Lake Aloha.

A much smaller Sno-Park at Taylor Creek, on the west side of Highway 89 near Camp Richardson, offers beginner-level cross-country skiing trails to Fallen Leaf Lake (530/573-2600). There is parking for about 15 cars, but again, you must have a Sno-Park permit. Those seeking more of a challenge can ski the hill leading up to the Angora Fire Lookout on Angora Ridge, or continue to the Angora Lakes.

South Lake Tahoe locals usually head to Oneidas Street, off Pioneer Trail, to ski the road/trail to Fountain Place, or a stretch of the Powerline Trail (both about four miles round-trip). High Meadows Road, also off Pioneer Trail, has more Nordic skiing opportunities.

If you need a place to rent equipment or take a few hours of lessons, your best bet is **Camp Richardson Resort** (1900 Jameson Beach Rd., South Lake Tahoe, 530/541-1801 or 530/542-6584, www.camprich.com). The resort has 35 kilometers of groomed trails bordering Highway 89, including a few trails along the shore of Lake Tahoe and on the grounds of the Tallac Historic Site. Equipment rentals cost $8–17 per day; a full-day trail pass is $10. Stay-and-ski packages that include cross-country ski equipment rentals, trail passes, lodging, and a continental breakfast start at $55 per person (double occupancy).

Snowshoeing

The great thing about snowshoeing is that you don't need any experience to do it, and you don't need to go anywhere special to do it. If there is snow on the ground and you have two feet, you can snowshoe. Sure, you can ride the gondola to Heavenly's Adventure Peak and snowshoe there, but you could just as easily (and much more cheaply) do so on any of South Lake Tahoe's bike paths, along the Baldwin Beach shoreline, or almost anywhere else.

Still, if it's your first time and you prefer to be led by the hand, try the groomed trails by the **Mountain Sports Center** at Camp Richardson Resort (530/542-6584, www.camprich.com), **Heavenly's Adventure Peak** (775/586-7000, www.skiheavenly.com), or

The shoreline near Camp Richardson Resort is a fine place for an easy cross-country ski.

© ANN MARIE BROWN

Sierra-at-Tahoe Ski Resort (530/659-7453, www.sierrattahoe.com).

The Mountain Sports Center at Camp Richardson has the largest selection of snowshoe rentals at Lake Tahoe, including children's sizes; they also hold fun events like snowshoe cocktail races and full-moon snowshoe parties. Snowshoe rentals cost $15–20 for a half day; $18–30 for a full day. Kids under 12 get a free trail pass when accompanied by an adult.

Sierra-at-Tahoe maintains three miles of groomed snowshoe trails. Interpretive signs along the route interpret the fauna and flora of the Sierra Nevada. Guides from the resort's Telemark and Backcountry Center occasionally lead guided nature walks on snowshoes.

Sledding and Tubing

There is nothing quite like going sledding to make you feel like you are eight years old again. If you are seeking an activity that will take decades off your personal clock, sledding is perfect. It is fun, low-tech, and it makes you laugh. What you choose as your sledding

SNOWSHOEING

Snowshoeing is one of the fastest-growing winter sports in the United States. It is low-impact, low-cost, and can be enjoyed by people of all ages. The sport is gentle on the environment and requires a bare minimum of equipment. Compared to skiing or snowboarding, the learning curve for snowshoeing is mercifully brief. Basically, if you can walk, you can snowshoe.

Today's snowshoes are nothing like the huge wood-and-wicker "tennis racquets" used to travel across the snow a generation ago. Built with heat-treated aluminum frames, modern snowshoes are remarkably light and durable, and allow you to "float" over deep snow. The attached toe and heel crampons give you traction to climb steep hills and travel across icy surfaces. Snowshoe bindings strap on to almost any kind of boots; just make sure that yours are waterproof and warm. If you find that snow gets in the tops of your boots, a pair of gaiters can solve the problem.

The few techniques you need to master are fairly intuitive. You will figure them out on your own in short order. For example, your stance needs to be wider than it normally is for walking, so you don't step on the inside of your snowshoe frames. To go up a short, steep hill, you may need to "herringbone," or place your feet in a V-shape – heels close together and toes spread out to the side. On very steep slopes, you may need to sidestep, or climb with your snowshoes parallel to the slope.

Many snowshoers like to use handheld poles to help their balance, especially on hills. Most poles are adjustable, and you'll quickly learn that you want to shorten them to go uphill and lengthen them to go downhill. If you are traversing a slope or "side-hilling," you can lengthen one pole (on the downslope side) and shorten the other (on the upslope side) to aid your balance.

There's only one important rule of snowshoeing etiquette: If you are snowshoeing in an area where people cross-country ski, stay off the ski tracks so you don't ruin their smooth surface. Usually running parallel to the ski tracks are a separate set of snowshoe tracks, which you may follow. If not, make your own tracks.

If you decide to buy a pair of snowshoes instead of renting them, you'll find that there are many different styles. Casual snowshoers require the least expensive models, which are called "recreational" snowshoes. Often these can be purchased for less than $100, and they are suitable for snowshoeing on relatively level terrain. If you plan to head into the backcountry on snowshoes, you'll want one of the sturdier models that have stronger bindings and more aggressive crampons. These can run as high as $300.

---

device is up to you. Many swear by round saucers, others insist on traditional rectangular models in plastic or wood, and still others buck tradition by sledding in large, inflatable inner tubes. In fact, the latter has become so popular it has spawned its own winter sport, known simply as tubing. Many snow-play resorts now allow only tubes on their sledding hills, since their insurance agencies believe this is a kinder, gentler, less accident-prone form of sledding.

An old-fashioned South Shore resort that offers tubing and sledding is **Hansen's Tube and Saucer Hill** (1360 Ski Run Blvd., South Lake Tahoe, 530/544-3361, www.hansens-resort.com), where the tubing hill is a whopping 400 feet long, with banked turns and smooth downhill runs. Equipment is furnished with the $6 per person per hour fee; no outside equipment is allowed. Hot chocolate and snacks are for sale.

If you are traveling with skiing friends, you can tube while they ski at **Heavenly's Adventure Peak.** This is an expensive choice for tubing, since you have to pay to ride the gondola to Adventure Peak and then shell out another $20 per hour to go tubing (thankfully, the tube is included in the price). For the more budget-minded thrill seeker, **Sierra-**

at-Tahoe brags of having 425 feet of smooth sailing and banked turns on its tubing run ($17 for two hours, $30 for all day, including equipment). Another sledding and tubing area is operated by **Lake Tahoe Adventures** (3071 Hwy. 50, South Lake Tahoe, 530/577-2940, www.laketahoeadventures.com) just south of Lake Tahoe Airport.

Do-it-yourselfers should head to one of the state-run Sno-Parks in the South Lake vicinity. Sno-Parks, which are basically plowed parking lots alongside or near the highway, are marked by distinctive brown signs. Here, for the price of a $5 daily permit or $25 annual permit, you can slide down the hills on any piece of equipment you like. Heck, bring along your garbage-can lid if that's all you have. Sno-Park permits are sold at sporting-goods stores, businesses located near Sno-Parks, and at many other locations. The Sno-Park program hotline (916/324-1222) has information on where to buy permits and where Sno-Parks are located.

Three Sno-Parks are found in the South Shore region, but only two have good sledding and tubing opportunities. **Taylor Creek Sno-Park** (530/573-2600), on the west side of Highway 89 near Camp Richardson, has a small sledding hill and parking for about 15 cars. This is the perfect spot to take very young children sledding. **Echo Summit Sno-Park** (530/644-6048), on the south side of Highway 50 at Echo Summit, is a popular snow-play and sledding area. Three separate slopes of varying inclines allow you to choose your risk level. For thrill seekers, the longest, steepest slope used to be a ski run in the days when a ski resort was located here. Only the most aerobically fit daredevils head for this run, since it is a long walk uphill to get to the top, especially dragging a sled. The Sno-Park has a large parking area for 120 cars; permits can be purchased on-site.

Snowmobiling

If you are craving a winter sport with some horsepower behind it, snowmobiling might fit the bill. Two companies at South Lake offer guided snowmobile tours on groomed trails that lead to impressive high vistas of the lake. The largest snowmobile tour center on the West Coast, **Zephyr Cove Snowmobile Center** (Hwy. 50 at Zephyr Cove Resort, Zephyr Cove, 775/589-4908 or 800/238-2463, www .laketahoesnowmobiles.com) has more than 100 touring snowmobiles (including double-rider machines, so even children as young as five can go along for the trip, with Mom or Dad driving). The company caters to first-time riders with free shuttle service from the casino area of South Lake Tahoe to Zephyr Cove, and bus service from there to the snowmobiling trailhead. If you forgot to bring along your warmest gloves and boots, clothing rentals are available for a few bucks. Helmets are provided free with all rides. The standard two-hour tour leaves four times a day in winter; all drivers must be at least 15 years old. Cost is $99 for a single rider or $145 for two double riders. Those seeking more adventure can sign up for the Peak Performance Tour, a three-hour ride for $259. If possible, try to make the trip on a weekday, as weekends are quite busy and tons of snowmobiles share the trails. The company that runs the snowmobile center is the same one that operates the cruising paddle wheelers MS *Dixie II* and *Tahoe Queen,* so ride-and-cruise packages are available for visitors who want to make a day of it. Other packages include dinner and/or an overnight stay in a cabin at Zephyr Cove.

Lake Tahoe Adventures (3071 Hwy. 50, South Lake Tahoe, 530/577-2940 or 800/865-4679, www.laketahoeadventures.com), located just south of Lake Tahoe Airport at the Lake Tahoe Winter Sports Center, specializes in introducing beginners to snowmobiling with their two-hour Summit Tour. Goggles, gloves, and boots are included in the price; tours cost $102 for single riders; $148 for two riders. More experienced riders can sign up for longer tours that leave the groomed trails behind and set out into fresh powder. Kids eight years old and up can try snowmobiling on their own on a special groomed track.

Currently only one company on the South Shore allows self-guided snowmobile rentals;

rental rates are generally around $250 per day. **Tahoe Snowmobiles** (Ski Run Marina, 900 Ski Run Blvd., South Lake Tahoe, 530/542-3294 or 800/696-7797, www.tahoesnowmobiles.com) provides the snowmobiles as well as safety tips, riding instruction, and a map. If you have a towing vehicle, a trailer is included with your rental, so you can tow the machines to any of the designated snowmobile areas.

Ice-Skating

From November to March, weather permitting, Heavenly Village's outdoor **ice-skating rink** is open daily from 10 A.M.–9:30 P.M. (530/541-2720). Where else can you practice your figure eights while your weak-ankled friends browse through the Village's exclusive shops? The rink is on the small side, so you might not be able to execute a triple camel, but lots of Tahoe locals bring their kids here to learn how to skate. Ice-skate rentals are available for $4 per hour.

More serious skaters can be found at the indoor **South Lake Tahoe Ice Arena** (1176 Rufus Allen Blvd., South Lake Tahoe, 530/542-6262, www.recreationintahoe.com). This full-service ice-skating facility consists of a regulation Na-

tional Hockey League–size ice arena, locker rooms, snack bar, retail store, arcade, and party rooms. Skating and hockey lessons are available, as well as public skate sessions.

Sleigh Rides

From December to March, longtime Tahoe residents the Borges family offer winter-wonderland-style sleigh rides in the big meadow across the road from **MontBleu** (Hwy. 50 and Loop Rd., Stateline, 775/588-2953 or 800/726-7433, www.sleighride.com). Rides last about 35 minutes and take place in one of five handmade sleighs, including a romantic two-seater and a party-style 20-passenger sleigh. Blankets are provided for snuggling with your loved one. The Borges' horses are celebrities—they frequently appear in Pasadena's Tournament of Roses parade.

On the opposite side of South Lake, the horses at **Camp Richardson's Corral** (Emerald Bay Rd. at Fallen Leaf Lake Rd., South Lake Tahoe, 530/541-3113, www.camprich. com, $20 per person) also carry passengers on sleigh rides through the snow-covered landscape. Reservations are required.

Entertainment and Shopping

CASINOS AND NIGHTLIFE

If you have wads of cash burning a hole in your pocket, you might as well donate some to the South Shore casinos. There are six to choose from on the Nevada side of the South Shore at Stateline, and all are within a few blocks of each other: Bill's Casino, MontBleu Resort, Harrah's Lake Tahoe, Harveys Resort and Casino, Horizon Casino Resort, and Lakeside Inn and Casino. What's the difference between them? Not a lot, since most are owned by two large gaming conglomerates. The gaming giant Harrah's owns Harrah's Lake Tahoe, Harveys, and Bill's. Columbia Sussex Corporation owns Horizon Casino Resort and in 2006 purchased the old Caesars Lake Tahoe for a cool $45 million. As this book goes to press, the old

Caesars is being remodeled, rebranded, and re-packaged as MontBleu Resort Casino and Spa. But in the end, its offerings will most likely be as indistinguishable as those of its neighbors, at least in terms of gaming. Blackjack, craps, keno, bingo, poker, slot machines, roulette wheels, and sports books are available everywhere, and in plentiful supply. Harveys has the largest amount of casino floor space (88,000 square feet) and most slot machines (more than 2,000), with Harrah's coming in second.

At least **Horizon Casino and Resort** (50 Hwy. 50, Stateline, 775/588-6211 or 800/648-3322, www.horizoncasino.com) can lay claim to an interesting piece of American history. It was originally known as the Sahara Tahoe, the resort where in the 1970s Elvis Presley often fired up the crowds. The Horizon is a bit lower key than the neighboring Harrah's-owned properties, and attracts more families, in part because of its eight-screen movie theater. The **Lakeside Inn and Casino** (168 Hwy. 50, Stateline, 775/588-7777 or 800/624-7980, www.lakesideinn.com) is worthy of note because it caters more to Tahoe locals. It is set off farther east from the larger casinos—it's the only one that is not quite within easy walking distance of the others, especially for older gamblers—so people who come here usually stay for the evening. Two-dollar drinks are standard fare at Lakeside, and their restaurant, the Timber House, is a locals' favorite.

Most people tire of gambling fairly quickly (or run out of cash), so the casinos wisely offer much more than roulette tables and one-armed bandits. Besides a huge selection of restaurants, there's also music, magic, cabaret, or comedy always happening at one or more of the casinos' nightclubs. Big-name performers usually appear on weekends only, but lesser-known singers, musicians, and dancers appear every night of the year. The most original of the nightclubs may well be **William's Back Door Blues Club** at Bill's Casino (25 Hwy. 50, South Lake Tahoe, 775/588-2455 or 775/588-6611, www.harrahs.com), which serves up some sizzling blues performances, usually without a cover charge. Shows generally start at 9:30 P.M. King-of-the-strip Harrah's is home to the **South Shore Room** (15 Hwy. 50, South Lake Tahoe, 775/588-6611 or 800/648-3773, www.harrahs.com), which has hosted a long line of famous American entertainers since it first opened in the 1950s. On weekends, the South Shore Room is transformed into **Altitude Nightclub** (775/586-6705), where dollar drinks are a common occurrence, the high-energy techno music pumps at deafening volumes, and go-go dancers do their hip-swinging acts in a variety of box, pole, and cage contraptions. If you're not a drinker, you can always go take a hit at the oxygen bar.

As this book goes to press, the new **Mont-Bleu Resort Casino** (55 Hwy. 50, Stateline, 800/648-3353, www.montbleuresort.com)

has not yet unveiled its plans for nightlife entertainment. With the change in ownership, long-time Caesar's fans mourned the loss of its popular Club Nero disco, which was famous (or infamous) for its go-go cages and cutting edge hip-hop music. Club fans can dry their tears, though, because the new MontBleu has hired Paul Reder, the original creator of Club Nero, to manage, operate, and maintain the casino's nightlife operations. A total of four new clubs are promised, of which at least two will feature live music. Expect great things.

Harveys (30 Hwy. 50, Stateline, 775/588-2411 or 800/427-8397, www.harrahs.com) has four nightclubs: the **Hard Rock Cafe** with live music on weekends, Dueling Pianos, The Improv (usually featuring top-name comics), and the tequila-obsessed **Cabo Wabo Cantina,** owned by none other than the Red Rocker himself, Sammy Hagar. If you're a real party animal, ask the bartender for a "body shot." If you aren't, order a Cabo Waborita and sip it very, very slowly. Harveys also sponsors an outdoor concert series at its 5,000-seat amphitheater in summer, with big-name headliners like Loggins and Messina, the Eagles, and of course, Sammy Hagar.

If you prefer to get away from the casino part of town but still want to enjoy great entertainment, several other spots around the South Shore offer live music and nightlife. The young and athletic flock to **Divided Sky** (3200 Hwy. 50, South Lake Tahoe, 530/577-0775, www.thedividedsky.com) located above the Downtown Cafe in Meyers. This popular hangout for rock climbers and snowboarders looks and feels a lot like a San Francisco South-of-Market bar, but without any suits. Happy hour takes place daily 3–6 P.M.

For something more stylish, **Fire and Ice** (in Marriott Timber Lodge, 4100 Hwy. 50, South Lake Tahoe, 530/542-6650, www.fire-ice.com) is adjacent to the gondola in the heart of Heavenly Village. Drinks are huge and colorful, customers are hip, and the music is high-energy. The beer-drinking, pool-playing set heads to **Turn 3 Sports Bar** (2227 Hwy. 50, South Lake Tahoe, 530/542-3199), a place where you can let your hair down, play a few games of pool, and toss your peanut shells on the floor.

Live music featuring local bands is a common occurrence at several South Lake bar/restaurants: Beacon Bar and Grill at Camp Richardson Resort (530/541-0630), Fresh Ketch in the Tahoe Keys Marina (530/541-5683), The Pub Tahoe (530/542-4435), Rojo's Tavern (530/541-4960), and The Tudor Pub at Dory's Oar (530/541-6603).

And if your idea of nightlife is snuggling up with your sweetie and a bag of popcorn at the **movie theater,** there are two on the South Shore: the eight-plex at Horizon Stadium Cinema inside Horizon Casino (775/589-6000) or Heavenly Village Cinema (530/544-1110, www.heavenlyvillagecinema.com).

SHOPPING

Seasoned factory outlet shoppers will want to head straight to the Y at South Lake Tahoe, where more than a dozen outlet stores are bunched together for easy browsing. The **Factory Stores at the Y** (junction of Hwy. 50 and Hwy. 89, 530/573-5545, www.tahoefactorystores.com) outlet center includes Bass Shoes, Izod, Oneida, Adidas, Big Dog, Geoffrey Beene, Samsonite, and other major brands.

The **Village Center** at Stateline (corner of Hwy. 50 and Park Ave.), features a huge variety of stores ranging from a Raley's supermarket and Starbuck's Coffee to High Country Comforts, 1000 Bathing Suits, Jon Paul Gallery, Neighbors Book Store, and Tahoe Sports Ltd. If you haven't been to Tahoe in a few years, you'll be amazed at this shopping complex, which used to be the run-down Crescent V Center. After a multimillion-dollar renovation designed to tie in this property with the adjacent Heavenly Village and Marriott complexes, it's now a pleasant place to stroll and shop.

A similar but more upscale venue is the après-ski shopping complex built around the Heavenly ski gondola. At **Heavenly Village** (1001 Heavenly Village Way, South Lake Tahoe, www.theshopsatheavenlyvillage.com), 50-plus shops and art galleries and 14 restaurants cater more to tourists than locals. A half dozen galleries and jewelry stores are mixed with clothing stores, sporting goods stores, and eateries such as Cinnabon, Cold Stone Creamery, Quizno's Subs, and even a few that you won't find in every other mall in America. (Try Kalani's for a wonderful Hawaiian-influenced meal.) The Heavenly Village center also has a day spa, movie cineplex, tanning salon, and other shops that serve life's not-so-essential needs. The "shopping village" was creatively designed and features heated cobblestone sidewalks, covered walkways, open bonfire pits, and a clock tower.

A smaller, more intimate shopping area is found in the **Ski Run Marina** complex (900 Ski Run Blvd., South Lake Tahoe, www.skirunmarina.com), which also has two good restaurants: Riva Grill and Watermark Cafe.

FESTIVALS AND EVENTS

A few annual events on the South Shore are worth planning your vacation around. Don't miss attending some part of the **Valhalla Arts and Music Festival** at the Tallac Historic Site, a series of concerts featuring jazz, bluegrass, New Age, folk, Latin, and classical artists. Concerts and theater performances are held inside the 200-seat Boathouse Theater and the Valhalla Grand Hall. The festival usually begins in mid-June and runs until late August. For program information, contact the Tahoe Tallac Association (530/541-4975 or 888/632-5859, www.valhalla-tallac.com). Ticket prices for shows range from free to $25. Another wonderful event at the Tallac Historic Site is the **Great Gatsby Festival** (530/544-7383, www.tahoeheritage.org, free), a celebration of the roaring '20s at Lake Tahoe, which takes place in mid-August.

If you have a latent lusty Elizabethan peasant hiding inside you, don't miss the **Heart of the Forest Renaissance Faire** (800/510-1558, www.forestfaire.com, $20 adults, $8 children) at Camp Richardson, usually held for two weekends in June. Costumed players offer arts and crafts demonstrations, cook and serve hearty English food, test their skills in games and races at the tournament field, hawk their wares, and generally make merry. The city of South Lake Tahoe pulls out all the stops for its annual **Fourth of July** celebration. Each year, extravagant pyrotechnics burst into air over the surface of Lake Tahoe. For information on special Fourth of July events, contact the Lake Tahoe Visitors Authority (530/544-5050).

As fall approaches, prepare to celebrate the salmon at the annual **Kokanee Salmon Festival** at the Taylor Creek Visitor Center (530/573-2600 or 530/573-2674). The kokanee, a species of landlocked salmon and a popular Tahoe sport fish, performs its annual spawning rites in Taylor Creek every October, when the adult fish travel upstream to spawn and die. (In spring, their offspring travel downstream back to Lake Tahoe.) From the trail alongside the creek, visitors can watch the female salmon lay her eggs and the male salmon fertilize them. During the course of this free two-day event, usually held on the first weekend in October, there are a wide variety of educational programs, nature walks, and informational tours related to the ecology of Lake Tahoe.

FAMILY FUN

Those folks who run the Stateline casinos are no dummies; they quickly figured out that it was smart to provide the kids with something to do while Mom and Dad gamble away the family nest egg. Each of the big casinos has its own game arcade, or, as the casinos prefer to call it, Family Fun Center.

For some family fun that isn't attached to a casino, go play a few rounds of pee-wee golf at **Magic Carpet Golf** (2455 Hwy. 50, South Lake Tahoe, 530/541-3787). Or check out the summertime action at the **Tahoe Amusement**

Park (2401 Hwy. 50, South Lake Tahoe, 530/541-1300, www.laketahoeamusementpark.com, open 10 A.M.–9 P.M. May–Oct., weather permitting, free admission), which has a variety of carnival-type kiddie rides and games in an outdoor setting alongside Highway 50. Tilt-a-whirl, superslide, carousel, roller coaster, go-karts—all the good old-fashioned rides are represented. There is no admission charge, but rides require the purchase of tickets.

If bowling is your bag, head to the lanes at **Tahoe Bowl** (1030 Fremont St., South Lake Tahoe, 530/544-3700) and teach your kids how to roll a few strikes or spares. And for arcade gaming on the nongambling side of the California/Nevada state line, visit **The Village Arcade,** at The Shops at Heavenly Village (530/541-2755), Magic Carpet Golf, and Tahoe Amusement Park.

Or, if you think it's a better plan to just get rid of the kids altogether for a few hours or even a day, consider sending them to **Kids' Camp Lake Tahoe** (775/267-6399, www .tahoekids.com, $80 per child), available for children ages 6–13. Reservations are required. The camp meets at Harveys or Harrah's casino or the Embassy Suites Hotel; kids take part in a host of activities, including movies, bowling, and arcade games. Evening sessions, 6–10 P.M., are offered nightly year-round; the fee is $50 per child. Daytime sessions run 9 A.M.– 7 P.M. in summer only; kids spend the day going for short, educational hikes, playing outdoor games and sports, and swimming.

In the summer months, be sure to take the whole clan on the *Tahoe Queen's* **Family Fun Cruise,** which has "Tahoe Tessie" on board to entertain the kids. And in winter, spend a few hours on one of the local sledding or tubing hills with the kids, or take them on a horse-drawn sleigh ride.

SOUTH SHORE

Accommodations

STATELINE AND CASINO AREA
Casinos and Hotels

If you want to gamble without a long commute from your bed, you have a half-dozen choices in Stateline. The hippest of those is the new **MontBleu Resort Casino and Spa**, (55 Hwy. 50, Stateline, 800/648-3353, www. montbleuresort.com, $199-399). MontBleu is the new name and look of the old Caesars Tahoe, which was taken over by Columbia Sussex Corporation in 2006. The fallen— Caesar's faux marble columns and toga-clad statues are ancient history. The Casino resort stil has 440 rooms and suites, including some with in-room spas, but the décor is contemporary and sophisticated, with cool colors and creative lighting. With 40,000 square feet of casino space, four nightlife venues, a half-dozen restaurants, and a luxurious spa facility, guests could easily spend a weekend at Mont-Bleu and never set foot outside its doors.

Just a stone's throw away, **Harrah's** (15 Hwy. 50, Stateline, 775/588-6611 or 800/648-3773, www.harrahs.com, $199-399) scores high marks for its customer service, which has always been a cut above that of the other Stateline casinos. The resort has 525 rooms spread out over 18 stories, and key to enjoying your stay is to get the best lake view you can afford. That way when your wallet has been cleaned out at the casino, you will still be able to look out the window and enjoy the view. The large (500 square feet and up), tastefully decorated rooms have odd luxuries like two bathrooms and multiple telephones, which are intended to make you feel like you are very rich.

It's all about excess at **Harveys** (30 Hwy. 50, Stateline, 775/588-2411 or 800/648-3361,

© ANN MARIE BROWN

The Borges' horses wait near the Stateline casinos to take visitors for an old-fashioned carriage ride.

www.harrahs.com, $199–399), which is right across the street from Harrah's. This four-diamond resort hotel has eight restaurants and 10 cocktail lounges. In addition to 24-hour gaming, Harveys also has a health club, heated outdoor pool and hot tub, full-service wedding chapel, and sprawling video arcade. But aside from the 740 nicely appointed rooms, most with excellent lake views, most people come to Harveys for the 100-plus tequila varieties at the Cabo Wabo Cantina, or the 300 seafood selections at the Pacifica Seafood Buffet. Or maybe it's the fact that Harveys has a monumental 88,000 square feet of casino floor space. It's all about the numbers here.

One of the Big 3 Hs on the South Shore (Horizon, Harveys, and Harrah's), the monolithic **Horizon Casino Resort** (50 Hwy. 50, Stateline, 775/588-6211 or 800/648-3322, www.horizoncasino.com, $49–199) has 539 hotel rooms in two separate towers, one reaching 15 stories high and the other merely 9. Generally speaking, the Horizon is less expensive than the other Hs, and its decor is less over-the-top. Higher-priced rooms feature floor-to-ceiling windows with views of Lake Tahoe; lower-priced rooms look out at the mountains or the pool, which happens to be the largest outdoor heated pool on the South Shore. If you want to break the bank, rent the suite that Elvis Presley used to stay in. The Horizon bills itself as being more "subdued" than other South Shore casinos, but you'd never guess it from the glare of its 40,000-square-foot gaming floor. As with all the other casinos, 24-hour gaming is available, plus cabaret shows and an eight plex movie theater. If you feel like stuffing your gut like a true gourmand, the resort has Le Grand Buffet and two other restaurants.

The **Lakeside Inn & Casino** (168 Hwy. 50, Stateline, 775/588-7777 or 800/624-7980, www.lakesideinn.com, $75–149) is not the busiest casino resort at Lake Tahoe, but it's a fine place to stay for easy access to gaming, skiing, and South Shore nightlife. With 124 recently renovated rooms with amenities like wireless Internet access and in-room ski racks, plus huge portions at the in-house Timber House Restaurant and Bar, lots of folks come to the Lakeside for quick weekend getaways consisting of wanton gambling, overeating, and imbibing $2 drinks. South Shore locals flock to the restaurant here, especially on prime rib nights. Rates are reasonable, but they'll get plenty more out of you at the craps table.

Families enjoy the **Embassy Suites Hotel** (4130 Hwy. 50, South Lake Tahoe, 530/544-5400 or 800/988-9820, www.embassytahoe .com, $150–250), which has all the amenities of a full-service hotel but no casino downstairs to pollute the little ones' minds. Each of the hotel's 400 rooms are two-room suites with a king or two double beds, and most have a pull-out couch in the living room for the kiddies. If you like having some room to spread out, the spacious accommodations here will satisfy. The hotel sits right on the California/Nevada state line (but still on the no gaming California side), so the Heavenly gondola and Village shops are a short walk away and the casinos are right next door. Rates include a full cooked-to-order breakfast in the morning and other nice touches, like a newspaper delivered to your door.

Condominium-Style Resorts

Located a few miles from the bustle of downtown Stateline, high up on Kingsbury Grade and immediately adjacent to Heavenly Ski Area's Nevada side, **The Ridge Tahoe** (400 Ridge Club Dr., Stateline, 775/588-3131 or 800/334-1600, www.ridgetahoeresort.com, $100–290) is a full-amenity condominium resort set on 11 acres, with more than 300 condo units providing everything you'd expect when you rent a ski condo: health club, indoor/outdoor swimming pool, whirlpool spas and saunas, scheduled activities for kids and adults, the Hungry Bear restaurant and bar, full-service spa, on-site ski shop, and shuttle transportation to the casinos. One- and two-bedroom units are available with living rooms, full kitchens, and gas fireplaces. Deluxe hotel rooms and junior suites are also available.

If you'd prefer something a little more low-key, the two-bedroom condos at **Tahoe Summit Village** (750 Wells Fargo La., Stateline, 775/588-8571 or 866/265-2041, www.tahoesummitvillage.com, $105–235) provide easy access to skiing—they are right between the North Boulder and Stagecoach chairlifts on Heavenly's Nevada side, but you'll have to leave the condo complex for meals, groceries, and the like. The condos have wood-burning fireplaces, whirlpool tubs, fully equipped kitchens, washers and dryers, and plenty of room for six to eight people.

Cabins

If you're the type who wants to stay busy on your Tahoe vacation and have lots of activities available right at your doorstep, book at stay at one of the 29 lakeside cabins or four lodge rooms at **Zephyr Cove Resort** (760 Hwy. 50, Zephyr Cove, 775/589-4907, www.zephyrcove.com). This old-style Tahoe resort has been in business since the 1900s, and despite the modern recreation offerings (jet skiing, beach volleyball, parasailing, personal watercraft rentals, and much more), it still manages to retain a bit of its historic feel. Rates are $69–169 for lodge rooms and $119–469 for cabins, depending on cabin size. Some cabins sleep as many as 10 people. A few cabins are lakefront; the others are lake view or no view at all, so make sure you ask for what you want. Everything is available here: a restaurant, bar, horseback riding, snowmobiling, sportfishing, boat rentals, lake cruising on the MS *Dixie II* or *Woodwind II,* and a sandy beach for swimming and sunning. The casinos of Stateline are only five miles away.

Motels and Lodges

Few Lake Tahoe motels can brag of being right on the lakeshore, but the **Royal Valhalla** (4104 Lakeshore Blvd., South Lake Tahoe, 530/544-2233 or 800/999-4104, www.tahoeroyalvalhalla.com, $89–199) can. Many of the 80 one-, two-, and three-bedroom suites have private balconies, some have full kitchens, and most have a fine lake view. The decor is standard motel issue and nothing to brag about, but a short stretch of private Tahoe beach more than makes up for it. A donuts-and-coffee-style continental breakfast is complimentary. Located right next door to Edgewood Golf Course and within a short walk of the casinos, the Royal Valhalla is a dependable bet for a stay in South Lake.

For those who want a moderately priced motel that isn't of the bland chain variety, the **Viking Motor Lodge** (4083 Cedar Ave., South Lake Tahoe, 800/288-4083, www.tahoeviking.com, $75–135) is a pleasant option. Run by the same people who manage the nearby Royal Valhalla, the Viking's 76 guest rooms, some with kitchenettes and/or electric fireplaces, are clean and comfortable without having the cookie-cutter feel of a Motel 6 or Super 8. A free continental breakfast is served (donuts, fruit, and coffee), and the swimming pool is popular with families on summer afternoons. The Viking is within walking distance of the casinos and Edgewood Golf Course, but its biggest draw is its short stretch of private Lake Tahoe beach, a few blocks away.

Adjacent to the Stateline casinos are city blocks full of nondescript motels, lined up side by side, one after another. One that stands out (among many that don't) is the **Alpenrose Inn** (4074 Pine Blvd., South Lake Tahoe, 530/544-2985 or 800/370-4049, www.alpenroseinntahoe.com, $59–149), a charming place with only 18 rooms that reflects the European refinement of its owner, Hannelore Conrad. All of the rooms at Alpenrose are nonsmoking and immaculately clean. Some have fireplaces. A shuttle service can take you to the ski resorts, tour boats, or casinos (although most are within easy walking distance), and the inn has access to a small private beach. A complimentary continental breakfast is served each morning.

The **7 Seas Inn** (4145 Manzanita Ave., South Lake Tahoe, 530/544-7031 or 800/800-7327, www.sevenseastahoe.com) wins the prize for "Most Ridiculous South Shore Motel Name." Nothing about its moniker or its ocean-blue exterior tells you you're in the mountains, but that doesn't seem to bother the legions of repeat customers at this no-nonsense, low-budget motel. Cheap ski packages are a big attraction here, with rates as low as $155 per person for two days' worth of lift tickets and three nights of lodging (based on double occupancy). The 7 Seas is only two blocks from the Heavenly gondola, but if you are too lazy to walk, a shuttle will take you there. Donuts and coffee are offered free of charge in the morning, and the owners, Marv and Dolores, are extra-nice folks.

If you want the convenience and no-frills of a motel but don't like staying at the big chains, you'll like the **Ambassador Motor Lodge** (4130 Manzanita Ave., South Lake Tahoe, 530/544-6461, www.ambassadorcapritahoe .com, $59–149). Harveys and Horizon casinos are just a stone's throw away, but the motel is far enough off busy Highway 50 to be quiet at night. The 57 units have all the basics, and a few even have kitchens. A large heated pool will keep the kids happy in summer, and a shuttle bus will whisk you to the ski areas in winter. Dogs are permitted in some rooms with advance reservations.

When is a motel better than a motel? When it's the **Avalon Lodge** (4075 Manzanita Ave., South Lake Tahoe, 530/544-2285 or 800/659-4185, www.avalonlodge.com, $59–149). From the outside, Avalon looks like a typical South Shore motel. But inside, its rooms are more hotel-like than motel-like, with tasteful furnishings like canopy and four-poster beds, plush bedding, oversized bath towels, gas fireplaces, refrigerators, coffeemakers, and microwaves. It's worth the extra money to get a spa room if one is available. Heavenly's gondola and the Stateline casinos are just two blocks away, but it is peaceful and quiet here on Manzanita Avenue. A complimentary breakfast is served each morning.

A South Shore lodging that caters to the young and the reckless, **The Block** (4143 Cedar Ave., South Lake Tahoe, 530/544-2936 or 888/544-4055, www.blockattahoe. com, $49–179) was designed by snowboarders for snowboarders. Located less than two blocks

from Heavenly's gondola and a stone's throw from Harveys casino, The Block features big windows, original art, vaulted ceilings, and hip wall colors. This is a Generation Xers version of heaven, with a cybercafe, wireless Internet, computer work screens, and a hot tub located on the roof of the building. Additionally, some rooms come with snowboard racks, boot dryers, and/or video games. If you've come to Tahoe to shred the slopes, this is your place. If you're looking for a romantic getaway, stay someplace else.

The **El Dorado Motel** (4139 Hwy. 50, South Lake Tahoe, 530/544-5757 or 800/935-3672, www.wcf.com/eldorado, $59–109) is located in the shadow of monolithic Harveys Casino, and loyal vacationers at this ultrabasic motel like it that way. The El Dorado offers newly decorated, clean rooms that are a mere 100 feet from the casinos and 200 feet from the Heavenly gondola. If you want lodging with a "downtown" feel, you're right in the heart of it here, complete with all the accompanying noise and commotion. The motel's amenities are the no-frills variety, but at least the rates are cheap.

You're likely to hear a lot of "cheers" and "brilliant" at the **Pine Frost Inn** (4113 Manzanita Ave., South Lake Tahoe, 530/544-3479, $59–129). Remarkably popular with British and European travelers, this down-to-earth motel works well for skiers who want to enjoy the South Shore nightlife after a day on the slopes. The inn has 30 rooms on two floors, each with one king-size bed or two queen-size beds. The managers at the Pine Frost Inn are nice folks who offer their guests a few pleasant extras, like warm apple cider at the end of the day. The inn is located three blocks from Heavenly's gondola and the downtown casinos and restaurants.

Count on the **Tahoe Driftwood Lodge** (4115 Laurel Ave., South Lake Tahoe, 530/541-7400 or 800/833-4543, www.tahoedriftwood. com, $49–79) for good value and convenient transportation to the crap tables. The casinos are one block away; Heavenly gondola is less than one block away. The neighboring

Driftwood Cafe makes breakfast or lunch a snap (lodge guests receive a 10 percent discount off all menu items). The lodge has access to a small stretch of private Tahoe beach, three blocks away. The same owners have been running this place for nearly 30 years, and they are doing a fine job. All that and the rates are cheap. Rooms have one queen bed, one king bed, or two double beds.

Take your pick from two separate units of the **Travelodge** chain of motels in South Lake Tahoe. Both offer clean, simple accommodations at a reasonable price, and since they are located within 100 yards of each other (4003 and 4011 Hwy. 50, South Lake Tahoe, 530/541-5000 and 530/544-6000, www.travelodge.com, $59–129), they are basically indistinguishable. Rooms are fully equipped with all the basics: in-room coffee, refrigerators, and cable television. Guests receive passes to a private Tahoe beach located a few blocks away. The Heavenly gondola and Stateline casinos are within walking distance; the Heavenly Village shops and restaurants are right across the street.

Campgrounds and RV Parks

The privately operated **Zephyr Cove RV Park and Campground** (760 Hwy. 50, Zephyr Cove, 775/589-4907 or 775/589-4981, www.zephyrcove.com, $15–33 for tents, $41–53 for RVs; RV sites $26 in winter) is part of the huge Zephyr Cove Resort complex, which includes cabins, a restaurant, general store, marina, horse stables, and a host of vacation-oriented activities that make it a zoo on most summer days. Camping at Zephyr Cove is camping in style, with full hookup sites, a coin-operated laundry, showers, flush toilets, and the like. Set across the highway from the lake, the camp has 93 RV sites, 10 drive-in campsites, and 47 walk-in campsites. The walk-in sites are the farthest from the busy highway and by far the best bet.

Operated by the U.S. Forest Service, lovely **Nevada Beach Campground** (775/588-5562) is located just two miles northeast of the California/Nevada state line, off U.S. 50 at Elk Point Road. Nevada Beach is a popular day-use site with a long and wide stretch of precious Tahoe shoreline perfect for sunbathers and swimmers. The adjacent campground is bare-bones (no showers or dump station), but well loved due to its lakeside location. Some of the 54 sites have lovely lake views; all have some shade from big Jeffrey pines. RVs up to 45 feet long are permitted. Firewood is sold on site; gas, groceries, and laundry are a half mile away at the Round Hill Shopping Center at U.S. 50. Fees are $22–24. Reserve in advance at 877/444-6777 or www.reserveusa.com.

SOUTH LAKE TAHOE
Bed-and-Breakfasts

If you have wads of cash burning a hole in your pocket, book a stay at one of five rooms or three cabins at the **(Black Bear Inn Bed & Breakfast** (1202 Ski Run Blvd., South Lake Tahoe, 530/544-4451 or 877/232-7466, www.tahoeblackbear.com, $200–275, larger cabins $325–450), a luxurious B&B that was built in the 1990s, but has an old-style Tahoe look. The place was constructed to take advantage of Tahoe's beauty, with huge picture windows, river rock fireplaces, exposed wood beams, and tasteful mountain-style decor and landscaping. The owner Jerry is the most accommodating guy you'd ever hope to meet; he takes good care of his guests. Wine and cheese are served at sunset. Breakfasts, served in the common dining room, are lavish and tasty. If you stay in one of the cabins, breakfast is brought to your door each morning.

Dog-lovers of the world, rejoice. Here's a place in South Lake Tahoe where Fido is welcomed with open arms. The **Inn at Heavenly** (1261 Ski Run Blvd., South Lake Tahoe, 530/544-4244 or 800/692-2246, www.innatheavenly.com) is a cross between a motel and a bed-and-breakfast, with all the amenities of the latter—a common room with a continental breakfast and wine and snacks in the late afternoon—but the physical structure of the former-all 14 rooms are located in a motel-style building, with exterior doors that open out to the parking lot. A spa room with hot tub, steam bath, and sauna is on the property; guests can reserve this room for their private use for one hour each day. Rates are $135–175 per night; there is a small additional charge for pets. A few large cabins that sleep up to 14 people are also available; those rates are $295–400 per night.

Condominium-Style Resorts

Many of the privately owned condominiums at **Bavarian Village** (1140 Herbert Ave., South Lake Tahoe, 530/541-8191 or 800/822-6636, www.bavarianrentals.com, $125–375) are available as rentals year-round, providing Tahoe visitors with all the amenities of a small vacation home—a spacious living room with fireplace, fully equipped kitchen, one or more bedrooms, color cable television, and direct-dial phones—but without the property taxes and maintenance issues. If you are traveling with a family or planning to spend more than a couple of nights at South Lake, this type of lodging can be a lot more comfortable than a hotel or motel. Families will like the heated swimming pool, and playground facilities are located a short walk away. The Heavenly gondola and Stateline casinos are about a mile away.

Located within a few steps of Heavenly Ski Resort's gondola, the **Forest Suites Resort** (1 Lake Pkwy., South Lake Tahoe, 530/541-6655 or 800/822-5950, www.forestsuites.com, $100–299) is a great choice for serious skiers who want to be out on the slopes, not stuck driving the car. In additional to standard hotel rooms, the resort offers one- and two-bedroom suites with a living room, dining area, and kitchen, so you can fix your own coffee and be in the gondola line the moment it opens for business. A continental breakfast is offered daily, and ski rentals and a ski repair shop, a fitness center, heated outdoor pools, hot tubs and sauna, and a game room with pool and Ping-Pong tables are on-site. If you get tired of skiing at Heavenly, the resort also has a shuttle service that will take you to other Tahoe slopes. In summer, the resort offers access to a private stretch of Tahoe beach.

The **Inn by the Lake** (3300 Hwy. 50, South Lake Tahoe, 530/542-0330 or 800/877-1466, www.innbythelake.com) is not right on the lakeshore nor does it have any fabulous lake views, but what they do here, they do well. This 100-unit boutique resort sits on six acres of grounds across Highway 50 from Lake Tahoe and is well suited for vacations on the South Shore. Each room has its own private balcony, plus a small refrigerator and microwave; the deluxe suites have fully equipped kitchens. A continental breakfast is served each morning and the inn boasts a state-of-the-art fitness center, 2,000-square-foot event or meeting space, and year-round heated pool and bi-level spa (the two levels are connected by a small waterfall). Free shuttles go to the casinos and ski resorts, and if you want to borrow a bicycle or a pair of snowshoes, they'll happily loan them to you. Rates are $98–358 for rooms and one-bedroom suites, $308–780 for two- or three-bedroom suites or town houses. If you are traveling with your dog, Fido is welcome here for an extra $20 charge per night, and he or she will be treated like royalty with a silver bowl and doggy blanket.

One of the nicest lakefront condo resorts in South Lake Tahoe, **Lakeland Village Beach and Mountain Resort** (3535 Hwy. 50, South Lake Tahoe, 530/544-1685 or 800/822-5969, www.lakeland-village.com, $125–399) allows visitors the Tahoe vacation home experience at hotel prices. Set on 19 wooded acres including a quarter-mile stretch of sandy beach, each of the condos here has a fireplace, private balcony, and kitchen or kitchenette. The 210 units come in various configurations as small as studios and as large as five bedrooms. In summer, guests have use of two tennis courts, a small pier, a sand volleyball court, and two swimming pools and hot tubs. In winter, free shuttles run to Heavenly's gondola and all the South Lake Tahoe action. The place is run by Premier Resorts, a large conglomerate that also manages similar properties in resort destinations like Sun Valley, Idaho, and Hawaii.

At the base of Heavenly Ski Resort, the ◖ **Marriott Grand Residence Club** (1001

Park Ave., South Lake Tahoe, 530/542-8400 or 800/627-7468, www.marriott.com, $200–800) offers studios and one-, two-, and three-bedroom condominiums, or "residences," as they call them. These are arguably the most luxurious condo rentals in South Lake, with spacious living areas, tasteful decor, fully equipped kitchens, fireplaces, whirlpool tubs, and a host of extras, including a health club, ski storage area, valet parking, and concierge desk. But even if they were run-down shacks people would still flock here, because the Grand Residence is located right at the base of the Heavenly gondola and next to Heavenly Village's outdoor ice rink, shopping center, restaurants, and movie theater. Once you're here, you don't need your car at all. But you'll pay for your pleasure. Marriott also operates the **Timber Lodge,** a hotel-style property, on the opposite side of the gondola. Both Marriott properties are ideal places for a ski vacation.

There's only a narrow strip of sandy beach between the lodge rooms and the lake at the **{ Tahoe Lakeshore Lodge** (930 Bal Bijou Rd., South Lake Tahoe, 530/544-6390 or 800/448-4577, www.lakeshorelodge.com), so every room boasts a fine lake view. The lodge's offerings include 46 rooms with queen beds and gas fireplaces ($89–299), plus 26 one- and two-bedroom condominiums ($159–419) with full kitchens and fireplaces. A year-round heated pool is right next to a 500-foot stretch of private Tahoe beach, so you can swim in warm or cold water. In addition, the lodge is home to Elements, a full-service day spa, which offers an intriguing assortment of massage therapies, body wraps, facials, and the like.

Across from Heavenly Ski Resort (not the gondola but the resort itself) lies **Tahoe Seasons Resort** (3901 Saddle Rd., South Lake Tahoe, 530/541-6700 or 800/540-4874, www.tahoeseasons.com, $100–250), a full-service resort offering one-bedroom suites with private whirlpool tubs, wet bars, fireplaces, coffeemakers, microwaves, and cable television. Not every unit has a fireplace; make sure you get one that does. In winter, you can rent or buy skis at the sports shop, eat at the Nee-

dles Restaurant, buy stuff at the general store, hang out at the fireside lounge and pub, and generally not leave the premises except to go skiing. In addition to a year-round pool and hot tub, the resort also has summer-season sport offerings, like rooftop tennis and volleyball courts.

If you like to travel with your dog, **3 Peaks Resort & Beach Club** (931 Park Ave., South Lake Tahoe, 800/331-3570, www.3peakshotel.com, $115 and up plus $15 for dogs) is your kind of place. The sign out front bears a Saint Bernard wearing bathing trunks, so their message is clear: They are dog-friendly. Plus, 3 Peaks has a great location on Park Avenue, a few blocks from Heavenly's gondola, but far enough off the noisy main drag. It's also only two blocks from a gated, members-only Tahoe beach, which human guests can use, but unfortunately, not their dogs.

Cabins

Long ago at Lake Tahoe, there were lots of places like **Hansen's Resort** (1360 Ski Run Blvd., South Lake Tahoe, 530/544-3361, www.hansensresort.com, $50–220 for one- and two-bedroom units, $240–350 for four-bedroom cabin), family-run cabin resorts that offered hospitality first and foremost without all the "bling." Now places like Hansen's are few, but many families will be happier here than at a noisy casino resort. Hansen's has seven old-style green-and-white cabins and two motel rooms located about a half mile from Highway 50, near Heavenly Ski Resort. The cabins are modest and simply furnished; all have cable televisions and some have kitchens and fireplaces. In winter, guests can walk over to Hansen's Tube and Saucer Hill for some old-fashioned sledding fun (cabin guests get free use of the hill). If your kids aren't old enough to ski, tubing or sledding will get them hooked on snow.

Motels and Lodges

There are a couple of Best Westerns in South Lake Tahoe, and they are quite different in style and ambience. The **Best Western**

Station House Inn (901 Park Ave., South Lake Tahoe, 530/542-1101 or 800/822-5953, www.stationhouseinn.com, $108–195 high season) is located a few blocks off Highway 50 (great for peace and quiet) and a short walk from a private beach (great for summer fun). The Stateline casinos are within easy walking distance. Most of its 101 rooms have queen and king beds; some have two double beds. The inn offers summer and winter packages that include cruises on the lake, ski-lift tickets, and dinner coupons for the in-house restaurant, LewMarNel's. If you really want to save money, visit during the low-season months of April, May, and November, when rates drop 30–40 percent.

The **Best Western Timber Cove Lodge** (3411 Hwy. 50, South Lake Tahoe, 530/541-6722 or 800/972-8558, www.timbercovetahoe.com) enjoys a prime waterfront location in South Lake Tahoe. The lodge is divided into town-house-style clusters of buildings, and when you reserve, it's worth paying the extra money for a unit right on the lakeshore, especially one with a fireplace. Two restaurants are located at or adjacent to the lodge: the family-oriented Mama's Red Tomato and the more grown-up Blue Water Bistro. A small marina rents kayaks and pedal boats and offers sportfishing, parasailing, and Emerald Bay tours. Rates drop as low as $69 in the off-season but climb to $239 in the busy season. A continental breakfast is included in the price. If you can't bear to vacation without your dog, he or she is welcome here for an extra $25 per night.

The name sounds a bit cheesy, and the ceiling mirrors might be considered in bad taste, but everyone seems to be having fun at the **Fantasy Inn** (3696 Hwy. 50, South Lake Tahoe, 530/541-4200 or 800/367-7736, www.fantasyinn.com, $99–359). The inn's 52 cleverly designed rooms are set up for romance, with oversized whirlpool tubs for two, king beds, and seductive lighting. If you want something really unique, pay the higher tariff for one of the 15 one-of-a-kind theme rooms, including Romeo and Juliet, Graceland, and Caesars Indulgence. The best deals are had in

winter with the inn's stay-and-ski packages. Not surprisingly, a lot of spur-of-the-moment weddings and honeymoons take place here.

Located near the Heavenly gondola and casino area, the **Chateau Inn and Suites** (965 Park Ave., South Lake Tahoe, 530/541-2363 or 800/455-6060, www.chateausuites.com, $45–175) has a lot going for it at budget prices. A cross between a motel and a condo complex, the chateau offers standard motel-style rooms, spa suites for two people, or two-bedroom and two-bath suites, perfect for families or two couples traveling together. All rooms have microwaves and refrigerators; some suites have fireplaces. Ultra-affordable stay-and-ski packages are a big draw.

You'll recognize the **Mark Twain Lodge** (947 Park Ave., South Lake Tahoe, 530/544-5733, www.marktwainlodge.com, $60–249) by the moose sculpture out front. What does a moose have to do with Lake Tahoe, or with Mark Twain? Nothing. But the lodge is a perennial favorite of budget travelers at South Shore. Its 10 guest rooms and four two-bedroom suites were beautifully renovated in 2004, and some have fireplaces, whirlpools, and/or minikitchens. The suites can sleep up to eight people, although a maximum of six would be more comfortable. The lodge's heated outdoor pool is popular with guests in summer, as is the hot tub in winter. Room rates are based on the number of people and time of the year. Everything in Stateline is a short walk away.

A perennial favorite of purse-string-watchers, the **Holiday Inn Express** (3961 Hwy. 50, South Lake Tahoe, 530/544-5900 or 800/544-5288, www.holidayinnexpresstahoe.com, $64–169) may well be the best deal in town. The motel is set back far enough from Highway 50 to make it blissfully quiet at night, but still close enough to all the South Shore action to make it convenient for skiing, restaurants, nightlife, and the like. The 89 rooms are clean and comfortable, and the decor is a huge step up from similarly priced budget motels.

If you've stayed at a Howard Johnson's anywhere else in the United States, you'll know what to expect at the one in South Lake: clean but unremarkable rooms, cable television, in-room coffeemakers and refrigerators, a complimentary continental breakfast that will make your blood sugar soar, and a heated pool and spa. Besides the shuttle service to the ski areas, maybe the best thing about the **Howard Johnson Express Inn** (3489 Hwy. 50, South Lake Tahoe, 530/541-4000 or 800/446-4656, www.hojo.com, $64–169) is that a stay here won't break the bank.

You gotta love a place like the **Quality Inn** (3838 Hwy. 50, South Lake Tahoe, 530/541-5400 or 800/245-6343, www.visitlaketahoe.com, $59–189). It's clean, it's affordable, and it often has rooms available on weekends when the fancier places are filled up. Sure, the 120 queen- and king-bed rooms have the all-too-familiar vanilla flavor of a chain motel, but at least you know what you are getting. A few suites with kitchenettes are available. Located one mile from Heavenly's gondola and the casinos, the Quality Inn's rates are reasonable and include a high-sugar, high-carbohydrate continental breakfast. And if you have a craving for tandoori while you are staying here, you're in luck: The Taj Majal Indian restaurant is in the same location.

Budget travelers will also be pleased with a stay at the **Vagabond Inn** (3892 Hwy. 50, South Lake Tahoe, 530/544-3642 or 800/522-1555, www.vagabondinn.com, $55–179), with 36 rooms in the heart of South Lake Tahoe. A few of the higher-priced rooms have fireplaces and whirlpool tubs. All the typical motel conveniences are provided, plus free shuttle service to local ski areas (Heavenly is a half mile away). A continental breakfast is offered in the morning. Families love this place because children 18 and under stay free.

There are two separate **Days Inns** in South Lake Tahoe, so penny-pinching travelers looking for a dependable chain-motel experience can choose from one a smidge nearer to the casinos (968 Park Ave., South Lake Tahoe, 530/541-4800 or 800/448-0754) or another slightly closer to Heavenly (3530 Hwy. 50, South Lake Tahoe, 530/544-3445 or 800/350-3446, www.daysinnlake-tahoe.com). The latter

was recently remodeled and offers casino and ski shuttle service, plus a heated outdoor pool in summer and year-round hot tub. If you've stayed at a Days Inn elsewhere in America, you won't find any surprises at either establishment. Both motels are without frills and affordable ($59–149). Children under 12 stay free.

When you're on a strict budget, a place like the **Econo Lodge** (3536 Hwy. 50, South Lake Tahoe, 530/544-2036 or 800/895-7304, www.econolodgelaketahoe.com, $39–99) is mighty appealing. Their motto is "spend a night, not a fortune," and with rates so low you can sleep here and still have plenty of money left over for lift tickets. The 37 rooms don't come with a lot of extras, but you can enjoy the use of their hot tub and sauna, heated swimming pool in summer, and free shuttle service to the ski resorts and casinos. Since the Econo Lodge is right in the middle of South Lake Tahoe, everything you might want to do is within a few minutes' drive.

Ask for a room in the back, away from Highway 50, to ensure a good night's sleep at the **Motel 6 South Lake Tahoe** (2375 Hwy. 50, South Lake Tahoe, 530/542-1400 or 800/436-8356, www.motel6.com, $49–69). This ultrabasic motel has 143 rooms, a guest laundry, a small swimming pool, and low-budget rates year-round. And as most dog-lovers know, all Motel 6 locations welcome dogs (one per room) at no extra charge, but you are not supposed to leave him or her unattended in your room. At this particular Motel 6, walking Rover is a snap, because the Upper Truckee River is only about 50 yards to the east, accessible by following a paved trail that runs behind the motel.

Much like the Motel 6, but with a different number, South Lake's **Super 8 Motel** (3600 Hwy. 50, South Lake Tahoe, 530/544-3476 or 800/237-8882, www.super8tahoe.com, $49–69) provides all the basics for a decent night's sleep and nothing more. The 108 rooms here are clean, inexpensive, and have king beds or two double beds. An outdoor hot tub is popular year-round; a children's play area and swimming pool are available in summer. Dogs are permitted for an extra $10 per night charge. A complimentary shuttle service runs to the casinos and ski resorts.

Campgrounds and RV Parks

Operated by the city of South Lake Tahoe, the 170-site **Campground by the Lake** (1150 Rufus Allen Blvd., South Lake Tahoe, 530/542-6096, www.recreationintahoe.com, $23–32) has almost everything a camper could ask for: space for RVs and trailers up to 45 feet long (but no hookups), water, restrooms, showers, a boat ramp, and access to Lake Tahoe for swimming and fishing. The camp name is just a bit misleading; Lake Tahoe is across Highway 50 from the camp. Sites are set among a forest of pines. Try to get one as far back from the highway as possible.

EMERALD BAY ROAD
Bed-and-Breakfasts

Owned by the same dog-friendly folks who own the Inn at Heavenly, the **Fireside Lodge** (515 Emerald Bay Rd., South Lake Tahoe, 530/544-5515 or 800/692-2246, www.tahoefiresidelodge.com, $79–165) is an ideal choice for dogs and their people. The lodge looks like a motel but it's a whole lot nicer, and offers amenities you'd expect at a bed-and-breakfast inn: a large continental breakfast, wine and cheese in the afternoon, and river-rock gas fireplaces and kitchenettes in each of the nine rooms. There is a small additional charge for pets. In winter, you can snowshoe around the large field right behind the inn.

Cabins

It isn't easy to get reservations, but **C Camp Richardson Resort** (1900 Jameson Beach Rd., South Lake Tahoe, 530/542-6550 or 800/544-1801, www.camprich.com) is a great place for a taste of the "old" Lake Tahoe. Built in the 1920s, the family-style resort on 150 acres of private land has cozy cabins under the pines, plus a great restaurant and bar alongside the beach. Some cabins are lakefront; most have kitchens and woodstoves, fireplaces, or gas stoves. The cabins range in size from studios

for two to larger units that will sleep up to eight people. In summer, they are rented by the week only ($900–1850). In winter, you can rent them by the night ($95–225). The resort also has hotel rooms and beachside inn rooms for rent by the night year-round ($80–175). The Pope-Baldwin Bike Path runs right by the resort, a full-service marina is on-site, and horse stables are right across the highway. In winter, Camp Richardson has groomed cross-country ski trails. You'll never run out of activities here.

Motels and Lodges

Less than a half mile from the Pope Baldwin Bike Path on Emerald Bay Road lies the **Lazy S Lodge** (609 Hwy. 89, South Lake Tahoe, 530/541-0230 or 800/862-8881, www.lazyslodge.com, $59–159), a 20-unit cottage-style motel. Many of the studios and two-room accommodations come with fully equipped kitchenettes and fireplaces. All units share use of a large heated pool, hot tub, picnic tables, and barbecues. The Lazy S is just far enough from the hubbub of South Lake Tahoe to feel like a relaxed getaway, but still within five miles of Heavenly and the casinos. If you want to attend a musical event at Valhalla, it's practically right next door.

Campgrounds and RV Parks

A favorite of tent campers who want to hike right from their tent door, tiny **Bayview Campground** (530/544-5994, $11) has only 10 sites for tents and mini-RVs (up to 20 feet) and no reservations accepted. Located at Highway 89 at Emerald Bay, right across the highway from Inspiration Point, the Forest Service–managed camp is the site of a major trailhead into the Desolation Wilderness. The camp has water and chemical toilets.

The **Eagle Point Campgound at Emerald Bay State Park** (Hwy. 89 at Emerald Bay, South Lake Tahoe, 530/541-3030 or 530/525-7277, $25) is perched on a high point above Emerald Bay, and yes, some but not all of the sites have remarkable lake views. Many of the 100 sites are quite spacious, too. Eagle Point

Campground can accommodate small trailers and RVs (up to 21 feet long) and has restrooms, coin-operated showers, and water, but no hookups. Not surprisingly, this camp is quite popular during the short season that it is open (mid-June–Labor Day), so you must reserve far in advance at 800/444-7275 or www.reserveamerica.com. The best sites are 66–70 on the Emerald Bay side of the loop; a short trail leads from there down to the beach. Dogs can join you for camping but are not allowed on any of the park's trails.

If you have your own boat or kayak, you can stay at one of 22 sites at **Emerald Bay Boat-in Camp** (530/541-3030 or 530/525-7277 for more information, $22) on the northern shore of Emerald Bay. Each campsite has a mooring buoy. Boaters can either sleep on board their boat (a fine idea if you have a yacht but a bad idea if you only have a kayak) or camp in a designated site on shore. Each campsite has a table, storage locker, and fire ring. Water is available in the campground, and there are chemical toilets. The boat camp is usually open Memorial Day–Labor Day, depending on weather conditions. Reserve in advance at 800/444-7275 or www.reserveamerica.com.

A colossal 332 campsites for tents and RVs up to 35 feet long are found at **Camp Richardson Resort** (1900 Jameson Beach Rd., South Lake Tahoe, 530/541-1801 or 800/541-1801, www.camprich.com, $20–31 for tents and RVs), in addition to its cabin rentals, general store, ice-cream shop, restaurant and bar, horse rentals, bike rentals, cross-country ski trails, and so much more. With all this going on, you won't feel like you are alone in nature when you camp here, but for many people, that's just fine. The camp has all the full-service amenities: full RV hookups, a disposal site, water, showers, restrooms, and a boat ramp. One downer: No pets are allowed. Tent campers should be sure to reserve a site at Badger's Den Campground, which is on the lake side of the resort. Most other sites are across the highway.

The Forest Service–run **Fallen Leaf Lake Campground** (2165 Fallen Leaf Lake Rd., South Lake Tahoe, 530/544-0426, $20) has 206 sites for tents or RVs up to 40 feet long and a great location just a few hundred yards from Fallen Leaf Lake, three miles north of the Y. An easy trail leads from the campground to the lake. The camp has water and flush toilets, but no showers or RV hookups. Reserve in advance at 877/444-6777 or www.reserveusa.com.

SOUTH OF THE Y
Motels and Lodges

If you are planning to ski at Sierra-at-Tahoe, you might not want to get a motel in the heart of downtown South Lake Tahoe, where you will be an extra 20 minutes or so from the slopes. The **Ridgewood Inn** (1341 Hwy. 89, South Lake Tahoe, 530/541-8589, www.ridgewoodinn.com, $59–129) is a great lodging choice south of the Y that makes the drive to and from Sierra-at-Tahoe that much shorter. This is your basic one-story, L-shaped motel, with rooms opening out to the parking lot, but many of the units have kitchens and gas fireplaces, and they are clean and cozy. Dogs are permitted in some rooms for an additional $10 fee per night.

More than a dozen miles from South Lake Tahoe off Highway 50 in the Strawberry/Twin Bridges area, the rustic **Strawberry Lodge** (530/659-7200, www.strawberry-lodge.com, $55–70 for rooms with shared baths, $150–175 for river cabin) is a former Pony Express bunkhouse that is now a favorite of rock climbers at Lover's Leap and skiers at Sierra-at-Tahoe. Lacking telephones or televisions, this old-style lodge is the polar opposite of anything you'll find near the South Shore casinos. For many travelers, that's a good thing.

Campgrounds and RV Parks

The **KOA Kampground of South Lake Tahoe** (760 Hwy. 50, South Lake Tahoe, 530/577-3693 or 800/562-3477, www.laketahoekoa.com) has what all KOAs have: spaces for RVs and trailers up to 40 feet long, full hookups (even cable TV hookups), a disposal station, restrooms, showers, laundry, cable TV, a heated swimming pool, playground, and lots of things that should be spelled with a C but are spelled with a K, like the rental Kottages. There are 60 sites in all and this particular KOA has wireless Internet. The tent sites have picnic tables, campfire rings (or kampfire rings, if you prefer), and barbecue grills. If you forgot the ingredients for s'mores, you can buy them at the general store. Fishing in the Truckee River is possible just 100 yards from the door of your tent or RV. Tent sites are $36–42; RV sites are $46–53. The Kottages, which are small, cozy cabins, are $175–225. The camp is open year-round.

Located a stone's throw from the KOA, **Tahoe Pines Campground** (860 U.S. 50 at Upper Truckee Rd., Tahoe Paradise, 530/577-1653, www.tahoepinescampground.com, tent sites $34–39, RV sites $44–49) is similar in size (60 sites) and amenities: full hookups for RVs, sites that can accommodate RVs up to 40 feet long, showers, flush toilets, dump station, playground, store, and laundry. Even the rates are the same. The camp is situated along the Truckee River and Echo Creek, so if you're a fishing camper, you'll be happy here.

Huge, private **Tahoe Valley Campground** (1175 Melba Dr., South Lake Tahoe, 530/541-2222, $24–44) boasts a staggering 415 sites and can accommodate supersized RVs up to 60 feet long. It has all the standard RV park amenities: full hookups, a disposal station, restrooms, and showers, plus some luxuries you might not expect—a swimming pool, tennis courts, a small store, and laundry. The camp is open year-round, a rarity around Lake Tahoe.

Campers at **Wrights Lake Campground** (off Hwy. 50, 17 miles west of South Lake Tahoe, $20) may be a long way from the shores of Lake Tahoe, but they are situated right on the southwest edge of the Desolation Wilderness at 7,000 feet in elevation. For day hikers and backpackers, this is a swell location; a multitude of trails lead right from camp. For rock climbers, the spectacular Phantom Spires are nearby. For everybody else, there is easy access to swimming and fishing in Wrights Lake (great for fly-fishing in float tubes). The 67-site camp has water and vault toilets and is suitable for RVs or tents. Reserve in advance at 877/444-6777 or www.reserveusa.com. For more information, contact the Pacific Ranger District of Eldorado National Forest (530/647-5415, www.r5.fs.fed.us/eldorado).

Food

SOUTH LAKE TAHOE
Breakfast
If the chain restaurant Mel's Diner was the real McCoy, it would be the **Red Hut Cafe** (2749 Hwy. 50, South Lake Tahoe, 530/541-9024, 6 A.M.–2 P.M. daily, $5–10). This 1950s-era diner has been wildly popular since, well, the 1950s. Locals and visitors alike head here for breakfast, where they usually have to fight for one of the dozen or so booths, or settle for a counter stool. The place is so popular that in 1990 the owners gave in and opened a second location at 227 Kingsbury Grade. At both Red Huts, waffles are a hot ticket, usually served with fresh or frozen fruit (depending on the season) and heaps of whipped cream. Pancakes, eggs, and omelets are also popular; lunch consists of burgers and grilled sandwiches. Portions are large and the cholesterol factor is generally very high. When 2 P.M. rolls around and the restaurant closes its doors for the day, a sad sign lights up the window: The Hut is Shut.

You don't have to be a health-food nut to love **Sprouts** (3123 Harrison Ave. at Hwy. 50, South Lake Tahoe, 530/541-6969, $5–10). The food is so delicious that even junk-food devotees won't mind eating stuff that is good for them. Open for three meals, 8 A.M. to 9 P.M. daily, Sprouts is run by a husband-and-wife team who have a creative flair with wholesome food. Try the breakfast bowl (brown rice, beans, steamed eggs, salsa, and avocado), "killer nachos," tempeh burgers, salads, or one of several choices of fresh-squeezed juices: carrot, orange, wheatgrass, beet, and so on. You will feel healthier just perusing the menu.

On your way to or from Heavenly you can make a stop at the **Blue Angel Cafe** (1132 Ski Run Blvd., South Lake Tahoe, 530/544-6544, www.blueangeltahoe.com, 8 A.M.–8 P.M. Wed.–Sun., 8 A.M.–2 P.M. Mon.–Tues., $5–8) for gourmet food to go or to eat in. This stylish little cafe looks like something you might find in San Francisco's Marina District, with big arrangements of fresh flowers and light-yellow walls. If you aren't a traditional bacon-and-eggs eater, you'll love the breakfasts here: eggplant Benedict, lemon French toast, frittata of the day, pesto scrambled eggs. Lunch and dinner and good bets, too, and there is a children's menu for the little ones.

Seafood and Steak

When Tahoe locals want a seafood lunch or dinner, **The Fresh Ketch** (2425 Venice Dr., Tahoe Keys Marina, South Lake Tahoe, 530/541-5683, www.thefreshketch.com, 5:30 P.M. to close, $10–25) is where they go. It's far enough off the beaten track—tucked in among the town houses surrounding Tahoe's only inland marina, Tahoe Keys—that most casual tourists would never find it. The Fresh Ketch prides itself on a wide selection of fresh fish, from ahi tuna to smoked trout. On Thursdays and Saturdays they serve sushi as well. Two separate dining areas are available: the upstairs is more formal; the downstairs opens earlier at 11:30 A.M. and is more casual and less expensive. Both have views of the boats in the Tahoe Keys marina. Live music is often playing in the bar on weekends. In summer, even the kids will be comfortable dining here at the patio tables outside on the grass.

Owned and operated by the same folks who run Gar Woods on the North Shore, **Riva Grill** (900 Ski Run Blvd., Ski Run Marina, South Lake Tahoe, 530/542-2600, www.rivagrill.com, noon–9:30 P.M. Mon.–Thur., noon–10 P.M. Fri.–Sat., $23–30) offers fine dining at the Ski Run Marina. Just like at Gar Woods, Riva Grill is known for its long list of well drinks

with provocative, "wink-wink" names. The Wet Woody, a rum-and-fruit concoction, is their trademark elixir. Dinner may be a little expensive, but at least you don't have to add in the cost of valet parking—it's free. The menu includes several seafood dishes plus free-range chicken, braised lamb shank, and filet mignon. The dining room is decorated with lots of stylish, polished mahogany, just like those fast wooden boats of days gone by. The outside deck has only a so-so view of the lake; the upstairs windows offer a somewhat better view.

In the same complex, **Watermark Cafe and Wine Bar** (900 Ski Run Blvd., Ski Run Marina, South Lake Tahoe, 530/544-3300, www.watermarkcafe.com, $18–29) is located just a few feet from the lake. The busy lakeside patio is a scenic spot for lunch or dinner, with entrees including shrimp, halibut, salmon, lamb, and elk. When the evenings turn cool, the waiters fire up the outdoor fire pit. The indoor wine bar has an extensive selection of vintages; you can sample them by the glass, by the bottle, or in a selection of wine flights.

Located at the Best Western Station House Inn, **LewMarNel's** (901 Park Ave., South Lake Tahoe, 530/542-1101 or 530/542-1072, 5:30–9:45 P.M. daily, $18–30), is a restaurant catering to big eaters whose appetite is more discriminating than that of the average casino buffet diner. If you are tired of having to order à la carte everywhere you go, you'll be happy here. Dinner begins with complimentary cheese fondue and fresh-baked sourdough bread, and all entrees come with soup or salad and potatoes or rice. Steaks are the main event here, but several seafood, pasta, and poultry dishes are served as well. Amazingly, some diners save enough room to order apple pie à la mode for dessert. Wine lovers will be pleased with the extensive wine list, rated as "one of the greatest wine lists in the world" by *Wine Spectator Magazine.*

The Beacon at historic Camp Richardson Resort (1900 Jameson Beach Rd., South Lake Tahoe, 530/541-0630, www.camprich.com, 11 A.M.–9 P.M. daily, winter hours may vary, $9–28) is a Tahoe institution—the only "beach house"–style restaurant on the lake. In the warm months, diners covet the umbrella-shaded tables on the huge outdoor deck, which opens onto a sandy lakeshore beach. Summer lunches can be a bit of a zoo because of the multitudes of kids playing on the beach, but sunset dinners are a great experience. The fried calamari is wildly popular—almost as much as the Rum Runner, the restaurant's signature rum-laced well drink. Entrees include everything from hamburgers to fancy seafood dishes. Live music is offered on summer weekends.

If you're cruising from the South Shore up Highway 89, you can't miss the **Rockwater Bar & Grill** (787 Emerald Bay Rd., South Lake Tahoe, 530/544-8004, 11 A.M.–10 P.M. daily, www.rockwaterbarandgrill.com), just north of the Y. A traditional yet semicasual steak house, this is a great place to go after a long day of skiing when you want a big meat-and-potatoes meal and a chance to catch up on the sports scores. Five television sets are located in the bar. Even if you're not a red meat–eater, you'll find plenty of options here– fish-and-chips, fish tacos, shrimp scampi ($10–15). Sirloins, rib eyes, and New York strip steaks are pricier ($17–25), but you can always save money and order a sandwich or burger, served with crispy fries ($8). The dining room is decorated with beautiful Tahoe photographs and hand-painted murals; the outdoor patio and bar are heated and open year-round. Rockwater is owned by the same folks who run The Dory's Oar (see *Californian/Continental*), so you can be assured of a quality experience here.

American

For a serious burger, **The Burger Lounge** (717 Hwy. 89, South Lake Tahoe, 530/542-4060, 11 A.M.–8 P.M. daily June–Sept., 11 A.M.–9 P.M. daily Oct.–May, $6–12) is the place to go on the South Shore. Only half-pounders are served, plus ample options for non-beef eaters: grilled chicken sandwiches, a portabello mushroom sandwich, and five different kinds of veggie burgers. For novelty seekers, there's a peanut-butter-and-jelly burger, and a dazzling array of french-fry choices: garlic fries,

pesto fries, Cajun fries, chili fries, and so on. Customers order at the counter and have a seat at inside or outside tables. Lots of folks order takeout here, too.

Pilots and nonpilots alike will enjoy the food and fun at **Chase's** (1901 Airport Rd., South Lake Tahoe, 530/544 9080, www.chasesgrill.com, 8 A.M.–7 P.M. Tues.–Sun., $9–14). The large windows at this airport grill open out to surprisingly big views of the Upper Truckee Meadow, Freel Peak, and Job's Peak. And the food is far more interesting than you'd expect. The restaurant's motto is "where Tahoe meets New Orleans," so if you're hankering for a taste of the Big Easy, try one of the fried oyster po'boy sandwiches, jambalaya, or a big bowl of gumbo. Their crab cakes just might be the best west of the Mississippi, and they also make a mean London-style fish-and-chips.

The most commonly asked question at the **Shoreline Cafe** (3310 Hwy. 50, South Lake Tahoe, 530/541-7858, 8 A.M.–10 P.M. Sun.–Thur., 8 A.M.–11 P.M. Fri.–Sat., $12–20) is probably "Did this place used to be a Denny's?" The building has that trademark Denny's look to it, but the food is several cuts above. The Shoreline is open for three meals a day, and with an extensive kids' menu and casual decor, it's great for families. Prices are moderate—dinner entrees include chicken, pasta, and steak—and the lake view is a bonus, even though Highway 50 runs between the cafe and the lake.

If you want to meet the South Tahoe locals, go to **Steamers** (2236 Hwy. 50, South Lake Tahoe, 530/541-8818, www.steamersbar.com, 11 A.M.–11 P.M. Mon.–Sat., 9 A.M.–9 P.M. Sun., $7–8) after work hours, say 5–7 P.M. This small tavern is well known for its affordable Friday-night steak dinners, Saturday-night tacos, and reasonably priced beer selection. There's no pretension here—it's all about the brews, the bar food, and the three big-screen TVs. The place is named after the mighty steamships that once ruled the waves of Lake Tahoe. If the bar area is too dark for your taste, sit outside at the back patio tables in summer.

Located inside a 1960s-era strip mall,

Freshie's (3330 Hwy. 50, South Lake Tahoe, 530/542-3630, 11 A.M.–9 P.M. daily) wins the award for "most uninspiring restaurant location," but the owners have made the most out of what they had to work with. Beloved throughout the South Shore, Freshie's has a fun and creative atmosphere (a Hawaiian surfing theme) and outstanding food—Pacific Rim–style dishes, Hawaiian-style ribs, original salads, and a great selection of microbrews. The fish tacos are delectable. In the summer months, you can forgo the strip mall altogether and eat outside on the rooftop deck. Fun, casual, and surprising, Freshie's is a winner for dinner or lunch, and two can eat well here for about $30.

Californian/Continental

Affordable lakefront restaurants on the South Shore aren't easy to come by, but the 【 **Blue Water Bistro** (3411 Hwy. 50, South Lake Tahoe, 530/541-0113, 11:30 A.M.–9 P.M. Sun.–Thurs., 11:30 A.M.–10 P.M. Fri.–Sat.) takes up the slack in fine style. At the Timber Cove Marina, on a boardwalk pier built over the water, you can gaze at the azure waters of Lake Tahoe as the sun sinks over the western mountains. Pick an inside seat in the upstairs dining room colorfully decorated with Picasso prints, or choose a table outside on the pier or on the small upstairs deck. The food is classic California cuisine, with several creative fish, chicken, and beef dishes on the often-changing menu. Appetizers are $7–13, entrees are $18–28. For lunch, you can choose from gourmet sandwiches ($9–12) or a few pasta dishes. The only tricky part is finding this place—you have to drive into the Best Western Timber Cove Lodge driveway and then go around the back to find it.

From the outside, this intimate fine-dining restaurant looks like somebody's cozy cottage in the pines. But 【 **Evan's** (536 Emerald Bay Rd., South Lake Tahoe, 530/542-1990, www.evanstahoe.com, 5:30 P.M.–close daily, $21–30) is a long-standing success story on Tahoe's southwest shore, serving up classic continental cuisine just at the edge of the city limits. It's far from the madding crowds of downtown, but close enough to be an easy drive from anywhere in South Lake. Entrees include roast venison with wild-rice cakes, veal sweetbreads, rack of lamb, and fresh seafood. The seared foie gras is a standout appetizer. The wine list is outstanding. *Bon Appetit* magazine called this 11-table restaurant "a jewel."

When a restaurant has been written up by magazines like *Bon Appetit* and *Wine Spectator* and newspapers like *The New York Times* and the *San Francisco Chronicle,* diners should expect great things. 【 **Nepheles** (1169 Ski Run Blvd., South Lake Tahoe, 530/544-8130, www.nepheles.com, 5 P.M.–close daily, $20–32) will exceed your expectations. The restaurant has been serving California cuisine near Heavenly Ski Resort since 1977—before most chefs knew what California cuisine was. The swordfish egg rolls and seafood cheesecake are standout appetizers. Entrees include traditional foods like rack of lamb and filet mignon, and nontraditional foods like broiled elk, prepared in fresh, creative ways. (Nephele was the Greek goddess of epicurean delights.) As an unusual sideline, the restaurant also has three private hot tubs for rent by the hour, so you can finish out your meal with a soothing soak.

If you are craving fish-and-chips, or bangers-and-mash, **The Dory's Oar & Tudor English Pub** (1041 Fremont Ave., South Lake Tahoe, 530/541-6603 or 866/541-6603, www.dorysoar.com, 5–10 P.M. daily) does them right. Order these and other British favorites ($9–15) upstairs in the English pub and wash them down with a Guinness or Fuller's London Pride. Or, for something more formal, make a reservation for the downstairs dining room, where less proletarian seafood entrees like shrimp scampi, grilled swordfish, and broiled lobster tail are served, as well as a variety of steaks ($15–28). It's Merry Olde England upstairs, and a classy blend of California and continental cuisine downstairs. Owner Keith Simpson is an authentic Brit who has catered for the royal family. Two restaurants; one building—a winning combination.

Italian

If your stomach is set on classic Italian food, **Scusa** (1142 Ski Run Blvd., South Lake Tahoe, 530/542-0100, 5:30–9 P.M. daily, $15–25) is the place on the South Shore. For 15 years, the restaurant has been doling out their famous cream of roasted garlic soup, plus pasta dishes served with 10 different sauces, to hungry skiers coming off Heavenly's slopes. The atmosphere is casual; it's okay to show up in your ski parka. If you aren't in a pasta mood, the menu also includes fresh fish, veal, shrimp, chicken, and vegetarian entrees. The smoked chicken ravioli is legendary.

For celebrating a special occasion with your sweetie, the intimate **Cafe Fiore** (1169 Ski Run Blvd., South Lake Tahoe, 530/541-2908, www.cafefiore.com, 5:30–10 P.M. daily, $15–28) is the spot, with its fabulous Italian/Continental cuisine and meager half dozen tables. Don't imagine you will get in without reservations. The food at Cafe Fiore is miles away from the typical cannelloni and ravioli served at so many American Italian restaurants. Entrees include grilled lamb chops with shiitake mushrooms and pine nuts, and seafood linguine in a cognac, caper, and lemon butter sauce. Vegetarians always have a few interesting choices, and the garlic bread is to die for. The tiny restaurant is located in a cottage behind Nephele's off Ski Run Boulevard and is easy to miss if you don't know it's there.

For simple Italian food—nothing too cutting-edge—**Passaretti's** (1181 Hwy. 89, South Lake Tahoe, 530/541-3433, www.passarettis.com, 11 A.M.–9 P.M. daily, $11–19) serves up steaming plates of pasta, pasta, and more pasta in a wide variety of shapes and flavors. Lasagna, manicotti, ravioli—all the carb-loading basics are done well here. A few seafood, steak, and veal dishes will satisfy high-protein dieters. All meals begin with a trip to the hearty salad-and-soup bar—a great start when you are starving after a day on the slopes. The restaurant is located just south of the Y at South Lake.

There's something about pizza and skiing that just seems to go together. **Lake Tahoe Pizza Company** (1168 Hwy. 50, South Lake Tahoe, 530/544-1919, 4–9:30 P.M. daily) creates a memorable version of the old dough, cheese, and tomato sauce gambit. Several gourmet-style toppings are available in addition to the classics like pepperoni and mushrooms. Their meatball pizza is a winner, as is the salad bar. The restaurant's warm, friendly atmosphere and affordable prices attract locals and repeat customers. For about $25, four people could eat well here.

Mexican

Everybody is always happy with **The Cantina** (765 Emerald Bay Rd., South Lake Tahoe, 530/544-1233, www.cantinatahoe.com, 11:30 A.M.–9 P.M. daily, $9–16) nontraditional Mexican food, which includes smoked chicken polenta, Texas crab cakes, and a Southwestern Reuben sandwich. For the traditional, the menu also offers burritos, chile verde, and fajitas. Wash it all down with one of the Cantina's salt-rimmed margaritas or 30 different beer varieties. Drinks are a lot cheaper during the weekday happy hour, 3–6 P.M. The restaurant is always busy, but salsa and chips come to your table the moment you sit down. No wonder it's been voted "Best Mexican Restaurant" seven years in a row.

Asian

If you've just pulled into South Lake Tahoe from points west on Highway 50, **Orchid's** (2180 Hwy. 50, South Lake Tahoe, 530/544-5541, 11 A.M.–10 P.M. Mon.–Sat., 3–10 P.M. Sun., $5–15) is the first restaurant east of the Y. It's worth a stop here for a Thai dinner before heading downtown. Don't be discouraged by the restaurant's unappealing strip-mall location. Once you're inside, you'll be instantly transported to Southeast Asia. You can order all your favorites: lemongrass soup, pad thai, basil chicken, papaya salad, and the chef's special Similan Island red curry, and tell the chef how spicy to make them. The menu includes more than 70 items.

South Lake Tahoe locals have twice voted **Mandarin Garden** (2502 Hwy. 50, South

Lake Tahoe, 530/544-8885, 11:30 A.M.–9 P.M. daily) their favorite Chinese restaurant. If you're a fan of chicken with black bean sauce, moo shi pork, Szechuan tofu, tea-smoked duckling, or kung pao seafood, you'll be happy here. Most items are $6–12 for dinner; complete lunches are about $5.

One of the best things about a vacation in Tahoe is that in terms of dining, it's not that different from a vacation in San Francisco. Think you can't get good sushi in the mountains? Think again. **The Naked Fish** (3940 Hwy. 50 #3, South Lake Tahoe, 530/541-3474, 5–9:30 P.M. Mon.–Fri., noon–3 P.M. and 5–10 P.M. Sat.–Sun., $5–12) is located right on the main drag in South Lake Tahoe. From the outside, the setting doesn't look altogether promising. But step inside and you're in a blue-green world that shifts your mind-set, and your appetite, to ocean-fresh fish in no time at all. Sushi, sashimi, teriyaki, tempura-they do it all here, and they do it well.

South Lake is blessed with two other good sushi restaurants: **Samurai** (2588 Hwy. 50, South Lake Tahoe, 530/542-0300, www.sushitahoe.com, 5 P.M.–close daily, $5–12) has been serving sushi at the lake since 1984, so they know how to do it right. The restaurant's decor is a bit bland, but the gracious servers wearing kimonos brighten things up. And nearby **Off The Hook** (2660 Hwy. 50, South Lake Tahoe, 530/544-5599, 11:30 A.M.–2:30 P.M. and 4:30–9 P.M. Mon.–Fri., 2–9 P.M. Sat.–Sun., $5–12) can also satisfy your cravings for wasabi and pickled ginger.

STATELINE
Seafood and Steak
Located on the 16th floor of Harrah's Casino, **The Summit** (15 Hwy. 50, South Lake Tahoe, 775/588-6611, www.harrahs.com, 5:30–10 P.M. Fri.–Sat., 5:30–9 P.M. Sun., $30–65) offers sophisticated food in an intimate setting, with a pianist tinkling the ivories and a world-class view of Lake Tahoe from on high. Dinner entrees include filet mignon stuffed with gorgonzola cheese and wrapped in prosciutto, and grilled venison T-bone with brandied wild

mushrooms. The food is presented like an edible work of art, but nonetheless, the lake view from the penthouse restaurant's big windows steals the show. The two of you probably won't leave here without dropping $100 and up on dinner, but it's worth it. The adjacent Summit Lounge features an impressive wine list and more than 50 brands of cigars.

Yes, the **Chart House** (392 Kingsbury Grade, Stateline, 775/588-6276, www.charthouse.com, 5–9 P.M. Sun.–Fri., 5–10 P.M. Sat., $19–29) is a chain restaurant, but the views from this top-of-the-hill dining room on Kingsbury Grade make it feel anything but ordinary. A million-dollar renovation in 2004 has made this South Shore standby even better than before, with a tasteful, cozy decor. The food is basically the same as at all Chart Houses in resort towns across the United States—well-prepared seafood, prime rib, and steaks, and a salad bar that fills the length of the dining room—but it is the stunning lake view, framed by majestic pine trees, visible from almost every table that keeps the locals and visitors coming back for more. Sunsets are unforgettable.

Speaking of lake views, the restaurant at ◖ **Edgewood Golf Course** (180 Lake Pkwy., South Lake Tahoe, 775/588-2787, www.edgewood-tahoe.com, 6–9 P.M. daily in summer, $21–29) has a vista that will knock your socks off. With a high, vaulted ceiling and big windows overlooking the lake, it's hard to focus your eyes on the upscale steak-house-style menu. Most golf courses serve up basic fare for hungry golfers, but since it costs $200 to golf at Edgewood, the quality of the food is on par with the green fees. Appetizers include crab cakes, sautéed scallops, and ostrich medallions. Entrees are a variety of fresh seafood, plus elk chops, osso bucco, filet mignon, and aged rib eye.

Hearty appetites will achieve satisfaction—perhaps even heavenly delight—at the **Timber House Restaurant** (168 Hwy. 50, Stateline, 775/588-7777 or 800/624-7980, www.lakeside-inn.com, open 24 hours daily), without breaking the bank. A favorite of locals and visitors alike, this restaurant at the Lakeside Inn and Casino is not exactly fine dining, but the sourdough bread is brought to your table hot and plentiful, and the huge slabs of prime rib won't leave you feeling hungry. The Timber House's $2.99 breakfast has filled the bellies of more than a few local construction workers and the $8.95 prime rib comes in portions big enough to feed a crowd.

Diners willing to drive a few miles to Zephyr Cove may find culinary nirvana at **The Cedar Room** (178 Hwy. 50, Zephyr Cove, 775/588-9300, www.thecedarroom.com, 5–10 P.M. daily, $20–34). The menu is always changing, but expect to find many of the classics: filet mignon, rack of lamb, veal marsala, and lots of seafood (tiger prawns, sea bass, orange roughy, ahi, and sea scallops). The dining room is contemporary and stylish, and even the traditional entrees are prepared in fresh, creative ways.

A more casual choice in Zephyr Cove is the restaurant at the historic **Zephyr Cove Resort** (760 Hwy. 50 at Zephyr Cove, 775/589-4968, www.zephyrcove.com, 7 A.M.–3 P.M. Mon.–Wed., 7 A.M.–9 P.M. Thur.–Sun., $12–22). Housed in an 1860s-era building, the wood-paneled dining room and its menu have an "old Tahoe" slant: trout and eggs for breakfast, thick burgers for lunch, and an array of large-portioned entrees for dinner, like rainbow trout, New York strip steak, and Rubicon short ribs. The restaurant's milk shakes are legendary.

Barbecue

Got a hankering for hot links, black-eyed peas, ham hocks, and homemade sweet-potato pie? Since 1977, **Womack's** (4041 Hwy. 50, South Lake Tahoe, 530/544-2268, $10–15) has been serving up Southern comfort in the form of lip-smackin' barbecue ribs, chicken, beef, and brisket. Its setting in a strip mall of T-shirt and souvenir shops won't lure you in, and the dining room is small and nondescript, but most people aren't concerned about ambience when they are wiping barbecue sauce off their chins. Womack's is within walking distance of the casino district, so spend some money on tasty

Louisiana hot links and gumbo before you donate the rest to the slot machines. If Elvis were alive, he'd love this place.

Californian/Continental

Most casino food is, well, just casino food, but 19 Kitchen/Bar breaks that rule. On the 19th floor of Harveys Resort, **19 Kitchen** (30 Hwy. 50, Stateline, 775/588-2411 or 800/648-3361, www.harrahs.com, 5–9 P.M. daily) offers what has to be one of the best sunset dinner seats on the lake, at the site of what used to be Llewellyn's Restaurant. More than a few marriage proposals have taken place here. The menu is heavy with seafood selections, but with some eclectic, and maybe even eccentric, touches. In addition to $20–30 entrees, there are "small plates" in the $10–15 range: New England lobster chowder, lump crab cakes with green papaya salad, sea bass in a baby shrimp lobster broth, and a few oddities like "The Forks"—smoked salmon and caviar poppers, served on the tines of upright forks. Careful not to poke your eye out with that one.

Italian

Drive a couple of miles east to Zephyr Cove and you'll find **Ivano's** (605 Hwy. 50, Zephyr Cove, 775/586-1070, 6–10 P.M. Mon.–Sat., $12–20), which doles out tasty Italian dinners at night. Sit outside on the deck to enjoy the Tahoe summer evening air, or on cool nights choose a table inside next to the rock fireplace. Start your meal with a classic antipasto or mozzarella caprese ($8–10), then move on to a pasta course and/or a meat-based second course—veal scaloppini, beef tenderloin medallions, or chicken with prosciutto.

French

Once you're inside, **Mirabelle** (290 Kingsbury Grade, Stateline, 775/586-1007, 5:30–9 P.M. Tues.–Sun., $21–30) will make you feel like you're in a small cafe alongside the Seine. Chef/owner Camille Schwartz brings authentic *cuisine français* to the South Shore at this small dining room in a business park off Kingsbury Grade. The only thing that mars the French experience is the sight of the true-blue American sports bar next door. All the classics are served, from lobster bisque and an escargot appetizer to a Grand Marnier dessert soufflé. In between are a multitude of entrees, from bouillabaisse to venison. Don't miss the onion tart if it's on the menu when you visit.

Hawaiian
Maybe Hawaiian isn't the type of food that comes to mind after a day of skiing at Heavenly, but sometimes it's worth thinking outside the box. **Kalani's** (shop #26 at Heavenly Village, 1001 Heavenly Village Way, South Lake Tahoe, 530/544-6100, www.kalanis.com, 11:30 A.M.–3 P.M. and 5–9:30 P.M. Sun.–Thur., till 11 P.M. Fri.–Sat., $15–30) Pacific Rim fusion cuisine will put you in an aloha state of mind as fast as you can say "opakapaka." This award-winning restaurant features fresh fish flown in daily from Hawaii, a full-service sushi bar with a litany of signature rolls that change daily, and memorable Hawaiian-influenced entrées like blue crab crusted onaga fillet, or lomi lomi salmon-and-watercress platter laced with papaya-seed dressing. The restaurant is chic and stylish but still comfortable, and the food is elegantly presented.

Practicalities

INFORMATION
Several visitors centers are located on and around the South Shore. The **South Lake Tahoe Chamber of Commerce** (3066 Hwy. 50, South Lake Tahoe, 530/541-5255, www.tahoeinfo.com) is right next door to the Lake Tahoe Historical Society Museum. On the Nevada side of Stateline, the **Tahoe-Douglas Chamber of Commerce** (195 Hwy. 50, Zephyr Cove, 775/588-4591, www.tahoechamber.org) is at the Round Hill Shopping Center. There's also the **Lake Tahoe Visitors Authority** (1156 Ski Run Blvd., South Lake Tahoe, 530/544-5050, www.bluelaketahoe.com). These visitors centers are particularly helpful if you are looking for lodging, restaurants, tours, or businesses of any kind.

The **U.S. Forest Service** also has two visitors centers in South Lake Tahoe. At the main office (35 College Dr., South Lake Tahoe, 530/543-2600, www.fs.fed.us/r5/ltbmu) you will find tons of information on hiking, biking, and other outdoor activities on Forest Service land. Books on Tahoe's natural history are for sale, as well as hiking maps and guides. A much smaller Forest Service visitors center (on Hwy. 89, 530/573-2674), three miles north of the Y, is located at Taylor Creek by the parking lot near the Stream Profile Chamber.

The **League to Save Lake Tahoe,** a nonprofit organization, also has a small interpretive center (955 Hwy. 89, South Lake Tahoe, 530/541-5388).

SERVICES
Medical Care
South Lake Tahoe is served by **Barton Memorial Hospital** (2170 South Ave., South Lake Tahoe, 530/541-3420, www.bartonhealth.org) as well as two 24-hour emergency care centers: **Tahoe Urgent Care** (2130 Hwy. 50, South Lake Tahoe, 530/541-3277) and **Stateline Medical Center** (155 Hwy. 50, Stateline, 775/588-3561 or 530/543-5700).

Post Offices
Several post offices are conveniently located along the South Shore, including in Meyers, Tahoe Paradise, and at the west end of Fallen Leaf Lake. The main **South Lake Tahoe post office** (1046 Al Tahoe Blvd., 530/544-5867) is located at the Rite Aid Shopping Center.

Internet Access
Need to check your email or surf the Web? Do so at the South Shore's two public libraries:

the **El Dorado County Library** (1000 Rufus Allen Blvd., South Lake Tahoe, 530/573-3185) or the **Douglas County Library** (233 Warrior Way, Zephyr Cove, 775/588-6411). Or, buy a cup of java at one of two local coffeehouses that allow free Internet use for its customers: **Alpina Coffee Cafe** (822 Hwy. 89, South Lake Tahoe, 530/541-7449) and **Alpen Sierra Coffee Company** (3940 Hwy. 50, South Lake Tahoe, 530/544-7740).

If you are traveling with your laptop and it is enabled for wireless Internet, much of the South Lake Tahoe/Stateline area has wireless access. The BlueGo public transportation system, with on-demand kiosks at locations throughout the South Shore, has created more than 30 Wi-Fi hot spots.

GETTING THERE
By Air
The **South Lake Tahoe Airport** (1901 Airport Road, 530/542-6180 or 530/541-0480, www.laketahoeairport.com) is currently not operational for commercial flights. But visitors can fly into the **Reno/Tahoe International Airport** (2001 E. Plumb Lane, 775/328-6400, www.renoairport.com) and then rent a car, or take bus, shuttle, or limousine service to the South Shore. Several companies offer shuttle service between the Reno-Tahoe International Airport and the South Shore's casinos and hotels: Tahoe Casino Express (775/785-2424 or 800/446-6128), South Tahoe Express (866/898-2463, www.southtahoeexpress.com), Airport Minibus (775/786-3700 or 800/235-5466), or No Stress Express (775/885-7550 or 800/426-5644, www.nostressexpress.com).

On-demand limousine service is offered by Bell Limousine (775/786-3700 or 800/235-5466), Executive Limousine (775/333-3300), Aladdin Limousine (800/546-6009), and Sierra West Limousine (877/347-4789).

Visitors could also fly into Sacramento, Oakland, San Francisco, or San Jose airports, then rent a car to drive to Lake Tahoe. Sacramento Airport is two hours from the South Shore, the three other airports are about 3.5 hours away.

By Car
There are many possible driving routes to the South Shore of Lake Tahoe. From the San Francisco Bay Area or Sacramento, the primary route is to take Highway 50 east through Placerville and over Echo Summit to South Lake Tahoe (about two hours or 100 miles from Sacramento and 3.5 hours or 200 miles from San Francisco).

From Reno/Tahoe International Airport, take U.S. 395 south through Carson City, then take Highway 50 west to South Lake Tahoe (about one hour or 60 miles).

By Bus
Visitors can reach South Lake Tahoe by two major bus lines: **Greyhound Bus Lines** (530/587-3822 or 800/231-2222, www.greyhound.com) or **Amtrak Bus** (800/872-7245, www.amtrak.com). The bus depot is located at the South Y Transit Center (1000 Hwy. 50, South Lake Tahoe).

Other bus lines that travel to South Lake Tahoe include Amador Stage Lines (800/446-2928, www.amadorstagelines.com), Coach USA (775/329-0444, www.coachusa.com), and Sierra Nevada Gray Line (800/822-6009). The Tahoe Casino Express (775/785-2424 or 800/446-6128) runs daily service from Reno Tahoe International Airport to South Lake.

By Train
The nearest Amtrak train depots are in Truckee or Reno; both cities are a little more than an hour's drive from South Lake Tahoe. Amtrak buses and/or other bus services travel between Truckee and Reno and South Lake. The **Amtrak Thruway Station** is located at the South Y Transit Center (1000 Hwy. 50, South Lake Tahoe). For schedules and information, contact Amtrak (800/872-7245, www.amtrak.com).

GETTING AROUND
Public transportation services are easy to come by in South Lake Tahoe. Many casinos and ski resorts provide free shuttle service; low-cost buses, trolleys, and taxis are widely available.

DRIVING SAFELY IN WINTER

Lake Tahoe in the winter is a genuine snowy wonderland, but traveling in the white stuff presents its own unique challenges. It's important to be prepared before you go.

Before you head to the mountains, check your car to make sure your brakes, windshield wipers, exhaust system, and heater are in good working condition, and that your tires are inflated correctly and their treads are not worn. Make sure your radiator is filled with antifreeze. If you don't have chains that are sized properly for your car's tires, buy a set. Check the links and fasteners to make sure they work. If you haven't used chains before, practice putting them on under sunny skies and dry conditions. Chains should go on your car's drive wheels, so you need to know whether your car has front- or rear-wheel-drive.

Just in case roads are closed or an accident occurs and you are stranded, you should keep some emergency supplies in your car. At the minimum, carry one or two flashlights and extra batteries, warm blankets and clothing, water and snacks, an ice scraper, shovel, and sand or kitty litter (to pour on the snow around

your tires for extra traction if you get stuck). A clean towel is also useful for cleaning your hands after installing tire chains.

When you are ready to leave on your trip to Tahoe, allow yourself extra time in case the roads are icy. Make sure your gas tank is full, and keep it full (or close to it) for the duration of your trip. (If roads are closed, you may have to take a longer route than you planned.) As you drive, remember that shady areas of the road, bridge decks, and underpasses may be icy when the rest of the road is not, especially late at night and early in the morning. Allow plenty of stopping distance between you and the vehicles ahead. If you are driving an SUV, keep in mind that four-wheel-drive vehicles provide more power for traction but not for stopping. Go slow and avoid sudden stops and direction changes.

The best winter driving advice is always to check on road conditions before you go. California highway information is available at www.caltrans.com or 800/427-7623. Nevada highway information is available at www.nv-roads.com or 888/687-6237.

And with all of the traffic in the downtown area, public transportation is a much better way to go than driving your own car.

Shuttles and Buses

Public transportation is available by bus year-round from **BlueGo** (530/541-7149, www.bluego.org). Fixed bus routes run between Stateline and the Y 6 A.M.–midnight daily. Additional fixed-route buses travel in winter only to the ski resorts. BlueGo also offers casino shuttle service for $1 per person one-way (8:40 A.M.–1:30 A.M. daily). The casino shuttle travels from the bottom of Kingsbury Grade west to Al Tahoe Boulevard. You can also "order" door-to-door service on BlueGo through their on-demand shuttle service. Self-service touch-screen kiosks and phones are located at various locations throughout the South Shore from Meyers to Zephyr Cove, including

Zephyr Cove Resort, Horizon Casino, South Lake Tahoe Chamber of Commerce, Super 8 Motel, McDonalds at Ski Run and at the Y, Embassy Suites, Camp Richardson Resort, and many other spots. Order service by kiosk or phone, or on the Internet at www.bluego.org. "On-demand" service costs $3 per person one-way. Advance reservations are advised. If you order service and wish to get a ride as soon as possible, the reservation system will inform you of your estimated wait time.

The **Nifty Fifty Trolley,** operated by BlueGo, offers narrated tours combined with shuttle service in summer only 10 A.M.–9 P.M. throughout the length of South Lake Tahoe. The trolleys are open-sided buses—replicas of 19th-century streetcars with polished oak seats and brass poles—that allow riders to enjoy the fresh mountain air while they travel. The trolley drivers provide tips of things to see and do, and give out information on Tahoe's history, flora, and fauna. Riders can get on and off as often as they like with a $3 all-day pass. The pass is also good on BlueGo's fixed bus routes.

The South Shore casinos offer their own free shuttles to and from most lodgings along the Highway 50 corridor. Phone the individual casinos for schedules and information: Harrah's (775/588 6611), MontBleu (775/588-3515), Harveys (775/588-2411), Horizon (775/588-6211), and Lakeside Inn (775/588-7777). Cruise guests on the *Tahoe Queen* or MS *Dixie II* can also take advantage of free shuttle service from the South Shore area to the boats' respective marinas at Zephyr Cove and Ski Run. Most major ski resorts also offer free winter ski shuttles from various locations along Highway 50 and the South Shore to the slopes. Phone the individual resorts for more information.

Surprisingly, there's only one water shuttle that runs along the south end of the lake, the **South Shore Shuttle,** which travels from Lakeside Marina (530/541-9800) near the casinos to Camp Richardson Marina (530/542-6570) to Timber Cove Marina (530/544-2942). The shuttle runs June–September; fares are $6 one-way or $9 round-trip. The return-trip ticket can also be used on the Nifty Fifty Trolley. However, there is no public parking at any of these marinas, so you'll have to walk there or take the BlueGo bus. Or, if you are staying in the casino area, you can get a free shuttle to Lakeside Marina (530/541-9800 for reservations and information).

If you'd like to get from the South Shore to the North Shore in the summer months, the **Tahoe Trolley** (800/736-6365, www.laketahoetransit .com) travels from Emerald Bay northward to Squaw Valley and Crystal Bay. The service usually runs late June–Labor Day only.

By Car

To get current updates on road conditions on the California side of South Shore, phone 800/427-7623. To get current updates on Nevada road conditions, phone 877/687-6237.

For **car rentals** in South Lake Tahoe, try Emerald Bay Car Rentals (948 3rd St., 530/544-8837), or National Car Rental (1101 Hwy. 89, 530/541-7994 or 800/227-7368). Avis Rent-a-Car (775/588-4450 or 775/588-3361) is located inside Harrah's Casino. Enterprise Rent-a-Car (775/586-1077 or 800/325-8007) is located inside Horizon Casino. Hertz Rent-a-Car (775/586-0041 or 800/654-3131) is located inside Harveys Casino. All the major car-rental agencies are also available at Reno/Tahoe International Airport.

And if Harley motorcycles are your thing, you can rent one at Thunder Road (775/588-1181 or 866/323-7433), inside MontBleu Resort.

By Taxi

Yellow Cab Company (530/544-5555 or 775/588-1234) offers taxi service in South Lake Tahoe and Stateline. Two other local taxi services are Clue Taxi (530/577-CLUE or 530/577-2583) or Domino Taxi (530/544-6666).

NORTH AND WEST SHORES

While the South Shore is known as the high-energy, nightlife-and-action side of the lake, the North and West Shores have always been more sedate. A wealth of outdoor activities are available here, including skiing at 10 alpine resorts, hiking in Sugar Pine Point or D. L. Bliss state parks, biking along a wealth of paved and dirt trails, or golfing at one of eight courses. Two good-sized cities are found on the North Shore—Tahoe City and Truckee—but both are only a few blocks long. Beyond the towns are miles of river, forest, and lake shoreline, and the people who live here like it that way. Although there are ample tourism-related businesses—restaurants, lodgings, and the like—the area is characterized by public parkland, cozy knotty-pine cabins, and lakefront estates, including some of Tahoe's grandest mansions,

both publicly and privately owned. The West Shore in particular has an "old-money" ambience. This is classic Tahoe, with giant conifers and massive timber-and-stone lodges, including Fleur du Lac, the estate of Henry Kaiser and the movie location for *The Godfather II.*

Still, the North Shore does experience its share of crowds. The Y in Tahoe City is one of the busiest spots around the lake, where the highways, bike paths, and the Truckee River convene. Visitors rent rafts for a leisurely float down the river, a cluster of restaurants feed hungry tourists, sightseers lean over the railing of Fanny Bridge to watch the fish in the river below, history buffs tour the Gatekeeper's Museum, and bike riders pedal off on a network of trails. Some of the lake's best people-watching takes place near the Y, where Highways 28 and

HIGHLIGHTS

◖ *Tahoe Gal* **cruise:** The locals' favorite tour boat, this small paddle wheeler plies Tahoe's waters for a romantic sunset dinner cruise, a happy-hour cruise, and a scenic shoreline breakfast cruise (page 95).

◖ **Ehrman Mansion:** There is something for everyone at the Ehrman Mansion property at Sugar Pine Point State Park – free tours of the elegant, 11,000-square-foot, stone-and-timber lodge, a nature center and a few short interpretive trails, and a marvelous stretch of West Shore beach (page 96).

◖ **Martis Peak Lookout:** For a bird's-eye view of Lake Tahoe and points north, you can't do much better than the scene from Martis Peak Lookout, where a Forest Service fire spotter will welcome you to his/her perch (page 101).

◖ **Rubicon and Lighthouse Loop:** For a taste of Tahoe's spectacular shoreline scenery, take this easy two-mile loop hike at D. L. Bliss State Park. After only a short walk on the Rubicon Trail, you'll find yourself at dramatic Rubicon Point where you can peer several hundred feet down into the lake's depths before looping back past a restored 1916 lighthouse (page 115).

◖ **Truckee River Recreation Trail:** The most scenic of the multiple paved bike paths around Lake Tahoe, the Truckee River Recreation Trail runs 5.5 miles from Tahoe City to Squaw Valley USA, following within a few feet of the river's edge for its entire distance (page 116).

◖ **Rafting on the Truckee River:** Take a mellow float down the Truckee River in a raft or inner tube from Tahoe City to River Ranch Lodge, where you can sit out on the deck and enjoy lunch (page 121).

◖ **Sleigh Rides:** The best way to enjoy the North and West Shores' winter wonderland, without putting out any effort of your own, is to dash through the snow in an open sleigh drawn by handsome horses or eager huskies (page 135).

LOOK FOR ◖ TO FIND RECOMMENDED SIGHTS, ACTIVITIES, DINING, AND LODGING.

NORTH AND WEST SHORES

89 meet, but head south or east and the throngs disappear. On the West Shore, communities like Tahoe Pines, Tahoma, and Meeks Bay are separated by scenic beaches offering opportunities for boating and swimming. To the east of Tahoe City, the charming hamlets of Kings Beach and Tahoe Vista boast a collection of great restaurants and places to stay.

Frequently overlooked in favor of the cities on Lake Tahoe's shoreline, the quaint town of Truckee is worth a stop for railroad and history enthusiasts, browsers, and casual strollers. The town burgeoned during the construction of the transcontinental railroad through Donner Pass in 1868. In 1900, the Lake Tahoe Railway was completed between

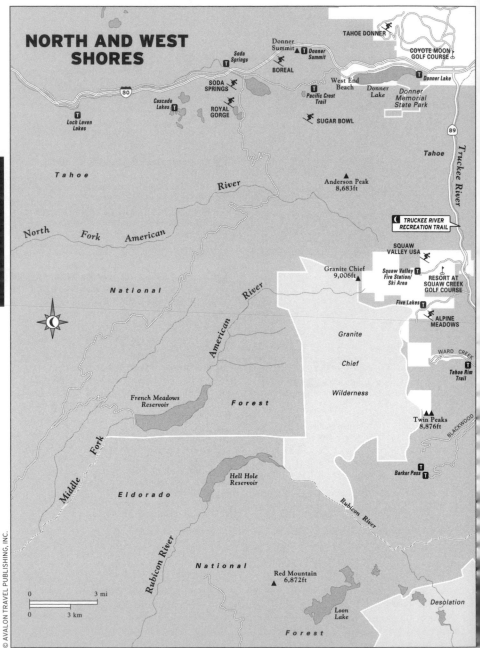

NORTH AND WEST SHORES

TAHOE DONNER

COYOTE MOON
GOLF COURSE

Donner
Summit   Donner
Summit

Soda
Springs

BOREAL

SODA
SPRINGS

Cascade
Lakes

West End
Beach   Donner Lake
Pacific Crest
Trail

Donner Lake

Donner
Memorial
State Park

ROYAL
GORGE

Loch Leven
Lakes

SUGAR BOWL

Tahoe

Tahoe

Truckee River

River

Anderson Peak
8,683ft

**TRUCKEE RIVER
RECREATION TRAIL**

North Fork American

SQUAW
VALLEY USA

Granite Chief
9,006ft

Squaw Valley
Fire Station/
Ski Area

RESORT AT
SQUAW CREEK
GOLF COURSE

National

River

Five Lakes

ALPINE
MEADOWS

American

Granite

WARD CREEK

Tahoe Rim
Trail

Chief

French Meadows
Reservoir

Wilderness

Forest

Twin Peaks
8,876ft

BLACKWOOD

Hell Hole
Reservoir

Middle Fork

Barker Pass

Rubicon River

Eldorado

National

American River

Red Mountain
6,872ft

Rubicon River

Desolation

Loon
Lake

Forest

0   3 mi
0   3 km

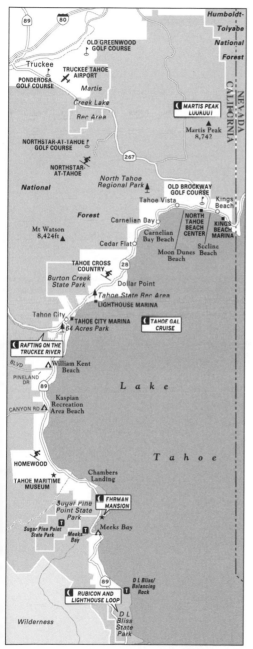

Truckee and Tahoe City, allowing tourists a much easier route to the lakeshore. The original train depot, now more than a century old, still serves railway passengers. But it's not just the lovingly restored buildings and gentrified hipness of Truckee that attract visitors. The region around Truckee and Donner Pass offers some of the best outdoor recreation of the entire Tahoe region, including world-class alpine ski resorts such as Squaw Valley USA and Northstar-at-Tahoe, North America's largest cross-country ski resort at Royal Gorge, and almost limitless rock-climbing and hiking opportunities.

PLANNING YOUR TIME

Many visitors spend a week or more in and around the North and West Shores, both in the winter and summer seasons. This is especially true if you are interested in outdoor recreation—skiing or other winter sports, hiking, rock climbing, mountain biking, golfing, and water sports. Just visiting some of the North or West Shore's sightseeing highlights, and dining at a few of its fine restaurants, will require a minimum of two days. In the summer months, be sure to visit the **Ehrman Mansion** at Sugar Pine Point State Park and take a walk on one of the park's short nature trails, or have a picnic on the mansion's beach. Stroll around the Tahoe City Y and stop in at the **Gatekeeper's Cabin Museum** to see its marvelous collection of Native American baskets. Allow some time for a few hours of fun recreation, like a lazy float down the Truckee River in a raft or inner tube, or an easy bike ride along the paved **Truckee River Trail** followed by lunch at River Ranch Lodge. And don't miss the chance for a few meals at some of the North and West Shores' fine restaurants, especially those with big lake views.

TOUR BOATS AND CRUISES
◖ *Tahoe Gal*

For a romantic sunset dinner cruise, happy-hour cruise, or a scenic shoreline breakfast cruise, you can't go wrong with **North Tahoe Cruises** (850 N. Lake Blvd., Tahoe City,

800/218-2464, www.tahoegal.com, $26–30 adults, $14–18 children), which operates the paddle wheeler *Tahoe Gal*. Smaller than the paddle wheeler cruise boats on the South Shore, the *Tahoe Gal* provides a more intimate cruising experience with a maximum of 150 people on board. Tours depart from Lighthouse Marina, behind the Safeway supermarket. For a special experience, book the full-moon cruise, which takes place only once a month.

Tahoe Sailing Charters

If you prefer wind power to paddle-wheel power, Tahoe Sailing Charters (700 N. Lake Blvd., Tahoe City, 530/583-6200, www.tahoe-sail.com, $40–75 adults, $30–60 children) offers daily two-hour afternoon and sunset cruises, as well as Sunday brunch cruises to Emerald Bay. Tours depart from the Tahoe City Marina; passengers can elect to help with the hands-on sailing or just sit back and relax on the 35-foot sailboat *Avalanche*.

© ANN MARIE BROWN

A sunset cruise on the North Shore's *Tahoe Gal* provides abundant photo opportunities.

Sights

◖ EHRMAN MANSION

Addicts of home-and-garden television shows should pay a visit to the Ehrman Mansion (7360 Hwy. 89/W. Lake Blvd., Tahoma, 530/525-7982, www.parks.ca.gov) at Sugar Pine Point State Park, 10 miles south of Tahoe City to see how the Tahoe rich lived at the start of the 20th century. This three-story, timber-and-stone lodge was built in 1903 as the summer home for Isaias W. Hellman, a San Francisco financier. Over the course of his lifetime, Hellman acquired 2,000 acres of land around Lake Tahoe, much of which is now Sugar Pine Point State Park. His grand, 11,000-square-foot house, which he called "Pine Lodge," was equipped with three porches covered in Oriental rugs, a circular staircase, leaded-glass windows, and fine furnishings in each of its eight bedrooms. The grounds were carefully landscaped with trees, lawns, flower beds, and a vegetable garden. A pier and two boathouses were built for the family's speedboats. Much of the construction materials for the estate had to be transported across the lake by steamship, as no road existed in the early 1900s between this site and Tahoe City.

The mansion was later inherited by Hellman's daughter, Florence Hellman Ehrman, who spent summers here with her husband, accompanied by an army of more than 30 servants, all of whom were housed in various buildings on the property. Tours of the mansion are offered 11 A.M.–4 P.M. daily in summer (530/525-7982 or 530/525-3345, www.sierraspf.org). A nature center with wildlife displays is housed in the mansion's old water tower. The estate enjoys a gorgeous setting on the shore of Lake Tahoe—an inviting spot for a picnic or a quick, cold swim. A $6 day-use fee is charged per vehicle.

© ANN MARIE BROWN

NORTH AND WEST SHORES

The elegant three-story Ehrman Mansion, also called Pine Lodge, was built as a summer home in the early 1900s.

GATEKEEPER'S CABIN MUSEUM

Located right next to the Truckee River outlet in William B. Layton Park at the Tahoe City Y is the Gatekeeper's Cabin Museum (130 Hwy. 89/W. Lake Blvd., Tahoe City, 530/583-8717 or 530/583-1762, www.northtahoemuseums. org, 11 A.M.–5 P.M. May–mid-Oct., $3 adults, $1 children 12 and under), which depicts Tahoe's reign as the queen of the California resort destinations in the late 19th century. In those days, before roads were built along the lakeshore, travelers crisscrossed the lake by passenger steamships. Scale models of four of these ships are on display, along with other bits and pieces of Tahoe memorabilia, including period clothing and winter sports equipment. Serious historians will be interested in the Ellen Attardi research library, which includes books, oral histories, photographs, and newspapers from Tahoe's pioneer era to more modern times. The museum building itself is an authentic log cabin. The original cabin on this site, built in 1909, was the home of

the river gatekeeper, whose job was to measure and regulate Tahoe's water level. Five different men held this duty from 1910 to 1968. When the gatekeeper's cabin was destroyed by fire, the present-day museum was hand-carved from lodgepole-pine logs on the same foundation.

In an adjoining building is the **Marion Steinbach Indian Basket Museum,** exhibiting more than 800 Native American baskets made by more than 85 different tribes, including the local Washoes and Pauites. The woven baskets are as large as three feet in diameter and as small as one-quarter inch. This world-class collection, which belonged to Marion Steinbach and was donated after her death in 1991, also includes Native American pottery, dolls, rattles, hats, and artifacts. The museum may be closed Mondays and Tuesdays.

TRUCKEE RIVER OUTLET/ FANNY BRIDGE

Situated at Outlet Point, the only spot where the waters of Lake Tahoe find an escape from

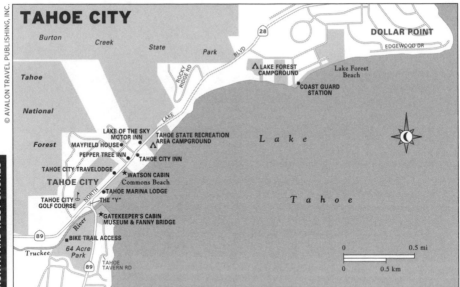

the lake's basin, tiny Truckee River Outlet State Park is comprised of the land surrounding the Lower Truckee River at Tahoe City. Here the river is crossed by a dam and Fanny Bridge, named for the tourists who lean over the bridge's railing to see the trout in the river below. The Donner Lumber Company built the first dam across the Truckee River outlet in Tahoe City in 1872. Water released through the dam controlled the flow of logs to lumber mills downstream. This led to long-running conflicts and a court battle, known as the Tahoe Water War, over who had the right to regulate the flow of water—the lakeshore landowners or the downstream Truckee River water users. Today the water is controlled by the Federal Watermaster in Reno, Nevada, but the dam's 17 gates are still raised and lowered on this site using the same hand-turned winch system employed since 1913. The Gatekeeper's Cabin Museum is a few feet away, and the paved Tahoe City Lakeside Trail passes by and continues to the Commons Beach area.

WATSON CABIN

Perched on a bluff alongside busy North Lake Boulevard and above Commons Beach, the Watson Cabin (560 N. Lake Blvd./Hwy. 28, Tahoe City, 530/583-8717 or 530/583-1762, www.northtahoemuseums.org, noon–4 P.M. weekends Memorial Day–June 30, noon–4 P.M. Wed.–Mon. July–Labor Day, free) is the oldest log structure remaining in the North Tahoe area. The cabin was built in 1908 by Robert Montgomery Watson, Tahoe City's first policeman, and his youngest son, using local materials such as hand-hewn logs, native stone, and deer antlers. Part of the structure's claim to fame is that it had the area's first indoor bathroom. The cabin was given to the son, Robert, as a wedding present in 1909, and he and his wife Stella used it as a summer retreat and occasionally as a year-round home, although they found the Tahoe winters difficult. By the 1940s, the Watsons were dismayed by the traffic and noise of downtown Tahoe City, so they leased out the cabin. From the late 1940s until 1990, the building was used as a gift shop.

Today at the Watson Cabin docents from the North Lake Tahoe Historical Society dress in period costumes and tell stories of early-20th-century Tahoe life.

SQUAW VALLEY USA

Although the 1960 Winter Olympics are a long-vanished memory for most, the host of those games, Squaw Valley USA (1960 Squaw Valley Rd., Olympic Village, 530/583-6955 or 800/545-4350, www.squaw.com), has parlayed its Olympic glories into its raison d'être for being a year-round destination. Located five miles northwest of Tahoe City, and with the symbolic Olympic flame still greeting visitors at is entrance, Squaw boasts an extraordinary 4,000 acres of skiing terrain serviced by nearly three dozen chairlifts. The full-service resort offers a wide range of summer activities, too. A cable car sails 2,000 feet above the ground to the **High Camp Bath and Tennis Club,** elevation 8,200 feet, where an artificial lagoon lures swimmers and bathers, and a cafe serves meals on an outdoor deck above the pool. Plenty of parents let their kids play in the water while they order a Blue Lagoon margarita, put on their shades, and enjoy the show. An open-air **ice-skating rink** is open year-round for those who wish to do a few pirouettes (to keep the ice from melting, the rink is partially covered in summer). Hiking trails lead from the cable car station to surrounding high peaks, and outdoor concerts are held on weekends. Summer cable car hours of operation are 9:40 A.M.–9 P.M. daily mid-June –Labor Day; open weekends only the rest of the year. Fares are $9–19, but drop after 5 P.M. Skate and/or swim passes are extra. For a wonderful sunset dinner, ride the cable car to Alexander's Cafe at High Camp. A three-course dinner and cable car ride package is $29 per person.

While at High Camp, the curious can visit the **1960 VIII Olympic Winter Games Museum.** It's mostly just a room full of photographs and posters that commemorate what was at that time the largest Olympics ever held, with 34 nations sending more than 1,000 ath-letes, all of whom were housed on-site in the first-ever Olympic Village. The 1960 Olympics were also the first winter games to be nation-ally televised, and the first to use electronic computers to tally scores.

Down below at Squaw Valley and Squaw Creek, visitors can play 18 holes of golf, ride horseback, or browse the upscale shops at The Village at Squaw Valley. Then again, some visitors just take a look at this beautiful alpine valley and wonder what it would have been like if they hadn't altered the landscape for the sake of recreational sports.

TAHOE MARITIME MUSEUM

Lake Tahoe's colorful maritime history is memorialized at this West Shore museum located just south of Homewood ski area (5205 W. Lake Blvd./Hwy. 89, Homewood, 530/525-9253, www.tahoemaritimemuseum.org). The collection includes eight antique watercraft, including the *Shanghai,* an 1890s-era launch that was discovered on the bottom of Lake Tahoe in 2000, and a Gar Wood runabout. Several outboard engines on display date back to the early 20th century. Exhibits highlight the famous steam-powered vessel *Tahoe,* which plied the lake's waters in the late 19th century. A special children's room encourages kids to learn about boating with activities like line tying, boat-building, watercolor painting, and other arts and crafts. Open 11 A.M.–5 P.M. Thur.–Mon., Memorial Day–June 30 and daily July–August; days and hours vary the rest of the year.

EMIGRANT TRAIL MUSEUM

When Californians get hungry on a hiking trip, inevitably someone cracks a sorry joke about the Donner Party, an ill-fated group of emigrants who took what they thought was a shortcut while trying to make their way westward from Illinois in 1846. Caught in a series of early snowstorms at what is now known as Donner Lake, members of the wagon train were forced to eat the bodies of their deceased companions in order to survive the premature winter. The tragedy is remembered at the

TRUCKEE AND
DONNER LAKE

© AVALON TRAVEL PUBLISHING, INC.

To Reno

TRUCKEE TAHOE
AIRPORT

To North
Lake Tahoe

SCHAFFER MILL RD

BEST WESTERN
TRUCKEE TAHOE INN

Prosser Creek
Reservoir

80

RD

DAM

PROSSER

DR

267

GLENSHIRE

Ponderosa
Golf Course

BROCKWAY RD

DONNER PASS RD

Truckee River
Regional Park

MARTIS VALLEY DR

89

COACHLAND
RV PARK

RD

TRUCKEE HOTEL

RIVER
STREET INN

US FOREST SERVICE
RANGER STATION

HIBOOM ST

TRUCKEE

TRUCKEE VISITOR
CENTER

RICHARDSON HOUSE

80

National

Forest

89

Truckee River

National

To Tahoe
City

Alder Creek

CREEK

RD

Trout Creek

Coyote Moon
Golf Course

SITZMARK WY

LAISENNE WY

SCHUSSING WY

Forest

Tahoe

DONNER PASS RD

NORTHWOODS BLVD

Tahoe

TAHOE DONNER

ALDER

HANSEL

DR

Tahoe Donner
Golf Course

BLVD

SKISLOPE WY

NORTHWOODS RD

Creek

TRUCKEE HOLIDAY
INN EXPRESS

Donner

Creek

0.5 mi

0.5 km

0

0

Memorial

State

Park

COLD STREAM RD

Cold

TAHOE DONNER
DOWNHILL SKI AREA

80

DONNER

PASS

RD

To Sacramento

Donner

Lake

Donner

Emigrant Trail Museum at Donner Memorial State Park (12593 Donner Pass Rd. off I-80, Truckee, 530/582-7892, www.parks.ca.gov, park open year-round, museum 10 A.M.–4 P.M. daily, $3 adults, $1 children). The museum highlights the mid-1800s emigrant movement with a collection of displays, including a fully loaded covered wagon and a slide show detailing the tragic Donner story. Exhibits also interpret the history of Donner Pass, including the building of the transcontinental railroad, the ice harvesting and lumber business, and the lifestyles of the local Native Americans. A few hundred feet away is the **Pioneer Monument,** an impressive bronze statue that honors the thousands of emigrants who attempted the arduous trek across the western mountains. Its 22-foot-high pedestal marks the depth of snow that trapped the Donner Party in this valley. The cabin site of the Murphy family, where 16 Donner Party members from three different families spent the winter of 1846–1847, is a short walk away. Built in haste as the snow fell, a large boulder was used as one wall of the earthen-floor cabin.

A few miles away, the Donner Party is also remembered at the **Donner Historical Site,** four miles north of Truckee and I-80 on Highway 89. A short interpretive trail leads you to the tree where other members of the Donner Party pitched their tents and struggled through winter.

DOWNTOWN TRUCKEE

The historic town of Truckee, 12 miles northwest of Tahoe City, was settled in 1863 and named for a Paiute Indian Chief. It came into existence as a way station serving wagon traffic traveling over Donner Summit's emigrant routes, and thrived due to the construction of the transcontinental railroad. The first train passed through Truckee in 1868; Amtrak still travels through the town. An enjoyable historic walking tour of the downtown's wooden sidewalks will take most visitors an hour or two, although serious shoppers could easily spend a day browsing Commercial Row's many stores. Start by picking up the walking tour brochure

© ANN MARIE BROWN

The streets of downtown Truckee are a mix of historic buildings and gentrified shops and restaurants.

at the Truckee visitors center (10065 Donner Pass Rd., Truckee, 530/587-2757, www.historictruckee.com, 8 A.M.–6 P.M. daily), located at the century-old train depot. Among the town's many historic buildings, don't miss the two-story **Old Truckee Jail Museum** (10142 Jibboom St., 530/582-0893), one block north of Commercial Row. It showcases the longest operating jail in California, which incarcerated criminals from 1875 to 1964. The museum is usually open 11 A.M.–4 P.M. weekends in summer.

◖ MARTIS PEAK LOOKOUT

For a bird's-eye view of Lake Tahoe and points north, it's hard to do better than Martis Peak Fire Lookout. In summer and fall, drive your car or ride your bike to the lookout tower at elevation 8,650 feet. In winter and spring, you can get there on snowshoes or cross-country skis. No matter what time of year, the expansive view from the top will wow you. The tower is staffed by a Forest Service worker during daylight hours in summer and fall. When the lookout is not busy spotting fires, he or she will be happy to interpret for you the expansive high view of Lake Tahoe and Carnelian Bay to the south, Boca and Stampede Reservoirs to the north, Donner Lake, Mount Tallac, the Truckee airport, Twin Peaks, and dozens of other landmarks. On clear days you can even see Mount Lassen, 100 miles to the north.

From Highway 28 at Kings Beach, drive northwest on Highway 267 for 3.7 miles. Just beyond Brockway Summit, turn right on Martis Peak Lookout Road and continue four miles to the lookout.

Recreation

HIKING

The following hikes are listed from west to east along the I-80 corridor, and from north to south along the Highway 89/Emerald Bay Road corridor.

For more information on the trails described below, contact Tahoe National Forest, Truckee Ranger District (10342 Hwy. 89, Truckee, 530/587-3558, www.fs.fed.us/r5/tahoe). Or contact Lake Tahoe Basin Management Unit (35 College Dr., South Lake Tahoe, 530/543-2600, www.fs.fed.us/r5/ltbmu). For trails in Sugar Pine Point State Park or D. L. Bliss State Park, contact California State Parks Sierra District (7360 W. Lake Blvd., Tahoma, 530/525-7277 or 530/525-7232, www.parks.ca.gov).

Loch Leven Lakes

- Distance: 7.8 miles round-trip
- Duration: 4 hours
- Rating: Moderate
- Elevation change: 1,100 feet
- Trailhead: Loch Leven Lakes
- Directions: From I-80 near Soda Springs, take the Big Bend/Rainbow Rd. exit and drive 1 mile west on Hampshire Rocks Rd. to the trailhead parking area, which is 0.2 mile east of the Big Bend Visitor Center and 0.5 mile west of Rainbow Lodge. The trail begins across the road from the parking area.

The Loch Leven Lakes are like a little slice of heaven on earth—three granite-backed bodies of water that can be reached by a moderate hike of only 3.9 miles one-way. If only the trailhead wasn't right off I-80, this hike truly would be heaven. Unfortunately, because of the too-easy trailhead access, this is one of the most heavily trampled destinations in the North Tahoe region. Another problem is that for the first mile or so, you can't escape the constantly annoying sound of I-80 traffic. But once you top the ridge, you leave all sounds of civilization behind and are able to focus on the gorgeous Sierra scenery. Trailhead elevation is 5,700 feet and the path leads through a glaciated landscape of huge granite boulders scattered amid Jeffrey and lodgepole pines. After crossing a creek and a set of railroad tracks, the path climbs a steep 800 feet in only 1.3 miles, then reaches the ridgetop and descends slightly to the lowest of the three Loch Leven Lakes, 2.7 miles from the trailhead. A crowd is usually congregated here, so go left at the junction by the lake and continue another 0.5 mile to the middle Loch Leven Lake, or better still, another 1.2 miles to the upper lake, High Loch Leven, 3.9 miles from the start and the most beautiful of them all. Because much of the last stretch of trail traverses granite slabs, some hikers have difficulty locating the upper lake, but there is usually someone around who can show you the way. If not, keep your eyes peeled for trail cairns; they'll guide you right to the lakeshore. If you have the energy to add a fourth lake to your itinerary, you can follow a side trail leading west (right) from the lowest Loch Leven Lake to Salmon Lake, just under a mile away.

Lower Lola Montez Lake

- Distance: 6.6 miles round-trip
- Duration: 3 hours
- Rating: Moderate
- Elevation change: 500 feet
- Trailhead: Soda Springs
- Directions: From I-80 near Soda Springs, take the Soda Springs/Norden exit and cross over the overpass to the north side of the freeway. Follow the paved road east, past the fire station, for 0.3 mile to the trailhead parking area.

At 7,200 feet in elevation, Lola Montez Lake has all the scenic qualities of a high alpine lake, but without the frigid water. The lake is shallow enough so that in most years it warms up enough for swimming by July, making it a favorite destination for vacationers and locals alike in the Soda Springs area. However, partly because the trail is so easy, partly because it is right off I-80, and partly because it is favored by mountain bikers, this path is a bad choice for a summer weekend afternoon. For hikers who enjoy peace and quiet, save this hike for the off-season (autumn is lovely), or in summer, stick to weekday mornings only. The first couple of miles of the route cuts through a private housing development called Toll Mountain Estates on a mix of wide dirt road and single-track trail. In order to keep hikers and mountain bikers off private property, the path is well signed, so you're in no danger of getting lost. After about an hour of walking along alternating trail and dirt road, you come out to a meadow and a trail fork. Bear right for the lake, which is now only 0.25 mile ahead. Fishing in Lower Lola Montez Lake is decent, but swimming is the main event. Who was Lola Montez, anyway? One of the most colorful characters of the Old West, she operated a saloon in the 1950s in the mining town of Grass Valley.

Mount Judah Loop

- Distance: 5.2 miles round-trip
- Duration: 2.5 hours
- Rating: Moderate
- Elevation change: 1,200 feet
- Trailhead: Pacific Crest Trail/Sugar Bowl Academy
- Directions: From I-80 near Soda Springs, take the Soda Springs/Norden exit and follow Old Hwy. 40 east for 4 miles to just beyond Donner Ski Ranch. Turn right into the parking lot for Sugar Bowl Academy, then turn right on a dirt and gravel road and drive 100 yards to the Pacific Crest Trail on the left, at a gated road. (You can also access the trailhead by driving from Donner Lake west up to the original Donner Pass along Old Hwy. 40; the trailhead is just beyond the pass.)

If you don't mind the appearance of ski-lift operations marring your nature experience, the Mount Judah Loop is a fine hike that offers outstanding views of Lake Mary, Donner Lake, Martis Valley, Castle Peak, and Lake Van

© ANN MARIE BROWN

The multiple spires and slabs of Donner Peak are a worthy destination on the Mount Judah Loop Trail.

NORTH AND WEST SHORES

Norden, among other landmarks. The trail begins by following the Pacific Crest Trail from near Donner Summit off Old Highway 40, and it climbs gradually but steadily all the way to the top of Mount Judah. One mile from the trailhead, bear left on the Mount Judah Trail to start along the loop. A few spur trails lead off to the left, heading to high overlooks above the Donner basin, but just stay on the main path, which soon becomes an old dirt road. At 1.6 miles the climb tops out at a saddle below the multiple granite spires of Donner Peak, elevation 8,019 feet. Look just to the left of the trail to find an Emigrant Trail marker that designates Emigrant Pass, elevation 7,850 feet. Don't miss the chance to climb up and explore Donner Peak's odd collection of summit pinnacles, where you'll enjoy marvelous views, especially of Donner Lake far below. (The highest pinnacles require climbing equipment and experience to reach, but some of the lower ones are an easy walk up.) From the saddle, continue south along the trail for another mile to Mount Judah's 8,243-foot summit, a bald, windswept high point along a view-filled volcanic ridge. Beyond the summit, the loop trail switchbacks downhill and westward for 0.7 mile until meeting up with the Pacific Crest Trail, where you head right. You'll pass underneath the Sugar Bowl chairlift on your return, then walk through an impressive grove of big red firs on your way back to the trailhead.

Palisade Creek Trail to Heath Falls

- Distance: 10 miles round-trip
- Duration: 6 hours
- Rating: Moderate/strenuous
- Elevation change: 1,700 feet
- Trailhead: Cascade Lakes
- Directions: From I-80 near Soda Springs, take the Soda Springs/Norden exit and follow Old Hwy. 40 east for 0.8 mile to Soda Springs Rd. Turn south (right) and drive 0.8 mile to Pahatsi Rd. Turn right. Pahatsi Rd. turns to dirt in 0.2 mile and its name

changes to Kidd Lakes Rd. At 1.5 miles, you'll reach a fork. Continue straight for 2.3 more miles, then bear left at a fork and drive 0.5 mile farther. The trailhead is on the north side of the Cascade Lakes.

A hike to Heath Falls is like going on vacation on your credit card. You can have all the fun you want, but when you return home, you have to pay up. That's because the trip is downhill nearly all the way, dropping 1,700 feet over five miles through lovely alpine scenery. But alas, eventually it's time for the return trip—a long and steady climb over those same five miles.

The trail begins at the dam between the two Cascade Lakes, the first of many lakes you'll pass on this trip. Walk across the dam and spillway, then follow the trail through a lodgepole-pine forest, heading to your right at a sign for the North Fork American River. Prepare for a steady diet of granite, lakes, and vistas. You'll hike past 7,704-foot Devil's Peak and pretty Long Lake, as well as several smaller, unnamed lakes and ponds. At 2.2 miles, the trail leaves this exposed, glaciated landscape behind and moves into a dense forest of cedars and firs, then switchbacks downhill for two miles to the Palisade Creek Bridge. Look for a junction 300 yards beyond the bridge where the Heath Falls Overlook Trail heads east. Follow it for 0.5 mile to the trail's end at a vista of Heath Falls on the North Fork American River. The overlook is a fair distance from the falls, which are sheltered deep in the canyon, but you can still hear and see the white water thundering over rock cliffs and into big pools. The land surrounding the waterfall is private property, so exploring any closer than the overlook is forbidden. After soaking in the scenery for as long as you wish, prepare yourself for the long uphill return trip.

Summit Lake

- Distance: 4.4 miles round-trip
- Duration: 2 hours
- Rating: Easy

FEELING THE ALTITUDE

Many hikers experience a shortness of breath when hiking only a few thousand feet higher than the elevation where they live. If you live on the coast, you may notice slightly labored breathing while hiking at an elevation as low as 4,000 feet. As you go higher, it may get worse, sometimes leading to headaches and nausea. Since the lakeshore of Tahoe is at 6,200 feet, and the mountains surrounding the lake top out above 10,000 feet, the high elevation can be problematic for some people. It takes a full 72 hours to acclimate to major elevation changes, although most people feel better after 24 to 48 hours.

The best preparation for hiking at high elevation is to sleep at that elevation, or as close to it as possible, the night before. If you are planning a strenuous hike at 7,000 feet or above, spend a day or two beforehand taking easier hikes at the same elevation. Get plenty of rest and drink plenty of fluids. Lack of sleep, dehydration, and drinking alcohol can contribute to a susceptibility to "feeling the altitude."

When you get to the trailhead and start hiking, take it slower than you would at lower elevations. Give yourself a half hour of warm-up time so that your legs and lungs start working in sync. (Your legs will want to move at their usual swift pace, but your lungs may be lagging behind.) Keep drinking a lot of water during your hike – more than you think you need.

Serious altitude sickness typically occurs above 10,000 feet. It is generally preventable by simply allowing enough time for acclimation. Staying fully hydrated and fueled with food will also help. If you start to feel ill (nausea, throwing up, severe headache), you are experiencing altitude sickness. Some people can get by with taking aspirin and trudging onward, but if you are seriously ill, the only cure is to descend as soon as possible. You'll feel better as soon as you get to a lower elevation.

- Elevation change: 400 feet
- Trailhead: Donner Summit/Pacific Crest Trail
- Directions: From I-80 west of Donner Summit, take the Boreal Ridge/Castle Peak exit. Drive to the frontage road on the south side of I-80, then continue 0.3 mile east to the road's end at the trailhead for the Pacific Crest Trail.

This easy hike is a perfect leg-stretcher for families who have grown weary of the drive to Tahoe and want to get out of the car before reaching their final destination. The trail begins at the Pacific Crest Trail (PCT) trailhead at Donner Summit and ends two miles later at a pretty alpine lake at 7,395 feet. The numerous junctions along the way are clearly marked. A half mile from the start, you must turn left and follow the PCT Access Trail north (signed for Castle Pass and Peter Grubb Hut) through a tunnel underneath I-80. On the north side of the freeway is another junction; bear right for Summit and Warren Lakes. The trail climbs gently through a fir forest and occasionally breaks out of the trees to wide granite slabs that allow views to the south and east. At 1.7 miles you reach the start of the Warren Lake Trail; take the right fork for Summit Lake and travel the final 0.5 mile to the mostly forested lakeshore. Swimming, fishing, and picnicking are common activities here. The only thing that mars the scenery is the distant sound of car traffic moving along I-80. Those seeking a longer trip and a stiff climb can bear left instead at the 1.7-mile fork and follow the Warren Lake Trail to a high overlook atop the bald granite cliffs above Frog Lake, 1.8 miles farther (follow the 150-yard spur trail on the right to the best views). Or, for the truly hard-core, the trail continues another 3.5 miles beyond the overlook to Warren Lake, which is popular with backpackers but rarely visited by day hikers. The round-trip hike to Warren Lake is a full 15 miles with a butt-kicking 3,800 feet of elevation gain (1,900 feet in each direction).

Castle Peak

- Distance: 5.4–9.4 miles round-trip
- Duration: 3–5 hours
- Rating: Moderate/strenuous
- Elevation change: 2,100 feet
- Trailhead: Donner Summit/Pacific Crest Trail
- Directions: From I-80 west of Donner Summit, take the Boreal Ridge/Castle Peak exit. Drive to the frontage road on the south side of I-80, then continue 0.3 mile east to the road's end at the trailhead for the Pacific Crest Trail.

The turreted summit of 9,103-foot Castle Peak is a worthwhile destination for any crystal-clear day, when the peak's panorama can extend for 100 miles north to Lassen Peak and west to the Diablo Range. The throat of an ancient volcano, Castle Peak is a well-known destination for backcountry skiers and snowshoers in winter, but an equally worthwhile summer trek. The trail is the same as that to Summit Lake (see above) for the first mile to the junction after the tunnel crossing underneath I-80. Here you'll leave the Summit Lake Trail behind and head west (left) for Castle Pass, staying on the Pacific Crest Trail. As the trail nears the Donner Summit Rest Area on I-80 (keep right at all junctions, still heading west), you'll pass a small pond and finally leave the highway behind as you hike northwest along the PCT to Castle Pass. The path crosses a dirt road at slightly more than two miles out, as well as several seasonal streams, causing potential wet feet as late as July. At Castle Pass, 3.5 miles from your start, look for an obvious side trail heading right (northeast) off the PCT, and follow it for 1.2 memorably steep miles to the west summit of Castle Peak. Use caution on the loose volcanic rock; the last half mile or so requires some scrambling, but the wide summit view is more than worth the effort. The eastern turret of the "castle" is the highest summit.

Note that many people cut two miles off the length of this hike (or four miles round-trip) by parking on the north side of I-80 along Castle Valley Road, which turns to dirt and gets progressively rougher after the first 0.25 mile. Park alongside the road and then hike to Castle Pass via the dirt road/trail instead of the Pacific Crest Trail. The dirt road and PCT junction at the pass.

Donner Lakeshore Trail

- Distance: 2 miles round-trip
- Duration: 1 hour
- Rating: Easy
- Elevation change: 50 feet
- Trailhead: Donner Lake
- Directions: From I-80 near Donner Summit, drive 0.8 mile west on I-80 to the Donner Pass Rd. exit (not the Donner Lake exit). Turn left and cross over I-80, then continue along the frontage road for 0.5 mile to the state park entrance on the left ($6 day-use fee per vehicle). Once you pass through the entrance kiosk, take the right fork for the picnic and day-use area at China Cove. Park at the far end of the picnic area lot and walk to the lakeshore to pick up the trail.

The Donner Lakeshore Trail begins at the sandy swimming area at China Cove and parallels the southeast shoreline of three-mile-long Donner Lake. The path travels for a mile along the Jeffrey-pine-dotted shoreline and features more than a dozen interpretive plaques with information about the area's history, geography, and ecology. Among many other facts, you'll learn about the amphibians that reside in and around Donner Lake, how the lake was formed by the movement of glaciers, and why and how the train tracks were built on the steep slopes of Donner Summit. The hike is level and easy and the lakeside scenery is lovely every step of the way; the only downer is that you never quite escape the sound of I-80 across the canyon. Every now and then, you'll even hear the wail of a train churning up the tracks to Truckee or Reno. The trail ends by the lagoon on the east side of the lake, along the banks of Donner Creek. Before or after walking this pleasant trail, be sure to stop in at the Emigrant Trail Museum at the park; it offers some fascinating insights into this history-rich area.

Granite Chief Trail to Tinker Knob

* Distance: 15 miles round-trip
* Duration: 8 hours
* Rating: Strenuous
* Elevation change: 3,200 feet
* Trailhead: Squaw Valley Fire Station
* Directions: From Tahoe City, drive north on Hwy. 89 for 5 miles and then turn west on Squaw Valley Rd. Drive 2.2 miles to the Squaw Valley Fire Station on the right side of the road, just before the Olympic Village Inn. The trail begins on the east side of the fire station, but you must park your car in the large parking lot by the ski-lift buildings, then walk back to the trailhead.

Tinker Knob is not an easy summit to attain, but those who reach it always remember it. From the Squaw Valley Fire Station, it's a challenging 3.8-mile hike on the Granite Chief Trail to a junction with the Pacific Crest Trail, gaining 2,000 feet along the way. (You can "cheat" on this section of trail by riding the cable car at Squaw Valley uphill to the PCT, cutting your mileage nearly in half and knocking off three-fourths of the elevation gain.) Much of the ascent is forested, but occasional openings through the trees allow views of Squaw Valley, Lake Tahoe, and surrounding peaks. At just over two miles out, the trail crosses a massive granite slab divided into a series of wildflower-decorated benches; the path is marked by yellow paint.

When you reach the PCT, turn right (north) toward Tinker Knob. The next 3.5 miles follow an easier grade along the ridgetop, but with a cruel twist of fate the trail actually descends, losing 500 feet of hard-won elevation that will have to be regained later. The last stretch of trail follows a series of switchbacks up to Tinker Knob Saddle, where impressive views await

and a trail on the right heads off Coldstream Valley. Continuing another 0.25 mile northwest on the PCT leads to a high point from which you can leave the trail and climb 0.25 mile south to Tinker Knob's volcanic summit at 8,960 feet. A few rock cairns mark the top, where a head-swiveling vista of Anderson Peak, Painted Rock, Silver Peak, Mount Rose, Granite Chief, the Royal Gorge of the American River Canyon, Donner Lake, and of course, Lake Tahoe—awaits weary hikers.

Note that it is possible to shorten this hike by making a one-way shuttle trip. You'll need a second car waiting for you at the Coldstream Trailhead near Donner Memorial State Park. The Coldstream Trail meets the PCT just below the summit of Tinker Knob, so after gaining the summit via the route described above, you simply follow Coldstream Trail 5.5 miles down to its trailhead. This makes a 13-mile one-way hike with a car shuttle. Some people also arrange a shuttle hike from the PCT Trailhead near Old Donner Pass (Old Highway 40), making a 15-mile one-way trip.

Granite Chief Trail to Granite Chief Summit

* Distance: 11 miles round-trip
* Duration: 6 hours
* Rating: Strenuous
* Elevation change: 2,800 feet
* Trailhead: Squaw Valley Fire Station
* Directions: From Tahoe City, drive north on Hwy. 89 for 5 miles and then turn west on Squaw Valley Rd. Drive 2.2 miles to the Squaw Valley Fire Station on the right side of the road, just before the Olympic Village Inn. The trail begins on the east side of the fire station, but you must park your car in the large parking lot by the ski-lift buildings, then walk back to the trailhead.

As with the trail to Tinker Knob (see above), it is possible to utilize a "hiker's handicap" by riding the Squaw Valley cable car to cut off more than four miles of hiking (each way), plus most of this trip's elevation gain.

But if you decide to hike those miles instead, you'll know that you've truly earned the summit of 9,086-foot Granite Chief, one of the highest points in the Granite Chief Wilderness and the highest point in Placer County. From the Squaw Valley fire station, follow the Granite Chief Trail uphill for 3.8 miles, gaining a stiff 2,000 feet along the way as the trail alternates through dense forest and a series of exposed granite slabs. When you reach the PCT, go left (south) toward Twin Peaks. The distant view of Lake Tahoe is stunning from here, but keep ascending and more views will be your reward. (Try to ignore the ski-lift towers and other manufactured structures that mar the natural scenery.) After a sustained climb of about a mile, you reach the eastern flank of Granite Chief, and the PCT starts to descend. Leave the trail here and head right for 0.4 mile, following any of several use trails that lead to the summit of Granite Chief. On top of "the Chief" a banquet of peaks come into perspective, including Twin Peaks, Tinker Knob, Castle Peak, Needle Peak, and those of the jagged Crystal Range in Desolation Wilderness. Some of Lake Tahoe can also be seen.

If you still have energy to burn after visiting Granite Chief, return to the PCT and hike southward for another 150 yards to a junction with the Emigrant Trail leading 0.3 mile east to the Watson Monument on the saddle of Emigrant Peak. (This trail then continues to High Camp at Squaw Valley, so those who took the cable car instead of hiking up Granite Chief Trail will have already passed this way). A short side trip to the stone Watson Monument provides a slightly different view of the North Tahoe basin, but don't expect much from the monument itself. Built by Bob Watson in 1931 to commemorate the pioneers who traveled this hazardous route through Emigrant Pass in the 1850s, the monument has deteriorated to the point that it is little more than a pile of rocks.

Loop-lovers who wish to return to the base of Squaw Valley via a different route can continue to High Camp, get a meal or a snack

if they so desire, and then follow the Shirley Lake/Shirley Canyon Trail back downhill (see the trail description below).

Shirley Lake and Squaw Creek

- Distance: 2.5–5 miles round-trip
- Duration: 1–3 hours
- Rating: Moderate
- Elevation change: Varies
- Trailhead: Squaw Valley Ski Area
- Directions: From Tahoe City, drive north on Hwy. 89 for 5 miles and then turn west on Squaw Valley Rd. Drive 2.2 miles to where the road curves left into the main ski area parking lot. Turn right on Squaw Peak Rd. and follow it past a condominium complex to its junction with Squaw Peak Way. Park alongside the road near this junction. Or, for a one-way downhill trip, park in the ski-area lot and ride the cable car to High Camp ($14–19 fee). Begin your hike there.

You have a couple of choices for this hike in lovely Shirley Canyon, which follows Squaw Creek past a series of waterfalls, cascades, and swimming holes. If you just want to take a short out-and-back hike and perhaps have a picnic or swim in Squaw Creek, you can start at the Squaw Peak Road/Squaw Peak Way junction and follow the trail as far as you like. Most people just go for a mile or so up this watery, flower-filled canyon, which is laced with a spider web of use trails. Some hikers travel as far as Shirley Lake, 2.5 miles up the trail and with 1,500 feet of elevation gain. Or, if you'd like to enjoy a scenic gondola ride with your hike, you can take the Squaw Valley Cable Car to High Camp (your leashed dog is allowed to join you, at no charge), then head out the back of the station and follow the ski-lift maintenance road to the right and steeply downhill to Shirley Lake, 1.5 miles from High Camp. Although the ride on the aerial tramway is a winner, this is a somewhat forbidding stretch of trail—the dirt road is wide, exposed, and hot. Fortunately it is over with quickly since you are going downhill. Shirley Lake is small but

On warm summer days at Squaw Valley, the boisterous cascades of Shirley Canyon are a popular destination.

pretty, with low granite cliffs on one side that invite jumping off. From the lake, continue 2.5 miles downhill through gorgeous Shirley Canyon, now on a narrow trail, eventually returning to the end of Squaw Peak Way, where you have an easy walk on the road back to your car. Note that although the trail is quite obvious in lower Shirley Canyon, it is a little harder to find in upper Shirley Canyon, especially in the first mile below the lake where the trail traverses granite slabs and travels over and around rock boulders. Dabs of paint and trail cairns mark the way. Watch for them, and remember to keep the creek on your left.

Five Lakes

- Distance: 4.2 miles round-trip
- Duration: 2–3 hours
- Rating: Easy to moderate
- Elevation change: 1,000 feet
- Trailhead: Five Lakes
- Directions: From Tahoe City, drive north

on Hwy. 89 for 3.6 miles and turn west on Alpine Meadows Rd. Drive 2.1 miles to the Five Lakes trailhead on the right side of the road. Park alongside the road.

Some say that this trek into the Granite Chief Wilderness is so easy that it is actually *too* easy, and they may be right. Although the trail has a moderately steep grade, it is mercifully short, which makes it incredibly popular with casual weekend hikers. If possible, visit here in the off-season or on a weekday to experience the least amount of crowds along the trail. The trail takes off from Alpine Meadows Road and the first 0.5 mile has the steepest grade. The next 0.75 mile continues uphill more gradually to the top of a granite ridge, completing a total 1,000-foot ascent. Switchbacks make the climb quite manageable, but welcome shade from occasional Jeffrey pines and white firs is in short supply along the route, so the trail can be hot. Views of the steep canyon below the ridge are impressive. At 1.8 miles, you reach the Granite Chief Wilderness boundary and enter a land of red fir and gray granite. A signed junction 0.25 mile farther points you left toward the lakes. The trail heads directly downhill to the largest of the five bodies of water at 7,500 feet in elevation. From there, you can follow side trails to the four other lakes, all east of the big one. Most people don't go any farther than the first big lake, where the swimming is nonpareil—the shallow water is clear and remarkably warm. A few white pines and hemlocks line the lakeshore, interspersed with stretches of grassy marsh and big, rounded boulders.

Ward Creek to Twin Peaks
- Distance: 12 miles round-trip
- Duration: 6–7 hours
- Rating: Strenuous
- Elevation change: 2,400 feet
- Trailhead: Tahoe Rim Trail/Twin Peaks
- Directions: From Tahoe City, drive 2.5 miles south on Hwy. 89 to Pineland Dr., which is 0.2 mile south of William Kent campground. Turn west on Pineland Dr. and drive 0.4 mile, then bear left on Twin Peaks Dr.

Drive 1.6 miles (the road becomes Ward Creek Blvd., also signed as Twin Peaks Blvd.) to the Tahoe Rim Trail/Twin Peaks trailhead on the left side of the road.

It's hard to believe, but during July and early August, the wildflower show along the trail to Twin Peaks often steals the show from the double peaks' spectacular summit view. Time your trip for the peak of the flower bloom and decide for yourself which feature is the most memorable aspect of this trip. Begin your hike by walking around the Twin Peaks trailhead gate and following the old dirt road alongside coursing Ward Creek. The flower show is just beginning as you travel the pleasant first two miles of road/trail on a nearly level course. Shortly after crossing a small creek where old bridge foundations can be seen, the dirt road narrows to a trail, and at 2.3 miles from the start, you'll reach a crossing of Ward Creek. Hikers out for a casual stroll usually turn around here, but those heading for Twin Peaks must rock-hop their way across the stream, then begin a more noticeable ascent alongside Ward Creek. The flower gardens become increasingly showy over the next mile, as the trail sticks close to the creek's south side. During the peak bloom, more than two dozen species are in full color here.

After passing a boisterous waterfall at 3.3 miles, you leave the creek behind and begin a breathless climb through increasingly short and steep switchbacks. This is where much of the work lies in this trail. At 5.2 miles from the start, the trail gains the top of a ridge at 8,000 feet. Here, at a junction, a trail on the left leads one mile to Stanford Rock, a worthy destination in its own right with a view almost as fine as Twin Peaks. For Twin Peaks, go right instead and climb more gently for one mile to a junction with a narrow use trail on the right. Follow this trail northwest to the eastern summit of Twin Peaks, elevation 8,878 feet. Because of the loose talus rock and steep incline, the last stretch to the east summit requires careful scrambling using two hands and two feet. Those who feel uncomfortable with the risk factor may prefer to ascend the western

summit of Twin Peaks. The view from either peak is no disappointment; both deliver a full panorama of easily identifiable landmarks covering the entire Tahoe basin. Be sure to bring a map with you so you can pick out Granite Chief, Tinker Knob, Mount Rose, Freel Peak, and Mount Tallac, amid a host of lesser-known peaks and precipices.

Barker Pass to Twin Peaks

- Distance: 10 miles round-trip
- Duration: 5–6 hours
- Rating: Moderate
- Elevation change: 1,600 feet
- Trailhead: Barker Pass
- Directions: From Tahoe City, drive 4 miles south on Hwy. 89 to Barker Pass Rd. (Forest Rd. 03), just south of Kaspian Campground and picnic area. Turn right (west) and drive 7 miles to the end of the pavement, then continue on the dirt road for 0.3 mile to the Barker Pass/Pacific Crest Trail/Tahoe Rim Trail Trailhead. Begin hiking on the right (north) side of the road.

Although the Ward Creek route to Twin Peaks (see above) delivers the most scenic punch during the wildflower season, when the bloom is over you might want to choose a somewhat easier route to the 8,878-foot peaks and their world-class summit view. From Barker Pass, you can follow the Pacific Crest Trail/Tahoe Rim Trail north for five miles to Twin Peaks, enjoying a relatively mellow grade and views much of the way. Flower-lovers will still be able to find some color on this trip, especially from the prolific mule's ears that favor the volcanic soils in this area.

The trail from Barker Pass begins with a climb up the slopes of 8,166-foot Barker Peak to a ridgeline with fine views of the surrounding volcanic landscape. It then descends into a dense forest of hemlock, white fir, and massive red firs. Over the next 1.5 miles the trail loses almost 500 feet in elevation, which then must be gained back in a series of well-graded switchbacks that curve upward to a high point,

© ANN MARIE BROWN

A bevy of mule's ears greet hikers along the trail to Barker Peak.

4.2 miles out. Here, you are rewarded with impressive vistas every way you look. Enjoy the view, and look forward to an even better one from the twin summits of Twin Peaks, now less than a mile away. Depart the Pacific Crest Trail at the right turnoff for the Tahoe Rim Trail; turn right and walk a short distance to the obvious use trail on the left heading up to Twin Peaks. The western summit is the closest and easiest to attain; both summits offer a classic Tahoe view, with dozens of easily recognizable peaks in sight.

Ellis Peak

* Distance: 8.2 miles round-trip
* Duration: 3–4 hours
* Rating: Strenuous
* Elevation change: 1,400 feet
* Trailhead: Barker Pass
* Directions: From Tahoe City, drive 4 miles south on Hwy. 89 to Barker Pass Rd. (Forest Rd. 03), just south of Kaspian Campground and picnic area. Turn right (west) and drive 7 miles to the end of the pavement (0.3 mile

before the Barker Pass/Pacific Crest Trail Trailhead). The trailhead and a dirt parking area are on the left (south) side of the road.

This short but memorably steep trip leads to the top of 8,740-foot Ellis Peak, where peak-baggers are rewarded with a fabulous view of Lake Tahoe, Granite Chief and Desolation Wildernesses, and Hell Hole Reservoir. In fact, the hike is rewarding all the way, not just at the top, as the trail's wildflower displays rival its far-off views. The initial 0.7 mile of trail is the steepest part, but there is plentiful shade from big red firs along this stretch. When you reach the ridgetop, the vistas spread wide, with Lake Tahoe to the east and Hell Hole Reservoir to the west. Mule's ears and other wildflowers bloom in profusion on this sunny, windswept ridge. The trail continues climbing gently along the ridgeline for a half mile, then heads abruptly downhill through a lodgepole-pine and fir forest, dropping 400 feet in elevation. At a junction with a wide dirt road, bear left to head for Ellis Peak, and prepare to face a confusing

EXPLORING THE TAHOE RIM TRAIL

The Tahoe Rim Trail (TRT) is one of the greatest achievements in the history of trail building in California. Completed in 2001 after nearly 20 years of effort, the 165-mile trail makes a complete circuit around Lake Tahoe, ranging in elevation from 6,300 feet to 10,338 feet. Marked with light blue triangular TRT markers, the trail is accessible most years mid-June–late October, depending on snow levels.

The trail is accessed by nine major trailheads. Starting at Tahoe City and going clockwise around the lake, they are: Truckee River Access/64 Acres Park in Tahoe City, Brockway Summit, Tahoe Meadows, Spooner Summit, Kingsbury Grade, Big Meadow, Echo Summit, Echo Lakes, and Barker Pass. A half dozen other trailheads also provide access to the trail. On much of the west side of the lake, the TRT and the long-distance Pacific Crest Trail are one and the same.

Although the vast majority of trail users hike or bike on only short stretches of the Tahoe Rim Trail, it is possible to hike the entire thing, and many have done it. Most take 10-20 days to complete the circuit. This requires walking a few short stretches on roads or highways, but the vast majority of the route is on trail. Camping is permitted on all parts of the trail except in Lake Tahoe Nevada State Park, where it is limited to two designated areas, and in the Desolation Wilderness portion of the trail, where overnight permits are required. Since in a few places the trail passes right through a town (as in Tahoe City), it is relatively easy to restock your pack with food and supplies. At several points the trail crosses roads or highways where you could arrange for friends or family to meet you with a food drop. The trail is subject to temporary closures due to weather conditions or trail work, so if you are planning a multiday trek, always check the website www.tahoerimtrail.org for the latest updates.

The TRT is maintained completely by volunteers who do everything from office support to trail work, and the nonprofit Tahoe Rim Trail Association can always use additional volunteers and/or donations. Donors can become a member of the association for as little as $35 per person or $45 per family. For more information, go to www.tahoerimtrail.org or phone 775/298-0012.

series of dirt road and trail junctions. In 0.25 mile, you'll note a left spur trail, but stay on the road until you reach a signed junction, 2.8 miles from your start. A left turn here will take you downhill to Ellis Lake in less than a half mile, a worthwhile side trip. Staying straight at the junction, you'll follow a narrower trail steeply uphill and then shortly rejoin the dirt road, which continues its ascent to Ellis Peak. As you gain Knee Ridge, Ellis Peak's summit is clearly visible; a little more huffing and puffing and you arrive at the top. The summit view extends from Pyramid Peak in the Desolation Wilderness to the eastern shores of Lake Tahoe, with a few close-up landmarks like nearby Twin Peaks adding dimension to the scene. Note that you may share this trail with mountain bikers or possibly even off-highway-vehicle users.

General Creek to Lily Pond

• Distance: 6.6 miles round-trip
• Duration: 4 hours
• Rating: Moderate
• Elevation change: 400 feet
• Trailhead: Sugar Pine Point State Park
• Directions: From Tahoe City, drive 8 miles south on Hwy. 89 to the Sugar Pine Point State Park General Creek Campground entrance on the right. Park in one of the day-use lots near the entrance kiosk ($6 fee), then follow the trail to the far end of the campground and site number 149.

Campers at Sugar Pine Point State Park who want to hike right from their tent flaps can do so on the General Creek Loop Trail (as can any noncampers who are willing to pay

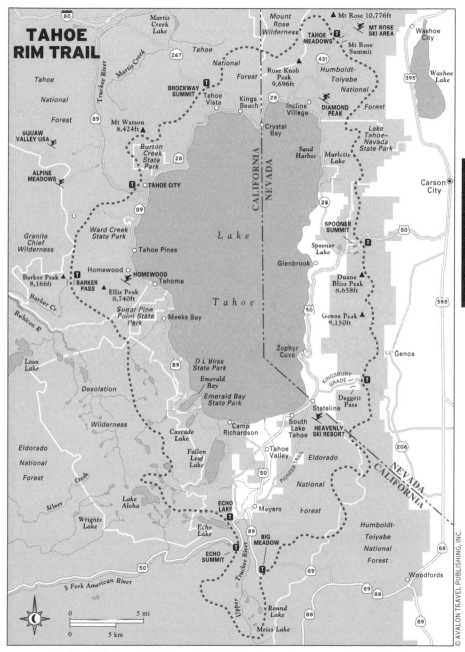

TAHOE RIM TRAIL

80 · Martis Creek Lake · Tahoe · 267 · Mount Rose Wilderness · ▲ Mt Rose 10,776ft · MT ROSE SKI AREA · Washoe City

Tahoe · National · Forest · Truckee River · Martis Creek · TAHOE MEADOWS T · Mt Rose Summit · 431 · Rose Knob Peak 9,696ft · Humboldt-Toiyabe · 395 · Washoe Lake · 395

Tahoe · National · Forest · BROCKWAY SUMMIT T · Tahoe Vista · 89 · Mt Watson 8,424ft ▲ · Kings Beach · 28 · Incline Village · DIAMOND PEAK · National · Forest · Lake Tahoe–Nevada State Park

SQUAW VALLEY USA · Burton Creek State Park · 28 · Crystal Bay · Sand Harbor · Marlette Lake · Carson City

ALPINE MEADOWS · T · TAHOE CITY · CALIFORNIA · NEVADA

Granite Chief Wilderness · 89 · Ward Creek State Park · Tahoe Pines · Lake Tahoe · 28 · SPOONER SUMMIT · 50

Barker Peak ▲ 8,166ft · Homewood · T · BARKER PASS · HOMEWOOD · Tahoma · Spooner Lake · 395 · T · Glenbrook · Duane Bliss Peak 8,658ft

Barker Cr · Ellis Peak 8,740ft ▲ · Tahoe · Genoa Peak ▲ 9,150ft

Rubicon R. · Sugar Pine Point State Park · Meeks Bay · Genoa

Loon Lake · 89 · D L Bliss State Park · Emerald Bay · Zephyr Cove · KINGSBURY GRADE · T · Daggett Pass · 206

Desolation · Emerald Bay State Park · Stateline · NEVADA · CALIFORNIA

Wilderness · Cascade Lake · Camp Richardson · South Lake Tahoe · HEAVENLY SKI RESORT

Eldorado National Forest · Silver · Creek · Fallen Leaf Lake · Tahoe Valley · 50 · Eldorado · National · Forest · PIONEER TRAIL

Wrights Lake · Lake Aloha · ECHO LAKE · T · Meyers · Humboldt-Toiyabe National Forest · 88

Echo Lake · 89 · BIG MEADOW · Woodfords

S Fork American River · 50 · ECHO SUMMIT T · Upper Truckee River · T · 89 · 89 · 88 · 89

0 · 5 mi · 0 · 5 km · Round Lake · 88 · Meiss Lake

the state park day-use fee). The trail begins by site number 149 and forms a loop heading up one side of General Creek and back on the other. A wide and level dirt road, the loop is popular with cross-country skiers in winter. For this hike to Lily Pond, follow the north side of the General Creek Loop for 2.7 miles through a pleasant forest of white fir, incense cedar, and Jeffrey and sugar pines to its junction with a single-track trail on the right to Lily Pond. Leave the loop and follow the narrow trail uphill for 0.6 mile, through a dense and rocky forest, to small, tranquil Lily Pond, which is indeed covered with lilies. This peaceful spot is a good place to look for birds or amphibians. For your return, you can opt to take the south side of the General Creek Loop for variety. Turn left on the bridge over General Creek to head back to the campground. Those looking for a much longer hike can continue on the main trail along General Creek for as long as they wish. The forested shore of lovely Lost Lake is a total of 6.5 miles from the campground and makes a fine destination for a long day hike. If you visit both Lily Pond and Lost Lake, you'll complete a round-trip of 14.2 miles.

Meeks Bay to Genevieve, Crag, and Stony Ridge Lakes

- Distance: 10–12.4 miles round-trip
- Duration: 5–6 hours
- Rating: Moderate
- Elevation change: 1,200–1,600 feet
- Trailhead: Meeks Bay
- Directions: From Tahoe City, drive 11 miles south on Hwy. 89 to the Meeks Bay Trailhead on the west side of the highway, across from the entrance to Meeks Bay Resort. Park in the small dirt parking lot. Day hikers must fill out a self-serve permit at the trailhead.

The Meeks Bay Trailhead offers one of the easiest entrances to Desolation Wilderness, and the Meeks Creek Watershed contains half a dozen scenic lakes—two reasons why this trail is quite popular with day hikers and backpackers alike. The first 1.3 miles of the Meeks Creek Trail (also known as the Tahoe–Yosemite Trail) to the wilderness boundary follow an old dirt road that runs alongside Meeks Creek and is almost completely level. It's a perfect warm-up for hikers who have just driven to the trailhead and gotten out of their cars. At the Desolation boundary sign, the trail forks right off the dirt road and begins a gradual, forested climb. As you gain the ridge, the white fir and Jeffrey pines are replaced by higher-elevation red fir and western white pine. After crossing Meeks Creek on a footbridge at 3.2 miles, the trail climbs some more until the forest opens up to views of the surrounding glaciated landscape. You arrive at the pine-forested shore of shallow Lake Genevieve at 4.6 miles from the start. This small lake is worthy of a brief rest stop, then follow the trail to the left around its eastern shoreline to Crag Lake at 5 miles. As you might expect, a craggy peak looms behind it. Most day hikers make this scenic, swimmable lake their final destination, but those with extra energy can continue the ascent to lily-covered Shadow Lake at 5.3 miles or Stony Ridge Lake at 6.2 miles. The largest of the lakes in this basin, long and narrow Stony Ridge Lake at 7,800 feet is marked by reddish-colored granite and framed by Rubicon Peak and Jakes Peak.

Rubicon Trail

- Distance: 5.5 miles one-way
- Duration: 2.5 hours
- Rating: Moderate
- Elevation change: 500 feet
- Trailhead: D. L. Bliss
- Directions: From Tahoe City, drive 15.5 miles south on Hwy. 89 and turn left at the sign for D. L. Bliss State Park. Drive 0.5 mile to the entrance station ($6 day-use fee per vehicle), then continue for 0.7 mile to a fork. Bear right at the sign for Camps 141–168 and Beach Area and drive 0.7 mile to the Calawee Cove Beach parking lot. The Rubicon Trail begins on the far side of the lot.

The Rubicon Trail is Tahoe's premier lakeshore hike. If you want to get the maximum dose of Lake Tahoe eye candy, with lots of postcard-perfect views of rocky inlets, sandy coves, and boats bobbing in the water, this is your trail. The hike runs 4.5 miles one-way from D. L. Bliss State Park to Vikingsholm Castle, and then an additional 1.6 miles from Vikingsholm to Eagle Point Campground at Emerald Bay State Park. Since there is no day-use parking at Eagle Point Campground, most hikers just follow the stretch of trail between D. L. Bliss and Vikingsholm Castle, then hike up the Vikingsholm trail/road for one mile to its trailhead parking lot on Highway 89, making a total one-way hike of 5.5 miles. You'll need a shuttle car waiting to pick you up, or, in the summer months, check with the Tahoe Trolley (800/736-6365, www.laketahoetransit.com) to see if they are running bus shuttle service between the two trailheads. Of course, ambitious hikers can follow the trail out-and-back instead of one-way, completing a round-trip of up to 12 miles.

No matter how you do it, the path stays close to the lakeshore, although often high above it, and has a very relaxed grade. Highlights along the trail include Rubicon Point, Emerald Point, and Vikingsholm Castle, but really, the entire path is a highlight. Don't miss taking the short side trail that curves around the shoreline at Emerald Point, where the 1920s-era Emerald Bay Resort once stood, and allow some extra time so you can take the short tour of Vikingsholm Castle ($5 fee).

Not surprisingly, the trail is extremely crowded, especially in the peak season, so you might want to plan this trip for after Labor Day. The most jammed-up section occurs near the start of the trail in D. L. Bliss State Park by Rubicon Point, where the drop-offs into the lake are so steep that the trail is lined with chain-link fencing, and the path is so narrow that only one person can pass through at a time. Still, even on the busiest days, everybody is in high spirits as they enjoy this eye-popping, film-burning lakeside scenery.

◖ Rubicon and Lighthouse Loop

- Distance: 2 miles round-trip
- Duration: 1 hour
- Rating: Easy
- Elevation change: 500 feet
- Trailhead: D. L. Bliss
- Directions: From Tahoe City, drive 15.5 miles south on Hwy. 89 and turn left at the sign for D. L. Bliss State Park. Drive 0.5 mile to the entrance station ($6 day-use fee per vehicle), then continue for 0.7 mile to a fork. Bear right at the sign for Camps 141–168 and Beach Area and drive 0.7 mile to the Calawee Cove Beach parking lot. The Rubicon Trail begins on the far side of the lot.

This short and easy loop follows a scenic stretch of the Rubicon Trail, then visits an interesting piece of Lake Tahoe's history, the Rubicon Point Lighthouse. You can start this loop at one of two parking lots at D. L. Bliss State Park—the Calawee Cove Beach parking lot, which is the official start of the Rubicon Trail, or the Lighthouse parking lot, at which the Lighthouse Trail begins. The route described here begins at Calawee Cove, but it really doesn't matter where you start.

Pick up the Rubicon Trail from the southeast end of the Calawee Cove parking lot. Scenic rewards are delivered almost immediately; from Rubicon Point, just 0.25 mile in from the parking lot, you can peer several hundred feet down into the lake's depths. The steep drop-offs from the trail to the lake are so vertical that the park has installed cables and chain-link fencing to keep hikers from inadvertently taking a tumble.

At 0.5 mile, you'll see a right spur trail to the old lighthouse. Ignore it; you'll visit the lighthouse on the return leg of your loop. Stay on Rubicon Trail for another 0.5 mile, enjoying nonstop lake views and the constant companionship of a bevy of chipmunks. At the next junction, one mile from your start, turn right and head for the Lighthouse trailhead parking lot, where you walk a short distance through the lot (to your right) and then pick up the Lighthouse Trail and head northeast to complete your loop. A half mile along this trail you'll see a right spur leading down granite stairsteps to the restored Rubicon Point Lighthouse. The Coast Guard built a gas-powered lighthouse on Rubicon Point in 1916, but keeping the light supplied with fuel proved too difficult. Even when lit, the lighthouse was so high above the shoreline that it just confused everybody. It was shut down in 1919 and replaced by a newer lighthouse, which still stands at Sugar Pine Point. The original Rubicon Point Lighthouse fell into ruins and wasn't much of a tourist attraction until 2001, when the short-but-stout structure was rebuilt. Pay a visit here and admire the site's spectacular lake view, then finish out the last half mile of your loop.

Balancing Rock Nature Trail

• Distance: 0.5 mile round-trip

• Duration: 30 minutes

• Rating: Easy

• Elevation change: 50 feet

• Trailhead: Balancing Rock

• Directions: From Tahoe City, drive 15.5 miles south on Hwy. 89 and turn left at the sign for D. L. Bliss State Park. Drive 0.5 mile to the entrance station ($6 day-use fee per vehicle), then continue for 0.7 mile to a fork. Bear left and drive 0.25 mile to the Balancing Rock parking lot on the left.

The Balancing Rock is a big hunk of granite that has been a curiosity at Lake Tahoe for centuries. It's a 130-ton rock that sits precariously balanced on a small rock pedestal, like a giant golf ball on an itty-bitty golf tee. Visitors to Lake Tahoe in the late 1800s took pleasure in having their photographs taken next to this geologic oddity, and today most people enjoy the same pastime. The trail's interpretive brochure explains that eventually erosion will wear away the pedestal and cause the Balancing Rock to lose its balance. But don't hold your breath, because it probably won't happen in our lifetime. In addition to Balancing Rock, the trail shows off many of the native plants and trees of the Tahoe area.

BIKING

Cyclists looking for an easy, pedal-spinning ride will want to explore the paved bike trails that travel the West and North Shores. A major hub for these trails is located at 64 Acres Park, also known as the Truckee River Access parking lot, 0.25 mile south of the Y off Highway 89. At this large parking lot, you'll find signboards that map out the various trails leading from this hub.

If you don't feel comfortable mountain biking around the North and West Shores on your own, guided trips are provided by the **Tahoe Adventure Company** (530/913-9212 or 866/830-6125, www.tahoeadventurecompany.com). All trips include a van shuttle to and from the trailheads, lunch, front-suspension bikes, and helmets. Rides are about 10–12 miles in length and are offered at various locations, the fee is $85–100 per rider.

Bike rentals are available at several locations on Tahoe's North and West Shores. The Back Country has two locations; one in Truckee (11400 Donner Pass Rd., 530/582-0909) and the other in Tahoe City (690 N. Lake Blvd., 530/581-5861). Also in Tahoe City, rentals are available at Cycle Paths (1785 W. Lake Blvd., 530/581-1171) and Olympic Bike Shop (620 N. Lake Blvd., 530/581-2500). Farther to the east, you can rent bikes at Enviro-Rents in Tahoe Vista (6873 N. Lake Blvd., 530/546-2780) or Tahoe Bike and Ski in Kings Beach (8499 N. Lake Blvd., 530/546-7437). Typical bike rental rates are $8–12 per hour, $18–30 per half-day, and $24–40 per day.

◖ Truckee River Recreation Trail

This is the most scenic trail of them all. It crosses a bridge by the trailhead, then continues alongside the Truckee River for 5.5 miles to the entrance road to Squaw Valley USA. Many bicyclists follow the trail only as far as River Ranch Lodge at Alpine Meadows Road, 4.5 miles out, where they enjoy lunch or dinner on the riverside deck, then ride back. But

Cyclists pedal alongside colorful aspen groves in Blackwood Canyon on the paved road to Barker Pass.

you could pedal farther by following the trail for another mile to Squaw Valley Road, crossing picturesque Midway Bridge along the way, then riding up Squaw Valley Road to meet up with its two-mile-long paved bike path.

Another option from the same trailhead parking lot is to ride south along the **West Shore Bike Path,** which parallels Highway 89 for nine miles to Sugar Pine Point State Park. Despite its terrific lakeshore views, the trail has one major drawback: It crosses Highway 89 dozens of times, and occasionally is merely a bike lane on its shoulder, not a separate trail. Riders must exercise caution during heavy summer traffic. A third option from 64 Acres is to follow the **Tahoe City Lakeside Trail** to Commons Beach and then connect to the 2.5-mile **Dollar Point Trail,** which travels from Tahoe State Recreation Area to Dollar Point. This is a great way to access some of Tahoe City's lovely shoreline without driving your car and fighting for parking.

Barker Pass/ Blackwood Canyon Road

For a more challenging paved ride with an athletic hill climb, park near Kaspian Campground, 4.2 miles south of Tahoe City on Highway 89, and ride up Barker Pass/Blackwood Canyon Road. The route is smooth pavement all the way and gradually gains 1,400 feet in elevation over its seven-mile course to Barker Pass. Car traffic is generally very light. Streams, wildflowers, and aspen groves accompany you on the ascent, and when you reach the top, you have a seven-mile downhill cruise to look forward to.

Martis Peak Fire Lookout Road

The Martis Peak Fire Lookout Road, which takes off from Highway 267 just north of Brockway Summit, provides a similar solid hill workout, but on a much shorter ride—only eight miles round-trip. From Highway 28 at Kings Beach, drive northwest on

A BIKER'S EQUIPMENT LIST

Like the Boy Scout motto says, "you must be prepared." It's easy to set off on a bike ride carrying nothing except your wallet and keys. But even for the shortest spin, it's wise to have a few items with you. Some riders carry all of the following items on every ride, some carry only some of the items some of the time. Each of these could prove to be a real lifesaver.

1. A helmet. They don't call them "brain buckets" for nothing. Don't get on your bike without one. Just as you wear your seat belt when you drive, wear your helmet when you ride. Make sure yours fits properly and strap it on securely.

2. Food and water. Being hungry or thirsty spoils a good time, and it can also turn into a potentially dangerous situation. Even if you aren't the least bit hungry or thirsty when you start, you will feel completely different after 30 minutes of riding. Always carry at least two water bottles on your bike, and make sure they are full of fresh, clean water when you head out. Add ice on hot days, if you wish. For a two- to three-hour ride, 100 ounces of water is not overkill, especially in the dry, high-elevation air at Lake Tahoe.

Many riders prefer to wear a bladder-style backpack hydration system, which has the extra advantage of providing room to carry a few snacks or car keys. Always bring some form of calories with you, even if it's just a couple of energy bars. If you carry extras to share, you'll be the hero or heroine when you give them to a rider in need.

3. Cycling gloves and cycling shorts. These make your trip a lot more comfortable. Cycling gloves have padded palms so the nerves in your hands are protected from extensive pressure when you lean your upper body weight on the handlebars. Cycling shorts have chamois or other padding in the saddle area.

4. A map of the trails where you are riding. Sometimes trails and roads are signed, sometimes they're not. Signs get knocked down or disappear with alarming frequency, due to rain, wind, or souvenir hunters. Always carry a good map.

5. A bike repair kit. How much and which tools to carry is a great subject of debate. At the very least, if you're going to be farther than easy walking distance from your car, carry what you need to fix a flat tire. Great

---

Highway 267 for 3.7 miles. Just beyond Brockway Summit, turn right on Martis Peak Lookout Road (Forest Service Road 18N02) and park in any pullout alongside the road. Route-finding is easy, because you simply stay on the paved fire lookout road and ignore the numerous dirt road junctions. You climb, climb, and climb some more, and after gaining 1,500 feet in a mere four miles, you're at the fire lookout at elevation 8,750 feet. The view from here is one of the best on the North Shore, encompassing several distinct peaks—Lassen Peak, Castle Peak, and Round Top—and the Tahoe basin.

Old Donner Summit Road

Experienced road cyclists head for the Old Donner Summit Road, also known as Old Highway 40, for an out-and-back training ride of nearly 40 miles. The best place to start

is at Donner Memorial State Park, pedaling alongside the North Shore of Donner Lake for a warm-up. Then it's a strenuous climb up to Old Donner Pass (wave to the rock climbers as you spin by) and beyond to Sugar Bowl Ski Resort. The worst of the work is over now, and you enjoy a mostly downhill cruise along Old Highway 40 through Norden and Soda Springs to Rainbow Lodge. Most riders turn around at Cisco, then head back for a mellower climb up the west side of Donner Summit and a fast, twisting descent back to Donner Lake.

Hole in the Ground Trail

Mountain bikers have an untold wealth of trails to choose from on the North and West Shores. Fat tires are allowed, even welcomed, on an abundance of trails, including large sections of the Tahoe Rim Trail. The biggest problem distances are covered quickly on a bike. This is never more apparent than when a tire goes flat 30 minutes into a ride and it takes two hours to walk back. So why walk? Carry a spare tube, a patch kit, tire levers, and a bike pump attached to your bike frame. Make sure you know how to use them.

Many riders also carry a small set of metric wrenches, Allen wrenches, and a couple of screwdrivers, or some type of all-in-one bike tool. These are good for adjusting derailleurs and the angle on your bike seat, making minor repairs, and fidgeting with brake and gear cables. If you're riding on dirt trails, carry extra chain lubricant with you, or at least keep some in your car. Some riders carry a few additional tools, such as a spoke wrench for tightening loose spokes, or a chain tool to fix a broken chain.

6. Extra clothing. At Lake Tahoe, weather and temperature conditions can change at any time. It may get windy or start to rain, or you can get too warm as you ride uphill in the sun and then too cold as you ride downhill in the shade. Wear layers. Bring a lightweight jacket and a rain poncho with you. Tie your extra clothes around your waist or put them in a small day pack.

7. Sunglasses and sunscreen. Because of the high elevation around the lake, you need much more sun protection than you would at sea level. Put on a high-SPF sunscreen 30 minutes before you go outdoors, so it has time to take effect. Reapply if you are out for more than a few hours.

8. First-aid kit. Like most of life, bicycling is a generally safe activity that in the mere bat of an eye can suddenly become unsafe. The unexpected occurs – a rock in the trail, a sudden change in road surface, a misjudgment or momentary lack of attention – and suddenly, you and your bike are sprawled on the ground. Usually you look around nervously to see if anybody saw you, dust yourself off, and get back on your bike. But it's wise to carry a few emergency items just in case your accident is more serious: A few large and small bandages, antibiotic cream, and an elastic bandage can be valuable tools. A Swiss Army knife – one with several blades, a can opener, and scissors – can be used both for first aid and also for emergency bike repairs.

for bikers is deciding which trail to ride. In the Donner Summit area, one that shouldn't be missed is the Hole in the Ground Trail, a 16.5-mile loop that begins and ends just off I-80. This incredibly popular trail was completed in 1998 to the cheers of mountain bikers everywhere. Today, more than 300 people ride it every summer weekend. The loop has a total 2,100-foot elevation gain, passes near two granite-bound swimming lakes (Sand Ridge and Lower Lola Montez) and doles out 10-plus miles of exciting single-track. To get to the trailhead, take the Castle Peak/Boreal Ridge Road exit. Cross over to the north side of I-80 and follow the pavement to its end at a metal gate. One mile of riding on a rocky jeep road leads you to the official start of Hole in the Ground. Nine miles of single-track follow. The first stretch includes a heart-pumping

climb up Andesite Ridge, with awe-inspiring views of Castle Peak and Squaw Valley. Next comes a long 2.5-mile descent on a knife-thin ridge; try to keep your eye on your front wheel and not the stunning Sierra scenery. After more ups and downs, plus two potential side trips to the lakes, the route joins Lower Lola Montez Lake Trail and cruises downhill to the Soda Springs fire station, then loops back on pavement to the starting point.

Stanford Rock Loop

Fat-tire riders seeking both a physical and technical challenge will enjoy the Stanford Rock Loop, a 14-mile ride with 2,200 feet of elevation gain that may require a good dose of bike-hiking, i.e. carrying your bike. The trailhead is at William Kent Campground on Highway 89, three miles south of Tahoe City and 0.2 mile north of Pineland Drive. The first 2.3 miles are a warm-up on paved roads as you head out to the Twin Peaks Trailhead; just follow Pineland Drive to Twin Peaks Drive to Ward Creek Boulevard. The next three miles are a gentle streamside ride on a smooth dirt road, which then narrows into single-track and begins to climb alongside Ward Creek. At mile 5.8, the trail moves away from Ward Creek and the serious ascent begins. The next 1.5 miles are on the miserable side, unless you possess thighs of steel. When at last you reach a trail junction, bear left for Stanford Rock. You have one more climb and a ridgeline ramble to get there. When you do, you'll enjoy a well-earned vista of Lake Tahoe, Desolation Wilderness, and Ward Creek Canyon. From the rock, you have five miles of mostly downhill cruising on wide trail to bring you back to Ward Creek Boulevard, which you then follow back to Highway 89.

General Creek Loop

If you want to get the kids interested in mountain biking, Sugar Pine Point State Park is a great place to do it. A five-mile loop on smooth dirt roads will bestow confidence in novice riders and leave them yearning for more. The General Creek Loop begins by campsite 149 in General Creek Campground. By heading straight past the first bridge, you ride the loop counterclockwise. The road/trail runs through a dense mixed conifer forest on the north side of General Creek and open meadows on the south side. One of the prettiest stretches is where the trail crosses over a marsh area and wooden bridge at mile 2.4; look for blooming corn lilies and wildflowers in spring. If after completing this short loop you want to keep on riding, it's simple to connect to Lake Tahoe's West Shore bike path (paved). Just follow the park road out to Highway 89 and pick up the trail heading north. Another place for kid-friendly mountain biking is at North Tahoe Regional Park in Tahoe Vista. Follow National Avenue uphill to where the road ends at the park. The bike trail begins at the far end of the parking lot.

© ANN MARIE BROWN

The General Creek Loop at Sugar Pine Point State Park is an easy mountain-bike ride for families.

Northstar-at-Tahoe Resort

Last but not least, for those who just want to coast downhill, not crank uphill, Northstar-at-Tahoe Resort (Hwy. 267 at Northstar Dr., 530/562-1010, www.northstarattahoe.com) operates a few of its chairlifts in summer so that mountain bikers can be *whisked* to mid-mountain, then cruise downhill on two wheels. Remarkably, some even choose to ride uphill as well as down. The largest mountain-bike park in northern California with more than 100 miles of trails, Northstar is usually open for biking from late June to early October (may be weekends only after Labor Day). All-day lift tickets are $34 adults, $21 children 12 and under. Bike rentals are also available for $32–47 per day or $24–34 per half day. Squaw Valley USA also usually offers mountain biking on its slopes in summer, although in 2005 the bike trails were closed due to erosion control projects. Trails are planned to reopen in the summer of 2006.

BOATING AND WATER SPORTS

C Rafting on the Truckee River

In terms of rafting opportunities, the Truckee River offers something for everyone, running the gamut from the mild to the wild. The most popular stretch, by far, is the 4.5 miles from Tahoe City to River Ranch, which can be navigated by almost any kind of boat—from inner tubes to kayaks and canoes—in midsummer. Because the river flow is controlled by the sluice gates of the dam at Fanny Bridge in Tahoe City, the ride is more like floating than rafting, but that's what makes it fun. There are sandy beaches and designated areas where you can pull up and have a picnic, and unlimited opportunities for jumping out of your boat for a swim. Portable toilets and picnic tables are available at points along the river.

This stretch of the Truckee is so tame that you don't need a guide. You can go when you want and where you want. Several companies

When the river level is just right, a float down the Truckee River is the perfect way to spend a summer afternoon.

rent rafts, inner tubes, and other suitable floating devices. Drive up to the Y in Tahoe City and you'll find them at the highway junction. **Truckee River Rafting/Mountain Air Sports** (55 W. Lake Blvd., 530/583-7238 or 888/584-7258) is the biggest of the lot and has the most obvious location, right across from Albertson's. Another good company is the **Truckee River Raft Company** (185 Hwy. 89/River Rd., Tahoe City, 530/581-0123, www.truckeeriverraft.com).

No matter which company you rent from, at the end of the float at River Ranch a bus will pick you up and take you back to Tahoe City. Most people take two or three hours to float the 4.5 miles, but you could do it faster if you don't make any stops. The raft rental fee is $8–11 per person. Reservations usually aren't needed; most companies rent rafts 9 A.M.–3:30 P.M. daily in summer.

If you have your own raft or floating device, you can put in at the free **Public Raft Launching Facility,** which is located at the parking access for the Truckee River Recreation Trail in Tahoe City, otherwise known as 64 Acres Park (0.2 mile south of the Tahoe City Y). A concrete boat-launch pad is located right next to the bicycle bridge over the Truckee River. At the end of your float, you'll need to have a shuttle car waiting for you, or someone in your party will have to walk back four miles along the paved Truckee River Recreation Trail to get the car. A better choice is to plan carefully so that you arrive at River Ranch in perfect synchronization with the Tahoe Area Regional Transit (TART) bus (800/736-6365, www.laketahoetransit.com), which makes the run from River Ranch to Tahoe City several times a day. One person in your party can ride the bus back to retrieve your car, then return to pick up the rest of the party and the raft.

Rafting is only permitted when the river flow is moderate enough to be safe, which is usually in the months of July and August. When the river is too high or fast, signs are posted to alert people to stay out of the water. And even when the river is safe to float, this adventure is not suitable for nonswimmers or very

NORTH AND WEST SHORES

young children, as the river is deep in places and a few minirapids could tip your raft.

For something more adventurous, the lower Truckee River (below River Ranch) offers Class II and III rapids almost all summer long. Several tour companies offer **guided white-water trips** on the lower Truckee. Tahoe Whitewater Tours (303 Alpine Meadows Rd., 530/581-2441 or 800/442-7238, www.gowhitewater.com, $65–75 adult, $55 child) leads half-day and full-day trips mid-May–mid-September. Guided white-water rafting trips are also available from Truckee Whitewater Adventures in Tahoe City (530/583-1373 or 888/969-4743) or Tributary Whitewater Tours in Grass Valley (800/672-3846, www.whitewatertours.com).

Kayaking

As at other points along Lake Tahoe's massive shoreline, kayak tours and rentals are available in and around Tahoe City. **Kayak Tahoe** (east of Sierra Boat Company in Carnelian Bay, 530/544-2011 or 530/546-7008, www.kayaktahoe.com) leads kayak tours, rents kayaks to do-it-yourselfers, and operates a kayaking school. No experience is necessary, beginners are outfitted with a sit-on-top kayak and with only a few minutes of instruction can set out on their own. Rental rates are $38 per half day for single kayaks and $55 for doubles; kayaks can also be rented for one or two hours or all day. Reservations are required for guided tours along Tahoe's East Shore or Emerald Bay ($65–80 for a six-hour tour) or evening sunset or moonlight tours ($30–35 for a two-hour tour).

Tahoe City Kayak (1355 N. Lake Blvd., Tahoe City, 530/581-4336, www.tahoecitykayak.com) also offers tours, rentals, sales, and instruction. To the east at Kings Beach, **Tahoe Paddle & Oar** (North Tahoe Beach Center, 7860 N. Lake Blvd., Kings Beach, 530/581-3029, www.tahoepaddle.com) rents kayaks and canoes and provides guided kayak tours ($85–110 per person) along the boulder-lined shores of Crystal Bay and Sand Harbor.

To simply rent a kayak, not go for a tour, try any of the above companies or North Tahoe

Water Sports (by the pier at Kings Beach State Recreation Area, 530/583-7245, www.northtahoewatersportsinc.com) or Enviro-Rents Sports (6873 N. Lake Blvd., Tahoe Vista, 530/546-2780). In Truckee, go to The Sports Exchange (10095 W. River St., Truckee, 530/582-4510, www.truckeesportsexchange.com).

And if you brought your own kayak, you can put in at just about any public beach you can drive to. A popular area for beginner to intermediate kayakers to paddle is at **Rubicon Point** at D. L. Bliss State Park, one of the deepest parts of the lake at 1,200 feet.

Kayakers with bigger ambitions should check out the Lake Tahoe Water Trail map (530/542-5651, www.laketahoewatertrail.org), which shows available boat launches, campsites, lodging, dining, and more for all 72 miles of lake shoreline.

Hang Gliding

Just when you thought they had invented every possible water sport, they come up with another one. Boat-launched hang gliding is now available on Tahoe's North Shore courtesy of **Adventure Ambassadors** (Tahoe Vista Recreation Area, one mile west of the junction of Hwy. 28 and Hwy. 267 in Kings Beach, 530/581-2448 or 888/824-6322, $179–199 per person). The sport is a lot like parasailing, utilizing a boat and a long towrope. But with boat-launched hang gliding, once you're high in the air, the rope is untied and you soar, untethered, until you splash down on the lake on the glider's pontoons. Passengers fly tandem with a certified instructor to a height of more than 2,000 feet above the lake. Most flights last about 20 minutes. The adventure is suitable for all ages (maximum weight limit is 225 pounds).

Water Sports Outfitters and Marinas

Those interested in less natural but more thrill-oriented water sports should head for **North Tahoe Water Sports** (by the pier at Kings Beach State Recreation Area, 530/583-7245, www.northtahoewatersportsinc.com), where you can soar up to 1,400 feet above Lake Tahoe on a boat-driven parasail flight, rent aqua-cycles or jet skis, or just suffice with old-fashioned sailing or kayaking. Also in Kings Beach, the **North Tahoe Aquatic Center** (8290 N. Lake Blvd., 530/546-2419) rents personal watercraft. More serious powerboats can be rented at the **North Tahoe Marina** (7360 N. Lake Blvd., Tahoe Vista, 530/546-8248 or 530/583-1039). On the West Shore, **Action Watersports** at Meeks Bay Marina (530/525-5588, www.action-watersports.com) offers a full array of boat and water toy rentals.

If you've always wanted to learn how to water-ski or wakeboard, Lake Tahoe is a great place to do it. The **High Sierra Water Ski School** (530/525-1214 or 530/583-7417, www.highsierrawaterskiing.com) has been teaching the sport for 25 years, and they also rent jet skis, waverunners, small sailboats, powerboats, and the like. The school has two locations at two and seven miles south of Tahoe City, respectively: Sunnyside Marina (1850 W. Lake Blvd.) and Homewood Marina (5190 W. Lake Blvd.). On the North Shore, **Goldcrest Water Ski School** (760 N. Lake Blvd., Kings Beach, 530/546-7412) also teaches waterskiing in July and August only.

If you brought your own boat or personal watercraft to Lake Tahoe and just need to find a boat ramp where you can put it in the water, you can do so on the West Shore at Homewood Marina (530/525-5966), Obexer's Marina (530/525-7962), or Sunnyside Marina (530/583-7201). On the North Shore, you can launch your craft at Kings Beach Recreation Area (530/546-7248), Lake Forest Boat Ramp (530/583-3796), North Tahoe Marina (530/546-8248), Sierra Boat Company (530/546-2552), or Tahoe City Marina (530/583-1039).

And when it comes to water sports, don't forget that Lake Tahoe is not the only game in town. Over at Donner Lake, the marina at **Donner Lake Village Resort** (15695 Donner Pass Rd., Truckee, 530/582-5112) rents ski boats, fishing boats, personal watercraft, and canoes and kayaks. You can also launch your own boat here.

SWIMMING

On the North Shore, beach-lovers don't have to go far to find a strip of swimsuit-worthy sand. One of the nicest is just 1.5 miles east of town at **Lake Forest Beach Park** (Lake Forest Rd. and Hwy. 28, 530/583-3796). The beach has picnic tables, fire pits, restrooms, barbecue grills, and a playground for the kiddies. Good news for Fido—dogs are permitted at this beach. When you and/or your four-legged friend get tired of swimming, it's great fun to laze around on the beach and watch the windsurfers and kiteboarders. **Tahoe State Recreation Area** (on the eastern edge of Tahoe City next to the Boatworks Mall) also has a nice beach, if you are lucky enough to get a parking spot ($6 parking fee). And **Commons Beach,** just a few steps from Fanny Bridge and the Tahoe City Y, was revitalized in 2004 with a grassy area, a playground for the kids, including a mini–rock wall for junior rock climbers, barbecues, and a paved recreation trail. It's not a great swimming area because it's so rocky, but it's a fun beach for children.

In Tahoe Vista, the 600-foot-long sandy swimming beach at **Moon Dunes Beach** (across the highway from Rustic Cottages near Pino Grande) is a popular spot, with picnic tables and fire pits. There's no public parking lot, so you are on your own to find street parking. A short distance to the west lies Tahoe Vista Recreation Area (N. Lake Blvd. and National Ave.), another good place to take a dip.

In Kings Beach, the last town heading east on Highway 28 before California ends and Nevada begins, swimmers and beachgoers flock to the **Kings Beach State Recreation Area** (7360 W. Lake Blvd., Kings Beach, 530/546-7248), a great place to take the kids because of the shallow, calm water. The beach has boat and jet ski rentals, a barbecue area, a kids' playground, and a $5 parking fee. Also in Kings Beach is the **North Tahoe Beach Center,** directly across the street from the Safeway supermarket. The beach has grassy areas, a beach volleyball court, and picnic tables. For a fee, you can use the Beach Center's clubhouse, sauna, hot tub, and weight machines. **Secline Beach,** at the end of Secline Street in Kings Beach, is 50 yards off the highway and more secluded. The beach is rocky and blissfully free of development (no facilities here), but there isn't a lot of shoreline.

For those who want to bring their dog to the beach, **Carnelian Bay Beach** (on both the east and west sides of Sierra Boat Company, near Gar Woods Grill) is one of the few officially "dog-legal" stretches of sand. (You may see dogs on other North Shore beaches, but that doesn't necessarily mean they are allowed.) The shoreline may be rocky, but that means you can search for carnelian stones. The water is shallow and inviting; retrievers will fetch darn near anything you throw into the water here.

Over on the West Shore, a few beaches make an obvious appearance along Highway 89, including **William Kent Beach** and **Kaspian Recreation Area,** both right next to the highway a few miles south of Tahoe City. If you don't want everybody driving by to see you in your bathing suit, head to **Sugar Pine Point State Park** in Tahoma, where a lovely stretch of shoreline is found by the historic Ehrman Mansion ($6 parking fee). Adjacent to **Meeks Bay Campground,** 10 miles south of Tahoe City, the Forest Service manages a white-sand beach with a boat launch, restrooms, and picnic facilities ($5 parking fee). Just south of Homewood is **Chambers Landing,** where a historic bar and restaurant are set within a few feet of a sandy, swimmable cove ($5 parking fee). And finally, what is arguably the West Shore's most beautiful public beach is found at Calawee Cove and Lester Beach at **D. L. Bliss State Park** (between Meeks Bay and Emerald Bay, $6 parking fee).

If you're in the Truckee area, pay a visit to **West End Beach** at Donner Lake, one of the few beaches near Tahoe that actually has a lifeguard ($5 fee). Or, if you prefer to have your swimming activities take place in a pool rather than a sandy cove, head over to Squaw Valley USA and ride the cable car to **High Camp Bath and Tennis Club** ($20–25 for cable-car fare and swimming pass), where a manufactured lagoon entices swimmers.

FISHING

Lake Tahoe is open for fishing year-round, except for within 300 feet of its tributaries October 1–June 30. The best fishing for mackinaw trout is in spring and early summer, but they can be fished year-round. Brown and rainbow trout are also commonly caught in the lake. An excellent kokanee salmon fishery, with most action occurring around midsummer, is also on offer.

Because of the lake's massive size and depth, the best fishing is always done by boat and in the company of an experienced guide who knows the lake. Most **guide services** have a 90 percent or better catch rate, provide bait, tackle and beverages, plus your fish will be cleaned and bagged for you. Dozens of North Lake Tahoe guide services can take you out on the lake and greatly increase your chances of catching fish. Contact one of the following guides on the North or West Shores to learn more about their services: Kingfish Guide Service (5110 W. Lake Blvd., Homewood, 530/525-5360, www.kingfishtahoe.com), Mickey's Big Mack Charters (at Sierra Boat Company, Carnelian Bay, 530/546-4444 or 800/877-1462, www.mickeysbigmack.com), Chuck's Bait, Tackle, and Guide (8658 N. Lake Blvd, Kings Beach, 530/546-8425), or Mac-A-Tac Fishing Charters (1320 Alpine Way, Tahoe City, 530/546-2500). Additionally, three different guiding services operate out of Tahoe City Marina (700 N. Lake Blvd.) in the center of town: Reel Deal Sport Fishing (530/581-0924), Reel Magic Sportfishing (530/587-6027), and Captain Chris' Fishing Charter (530/583-4857).

The **Truckee River** and its environs is a world-famous fly-fishing area, but it, too, is not for the inexperienced. The river can be legally fished from the last Saturday in April to November 15, except for the section from the Tahoe City dam to 1,000 feet downstream, which is closed year-round. Streams in the area can be fished July 1–November 15, whereas lakes in the Truckee–Donner area, including Donner Lake, Boca Reservoir, Stampede Reservoir, and Prosser Creek Reservoir, can be fished year-round. Martis Creek Reservoir can also be fished year-round, but special rules apply. The lake is catch-and-release only, using artificial lures with single barbless hooks.

For expert local **fly-fishing** advice, contact one of these resources: California School of Fly-fishing (Truckee, 530/587-7005 or 800/588-7688), Randy Johnson's Tackle and Guide Service (Tahoma, 530/525-6575), Mountain Hardware and Sports (11320 Donner Pass Rd., Truckee, 530/587-4844), Thy Rod and Staff Fly Fishing (12611 Hillside Dr., Truckee, 530/587-7333), Truckee River Outfitters (10200 Donner Pass Rd., Truckee, 530/582-0900), or Truckee Trout Guides (16073 North-woods Dr., Truckee, 530/277-1686).

Those who just want to stand on the shore of a scenic lake and drop in a line and some Power Bait or salmon eggs can do so at **Donner Lake,** near the boat ramp or the west end of the beach; **Boca Reservoir,** near the rocky sections of the stream inlet; and **Prosser Creek Reservoir** and **Stampede Reservoir.** The usual catch in these lakes is brown or rainbow trout and occasionally kokanee salmon. Donner Lake has big mackinaw and kokanee salmon, but you have to go out in a boat and go deep to find them. Boat rentals are available at each of these lakes for those who prefer trolling.

Stream anglers using spinners or Power Bait can set out for Coldstream Creek, a half-mile hike from Donner Memorial State Park, the section of the Little Truckee River between Boca and Stampede reservoirs, or the main Truckee River between Tahoe City and Truckee along Highway 89.

If you need to buy a fishing license or bait or tackle supplies, head to Swigard's True Value Hardware (200 N. Lake Blvd., Tahoe City, 530/583-3738).

HORSEBACK RIDING

Several stables on the North Shore will let you borrow (okay, rent) Trigger or Seabiscuit for a few hours to ride across the open plains (okay, mountains and valleys). Three of the big ski resorts offer horseback riding as part of their summer activities. **Northstar Stables**

(910 Northstar Dr., Truckee, 530/562-2480, www.skinorthstar.com, 1-hour guided rides $30, 2 hours $50, 10-minute pony rides $10) offers pony rides, boarding, one- and two-hour guided trail rides, dinner rides, breakfast rides, and pack charters. Specializing in beginners and families, all rides include an extra half hour for you to get to know your guide and learn about horse behavior and safety. Children must be seven years old to participate in trail rides. More experienced riders can take part in a view-filled, all-day ride on the Tahoe Rim Trail from Brockway Summit (riders and horses are shuttled from Northstar to the trailhead).

Alpine Meadows Stables (2600 Alpine Meadows Rd., Alpine Meadows, 530/583-3905) also offers pony rides, guided trail rides, and multiday pack charters. Guided trail rides are $40 per hour per person; pony rides are $25 per half-hour. **Squaw Valley Stables** (1525 Squaw Valley Rd., Olympic Valley, 530/583-7433, www.squawvalleystables.com, $29 one hour, $55 two hours, $85 half day) offers pony rides, riding lessons, and guided one-hour, two-hour, and half-day trail rides. If your horse travels with you on vacation, you can even board it here.

Just outside of Truckee, **Tahoe Donner Equestrian** (15275 Alder Creek Rd., Truckee, 530/587-9470, www.tahoedonner.com) provides a similar array of equestrian activities, plus Friday-night barbecue rides and wagon rides. Guided trail rides are $40 per hour per person; pony rides are $25 per half-hour. The barbecue ride is $60 for adults and $40 for children and includes dinner. For the more serious rider, the equestrian center has five-day horsemanship camps in Western and English riding for children and adults.

ROCK CLIMBING

The clean granite cracks and faces of **Donner Summit,** located off old Highway 40 west of Truckee, are by far the most popular climbing spots on the North Shore. With about 350 different possible routes on a multitude of cliffs, the Summit has amazing variety, from easy scrambles to expert climbs. Donner doles out everything from bouldering to multipitch crack climbing. Plus, access is a snap—you can drive right up the old Donner Pass Road and find climbers scaling the rocks all around you, just a few feet from the pavement.

Coming in a close second for popularity is the **Big Chief** area, located between Tahoe City and Truckee in the river canyon. The rock here is volcanic, not granite, so it provides steep sport climbing over more than 60 possible routes, none suitable for beginners. Instead, novice climbers head to **Twin Crags,** just north of Tahoe City on Highway 89. Beginners use top ropes to sharpen their skills and gain some confidence on the rock. The south-facing crags are usually snow-free early in the year.

Climbers who just want to solve a few boulder problems head to Grouse Slabs at Donner Summit, Split Rock at the west end of Donner Memorial State Park (more than 25 routes possible here), or the house-sized boulders near Balancing Rock at D. L. Bliss State Park. Another good bouldering site is at the end of Old County Road, just east of Tahoe City off Highway 28.

For **climbing instruction** and/or guide service, contact Alpine Skills International (11400 Donner Pass Rd., Truckee, 530/426-9108, www.alpineskills.com). Their office is located upstairs at The Back Country outdoor store, but they conduct climbing classes at Donner Pass. Their two-day, $250 beginning class is offered June–September. More advanced courses are also offered, as well as a climbing clinic for women only. Or contact the Tahoe Adventure Company (530/913-9212 or 866/830-6125, www.tahoeadventurecompany.com), which offers a five-hour beginner's lesson for about $150. Tahoe Adventure's North Shore courses are taught at Donner Summit.

If you are heading out on your own and forgot your chalk bag at home, several stores sell rock-climbing equipment: Alpenglow Sports (415 N. Lake Blvd., Tahoe City, 530/583-6917), The Back Country (690 N. Lake Blvd., Tahoe City, 530/581-5861), and The Sports Exchange (10095 W. River St., Truckee, 530/582-4510).

And lastly, if a summer thunderstorm hits and there's no place outdoors where you can climb, you can always head to the 30-foot-high indoor climbing wall inside the cable car building at **Squaw Valley USA** (530/386-1375 or 530/583-7673, www.squawadventure.com). A day of climbing is $14, or $18 with equipment rentals.

GOLF

Golfers have almost as many options as skiers in the North Tahoe region, with a total of eight courses located within a 30-mile radius. For those who just want to hit a few balls without a lot of fanfare, the area has three nine-hole courses with green fees of $50 or less—Tahoe City Golf Course, Old Brockway, and Ponderosa. Located behind the Bank of America, **Tahoe City Golf Course** (251 N. Lake Blvd., Tahoe City, 530/583-1516, www.tcgc.com) is a par-33 course with views of Lake Tahoe and a long history on the North Shore. The course was built in 1917 by a female golf pro, May "Queenie" Dunn Hupfel, and was intended to be used by guests at the nearby Tahoe Tavern. The course brags of having fast and true greens that "break toward the lake," and with green fees of $30 for nine holes, a round of golf here won't break the bank. The course's bar and cafe serves a casual breakfast and lunch.

Even nongolfers will enjoy a trip to the historic **Old Brockway Golf Course** (7900 N. Lake Blvd., Kings Beach, 530/546-9909, www.oldbrockway.com), a par-36 course with an outstanding course restaurant, the Blue Onion. Old Brockway has been rated as one of the top 10 nine-hole golf courses in Northern California by *Golf Today* magazine. Its scenic, Jeffrey pine–studded layout covers more than 3,200 yards with tight fairways, postage-stamp greens, and views of Lake Tahoe. Built in 1924 by Harry Comstock, owner of the Brockway Hotel, the course retains much of its historic character and charm. In 1934, Old Brockway was home to the first "unofficial" Bing Crosby Golf Tournament, when Bing would invite his friends to Lake Tahoe to play golf while he was entertaining at the nearby Cal-Neva Resort. The course's Blue Onion restaurant serves three meals a day during the golfing season, which is usually April–early November. Green fees are $38 for nine holes.

The nine-hole **Ponderosa Golf Course** (10040 Reynold Way, Truckee, 530/587-3501) is a par-35 regulation course set amid the ponderosa pines. The course was designed by Robert Balbach. The layout is fairly open and typical of a municipal course, but the greens are fast and sloping. Afternoon winds can make the greens even tougher. Green fees are $32 for nine holes and no reservations are required.

For golfing with more glitz, the North Shore's big resorts have world-class courses designed for the serious golfer. The tree-lined course at **Northstar-at-Tahoe** (168 Basque Dr. off Northstar Dr., Truckee, 530/562-2490 or 800/466-6784, www.northstarattahoe.com) is a par-72, 18-hole beauty designed by Robert Muir Graves. The 6,897-yard course has water on 14 holes and gorgeous mountain and meadow views. It's a course for accurate hitters, especially on the back nine. Green fees are $99 (cart included) in summer, but substantially less mid-May–mid June and mid-September–mid-October. The resort also boasts the earliest twilight rate hours around the lake, reduced fees start at 2 P.M. ($65). If you'd like to improve your game but don't want to pay for private instruction, free lessons are offered on Wednesday afternoons June–September; call for reservations.

Designed by the legendary Jack Nicklaus, the scenic course at **Old Greenwood** (12915 Fairway Dr., Truckee, 530/550-7010 or 800/754-3070, www.oldgreenwood.com) winds through 600 acres of stately Jeffrey pines and sagebrush, and has received an Audubon International certification for its environmental friendliness. The par-72, 7,518-yard course comes with a big price tag—18 holes of golf will cost you $170, cart included. Twilight rates drop to $100. Also in Truckee, the **Tahoe Donner Golf Course** (12850 Northwoods Blvd., Truckee, 530/587-9440, www.tahoedonner.com) offers similar beautiful scenery. Designed by Roy Williams

and Bill Bell Jr., this semiprivate course has green fees of $120, cart included.

Over at Squaw Valley, the **Resort at Squaw Creek** (400 Squaw Creek Rd., Olympic Valley, 530/583-6300 or 800/327-3353, www.squawcreek.com) boasts an exceptionally challenging 18-hole championship course designed by Robert Trent Jones Jr. Rated as "one of the top ten courses you can play" by *Golf Magazine*, the par-72 links meander for 6,815 yards along the valley floor amid a wealth of wetlands. If you're not the world's most accurate hitter, bring a bag full of extra balls. The course has received Audubon International status as a certified cooperative wildlife sanctuary. Resort guests pay $50–100 to golf here (cart included); nonguests pay slightly more.

Last but certainly not least is the **Coyote Moon Championship Golf Course** (10685 Northwoods Blvd., Truckee, 530/587-0886, www.coyotemoongolf.com), which opened in 2000 and sits on 250 acres of undeveloped pine- and boulder-covered hills. The resort brags of having not a single house or structure to spoil its mountain and forest views, an exceptional rarity around Lake Tahoe. Golf great Brad Bell was the creative force behind the 7,117-yard, par-72 course, which meanders around and across Trout Creek. Green fees are $150 with cart ($95 twilight). The resort's restaurant serves three meals a day.

BALLOONING

In the Truckee area, balloon flights over Prosser Reservoir are offered by **Mountain High Balloons** (10867 Cheyenne Way, Truckee, 530/587-6922 or 888/462-2683). The cost is $95 for a half-hour flight and $165 for a one-hour flight. Children ages 10–16 are half price; children 9 and under are free when accompanied by an adult.

WINTER SPORTS
Downhill Skiing and Snowboarding

North Lake Tahoe is home to the largest concentration of alpine ski resorts in North America, including three giant, full-service, megaresorts—Squaw Valley, Alpine Meadows, and Northstar-at-Tahoe—and a half dozen smaller, more manageable ones—Homewood, Boreal, Sugar Bowl, Tahoe Donner, and Soda Springs. Add it all up and you have a whole lot of snow-covered slopes within a very few miles. Whether you choose to ski or ride, there is an abundance of choices here, from beginner-level bunny hills to near vertical runs that give envelope pushers a place to push themselves.

The undisputed king of the North and West Shore resorts is **Squaw Valley USA** (1960 Squaw Valley Rd., Olympic Valley, 530/583-6955, www.squaw.com). Located seven miles north of Tahoe city and 12 miles south of Truckee off Highway 89, Squaw's claim to fame is that it was the site of the 1960 Winter Olympics. Today it is one of the largest ski resorts in North America, and one of the most expensive places to ski around Lake Tahoe. Lift tickets are $65 for adults ages 19–64, and $39 for seniors 65 and up and teens 13–18. Here's the only bargain: Children 12 and under ski for only $5 all day. Daytime lift ticket holders get one freebie: They can ski free at night 4–9 P.M., but the only run that is lit up is Mountain Run, from High Camp to the village floor.

Squaw's summit elevation is 9,050 feet at Granite Chief, and it features more than 100 possible runs spread out over 4,000 acres of terrain. Six mountain peaks are accessed by 34 lifts, including an aerial cable car and North America's only high-speed Funitel. Riders have a wide choice of places to play, with three terrain parks, two standard half-pipes, and a mammoth superpipe. Even with all this, Squaw is not a place for skiers and riders who don't like crowds—on winter weekends, it is always the busiest resort on the north side of the lake.

The reason for Squaw's success is not the size and variety of its terrain (although that certainly helps), nor is it the fact that there is almost always abundant snow (although an average 450 inches per year certainly helps, too). It's the fact that the family-owned resort is an entire industry in and of itself. Squaw's High Camp offers mountaintop ice-skating, snow

tubing, and a summer swimming lagoon and spa. On the lower mountain, The Village at Squaw Valley includes dozens of shops and restaurants plus a host of winter sports activities: snowshoeing, cross-country skiing, sleigh rides, dogsled tours, an indoor climbing wall, and so on. Winter visitors who come to Squaw for a week's vacation could easily fill their time without ever leaving the valley.

Just a few miles down the road from Squaw is its mellower neighbor, **Alpine Meadows Ski Resort** (2600 Alpine Meadows Rd., Tahoe City, 530/583-4232 or 800/441-4423, www.skialpine.com, $39–49 adults, $15 children 7–12 and seniors over 70, free for children 6 and under). Although many skiers have made Alpine Meadows their "regular" resort, this is also the place that people who have driven to Squaw and been discouraged by the crowds choose as their alternate. Located six miles north of Tahoe city and 13 miles south of Truckee off Highway 89, Alpine Meadows features 2,400 acres with more than 100 possible runs. Its summit elevation is 8,637 feet (base is 6,835), and there is no shortage of snow here; the resort receives an average annual 495 inches. Alpine Meadows' snowmaking capacity covers a large network of runs, but most years, they don't have to use it much.

Alpine Meadows has a total of 15 lifts, including one high-speed six-passenger chair and one high-speed express quad. Except for the busiest holiday weekends, lift lines are generally not an issue. All the expected services are offered at the resort, including ski and snowboard instruction for adults and children, ski and snowboard rental and repair, guided out-of-bounds tours for skiers craving the slopes less traveled, special clinics for those interested in moguls, freestyle skiing, powder skiing, or telemarking, and plenty of on-mountain food service. Don't miss the chance to eat at least one hamburger on the large sundeck at the day lodge. Boarders will enjoy a variety of terrain parks that feature jumps, spins, half-pipes, and table tops; there is even a separate terrain park just for kids. Expert skiers like the amount of backcountry terrain that is accessible via the lifts. Beginners and intermediates can sharpen their skills on miles of scenic, groomed terrain. With all this, it's no wonder Alpine Meadows was rated one of America's top 25 winter resorts by *Skiing Magazine.*

On the West Shore, just five miles south of Tahoe City, is the locals' favorite **Homewood Mountain Resort** (5145 W. Lake Blvd., Homewood, 530/525-2992, www.skihomewood.com). Because of its proximity to the lake, Homewood is known for its extraordinary lake views from every run, and for its wind-protected location. Unlike at other Tahoe resorts, Homewood skiers and riders are never subject to "wind hold," when the resort closes down the lifts due to high winds. Homewood hasn't had such a closure in more than a decade.

Very little of the resort is visible from the highway (only one ski run), so first-timers are always surprised at how large Homewood is. The resort has 1,260 acres of diverse terrain, with 60 runs served by eight lifts. The longest run is two miles with a 1,650-foot drop. Powder is the thing here; Homewood sees an average snowfall of 482 inches. Weekend ticket prices are $45–48 adults, $33 kids ages 11–18, and children 10 and under ski free when accompanied by an adult. Seniors 62–69 pay $22, 70 and older pay $10. Mon.–Thur. are bargain days, when prices drop to $27 for anyone 11–61. If you buy lift tickets for two or more consecutive days, you get a $5 discount each day.

Midway between Kings Beach and Truckee off Highway 267, **Northstar-at-Tahoe Ski Resort** (Hwy. 267 and Northstar Dr., Truckee, 530/562-1010 or 800/468-2463, www.skinorthstar.com) is currently undergoing a renaissance, and longtime Northstar fans are somewhat divided in their opinions about it. A megamillion-dollar redevelopment project is underway at Northstar. The project includes the construction of a new village complex, which will include luxurious condominiums, a year-round outdoor ice rink, and a variety of restaurants and shops. Sound familiar? Right. This formerly unhyped resort will soon be transformed from a place that always attracted cross-country and alpine skiers who wanted a low-key experience, to something more on the order of Squaw Valley or Heavenly.

Currently, Northstar has 17 lifts and one gondola serving 2,420 acres. Of 70 possible runs, its longest is an impressive 2.9 miles with a vertical drop of well over 2,000 feet. Northstar has always limited its daily lift ticket sales, preventing the mountain from being overcrowded. If a sellout occurs in the morning, half-day tickets are not sold in the afternoon. Lift tickets are $63-66 adult, $53 youth ages 13-22 and seniors 65 and up, $22 children ages 5-12, under 5 free. Advanced intermediate skiers and riders enjoy free 75-minute "sharpen your skills" lessons on weekdays. Parents have been able to send their kids ages 2–10 to Minors Camp Happy Hour (5–7 P.M.) while they sneak off for an après-ski beverage or dinner for two. And riders have enjoyed a 17-foot superpipe and standard half-pipe at Ground Zero terrain park. In its new incarnation, what will Northstar hold for its future guests? At this point, it's anybody's guess, but they clearly intend to follow the motto "more is better." Along with the new condos, restaurants, and shops, the resort is also planning for expanded terrain and additional lifts.

Farther to the west, **Boreal Mountain Resort** (19455 Boreal Ridge Rd., Soda Springs, 530/426-3666, www.borealski.com or www.rideboreal.com) is a well-known snowboarder's paradise. Usually the first ski resort around Lake Tahoe to open each year, Boreal is located at the Castle Peak exit off I-80, three miles west of Donner Lake. Often Boreal starts making snow well before Thanksgiving. To encourage business throughout the ski season, tickets prices are kept relatively low: adults aged 13–59 are $38, seniors 60 and up are $25, and children 5–12 are $10. Boreal also offers a conditions guarantee: If for any reason the skiing or riding does not meet your expectations, you can return your lift ticket within a half hour of purchase and receive a full refund.

Since Boreal is popular with riders, terrain parks are a big deal here. In the 2005–2006 ski season, Boreal unveiled the first and only all-mountain terrain park in northern California.

The new Jibassic Park (www.jibassicpark.com) is comprised of 100 rails, jumps, and funboxes for every ability, and a 450-foot-long superpipe. Every run at Boreal now has something dedicated just to riders. For young riders, the Kidz X Park has smaller curves and rollers designed for the little shredders.

Because of Boreal's location far to the west of Tahoe's lakeshore, it's the place where thousands of Sacramento and San Francisco Bay Area kids have learned to ski and/or ride. The resort brags that more than 350,000 people have taken their first run on skis or boards here. For many urban and suburban families, Boreal is an easy day trip from home, and the resort capitalizes on its location by catering to young beginners with its innovative Children's Snow School. The Nugget Chair Lift operates at a slower pace, taking the pressure off beginners who are just figuring out how to get on and off the lift. The Boreal Kids Club offers skiing lessons for kids ages 4–10, and snowboarding lessons for kids ages 6–10. After the day's lessons are over, children are permitted to keep their equipment for the rest of the day, so they can show off what they have learned.

Boreal is also one of only a few resorts that offers night skiing and boarding, with night lift tickets available 3:30–9 P.M., usually Thanksgiving–Easter. And it is home to the **Western Ski Sport Museum,** which portrays the history of skiing from the 1850s to today. Old ski movies play in a small theater.

Not far from Boreal are three ski resorts located off Old Highway 40, the road that carried travelers across Donner Summit before I-80 was constructed. The most developed of the three is historic **Sugar Bowl** (629 Sugar Bowl Rd., Norden, 530/426-9000, www.sugarbowl.com), considered to be the grand old dame of Tahoe resorts. Due in part to the secluded Inn at Sugar Bowl, with guest rooms and a view-filled dining room located at the top of the mile-long gondola, this 1930s-era resort has a decidedly European feel. Most years, it can boast of having the most snow of any resort around Tahoe. Because of its high base elevation (6,883 feet), average snowfall is a whop-

ping 500 inches, and the resort is known for deep powder. Nearly 90 runs on four mountain peaks are serviced by 12 lifts, including the first gondola built in the United States. The longest run is three miles with a 1,500-foot vertical drop. All this and the resort is only two miles east of I-80 (Norden/Soda Springs exit), so getting here from Sacramento or the San Francisco Bay Area is a piece of cake.

If you experience a sense of déjà vu while skiing at Sugar Bowl, it might be because one of its founders was Walt Disney. Matterhorn-esque touches can be seen around the resort. Of all the alpine resorts at Lake Tahoe, this one exhibits the most alpine charm. But the quaintness of the place doesn't mean it isn't right for snowboarders who just want to carve the slopes. Sugar Bowl's Mount Judah features several terrain parks, including a half-pipe.

Sugar Bowl's ticket prices are $46–59 for ages 23–59, $46 for ages 13–22 and 60–69, and $15 for ages 6–12. Children 5 and under are free and seniors 70 and up are $5.

Also at Donner Summit, **Soda Springs Winter Resort** (Old Hwy. 40/Donner Pass Rd., Norden, 530/426-3901, www.skisodasprings.com, adults $25, kids 8–17 $16, kids 7 and under $10, seniors over 70 $5) is a great beginner hill, with gentle, wide open runs. Located just one mile off I-80 at Donner Summit, the resort is easy to reach, but you'll never find big crowds here. You won't find high-priced lift tickets, either. Lift tickets include access to all lifts, snow-tubing tows, snowshoeing trails, and sledding area. This place is all about family fun, with just as much emphasis placed on their tubing run as on skiing and riding. The resort has only four lifts—two for skiing, which access 16 runs, and two for tubing.

The last of the three resorts on the old Donner Pass Road is **Donner Ski Ranch** (19320 Old Hwy. 40/Donner Pass Rd., Norden, 530/426-3635, www.donnerskiranch.com, adults $25–32, teens and seniors 60–69 $20–25, children 6–12 $8–10, kids 5 and under and seniors 70 and older free), another historic, family-owned resort that believes staying small is a good thing. Uncrowded slopes and lots of beginner runs give novice skiers and riders a chance to gain confidence. The resort has six lifts that service 45 runs. The longest run is 1.2 miles with a 750-foot vertical drop. Like at nearby Soda Springs Resort, ticket prices are a bargain. On-site lodging is available at the Summit House (530/426-3622).

One additional low-key beginner area is located just north of Truckee. **Tahoe Donner Downhill Ski Area** (11509 Northwoods Blvd., Truckee, 530/587-9444, www.skitahoedonner. com) has a gentle, open bowl with almost no obstacles to intimidate novice skiers and riders. Four lifts service 14 runs on 120 skiable acres.

Smallest of them all and the most subdued is **Granlibakken** (625 Granlibakken Rd., Tahoe City, 530/583-4242 or 800/543-3221, www. granlibakken.com, ski hill Fri.–Sun., daily during Christmas and New Years holidays, lift tickets $20 adults, $12 children) on the West Shore of the lake. The oldest and least expensive ski "resort" at Lake Tahoe, Granlibakken was founded in 1931 as a training hill for Olympic ski jumpers. With only one run possible, skiers don't have to study the trail map before hitting the slope. Plus, if you are prone to falling, the vertical drop is only 300 feet. Learn-to-ski or -board packages, including rentals, are only $49. So what's a granlibakken? It is Norwegian for "hill sheltered by fir trees."

If you need to rent or buy ski or snowboarding equipment and you don't want to do so at the resorts, several shops in Tahoe City, Kings Beach, and Truckee can accommodate you. **Dave's Skis and Boards** (530/546-5800 or 530/582-0900) has a whopping five locations in the Tahoe City and Truckee area.

Cross-Country Skiing

Although some of the downhill ski areas listed above offer cross-country skiing terrain as well, they don't hold a candle to a few North Shore resorts that specialize in it. For serious Nordic skiers, the only resort worth considering is **Royal Gorge** (9411 Hillside Dr., Soda Springs, 530/426-3871 or 800/500-3871, www.royalgorge.com, all-day trail passes $24–28 adult, $15 ages 13–16, free for ages 12 and under and

75 and up). It's all about the numbers here at North America's largest cross-country ski resort. With a base elevation of 7,000 feet, the resort sees an annual snowfall that exceeds 600 inches. Ninety different trails (28 novice, 46 intermediate, and 16 advanced) crisscross 9,000 acres of terrain. The resort boasts 330 kilometers of wide, machine-groomed track, a snowmaking system, four surface lifts for practicing downhill technique, four trailside cafes, an overnight lodge, and 10 warming huts sprinkled around the mountain. All this and a big bonus: Because the resort is less than one mile from the Soda Springs/Norden exit off I-80, it is easily accessible. You have to experience this place to believe it. Beginner lesson packages are available, plus ski rentals.

Closer to the lake, **Tahoe Cross Country** (925 Country Club Dr., Tahoe City, 530/583-5475, www.tahoexc.com, all-day trail passes $20 adult 18–59, $15 junior 10–17 and senior 60–69, children under 10 and seniors over 70 free, dogs $3) is located three miles north of downtown Tahoe City. You can kick and glide on 15 groomed trails that cover 65 kilometers, and even dogs are welcome on a few trails—a rarity at most cross-country ski areas. (Dogs are permitted only on weekdays 8:30 A.M.–5 P.M. and weekends and holidays 3–5 P.M.) Three trailside warming huts provide shelter or a meeting point for a midday lunch. A day lodge has games for the kids, hot food and drinks, and a warm fire. **North Tahoe Regional Park** (at the end of National Ave./Donner Rd., Tahoe Vista, 530/546-0605) also has 11 kilometers of groomed cross-country skiing trails.

Just a few miles farther north, **Tahoe Donner Cross Country** (15275 Alder Creek Rd., Truckee, 530/587-9484, www.tdxc. com, all-day trail passes $21 adults, $16 seniors 60–69, free for seniors 70 and older and kids 12 and under) has 48 trails covering 113 kilometers and 48,000 acres of terrain. The vast majority are suited to beginners and intermediates. Five trailside warming huts give you a place to catch your breath; the Tahoe Donner Day Lodge offers terrific hot meals plus ski rentals and the like. On Wednesday nights in January and February, the resort lights up a 2.5-kilometer loop for night skiing (5–7 P.M.). Trail passes are $25 adult, $12 child.

Of the big downhill resorts that offer cross-country skiing, **Northstar-at-Tahoe** (Hwy. 267 and Northstar Dr., Truckee, 530/562-2475, www.skinorthstar.com) has the most extensive trail system (38 trails covering 50 kilometers), plus equipment rentals, lessons, and warming huts. Trail passes are $25 adult, $12 child. Half-day and full-day telemarking clinics are offered. **The Resort at Squaw Creek Cross Country Center** (400 Squaw Creek Rd., Olympic Valley, 530/581-6637) has 18 kilometers of groomed trails, plus an on-site rental and repair shop. Trail passes are $15 adult, $10 child.

Do-it-yourselfers should head to one of the state-run Sno-Parks in the vicinity. Sno-Parks, which are basically plowed parking lots alongside or near the highway, are marked by distinctive brown signs. Here, for the price of a $5 daily permit or $25 annual permit, you can ski on marked and unmarked trails. Sno-Park permits are sold at sporting-goods stores, businesses located near Sno-Parks, and at many other locations. The Sno-Park program hotline (916/324-1222) has information on where to buy permits and where Sno-Parks are located. Three are found in the vicinity of the North and West Shores. At **Donner Lake Sno-Park** (by the Emigrant Trail Museum at Donner Memorial State Park, Donner Lake exit off I-80, 530/582-7892), marked ski trails lead along the shore of Donner Lake and to the Donner Party historic sites. At **Donner Summit Sno-Park** (Castle Peak exit off I-80, just past the Boreal Inn, 530/587-3558), parking is on the south of the highway but skiing trails are on the north side (ski underneath the freeway on the frontage road). This is a very popular area, with many skiers heading up to Castle Peak. On the West Shore, three miles south of Tahoe City, **Blackwood Canyon Sno-Park** (Lake Tahoe Basin Management Unit, 530/543-2600) is open for cross-country skiing and snowmobiling.

Another good area for beginning to intermediate skiers are the ski trails at **Sugar Pine Point State Park.** The park's campground remains open in winter for intrepid snow campers, and the General Creek Loop makes a perfect easy ski trail.

Snowshoeing

Although most snowshoers prefer to set off on their own on backcountry trails, beginners and those seeking a tamer experience can head to one of Tahoe's big resorts to get some experience. At **Alpine Meadows** (2600 Alpine Meadows Rd., Tahoe City, 530/583-4232 or 800/441-4423, www.skialpine.com), marked snowshoe trails begin near the lodge and meander through the forests around the base of the mountain. At **Northstar-at-Tahoe** (Hwy. 267 and Northstar Dr., Truckee, 530/562-1010, www.skinorthstar.com), snowshoers can travel on all 60 kilometers of the cross-country ski trail system. The same is true of the 18 kilometers of cross-country trails at **The Resort at Squaw Creek** (400 Squaw Creek Rd., Olympic Valley, 530/581-6637). And at **Royal Gorge** (9411 Hillside Dr., Soda Springs, 530/426-3871, www.royalgorge.com), North America's largest cross-country ski resort, snowshoers can take their pick from 90 groomed trails that travel a total distance of 330 kilometers. At all sites, snowshoe rentals are available. Rates are typically $15–20 for a half day or $22–30 for a full day.

If you'd like to go on a guided snowshoe tour, contact **Tahoe Trips and Trails** (700 Hwy. 89, Tahoe City, 530/581-4453 or 530/583-4506, www.tahoetrips.com) and ask about their customized winter sport tours.

Sledding and Tubing

Sometimes the most fun in the snow comes from using the simplest equipment, and that's why tubing parks and sledding hills are a big hit around Lake Tahoe. In the Soda Springs area, **Kingvale Tubing and Sledding Center** (53010 Donner Pass Rd., Soda Springs, 530/426-1941, 10 A.M.–4 P.M. Fri.–Mon., $10 for two hours, $15 for three hours) carves and maintains not one or two but nearly a dozen tubing lanes. Five lanes are served by lifts, and the center also has groomed sledding lanes (but you can't bring your own equipment). Nearby, Boreal ski resort offers groomed sledding lanes (plastic saucer provided) at **Boreal's Playland Park** (19455 Boreal Ridge Rd., Soda Springs, 530/426-3666, www.borealski.com or www rideboreal.com). **Soda Springs** ski resort (Old Hwy. 40/Donner Pass Rd., Norden, 530/426-3901, www.skisodasprings.com) offers almost identical activities, plus for the wee tubers, there's the Little Dipper and the tube carousel for slower-paced (and less-scary) snow tubing. Open 11 A.M.–4 P.M. daily, both resorts charge about $15 for sledding and tubing.

On the West Shore, **Granlibakken Resort** (625 Granlibakken Rd., Tahoe City, 530/583-4242 or 800/543-3221, www.granlibakken. com) has a saucer hill; the cost is a mere $5 per person. No sleds or tubes are allowed, but you can bring your own saucer or rent one of theirs.

The monolithic ski resorts are in on the tubing action, too. **Squaw Valley USA** (1960 Squaw Valley Rd., Olympic Valley, 530/583-6955, www.squaw.com) has snow tubing at High Camp (but you'll have to pay for a cable car ride to get up there). **Northstar-at-Tahoe** has snow tubing lanes at mid-mountain. Rates are $17 for the first hour and $9 per hour thereafter.

The locals' favorite is the family snow play area at **North Tahoe Regional Park** (at the end of National Ave., Tahoe Vista, 530/546-0605 or 530/546-4212). For only $5 per person, families can play in the snow all day (saucers, tubes, or sleds provided; you can't bring your own equipment). The park also has a snack bar, bonfire pit, heated restrooms, and picnic area, plus panoramic lake views. Or bring your own equipment to the **Tahoe City Snow Play Area,** just a few hundred feet south of the Tahoe City Y, and the sledding is free.

Snowmobiling

Because of the proximity of miles of Tahoe National Forest lands, snowmobiling opportuni-ties abound on the North and West Shores. For those who have their own machines, two popular snowmobile trailheads are at Brockway Summit on Highway 267 (three miles north of Kings Beach) and Little Truckee Summit on Highway 89 (16 miles north of the I-80/Hwy. 89 junction in Truckee). Contact the Forest Service (530/994-3401) for more information. On the West Shore, three miles south of Tahoe City, **Blackwood Canyon Sno-Park** (530/543-2600) is also open for snowmobiling.

If you want to head out on your own but don't have your own snowmobile, rent one at **The Ski Barn** (8445 N. Lake Blvd., Kings Beach, 530/546-8774, www.skibarnbeach-barn.com, $250 for a half day, $325 for a full day). Rentals include a trailer, helmet, and first tank of gas. If your vehicle can't pull a trailer, the folks at The Ski Barn will tow your machine to a local trailhead for you.

Beginners and others who would like to take a snowmobile tour have several options. **Lake Tahoe Snowmobile Tours** (530/546-4280, www.laketahoesnowmobile.com, $80–110 for one person on a single-rider machine, $100–130 for two on a double-rider machine) operates from their base camp one mile south of North-star-at-Tahoe off Highway 267. They offer a 90-minute lake view tour and a two-hour summit tour several times daily, plus private tours by special arrangement. Helmets are included; snowsuits and boots can be rented for a small fee. Advance reservations are recommended.

Several other companies offer similar snowmobile tours on the North Shore. Typical rates for a two-hour tour are $100 for a single rider or $140 for two riders on a double machine. In Tahoe City, **T. C. Sno Mo's** (at Tahoe City Golf Course, 251 N. Lake Blvd., Tahoe City, 530/581-3906, www.snowmobilelaketahoe .com) offers a standard two-hour tour with spectacular lake views. **Eagle Ridge Snowmobile Outfitters** (530/546-8667, www.tahoesnowmobiling.com), operates on Tahoe National Forest land 14 miles north of Truckee. The company has 200 miles of groomed trails for beginners, and cross-country riding on untracked powder for more advanced riders. Tours are available of various lengths from two hours to two days. Moonlight rides are also available. **Snowmobiling Unlimited** (530/583-7192, www.snowmobilingunlimited.com) and **Coldstream Adventures** (530/582-9090, www.coldstreamadventures.com) also provide snowmobile tours in Tahoe National Forest. Those who don't want to sign up for an organized tour but would still like to experience the cheap thrill of revving up a snowmobile can head for North Lake Tahoe Regional Park in Tahoe Vista, where **Tahoe Snowmobile Adventures** (530/546-0605) will rent you a machine you can drive around their groomed track ($70 for one hour, $40 for 30 minutes).

Ice-Skating

For the graceful, several skating rinks operate around the North Shore. In the Squaw Valley area, the outdoor **Olympic Ice Pavilion** (1960 Squaw Valley Rd., Olympic Valley, 530/581-7246 or 530/583-6955, www.squaw.com, 11 A.M.–9 P.M. daily) has skating year-round

at its Olympic-sized rink (100 by 200 feet), but you must pay to ride the cable car to High Camp to skate there. The twilight "Cheap Skate" (after 5 P.M.) is the best bargain. Rates are $15–24 for adults and $12–20 for children and seniors 65 and over for a cable-car ride, two-hour skating session, and skate rental.

Down in the valley below, the **Resort at Squaw Creek** (400 Squaw Creek Rd., Squaw Valley, 530/581-6624 or 800/327-3353, www.squawcreek.com) has its own ice-skating rink, but it is sized more for beginning skaters and children. Mom and Dad can watch the action from a large sunny deck by the rink. Rates are $15 for adults and $10 for children 12 and under (including skate rental).

Northstar-at-Tahoe (Hwy. 267 and Northstar Dr., Truckee, 530/562-3689, www.skinorthstar.com) has a 9,000-square-foot ice rink at the Village at Northstar, complete with outdoor fire pits and a s'mores kiosk. Open daily 12–8 P.M.; skate rentals are $5 and skating is free. If you don't know how to skate, lessons are available.

© ANN MARIE BROWN

Open year-round, the outdoor ice-skating rink at Squaw Valley is a fun diversion for kids of all ages.

◖ Sleigh Rides

There's nothing like dashing through the snow in a horse-drawn open sleigh to make you feel like winter is the greatest season of them all. Snuggle up with your sweetie under a warm woolen blanket while Trigger and his friends, or Rover and her friends, trot through the white stuff. Watching the animals at work is as much fun as enjoying the scenery; the horses and dogs seem to enjoy the trip as much as their human passengers. Horse-drawn sleigh rides and/or dogsled tours are available at Squaw Valley/Squaw Creek, Sugar Bowl, and Truckee.

At Squaw Creek Resort, **Verdi Trails** (530/583-6300 or 800/327-3353, www.squawcreek.com, $20–25 per person) provides sleigh rides 11 A.M.–5 P.M. daily in winter.

If you'd rather have your sleigh pulled by a group of strong and friendly huskies, contact **Wilderness Adventures** (530/550-8133 or 800/468-2463, www.tahoedogsledtours. com). Their dogsleds can accommodate two adults and two children with a maximum weight of 500 pounds per sled. If you have more people in your party, the company can run two or more sleds simultaneously. One-hour tours are offered daily at the Resort at Squaw Creek and Sugar Bowl, weather permitting. Cost is $95 per person weighing more than 60 pounds; $45 for children weighing less than 60 pounds. Two other companies also provide dogsled tours, ranging from 45 minutes to a half day: Coldstream Adventures (530/582-9090, www .coldstreamadventures.com) and Sierra Sled Dog Adventures (530/412-3302, www .sierrasleddogadventures.com).

Entertainment and Shopping

NIGHTLIFE

Since the North and West Shores are on the California side of the lake, gambling casinos are nonexistent in this area. But there's still plenty of nightlife to be found. In Truckee, live music happens almost every night at the ultrahip **Moody's Bistro** (10007 Bridge St., 530/587-8688, www.moodysbistro.com). Even ex-Beatle Paul McCartney has shown up here and sung a few bars. Live music, lots of beer, and a dance floor are found a block away at the **Bar of America** (10042 Donner Pass Rd., 530/587-3110). More sedate nightlife happens at Truckee's **Cottonwood Restaurant** (10142 Rue Hilltop at Brockway Rd., 530/587-5711, www.cottonwoodrestaurant.com). Live acoustic music is usually featured on weekend nights.

At Squaw Valley, the après-ski action is at **Bar One** (530/583-1558), upstairs in the Olympic House, with live music on Friday and Saturday nights. And in downtown Tahoe City, the young and restless flock to **Pierce Street Annex** (850 N. Lake Blvd., 530/583-

5800, www.piercestreet.com), a saloon-style bar where you can dance to the DJ's driving music, watch sports on large-screen TVs, or play pool or foosball. If none of that appeals, you can always do what many people do here—just sit on a bar stool and drink yourself silly.

And if your idea of nightlife is snuggling up with your sweetie and a bag of popcorn at the **movie theater,** there are three on the North Shore: Brockway Theatre (8707 N. Lake Blvd., Kings Beach, 530/546-5951), Cobblestone Cinema (465 N. Lake Blvd., Tahoe City, 530/546-5951), and Opera House Cinema (1725 Squaw Valley Loop, Olympic Valley, 530/546-5951).

SHOPPING

A few good shopping options are found in Tahoe City. The **Boatworks Mall** (760 N. Lake Blvd.) has a dozen specialty shops and two good restaurants, Jake's on the Lake and Sierra Vista. **Cobblestone Center** (475 N. Lake Blvd., www.cobblestonetahoe.com), a

TAHOE IN THE MOVIES

Since the 1920s, more than 50 movies have been filmed along the shores of Lake Tahoe. The mountain scenery, glitzy casinos, and cobalt waters of the lake just seem to lend themselves to the Hollywood imagination.

Probably the most famous of the films shot on location at Tahoe were the early 1970s *Godfather* and *Godfather II,* the saga of the immigrant Corleone family's life in crime. While the first film was shot partly in Stateline and Crystal Bay, the West Shore was used as the location for the second *Godfather,* in particular the timber-and-stone lakeside estate known as *Fleur du Lac* near Tahoe Pines, which once belonged to the cement magnate Henry Kaiser. The first film won an Academy Award for Best Picture (1973). Director Francis Ford Coppola as well as actors Marlon Brando and James Caan also won Oscars. The second *Godfather* again won Best Picture (1975), and Coppola again won Best Director. Robert DeNiro was awarded an Oscar for Best Supporting Actor. Many fans insist that Al Pacino was the real star of the film, however. He was nominated for an award, but didn't win.

Another Academy Award winner filmed near Lake Tahoe was the 1990 thriller *Misery,* in which Kathy Bates won Best Actress for her role as a psychotic fan who rescues a romance novelist (James Caan again) from a car crash in a freezing blizzard. The movie was filmed near Donner Pass, a place where there is usually a good supply of freezing blizzards. However, it didn't snow when the movie crew was there, so they had to make snow to film the scene.

Some movies go down in history as classics, but many more don't, and that is certainly the case for a slew of other filmed-at-Tahoe movies, like the forgettable Chuck Norris film *Good Guys Wear Black* (1978), which was filmed on the South Shore and at Squaw Valley; or the hysterically campy (but not intentionally so) *Showgirls* (1995), filmed at Horizon Casino. Sometimes it's the actors who wish they could forget the film, and that is probably the case for Kevin Costner in *The Bodyguard* (1992), a sappy love story that also starred Whitney Houston. Parts of the movie were filmed at Fallen Leaf Lake.

Bavarian-style shopping village in the center of town, has a variety of unique retail shops situated below its quaint clock tower. Cap off a day of shopping with dinner in one of the local restaurants or a movie at the Cobblestone Cinema.

Over at Squaw Valley, dozens of shops and restaurants are found at **The Village at Squaw Valley** (877/297-2140, www.thevillageatsquaw.com). All the things you don't need but you really want can be found here, at shops like Rocky Mountain Chocolate Factory, Waxen Moon (a candle shop), Splash Bath and Body, Black Diamond Wine Exchange, and Squaw Valley Clothing Company. Several restaurants and cafes round out the offerings, and if you are feeling a bit worn down from all the shopping, an espresso at Starbucks will perk you right up.

Shopping in **Truckee's Commercial Row** (530/587-2757, www.historictruckee.com) is fun even for those who don't like to shop. The historic Victorian-era buildings on Truckee's main street are fascinating to see, and the row is lined with restaurants, bars, and art galleries as well as upscale, unique shops. For the hardcore shopper looking for serious bargains, there's the **Tahoe Truckee Factory Outlet Stores** (12047 Donner Pass Rd., Truckee) near the I-80 Donner Lake exit.

FESTIVALS AND EVENTS

Summer is festival season around Lake Tahoe, with special events happening almost every weekend. On the North Shore, the event season begins with the **Lake Tahoe Jazz Festival** (www.laketahoejazzfestival.com, $22–60) in mid- to late May, featuring more than 20 bands, a parade, a gospel breakfast, and lots more. Concerts take place in Kings Beach, Crystal Bay, and Incline Village. An even bigger musical event is the **Lake Tahoe Summer Music Festival** (530/583-3101, www.tahoemusic.org, $25–40), with concerts happening at Squaw Valley and various other North Shore locations over a period of weeks in late July and early August. The festival celebrates wide-ranging music genres from classical to blues.

If you are more into boats than Bach, you won't want to miss **Wooden Boat Week** (530/581-4700, www.tahoeyc.com, free) in Carnelian Bay, usually held in early August at the Tahoe Yacht Club and Sierra Boat Company.

Squaw Valley and its shopping village (www.thevillageatsquaw.com) find a litany of excuses to hold summer events each year. The Celtic Solstice Celebration takes place in June, followed by a big Fourth of July celebration, followed by the late July Squaw Valley Art, Wine, and Music Festival. Somewhere in the middle of summer they usually throw in a kite festival and a blues festival, too.

While summer festivals at Lake Tahoe tend to be about art, music, and culture, the winter **Snow Festival** is all about making merry. North Tahoe's Snow Festival, usually held in March, includes a lot of silliness—grown-ups racing on tricycles, a "polar bear" swimming race in Lake Tahoe, and lots of people wearing funny hats. For information about this fun, free, 10-day event, visit www.tahoesnowfestival.com.

FAMILY FUN

Squaw Valley USA may be the exclusive domain of skiers and riders in winter, but in the summer months, it becomes Familyville. The resort offers a multitude of activities that appeal to kids, from ice-skating and swimming at High Camp Bath and Tennis Club to ropes course at the **Squaw Valley Adventure Center** (530/386-1375 or 530/583-7673, www.climbing walls). A 30-footer indoors and a 45-footer outdoors attract kids of all ages (including adults). This is basically rock climbing in an artificial, gym-type environ-

ment, with the climbers on belay. An all-day pass is $14 per person. The ropes course consists of a mammoth-sized jungle gym that is built on and around 50-foot-high towers. A session on the course is $42 for kids ages 7–12 or $48 adults. As if that isn't enough to give Mom a heart attack, there's the Sky-jump Bungee Trampoline, where kids can do somersaults and flips while hanging tethered in midair. The cost is $10 for a five-minute session.

For a tamer activity that measures zero on the adrenaline level, you can always take the kids to play a round of miniature golf. On the North Shore, two pee-wee golf courses are open from Easter to Thanksgiving, weather permitting: **Boberg's Lake Tahoe Mini Golf** (8693 N. Lake Blvd., Kings Beach, 530/546-3196) and **Magic Carpet Golf** (5167 N. Lake Blvd., Carnelian Bay, 530/546-4279). Rates average $5–8 per person for a round of minigolf. Magic Carpet Golf also has a video arcade where kids can play all the latest games.

If you are looking for a place to take the kids to get their ya-yas out without having to visit the local automated teller machine, try **Commons Beach** (at Fanny Bridge and the Tahoe City Y) in Tahoe City, where a playground area includes a miniboulder for junior "rock climbers" ages six and older, plus swings and other playground equipment for kids of all ages.

For something more educational, children are sure to enjoy the **Sierra Nevada Children's Museum** (11400 Donner Pass Rd., Truckee, 530/587-5437, 10 A.M.–4 P.M. Wed.–Sat.), which has hands-on educational exhibits designed for the young ones, plus an art center and computer corner.

In winter, don't forget to spend a few hours on one of the local sledding or tubing hills with the kids, or take them on a horse-drawn carriage ride or a dogsled ride. And for a summertime family-bonding activity, be sure to rent a raft in Tahoe City and float lazily down the Truckee River, or take the whole family on a bike ride on the paved Truckee River Recreation Trail.

Accommodations

TAHOE CITY
Bed-and-Breakfasts

One of the most unusual B&Bs in North Tahoe is the four-room **Chaney House** (4725 W. Lake Blvd., Tahoe City, 530/525-7333, www.chaneyhouse.com, $155–245), which was built in the 1920s by an Italian stonemason. The lakefront home of Gary and Lori Chaney, this minicastle has 18-inch-thick stone walls, gothic arches, and many other Old World touches. If you want maximum privacy, reserve the Honeymoon Hideaway, the only room that is completely separate from the main house.

All guests at the **Mayfield House** (236 Grove St., Tahoe City, 530/583-1001 or 888/518-8898, www.mayfieldhouse.com, $150–290) are treated to a goody basket, turndown service, a hearty breakfast, afternoon tea, and all-around superb hospitality. The inn's downtown location makes it ideal for those who want to enjoy Lake Tahoe's "city" amenities (great restaurants, shopping, and galleries), which are located just a short walk away. Although the structure was built in 1932, all the modern conveniences are available in the six guest rooms, including wireless Internet.

Condominium-style Resorts

If you want to pretend you own a condo on the lakeshore in Tahoe City, book a stay at the **Tahoe Marina Lodge** (270 N. Lake Blvd., Tahoe City, 530/583-2365 or 800/748-5650, www.tahoeml.com). Located within a stone's throw of the Tahoe City Y, the complex has one- and two-bedroom condominiums for rent. Everything in Tahoe City is within walking distance, and the complex has its own tennis courts, heated pool, and sandy Tahoe beach. The units are completely furnished with everything you would need for a multiple-night stay, so all you need to bring are your clothes. One-bedroom units can sleep four and are $140–230 per night. Two-bedroom units can sleep six and are $175–315 (the lakefront condos are the priciest).

Motels and Lodges

The 19 river-view rooms at the **《 River Ranch Lodge** (Alpine Meadows Rd. at Hwy. 89, Tahoe City, 530/583-4264 or 800/535-9900, www.riverranchlodge.com, $70–170) are hard to come by but worth every penny. Located just three miles outside Tahoe City and on the road to Alpine Meadows ski area, the River Ranch Lodge exudes an "old Tahoe" feel that you won't find at any in-town lodgings. Most rooms have one king bed furnished with a down comforter or quilt. Some rooms have private balconies that overlook the river. Be sure to eat a few meals at the lodge's restaurant, and in summer, get a table outside on the river-view deck. Rates are generous and include a continental breakfast each morning. An additional bonus: Well-behaved dogs are allowed in some rooms in the summer months if you make prior arrangements.

The **Pepper Tree Inn** (645 N. Lake Blvd., Tahoe City, 530/583-3711 or 800/624-8580, www.peppertreetahoe.com, $69–199) has one big advantage over all the other downtown motels in Tahoe City: It's seven stories high. So even though it's across the busy highway from the lake, the third story and higher rooms have wonderful lake views. The motel was completely renovated in 2003, so you won't find any 1950s decor here. Each room comes with a king or two queen beds and has a microwave, small refrigerator, television, and coffeemaker with a bean grinder. You don't have to drink your freshly ground coffee out of Styrofoam cups, either; each guest is provided with a ceramic mug. If you can afford it, book one of the tower suites, which have whirlpool tubs for two.

Everything is about what you'd expect from a mid-scale chain motel at the **Tahoe City Travelodge** (455 N. Lake Blvd., Tahoe City, 530/583-3766 or 800/578-7878, www.tahoecitytravelodge.com), except for the price. Located right next to the Tahoe City Golf Course and right across the street from Commons

Beach, this Travelodge has an ideal downtown location, but even in the peak of the high season, king-bed rooms are still only $135–169. During the fall and spring rates drop as low as $75–100. A continental breakfast is included in the price, and all guests are given a 10 percent discount card that is good at most local restaurants.

The 23 rooms at the **Lake of the Sky Motor Inn** (955 N. Lake Blvd., Tahoe City, 530/583-3305, www.lakeoftheskyinn.com, $69–149) have either a forest view or a parking-lot view, so make sure you ask for the best view you can afford. This single-story motel supplies the basics—complimentary continental breakfast, large heated pool—and the rooms have airy, vaulted beam ceilings and nice furnishings. Rooms have one king bed or two queen beds.

The two-story **Tahoe City Inn** (790 N. Lake Blvd., Tahoe City, 530/581-3333 or 800/800-8246, www.tahoecityinn.com, $49–199) offers a choice of room types: deluxe spa rooms with one king bed or two double beds, family suites that will sleep up to six people in two separate bedrooms, and standard rooms, which are, well, standard. Romantics will like the heart-shaped spa in the king-bed rooms. Room rates vary widely depending on the season and day of the week, so phone ahead and work the best angle you can.

If you book a stay at **Tamarack Lodge** (2311 N. Lake Blvd., Tahoe City, 530/583-3350 or 888/824-6323, www.tamarackat-tahoe.com), make sure you ask for a room away from busy North Lake Boulevard. This wonderful old-style lodge is located a short distance east of Tahoe City, freeing it from the bustle of downtown, but it's also a bit close to the highway. Get a quiet room here and everything about your stay will be great. Most rooms are lined with knotty pine and have queen beds; some rooms have two queen beds and/or kitchens. Three cabins are also available. Even on holidays, rates for two people are usually well under $100, which is why legions of Tahoe travelers return to this place year after year.

Campgrounds and RV Parks

Tahoe State Recreation Area (530/583-3074, www.parks.ca.gov, $25) is set in the middle of Tahoe City and has 34 sites for tents or RVs up to 24 feet long and all the critical campground amenities: water, flush toilets, showers. But what really matters is its beachside location, just a few steps from Tahoe's blue waters. And a bonus: If you get tired of grilling your own hamburgers, you can take a short walk and eat at McDonald's. The campground also has its own fishing and boating pier. Given their lakeside location, these sites are coveted, so reserve way in advance at 800/444-7275 or www.reserveusa.com.

Just down the road apiece, the Tahoe City Public Utility District runs **Lake Forest Campground** (two miles east of Tahoe City at Hwy. 28 and Lake Forest Rd., 530/583-3796, $15), which enjoys a peaceful location outside town plus 20 tent or RV sites, a boat ramp, and public fishing access. No reservations are accepted; it's first-come, first-served.

Between two and four miles south of Tahoe City are two Forest Service run campgrounds (Lake Tahoe Basin Management Unit, 530/583-3642, $15–16), **William Kent** and **Kaspian**. William Kent is a 91-site camp that can accommodate RVs up to 40 feet long. Kaspian is a tiny 10-site camp that is better suited for tents. Unfortunately, both are right next to Highway 89, but that also gives campers easy lake access (right across the road). Reserve in advance at 877/444-6777 or www.reserveusa.com.

TAHOE VISTA AND KINGS BEACH
Bed-and-Breakfasts
If you must have lakefront lodging, stay at the **Shore House** (7170 N. Lake Blvd., Tahoe Vista, 530/546-7270 or 800/207-5160, www.shorehouselaketahoe.com, $180–315), which unlike a traditional bed-and-breakfast has guest rooms with private outdoor entrances—more in the style of a motel or lodge. Most of the inn's nine rooms have fabulous lake views, decks or balconies, gas fireplaces, private bathrooms,

and featherbeds. The exterior gardens and hot-tub area adjoin a sandy beach and pier on Carnelian Bay. This B&B is famous for its gourmet breakfasts cooked by the innkeeper, an award-winning chef. In summer, the food is served alfresco on the lawn next to the lakeshore.

There are only a handful of bed-and-breakfasts in the North Shore area, but **Shooting Star** (9315 Olive St., Carnelian Bay, 888/985-7827, www.shootingstarbandb.com, $225–250) takes up the slack in fine style. From the front door of this contemporary home, you can stroll to the lake or drive a few short miles for skiing or snowboarding. Three rooms are available for rent, one with a king bed and two with queens. Everything is done with an emphasis on quality: down comforters, lavish bathrooms, and a gourmet breakfast. Many people who stay here come back again.

Cabins

When the owners of a cabin resort are thoughtful enough to set out cookies and iced tea for their guests in the evening, you can bet it's a nice place. **Rustic Cottages** (7449 N. Lake Blvd., Tahoe Vista, 530/546-3523 or 888/778-7842, www.rusticcottages.com, $69–199 for a cottage) is a delightful place, with adorable cottages that were built in 1925 as the labor camp for the Brockway Lumber Company. Each of the cottages is different; some have kitchens or fireplaces or both. The place is popular for family reunions and small groups, but it's equally nice for couples. Cottages sleep two to six people.

The same nice folks run **Tahoe Vista Lodge and Cabins** about a mile away (6631 N. Lake Blvd., Tahoe Vista, 530/546-3523 or 888/778-7842, www.rusticcottages.com), which was known as the Burrough's Resort when it was first opened in the 1940s. The current owners saved the resort from demolition in 2002 and completed restored it to its original grandeur. In addition to cabins, Tahoe Vista also has rooms in a main lodge, suites, and duplexes. Cabins are $79–159 for two to five people, suites and lodge rooms are $119–139.

For lakefront accommodations, book a cottage at the **Franciscan Lakeside Lodge** (6944 N. Lake Blvd., Tahoe Vista, 530/546-6300 or 800/564-6754, www.franciscanlodge.com). Perched a few feet from the lapping waters of Lake Tahoe, this cute red-roofed cottage resort has everything you want for a summer vacation—most importantly sun, sand, and water. One rule is strictly enforced: Don't feed the Canadian geese who flock to the beach (or they might follow you back home to Poughkeepsie). Small cottages for two go for $60–120, larger units for four are $100–175. Lakefront units cost more than the rest, of course.

Condominium-style Resorts

If you want to stay in a condo that is as appealing in summer as it is in winter, **Brockway Springs Resort** (101 Chipmunk St., Kings Beach, 530/546-4201, www.brockway-tahoe .com, one-bedroom unit $116–199) has the ideal all-season location. It's right on the lake in Kings Beach, and the resort owns a full half mile of shoreline. The year-round swimming pool is heated by natural hot springs. Brockway Springs has tons of amenities: tennis courts, saunas, clubhouse, boat dock, and more. The condos and town houses come in configurations from one to four bedrooms, so you can bring your aunts and uncles. All units are completely furnished with everything you'd expect: fully equipped kitchens, televisions and VCRs, patio furniture, and barbecues. Most units have fireplaces. Brockway Springs brags of having the best lakefront prices on the North Shore, and it may be true. The price goes down if you stay for more than two nights.

The same company that runs the attractive Red Wolf Lodge at Squaw Valley also manages **Red Wolf Lakeside Lodge** (7630 N. Lake Blvd., Tahoe Vista, 877/477-736, www. redwolflakesidelodge.com). The lodge-like condominiums come in studio and one- and two-bedroom configurations, each with a private patio or balcony, Jacuzzi tub, fireplace, and fully equipped kitchen. Each unit is decorated in an upscale mountain style. The front desk has kayaks, sleds, snowshoes, and the like available for loan at no extra charge. Perhaps best of all, because Red Wolf is located on the lake side of the highway, the condos offer great sunset views over the water. Studios run $150–250 per night; larger units are $195–325.

Motels and Lodges

Located across the highway from the lake, the **Firelite Lodge** (7035 N. Lake Blvd., Tahoe Vista, 530/546-7222 or 800/934-7222, www .tahoelodge.com, $56–128) is a clean and affordable choice for lodging. The motel has all the usual amenities— heated pool and spa, guest laundry, free continental breakfast—and its rooms are equipped with microwaves, refrigerators, coffeemakers, and a choice of bed configurations: one or two queens or doubles or one king. A few units have lake views and/or fireplaces, and those are your best bet.

If you can get past the blinking neon crown out front, the **Crown Motel** (8200 N. Lake Blvd., Kings Beach, 530/546-3388 or 800/645-2260, www.tahoecrown.com, $69–199) is a good bet for a North Tahoe summer vacation. The 1950s-style motel has location, location, location— as in right on the lakeshore in Kings Beach. Some rooms have lake views, kitchenettes, spas, or gas fireplaces; the most expensive rooms are lakefront, meaning right on the water. A family-oriented place, the motel's swimming pool is always busy on summer days, as is their stretch of private beach. The owners also own the neighboring **Gold Crest Resort** (8194 N. Lake Blvd., 530/546-3388 or 800/645-2260, $69–199), a similar lakefront property. In winter, ski packages are a great bargain.

If you don't mind paying a higher tariff, excellent lakefront accommodations are also available at **Mourelatos Lakeshore Resort** (6834 N. Lake Blvd., Tahoe Vista, 530/546-9500 or 800/824-6381, www.mourelatosresort.com), a small motel-style lodge that sits right on the Tahoe sand. Studios and suites are either lake view or lakefront, and you can guess which costs more. Units with full kitchens are $215–345; units with wet bars only are $159–215.

Campgrounds and RV Parks

Two private RV parks on the North Shore are popular with the fifth-wheel crowd: **Sandy Beach** (6873 N. Lake Blvd., Tahoe Vista, 530/546-7682) and **Blue Waters** (221 Chipmunk, Kings Beach, 530/546-7884). Both provide full hookups, a dump station, restrooms, showers, and swimming. Sites are $20–29. Both parks are open in summer only.

WEST SHORE
Bed-and-Breakfasts

An ever reliable bet for West Shore lodging, **Tahoma Meadows Bed and Breakfast** (6821 W. Lake Blvd., Tahoma, 530/525-1553 or 866/525-1553, www.tahomameadows.com, $95–250) gets plenty of repeat business from satisfied customers who enjoy its 15 cottages and common breakfast room. This place offers all the comforts of a traditional B&B, including evening snacks and a full, hearty breakfast in the morning, but because the guest rooms are individual cottages, you have more privacy. For dinner, the Stony Ridge Cafe is located right next door. A few cottages are dog-friendly; request one in advance if you want to bring your four-legged friend. A few larger "family cottages" have kitchens; those go for $145–350 and you have to make your own breakfast.

If you prefer a more traditional B&B in which guests share the owner's home, the **Rockwood Lodge Bed and Breakfast** (5295 W. Lake Blvd., Homewood, 530/525-5273 or 800/538-2463, www.rockwoodlodge.com, $125–200) fits the bill. This is the kind of "old Tahoe" home we all wish we owned, built of native stone, hand-hewn beams, and knotty pine. The inn has five rooms, all with queen beds, down comforters, and sitting areas. Breakfast is served outside on the patio in summer. On winter evenings, you'll want to hang out by the huge fireplace.

Condominium-style Resorts

You don't have to host a corporate meeting or a huge wedding party to book a stay at **Granlibakken Resort and Conference Center** (625 Granlibakken Rd., Tahoe City, 877/552-6301 or 800/543-3221, www.granlibakken.com, $122–256), although that's how most people get introduced to the place. The resort also welcomes families, couples, and single travelers with condo-style studios, suites, and one- to five-bedroom town houses. Certain features come standard with every visit, like Granlibakken's well-loved hot breakfast buffet, so you won't have to flip pancakes and fry eggs on your vacation. Some units have kitchens, fireplaces, decks, and/or separate dining areas. The complex has a heated outdoor pool, hot tub, and tennis courts. Rates are for two people, but many visitors take advantage of stay-and-ski packages with lift passes for Homewood and other ski resorts (Homewood is just a few miles away). You can cross-country ski or snowshoe right from the property.

Cabins
The woodsy ◖ **Cottage Inn** (1690 W. Lake Blvd., Tahoe City, 530/581-4073 or 800/581-4073, www.thecottageinn.com, $150–330) is downright adorable. The moment you drive in your eyes glimpse immaculate, storybook gardens and cozy wood cottages with bear-clad exteriors. Bear-clad? That's right. Wooden bears carved by Jonathan "the Bear Man" of Wyoming are all over this place—hanging from the rafters, peeking in the windows, and clinging to the walls. The original 1938 cottage buildings were completely remodeled in the 1990s, with new knotty-pine interiors that have been decorated with great care. Pick your theme—fishing, hunting, skiing, sailing, and so on—and the Cottage Inn probably has a room or suite to match. The price tag comes with a lot of extras (in addition to the hand-carved bears): private beach access, a sauna, free ski shuttles, a full breakfast, fresh baked cookies, and afternoon wine and cheese.

For summer vacationers who want to be right on the beach, **Meeks Bay Resort** (7941 Emerald Bay Rd./Hwy. 89, Meeks Bay, 530/525-6946 or 877/326-3357, www.meeksbayresort.com, May–Oct., $109–199) has some world-class real estate along a sandy stretch of calm and shallow Meeks Bay. Owned and operated by the Washoe Tribe, the resort has a variety

of accommodations from log cabins to motel rooms to a grand rental "mansion," but they all have one thing in common: a location just a few steps from the lakeshore. The resort also has a marina on-site with water-sport rentals (kayaks, canoes, paddleboats, and the like), or you can bring your own boat and dock it here. Rooms cost less than cabins.

Dog-owners rejoice: Fido and Spot are permitted in the cabins at **Tahoma Lodge** (7018 W. Lake Blvd., Tahoma, 530/525-7721 or 866/819-2226, www.tahomalodge.com, $70–225). The 1940s-era cabins are nothing fancy, but they provide all the vacation basics: kitchens, private baths, fireplaces or woodstoves, and cable television. As the owners describe it, this is a "jeans-and-sneakers" kind of place. Cabins can accommodate two to five people.

Motels and Lodges
For lakefront accommodations on the West Shore, you won't do any better than ◖ **Sunnyside Lodge** (1850 W. Lake Blvd., 530/583-7200 or 800/822-2754, www.sunnysidetahoe.com, $100–295). Just two miles south of Tahoe City, but far enough from the hustle and bustle, Sunnyside's 23 lakeside rooms are perfectly suited for a night of romance. Some rooms have river rock fireplaces; others have wet bars. All are decorated in an elegant mountain-lodge style. Guests enjoy a gourmet-style continental breakfast in the morning (the pastries are baked fresh daily by their in-house chef, not wrapped in plastic and shipped from a factory in Des Moines) and afternoon snacks 3–5 P.M. Basically, this is a bed-and-breakfast disguised as a lodge. For dinner, guests don't have to travel far; the wonderful Sunnyside Restaurant is on the property. Rates depend on the season and day of the week. Discounted midweek ski packages are available in winter.

Like most places on the North Shore, the **Norfolk Woods Inn** (6941 W. Lake Blvd., Tahoma, 530/525-5000, www.norfolkwoods.com, $110–230) is pleasantly low-key. It's a cross between an old Tahoe lodge, a bed-and-breakfast, and a cabin resort, but whatever category you put it in, it's a pleasant place to stay. The three-story lodge has nine rooms and suites on the second and third floor and a restaurant on the first floor. A full breakfast is included with a stay in the lodge rooms. A handful of cabins, large enough for families and with full kitchens, are located behind the main lodge, as is the darling Amy's Cottage, a honeymoon cabin that was built in the early 1900s. Bed-and-breakfast rooms cost less than cabins.

Campgrounds and RV Parks

One of the few campgrounds around the lake that is open for year-round camping, **General Creek Campground at Sugar Pine Point State Park** (530/525-7982, www.parks.ca.gov, $25) is located 10 miles south of Tahoe City off Highway 89 in Tahoma. The camp has 175 sites for tents, trailers up to 24 feet, and RVs up to 30 feet, as well as restrooms with flush toilets, showers, and a dump station. There are also 10 group sites that can accommodate up to 40 people each. In winter, you can cross-country ski right from your tent, and in summer, you can hike or mountain bike through hundreds of acres of conifer forest, or swim at the beach by the park's historic Ehrman Mansion. General Creek flows near the camp and is open to fishing mid-July–mid-September. Reserve sites in advance at 800/444-7275 or www.reserveamerica.com.

Just a mile south of Sugar Pine Point State Park is the privately operated campground at **Meeks Bay Resort** (7941 W. Lake Blvd., Tahoma, 530/525-6946 or 877/326-3357, $25–30) and the Forest Service–run **Meeks Bay Campground** (530/583-3642, $17), both on the lake side of the highway. Beach-lovers will be happy at either one. Meeks Bay Resort's camp has 28 sites for tents or RVs up to 60 feet long and all the developed resort amenities: showers, flush toilets, full hookups, general store, and marina. The Forest Service's Meeks Bay Campground has 40 sites suitable for tents or small RVs (20 feet or less). Flush toilets are the only amenity besides a wonderful stretch of Meeks Bay shoreline, complete with

a boat ramp. Reserve in advance at 877/444-6777 or www.reserveusa.com.

Six miles farther south toward Emerald Bay, **D. L. Bliss State Park** (530/525-7277, www.parks.ca.gov, $25–35) has 168 campsites on the lake side of the highway. Most are tent sites, but small RVs or trailers up to 18 feet are welcome (there are no hookups). The camp has restrooms with flush toilets and showers. The main activities here are swimming in Lake Tahoe, hanging out at the park's beautiful beaches, and hiking the Rubicon Trail, which begins a short distance from camp. Reserve sites in advance at 800/444-7275 or www.reserveamerica.com.

TRUCKEE AND SQUAW VALLEY
Bed-and-Breakfasts

Built in 1885 in the heart of downtown Truckee, the **River Street Inn** (10009 E. River St., Truckee, 530/550-9290, www.riverstreetinntruckee.com, $100–160) is steeped in history. In its multiple past lives, it has served as a jail, a restaurant, a boarding house for workers in the ice-harvesting business, and a bordello. Restored and remodeled in 1999, the inn is now a cozy B&B with 11 guest rooms, each with a private bath, color television, VCR, and a comforter-covered queen bed. Rates include a continental-style breakfast.

Perched high above Truckee's historic district, **Richardson House** (10154 High St., Truckee, 530/587-5388 or 888/229-0365, www.richardsonhouse.com, $100–175, $200 for a two-room suite) is only one block from Commercial Row but has a top-of-the-world feel to it. This historic 1880s Victorian has been completely restored and offers eight guest rooms, six with private baths. A breakfast buffet is served in the dining room each morning, and snacks are available 24 hours a day.

Condominium-style Resorts

If you are coming to play at Squaw Valley, stay at the European-style **Olympic Village Inn** (1909 Chamonix Pl., Olympic Valley, 530/581-6000 or 800/845-5243, www.olympicvillageinn.com,

NORTH AND WEST SHORES

© ANN MARIE BROWN

Skiers and riders take a break from the slopes at The Village at Squaw Valley.

$189–329 in winter, $119–179 rest of year). The Tyrolean-esque structure is lovely to look at, inside and out, and offers 90 luxurious suites for the discriminating traveler (or for nondiscriminating travelers with sizable bank accounts). Most rooms have balconies with mountain views; some have fireplaces. All rooms include custom furnishings, well-equipped minikitchens, color televisions, down comforters, plush terry robes, morning newspapers, overnight ski check—you get the idea. After wearing yourself out skiing all day, you can soak in one of five outdoor hot tubs, or swim in the year-round heated outdoor pool. Holiday weekends are more expensive.

Another excellent lodging option at Squaw Valley is the **Squaw Valley Lodge** (201 Squaw Peak Rd., Olympic Valley, 530/583-5500 or 800/549-6742, www.squawvalleylodge.com), which is equally as upscale as the Olympic Village Inn, but less subtle about it. The lodge has a concierge, health club, sauna, and three spas, and its guest suites come in sizes from studios (560 square feet) to three bedrooms

(1,700 square feet). Each unit features a gourmet kitchenette, designer furnishings, and lots of other amenities that spell "expensive." The rate for a studio suite on winter holiday weekends is $395, or $265 for nonholiday winter days, but merely $140–210 during the summer "value season." The nicer one-bedroom suites go as high as $495 on winter holidays. Bring your personal banker with you.

Two other fine lodging options at Squaw Valley are the **Red Wolf Lodge** (2000 Squaw Loop Rd., Olympic Valley, 530/583-7226 or 800/791-0081) and **Plumpjack Squaw Valley Inn** (1920 Squaw Valley Rd., Olympic Village, 530/583-1578 or 800/323-7666, www.plumpjack.com). Both offer much the same type of pampering as the Olympic Village Inn and Squaw Valley Lodge. Rates for both are $110–299 in the low season, $199–459 in the high season. If you really want to break the bank, rent the penthouse at Plumpjack.

As this book goes to press, **Northstar-at-Tahoe Resort** (530/562-1010 or 800/466-6784, www.northstarattahoe.com, $118–199 for two people, $225–295 for four) is undergoing a major renovation—you might even call it a renaissance—with a new "village complex" of shops, restaurants, and condominiums under construction. When everything is completed, the resort's lodging options will likely expand considerably. At present the only rental accommodations are 260 privately owned condominiums, in various configurations from studios to three bedrooms, as well as larger privately owned homes. Most people who stay here purchase the affordable stay-and-ski packages, or in summer, "stay-and-play" packages that includes golf, tennis, mountain biking, or hiking. It will be interesting to see what the resort has to offer in its new incarnation.

Hotels

It may not be the best place for light sleepers, but the Victorian landmark **Truckee Hotel** (10007 Bridge St., Truckee, 530/587-4444 or 800/659-6921, www.thetruckeehotel.com, $49–169), is a pleasant and historical lodging choice in Truckee. Located a bit close to the train station in downtown Truckee, this grand old hotel was built in 1873 and remodeled in the early 1990s. With rates including a continental breakfast, it's the most affordable lodging around. Rooms with private baths cost more than rooms with shared baths, so make sure you know what you are getting. Moody's Bistro, a wonderful restaurant and jazz club, is located on the first floor.

Motels and Lodges

For those inclined toward chain-variety motels, the 100 rooms in the **Best Western Truckee Tahoe Inn** (11331 Brockway Rd., Truckee, 530/587-4525 or 800/824-6385, www.bestwesterntahoe.com, $110–184 for rooms, suites rates higher) provide a safe, dependable lodging experience. The motel is located outside the town of Truckee, so you'll have to drive to visit the shops and restaurants, but it's only one mile from Ponderosa Golf Course. If you feel like staying in for the evening and watching a little HBO, the motel has a Pizza Hut Express downstairs. A bonus: The complimentary continental breakfast has more than just the usual Danish-and-coffee; some of the foods are actually hot and mildly nutritious.

Another safe bet in the chain motel category is the **Truckee Holiday Inn Express** (10527 Coldstream Rd., Truckee, 530/582-9999 or 877/878-2533, www.hiexpesstruckee.com, $109–189). The motel is right off I-80 at the Donner Pass Road exit, which makes it a great choice for travelers driving up from Sacramento or the Bay Area for the weekend. The Coldstream Trailhead for Donner Memorial State Park is just a few yards from the front door.

Campgrounds and RV Parks

Between two and eight miles south of Truckee are three Forest Service–run campgrounds (530/587-3558, $15–16) on Highway 89: **Granite Flat, Goose Meadows,** and **Silver Creek.** Goose Meadows is the largest with 75 sites; the others each have about 25. All three camps are situated along the Truckee River, but unfortunately that also means they are right next to Highway 89 (of the three, Granite Flat is farthest from the road). The camps are on the primitive side: no hookups, showers, drinking water, or flush toilets (pit toilets only), but there is piped water. Still, for anglers, rafters, or kayakers, camping doesn't get much better than this. Reserve in advance at 877/444-6777 or www.reserveusa.com.

RVers who want amenities will do better at one of the 131 sites at privately operated **Coachland RV Park** (10100 Pioneer Trail, Truckee, 530/587-3071). The park offers all the necessities: full hookups including cable TV, water, restrooms, showers, laundry, and a general store. It has a pleasant 55-acre setting in a pine forest at 6,000 feet, just off Highway 89 and I-80. Sites are $37 per night for two adults, but weekly and monthly rates are cheaper.

Fly-fishing anglers enjoy 25-site **Martis Creek Campground** (on Hwy. 267 one mile south of Truckee Airport, 530/587-3558), which has water, restrooms, and catch-and-release fishing in Martis Creek Reservoir. For anglers who would rather go out in a boat, **Prosser Reservoir Campground** (530/587-3558) is two miles north of Truckee off Highway 89 and Prosser Dam Road. This camp has 29 sites and a boat ramp on Prosser Lake. Sites at both camps are $15–16.

And for those who just want to be left alone, **Sagehen Campground** (off Hwy. 89, one mile north of Truckee, 530/587-3558) has 10 sites, found at the end of the rough access road (passenger cars okay). The best thing about this camp is that it's free, and fishing in Sagehen Creek is not too shabby.

DONNER LAKE AND SODA SPRINGS
Motels and Lodges

Many California families have made Serene Lakes, near Donner Lake and Soda Springs, their summer or winter vacation destination for generations. Now those of us who don't own a vacation home in the area can stay at Serene Lakes, too, at the **(Ice Lakes Lodge** (1111 Soda Springs Rd., Serene Lakes, 530/426-7660, www.icelakeslodge.com, $130–195). Completed in the fall of 2000, the large chalet-style lodge has 26 lake-view rooms, each simply but elegantly decorated with one king or two queen beds, plus a spectacular restaurant that looks out on Dulzura and Serena Lakes. In the lounge in winter, logs are always burning bright in the huge granite fireplace. The lodge is less than five miles from Sugar Bowl's downhill slopes and one mile from Royal Gorge cross-country ski area.

Owned and operated by Royal Gorge Ski Resort, the romantic and historic **(Rainbow Lodge** (50080 Hampshire Rocks Rd., Soda Springs, 530/426-3871 or 800/500-3871, www.royalgorge.com) has been welcoming visitors to its 32 rooms and delightful Engadine Cafe since the 1920s. Set at a bend in the Yuba River, constructed of hand-hewn timbers and natural stone, and decorated in classic ski-chalet style, this place has "historic mountain lodge" written all over it. Many of the rooms are on the small side, but because of the scenic riverside location, great service, and wonderful breakfasts that are included in the room rates, no one complains. In recent decades the lodge

has become almost as popular in summer as it is in winter, due to the number of hiking, biking, and rafting recreation options nearby. In winter, of course, skiing is the main event, particularly cross-country skiing at Royal Gorge, five miles away. Rates are $140–195 per night for rooms with private baths (breakfast included), but most guests opt for rate packages that include dinner at Engadine Cafe or trail passes at Royal Gorge. You can also save money by reserving a room with a shared bath ($110–140). Midweek specials that include lodging, trail passes, and lessons are $85–100 per night per person.

Royal Gorge also operates the **Wilderness Lodge** (530/426-3871 or 800/500-3871, www.royalgorge.com) in the middle of its Nordic trail system. You can't drive there; instead you just relax and enjoy a sleigh ride from Summit Station. Despite its name, a stay at Wilderness Lodge is not roughing it. The lodge has 32 rooms, a sauna and hot tub, a full program of cross-country skiing for beginners to experts, and best of all, fabulous French country cuisine. (The lodge is undergoing a major renovation and will reopen in the winter of 2006–2007.) All this backwoods luxury comes with a price, but it is well worth it. Lodging rates, which include three meals a day and all skiing programs, are $159–189 per adult and $105–145 per child (16 and under). If you would rather stay in a private cabin instead of a lodge room, the rate goes up to $259 per person.

Most visitors to Donner Lake are fortunate enough to own their own vacation homes, but those who aren't so lucky can stay at the **Donner Lake Village Resort** (15695 Donner Pass Rd., Truckee, 530/587-6081 or 800/621-6664, www.donnerlakevillage.com) on the west end of the lake. This two-story motel-style resort offers "lodgettes" and studios, one-bedroom suites, and townhomes, most with kitchens and fireplaces. The resort has a private beach and a marina that rents ski boats, fishing boats, and personal watercraft, so you won't have to wonder what to do with your time. If you have your own boat, you can tie it up here. In winter, Royal Gorge is just a few miles away.

Rates for two people are $90–220 (higher for lakefront and lake-view units, and on weekends and holidays). Two-bedroom town houses go for $200–340.

Just down the road is **Loch Leven Lodge** (13855 Donner Pass Rd., Truckee, 530/587-3773 or 877/663-6637, www.lochlevenlodge.com), which has a similar setup on the shores of Donner Lake, except that all of its rooms are lakefront. The old-style lodge has been a popular vacation spot for more than 50 years. The lodge's best-loved feature is its 5,000-square-foot deck that overlooks the lake. Bring a book and settle in to your favorite beach chair. Rates are $100–140 for two in a room, suite, or studio; $190–240 for two in a town house.

For a European-style stay-and-ski experience, consider the 70-year-old **Inn at Sugar Bowl** (530/426-6742 or 530/426-9000, www.sugarbowl.com), located at the top of the resort's one-mile-long gondola. You won't be able to drive your car here, but you and your luggage will enjoy a magical ride up the snow-covered slopes to the inn's 27 guest rooms and beautiful dining room. Over the years, numerous celebrities have stayed here. Mountain-view rooms are $200–295 for two people; rooms without views are less.

On the opposite end of the ski lodging spectrum, there's the no-nonsense **Boreal Inn** (530/426-1012, www.rideboreal.com, $100–140), a basic three-story motel that is located 200 yards from the Boreal off-ramp at I-80, and about the same distance from Boreal's ski lifts, so skiers and riders can do their thing with the greatest of ease. Rooms can accommodate up to four people, so all your rider friends can pack in together to save money. A free continental breakfast is offered; children four and under stay free.

Campgrounds and RV Parks

Campers who want to be near three-mile-long Donner Lake stay at **Donner Memorial State Park** (Donner Lake exit off I-80, west of Truckee, 530/582-7892, $25). This popular state park campground has 140 sites that can accommodate RVs and trailers up to 28 feet. Camp amenities include water, restrooms, and showers, plus all the swimming and fishing you could ask for in Donner Lake.

Food

TAHOE CITY
Breakfast

Breakfast and lunch are the main events at the **Fire Sign Cafe** (1785 W. Lake Blvd., Tahoe City, 530/583-0871, 7 A.M.–3 P.M. daily), a cozy place known for its creative home-style cooking. Omelets are large and run $7–9. A stack of three huge pancakes or a pecan waffle is $6. Ditto for the **Sawtooth Ridge Cafe** (877 N. Lake Blvd., Tahoe City, 530/583-2880, 6 A.M.–3 P.M. daily), which serves breakfast until 2 P.M., plus salads, soups, and sandwiches for lunch. The lengthy breakfast menu includes egg burritos, veggie eggs Benedict, latkes and eggs, corned-beef hash and eggs, quiche of the day, a bunch of omelets, and even buckwheat pancakes.

If you want something quick and convenient before heading off to the slopes or the trails, **Tahoe Dam Cafe** (55 W. Lake Blvd., Tahoe City, 530/581-0278, 6 A.M.–3 P.M. Mon.–Sat., 7 A.M.–3 P.M. Sun., open till 5 P.M. in summer, $5) has a killer location—just a few steps from the Truckee River Outlet—and offers locally roasted coffee and espresso, fresh pastries, and bagels. The emphasis is on organic ingredients. Come back in the afternoon for sandwiches, salads, smoothies, or frozen yogurt. Early birds will like that the cafe opens at 6 A.M. almost daily. Another great place for a quick-stop breakfast is just down the road at the **Tahoe House Bakery** (625 W. Lake Blvd., Tahoe City, 530/583-1377, 6 A.M.–4 P.M. Sun.–Thur., until 6 P.M. Fri.–Sat. and in summer, $5–10). Their European-style breads, pastries, and bagels make the perfect breakfast-to-go. Everything is made on-site, including an extensive line of gourmet sauces and take-out dinners.

Seafood and Steak

Two restaurants are found in the Boatworks Mall, **Jake's on the Lake** (780 N. Lake Blvd., Tahoe City, 530/583-0188, www.jakestahoe.com, 4:30–9:30 P.M. Mon.–Fri., 11:30 A.M.–9:30 P.M. Sat.–Sun., mid-June–Sept. 30, $17–38) and **Sierra Vista** (700 N. Lake Blvd., Tahoe City, 530/583-0233, www.sierravistatahoe.com, $17–29), both with marina views and outdoor deck dining in summer. Jake's is well known for its weekday happy hour, when appetizers are half price, and you can order a mai tai or an Alpine Sunset and watch the sun go down. The attractive bar area is large and airy enough to host a live band every Friday night. Menu items include Idaho trout, lobster tail, giant scampi, filet mignon, and rack of lamb. You can save money by ordering from the cafe menu (burgers and salads). Across the parking lot, Sierra Vista has a wide range of international dishes, including Hungarian goulash, chicken cordon bleu, and Thai coconut shrimp, plus the American standards: New York steak, filet mignon, seared ahi, and grilled salmon.

American

A Tahoe City institution, the **Bridgetender Tavern** (65 W. Lake Blvd., Tahoe City, 530/583-3342, 11 A.M.–11 P.M. Sun.–Thur., till midnight Fri.–Sat., $5–10) moved across the street from its historic location next to Fanny Bridge in 2002, but the casual bar/cafe still doles out the same delectable half-pound burgers, tacos, soups, wraps, and salads, and now has an even better Truckee River view. The fish-and-chips are popular, too, but what everybody orders is something from the huge menu selection of draft beers. Diners can sit outside at round wooden tables or inside in the cozy log-cabin dining room. If you are craving onion rings or garlic fries, this is your place.

One of the more famous and most long-running restaurants in Tahoe City, **Rosie's Cafe** (571 N. Lake Blvd., Tahoe City, 530/583-8504, www.rosiescafe.com, 7:30 A.M.–9:30 P.M. daily, $7–17) is known as much for its decor as for its traditional American food. Check out the elk antler chandelier, moose head above the fireplace, antique skiing and sledding equipment, and assorted Tahoe memorabilia. Rosie's is open for three meals a day, and families will be happy here; the cafe has an extensive children's menu. Their smoked salmon omelet was featured in *Bon Appetit* magazine. If you don't have the time to eat here, at least stop in to the historic bar for a drink.

Californian/Continental

It isn't easy to pull off casual elegance, but the **Ⅽ Black Bear Tavern** (2255 W. Lake Blvd., Tahoe City, 530/583-8626, www.blackbearlaketahoe.com, 6–9 P.M. Sun.–Thur., till 10 P.M. Fri.–Sat., $20–36) does it right. This 1930s-era log-and-stone cabin is the perfect setting for a meal of wild game (try the grilled venison medallions, roast duck breast, or wild boar tenderloin), grandma's boardinghouse meat loaf and mashed potatoes, or more traditional entrees like steak, pasta, or seafood. On summer nights, you can dine inside or outside on the back deck. In winter, the dining room is warmed by three stone fireplaces. In a previous life, the Black Bear Tavern was known as the Forest Inn, a popular and elegant restaurant that served the Tahoe elite in the 1930s and 1940s.

Located in the center of Tahoe City, **Ⅽ Christy Hill** (115 Grove St., Tahoe City, 530/583-8551, www.christyhill.com, $19–35) has been satisfying hungry diners for nearly a quarter of a century. Lauded by the *San Francisco Chronicle, Los Angeles Times, Wall Street Journal,* and *Bon Appetit* magazine, the food here is worthy of its reputation. A mix of California and French cuisine, the menu changes often but certain favorites appear regularly: ahi sashimi, foie gras with chanterelle mushrooms, wild king salmon, and filet mignon with roasted shallots. It's not just the food that's worthy of laurels, it's also the view. The restaurant sits 100 feet above Tahoe's shoreline, offering a panoramic blue-water vista. Not surprisingly, sunsets are sublime. If you can't afford dinner here, come for the "express lunch," which consists of very fancy sandwiches for $7–8, served up with that gorgeous eye-candy view.

Savvy diners might normally steer away from a restaurant that boasts having a "cuisine unique," but **Wolfdale's** (640 N. Lake Blvd., Tahoe City, 530/583-5700, www.wolfdales.com, $22–39) has been successfully serving up mouthwatering dishes, accompanied by first-rate service and a big lake view, for nearly 30 years. The menu is California cuisine with a distinct Asian influence, as chef/owner Doug Wolfdale studied under master Japanese chefs. Try the roasted quail stuffed with fennel sausage, or the green Thai curry seafood stew. One thing comes standard on every plate: gorgeous presentation. The food looks so artistic it's a pity to eat it. On warm summer days, make a reservation for the outdoor dining area, and don't miss the trio of fresh sorbets for dessert.

Located a few miles north of Tahoe City near Alpine Meadows, the historic **River Ranch Lodge** (Hwy. 89 and Alpine Meadows Rd., Tahoe City, 530/583-4264, www.river-ranch-lodge.com, 3:30–9 P.M. daily, $17–32) restaurant is a good place for a classic Tahoe dining experience. Diners can choose between indoor seating or a spot outside on the patio alongside the rushing waters of the Truckee River. The menu includes roasted elk loin, venison osso bucco, wild salmon, sautéed scallops over black linguine, and portabella mushroom napoleon, and the riverside scenery can't be beat.

Another good spot for riverfront dining is the aptly named **River Grill** (55 W. Lake Blvd., Tahoe City, 530/581-2644, 5:30–9 P.M. daily, $15–25), which serves fresh seasonal entrees alongside the banks of the Truckee (adjacent to the Bridgetender Tavern). The cuisine is a California/American blend, including a variety of fresh seafood, butternut squash ravioli, grilled Angus burger, and roast Sonoma duck breast. A few surprises await, like the macaroni and cheese with apple-smoked bacon appetizer. In

For an al fresco lunch at River Ranch Lodge, you can arrive by raft, bike, or car.

summer, you can dine outside on the terraced riverside deck, or in the knotty-pine-paneled dining room.

Italian

For Italian food on the North Shore, **Fiamma Cucina Rustica** (521 N. Lake Blvd., Tahoe City, 530/581-1416, 5:30–10 P.M. daily, $15–25) sets the standard. This neighborhood trattoria serves up northern Italian country cuisine (they call it "rustic Tuscan") in a warm and artistic dining room. Try the pizza with rock shrimp, tomatoes, and red onion, or the ravioli stuffed with wild mushrooms and butternut squash.

If it's summertime and you like your pizza with a river view, head over to **Front Street Station Pizza Company** (205 N. Lake Blvd. Tahoe City, 530/583-3770, 11 A.M.–10 P.M. daily), which sits right alongside the Truckee River just northwest of Tahoe City's Y. This tiny little cafe makes tasty pizzas, salads, and Italian sandwiches, plus a family of four can eat here for $25. Everything tastes even better when you are sitting outside on the riverside deck, watching the rafters float by.

Mexican

At the **Blue Agave** (425 N. Lake Blvd., Tahoe City, 530/583-8113, 11:30 A.M.–9:30 P.M. daily, $8–15), they serve about a billion different kinds of tequila. Okay, it's actually only 180, but regardless, it would take a very long time to try them all. The authentic Mexican and Southwest cuisine is prepared on the health-conscious side (no lard here). Specialties include shrimp fajitas, fruit-marinated carnitas, and seafood quesadillas.

More-casual Mexican food is found at **Rock's Mesquite Rotisserie** (475 N. Lake Blvd., Tahoe City, 530/581-1401, 11 A.M.–8 P.M. Tues.–Sun., $5–10). This order-at-the-counter cafe is always hopping with hungry diners ordering food to go or eat in. In addition to mesquite-grilled chicken, ribs, and tri-tip, several kinds of burritos, tacos, tortas, and quesadillas are served, plus burgers and salads.

TAHOE VISTA AND KINGS BEACH
Breakfast

Yes, the **Old Post Office Cafe** (5245 N. Lake Blvd., Carnelian Bay, 530/546-3205, 6:30 A.M.–2 P.M. daily, $5–10) really used to be the post office in Kings Beach—for three decades beginning in 1942. That history is commemorated in the restaurant's wallpaper, which looks like stamps. It's been a breakfast-and-lunch joint since the 1970s, and on summer mornings, there is often a crowd waiting for a table. The menu is huge, and includes all the morning favorites—eggs Benedict, huevos rancheros, breakfast burritos, omelets, potato creations, even oatmeal-plus more than 30 varieties of sandwiches for lunch.

The **Log Cabin Caffe** (8692 N. Lake Blvd., Kings Beach, 530/546-7109, 7 A.M.–1:30 P.M. daily, $10) is another favorite for breakfast, and it's easy to see why. Instead of the same old same old, the Log Cabin serves up whole wheat griddle cakes, lobster eggs Benedict, trout egg scramble, and cranberry orange waffles. The lunch menu is equally tempting: a half dozen salads including a seared ahi tuna on baby greens, several grilled panini sandwiches, and traditional and nontraditional burgers (beef, chicken, veggie, crab, and more). Figure on spending about $10 no matter what you order. It's all good.

Seafood and Steak

Situated right next to the North Tahoe sands at Kings Beach State Recreation Area, **Jasons Beachside Grille** (8338 N. Lake Blvd., Kings Beach, 530/546-3315, www.jasonsbeachside-grille.com, 11 A.M.–10 P.M. daily, $12–22) is the kind of place where you'll feel comfortable wearing your flip-flops is summer or Ugg boots in winter. The menu is classic American (salmon, pastas, prime rib, baby back ribs, flatiron steak). For lighter eaters there is also a cafe menu with all kinds of burgers and appetizer-type foods ($7–12), and an overflowing salad bar. The restaurant's big deck is adjacent to the beach parking lot and 50 yards from the lakeshore, so the view of the beach action is usually quite entertaining. Live acoustic music is offered on weekend evenings at the adjacent Sand Bar. If you like fruity drinks, try the Huckleberry Finn, a frozen mudslide with huckleberries.

At **Gar Woods Grill** (5000 N. Lake Blvd., Carnelian Bay, 530/546-3366, www.garwoods. com, 5:30–9:30 P.M. Sun.–Thur., till 10 P.M. Fri.–Sat.), their claim to fame is the "Wet Woody," a rum concoction that could easily inspire you to jump in the lake. Run by the same folks who own Riva Grill in South Lake Tahoe, the menu includes several seafood dishes plus free-range chicken, braised lamb shank, and filet mignon ($21–36), but there is also a much lower-priced bar menu ($8–14). The lake view from the outdoor deck is divine, which is one reason why Sunday brunch is wildly popular in the summer months. In case you've missed the boat, so to speak, Gar Woods were the watercraft of choice for the Tahoe elite in the early part of the 20th century. Both Riva Grill and Gar Woods capitalize on that fact with heavy merchandising. A wealth of boating-related gifts, clothing, and gear are for sale.

Red-meat eaters will be right at home at the **Old Range Steak House** (7081 N. Lake Blvd., Kings Beach, 530/546-4800, open from 5 P.M. daily, $25–45), which cooks up a huge variety of steaks—porterhouse, filet mignon, rib eye, New York strip—plus a few token poultry items. Bring your appetite, because all entrees include Caesar salad and red-skin potatoes. If you decide to order veggies on the side (not that your stomach will have any space), they are served in family-style portions, enough for the whole table. The house specialty is salt-roasted prime rib. Don't tell your cardiologist that you ate here.

The atmosphere at **Spindleshanks** (6873 N. Lake Blvd., Tahoe Vista, 530/546-2191, open from 5:30 P.M. daily, $15–29) is best described as "upscale rustic." An award-winning wine list accompanies an array of comfort food, including a wonderful Caesar salad, baby back ribs, salmon Wellington, and oysters bienzo. The food, while excellent, plays second fiddle to the wine at this American bistro/wine bar. In the

summer months, sit outside on the patio. In winter, hang out at the bar with all the North Shore locals.

Californian/Continental

You don't have to play golf to enjoy a meal at the **Blue Onion** (400 Brassie Ave., Kings Beach, 530/546-3913 or 800/353-4050, www .blueonion.com, 7 A.M.–3 P.M. daily), you just have to like good food. The restaurant is situated in the clubhouse of Old Brockway, North Lake Tahoe's oldest golf course, and serves three meals a day. For breakfast, try the Belgian waffles, or a variety of sweet and savory crepes or egg scrambles ($5–10). For dinner, start off with one of the Blue Onion's signature salads (warm spinach and caramelized pecans, or grilled pear and goat cheese on mixed baby greens) and then move on to Tuscan seafood stew, grilled rosemary chicken or duck breast, or osso buco. It's all delicious and moderately priced ($20–25 for entrees). In summer, you can sit outside on the redwood deck, or inside in the bright and airy dining room.

Imagine crisp white tablecloths, black wooden chairs, and impeccably sparkling glassware and you have a snapshot of **Boulevard Cafe** (6731 N. Lake Blvd., Tahoe Vista, 530/546-7213 or 530/546-7214, $17–29), a favorite on the North Shore for more than 15 years. This tiny restaurant has just over a dozen indoor and outdoor tables, with the emphasis on quality, not quantity. The menu shows northern Italian and Mediterranean influences—osso buco is their pride and joy—but everything is prepared in fresh and creative ways. Expect the unexpected, like potato ravioli and house-made chocolate gelato.

With a motto of "don't just eat... dine," **Wild Goose** (7320 N. Lake Blvd., Tahoe Vista, 530/546-9480, www.wildgoosetahoe.com, 5–10 P.M. daily July–Sept, hours vary the rest of the year) will make you want to linger after one glance at its lake view and luxurious menu. The saliva response is automatic when you mull over caramelized sea scallops, pan-seared Kobe beef, Hawaiian red snapper poached in lobster butter, and duck prepared three different ways.

Save room for dessert, particularly the brioche French toast or butter-roasted dates. Unfortunately, Wild Goose's prices match the quality of the food. Expect to pay about $30 for entrees, but you can also order "small plates" for $10–15, or select from the tasting menu, which includes a five-course meal for $65.

Italian

Nothing tastes better after a day of skiing than some basic, hearty Italian food, and that's what they do best at **Lanza's** (7739 N. Lake Blvd., Kings Beach, 530/546-2534, 5–10 P.M. daily, $13–15), an always-packed restaurant that is a great place for families and friends. Choose a pasta from the menu and a sauce to put on it (marinara, pesto, and lots more), then add extras like Italian sausage or meatballs. Or go with rich, hearty Italian entrees like chicken or eggplant parmesan, baked penne, or lasagna. There's something for everyone here.

Asian

If you are yearning for wasabi, **Hiro Sushi** (8159 N. Lake Blvd., Kings Beach, 530/546-4476, www.hirotahoe.com, $5–12) will bring it on. This is where the North Shore locals go for the four S's: sushi, sashimi, saki, and Sapporo. The chef is also the owner, and he makes sure all his customers leave well satisfied.

WEST SHORE
Breakfast

An unassuming little place with surprisingly inventive food, the **Stony Ridge Cafe** (6821 W. Lake Blvd., Tahoma, 530/525-0905, www.stonyridgecafe.com) is a wildly popular breakfast spot. It's not just the tasty, eclectic food that packs them in here, it's also the inviting atmosphere and decor. This is a homey place, artfully decorated with colorful paintings, tile work, and knotty pine. All of their dishes are made with fresh, organic ingredients. Try the Turkey a la Stony, served over oatmeal wheat toast with country gravy, or go for one of the omelets or pancake dishes ($7–14). It's all good. If you can't make it for breakfast, fear not—they're open for lunch

and dinner, too. The dinner menu changes weekly, and entrees are about $20.

Seafood and Steak

The restaurant at **Sunnyside** (1850 W. Lake Blvd., Tahoe City, 530/583-7200 or 800/822-2754, www.sunnysidetahoe.com, 4:30–10 P.M. daily) is as nice as the adjacent lodgings, which means you'll certainly enjoy your meal. This lakefront restaurant features an expansive oudoor deck (they claim it's the largest lakeside deck in all of Tahoe) and several different menus: a casual grill menu with burgers, salads, and the like ($8–14), a full array of more formal lunch and dinner entrees ($18–36), and a separate children's menu. The food is fairly traditional, with steaks and seafood the main attractions. The hula pie dessert has spawned legions of fans. Lots of Tahoe boaters cruise up to Sunnyside's dock and tie up, then enjoy lunch, dinner, or a rum-filled cocktail on the deck. The boat-less must resort to driving their cars.

Californian/Continental

Situated at the end of a narrow access road off Highway 89, **Chambers Landing Restaurant** (6300 W. Lake Blvd., Tahoma, 530/525-7262, summer hours vary, $23–32) has the feel of a "secret spot" when in fact it is anything but. This charming river-rock-and-wood-beamed pavilion enjoys a parklike setting right on the beach, and its folding French doors allow it to be completely open-air on warm days. The bar here is reportedly Lake Tahoe's first, having opened for business in 1875. Open in summer only for lunch, dinner, and Sunday brunch, Chambers Landing's scenic location has long been a favorite spot for weddings; hundreds of brides and grooms have been photographed in front of the old boathouse by the restaurant. The menu is a mix of French, Italian, and Spanish, including a traditional Spanish fish stew, veal saltimboca, rack of lamb with port wine sauce, and several pastas. If you've eaten at Graham's at Squaw Valley you'll notice similarities: same owner, similar fabulous menu.

The oldest continually operating restaurant in Tahoe, **Swiss Lakewood Lodge** (5055 W. Lake Blvd., Homewood, 530/525-5211, www.swisslakewood.com, 5:30–10:30 P.M. Tues.–Sun., $22–35) is *très* European. With its faux painting of a wine cellar, a huge wine cask mounted into the wall, and Old World decor, you'll be convinced you are somewhere in western Europe, not California. This is the kind of place where beef Wellington and roast duck are standard issue, as well as Swiss-style fondue, rack of lamb, sweetbread, veal, and venison. If you ever had a hankering to try beef tartar, this is the spot to do it. Of course, vegetarians would be miserable here, especially when they see the mounted goat head that hangs over the stone fireplace in the bar. If you are dining with a group, reserve the private dining room.

TRUCKEE AND SQUAW VALLEY
Breakfast
Breakfast aficionados make headway for the dozens of omelet varieties at the diminutive and appropriately named **Squeeze In** (10060 Donner Pass Rd., Truckee, 530/587-9814, 7 A.M.–2 P.M. daily, $7–12). Dozens of omelets? Yup, there are no less than 62 omelet choices on the menu, and the folks at Squeeze In claim they are "the best on the planet."

American
A Truckee tradition for more than 30 years, **O.B.'s Pub and Restaurant** (10046 Donner Pass Rd., Truckee, 530/587-4164, www.obstruckee.com, 11:30 A.M.–2:30 P.M. and 5:30–9:30 P.M. daily, $9–25) is the kind of place where everyone can find something to eat. The huge menu includes a variety of burgers and salads for lunch, and a mélange of entrees for dinner, including six kinds of hamburgers, slow-roasted prime rib, filet mignon, drunken shrimp, seafood pasta, and wild mushroom and spinach strudel. Portions are huge, but many diners save room for the home-made mud pie dessert. You'll have to waddle home afterward. Meals are served in the rustic,

century-old dining room, which is decorated with historic bric-a-brac, including an antique barber's chair, old photographs, and an old-fashioned potbellied stove. It's worth having a meal here just so you can see the ornate antique wooden bar.

Of the plentiful dining choices in and around Truckee's gentrified Commercial Row, the **Truckee Diner** (10144 W. River St., Truckee, 530/582-5835, $7–12) anchors the more pedestrian end of the spectrum with its no-nonsense, meat-loaf-and-potatoes menu. The place is famous for its shakes and malts, not to mention its world-class banana splits. If Mom or Dad wants steak and the kids want peanut butter and jelly, everyone can be satisfied here.

Californian/Continental
With an impressive view that overlooks downtown Truckee and the river canyon beyond, summer outdoor dining, and a roaring fireplace in winter, **⟨ Cottonwood** (10142 Rue Hilltop at Brockway Rd., Truckee, 530/587-5711, www.cottonwoodrestaurant.com, 7 A.M.–9 P.M. Sun.–Thurs., till 10 P.M. Fri.–Sat.) is a winner for dinner in all four Tahoe seasons. The restaurant somehow manages to be rustic and sophisticated at the same time, as in "Truckee meets San Francisco." The decor (wooden skis, antique sleds, candlelight chandeliers) creates an inviting setting for the creative and tasty food, which includes an eclectic variety of salads—try the garlic-laden Caesar, which should be eaten with your fingers—plus entrees like Thai red curry prawns, rabbit cassoulet, tofu stir-fry, and a memorable seafood stew. If you're in Truckee, don't miss the chance to eat here. In summer, be sure to sit outside on the deck and order one of their incredible French martinis. Entrees run $19–28; salads are $7–11.

Situated right next to the Christy Inn, **Graham's** (1650 Squaw Valley Rd., Olympic Valley, 530/581-0454, www.dinewine.com, 6 A.M.–10 P.M. Tues.–Sun., $25–35) is a top pick for Squaw Valley diners. Housed in the first home constructed in Squaw Valley, which was built for the original owners of the ski resort, Graham's intimate dining room has a high pine ceiling and rock fireplace. Owner and chef Graham Rock is big on grilling things; a major portion of the brief menu consists of grilled meats—elk, veal, salmon, tuna, and lamb chops. A few appetizers shouldn't be passed by: the grilled quail over polenta ($14) and potato leek soup ($7). With more than 800 wines on its wine list, the restaurant has won the *Wine Spectator* Award of Excellence several times, as well as many other accolades.

Like its sibling restaurant in San Francisco, **PlumpJack Restaurant and Bar** at Squaw Valley (1920 Squaw Valley Rd., Olympic Village, 530/583-1578 or 800/323-7666, www .plumpjack.com, 7:30–10:30 A.M. and 6–10 P.M. daily, $20–30) serves elegant, seasonal cuisine in a chic setting. The restaurant has received high marks from the *San Francisco Chronicle* as well as numerous travel publications. The menu changes frequently, but count on creative dishes like almond-crusted halibut, bison short ribs, and Niman Ranch pork tenderloin ($20–30). If you can't afford dinner here, try breakfast or lunch, or order from the bar menu (11:30 A.M.–10 P.M. daily, $10–15). Since the restaurant is part of the Plumpjack Squaw Valley Inn, which hosts visiting skiing families, the restaurant even has a kids' menu.

As Northstar-at-Tahoe undergoes its major redevelopment program, longtime Northstar fans hope that one aspect of the resort stays the same: the wonderful food at **Timbercreek Restaurant** (at The Village at Northstar, Truckee, 530/562-1010 or 530/562-2252, www.northstarattahoe.com, 7:30 A.M.–9 P.M. daily, $22–36). The dining room was completely restyled in 2004 in an earthy decor intended to reflect the organic, environmentally sustainable ingredients used on the menu. Only all natural Niman Ranch beef and pork, sustainable "ocean-safe" seafood, and fresh organic produce appear on the menu, which changes daily based on local availability. If you aren't especially concerned about eating environmentally conscious health food, order one of their fabulous martinis.

Located in the Truckee Hotel, **Moody's Bistro and Lounge** (10007 Bridge St., Truckee, 530/587-8688, www.moodysbistro .com, 11:30 A.M.–9:30 P.M. daily, $19–29) has a swank feel that you wouldn't expect to find in downtown Truckee. The scene here is almost as much about jazz as it is about food; live music is offered several nights a week with no cover charge. Dinner entrees include Idaho trout, beef short ribs, Niman Ranch pork chop, lamb shank, and venison. Vegetarians always have a few excellent selections, too, like an eggplant and coconut red curry. Lunch is mostly soups, salads, and burgers ($10–15), and the Sunday brunch is a winner. Chef and co-owner Mark Estee prides himself on a fresh, season-specific menu that changes daily.

Casual diners who enjoy well-prepared food will like the **Pacific Crest Restaurant,** a hip, friendly bistro located adjacent to the Bar of America in downtown Truckee (10042 Donner Pass Rd., Truckee, 530/587-2626, 10:30 A.M.–3 P.M. and 5:30–9 P.M. Mon.–Fri., 9 A.M.–3 P.M. Sat.–Sun., $12–20). A selection of creative wood-fired pizzas, sandwiches, and pastas are served for lunch and dinner, without any accompanying hype. Be sure to try the roasted portabella mushroom appetizer, or the cassoulet entree. Weekend brunches are popular.

Mexican

Located on the far west end of Commercial Row in Truckee, **El Toro Bravo** (10186 Donner Pass Rd., Truckee, 530/587-3557, 11:30 A.M.–10 P.M. daily, $5–10) is housed in a small historic cottage. In addition to many traditional Mexican entrees (steak or chicken fajitas, chimichangas, enchiladas, chili rellenos, and the like), the restaurant serves a number of seafood specialties, like seviche, snapper Santa Cruz, grilled prawns, and oysters. Happy hour, 4–6 P.M., is popular with Truckee locals. If you've ever been to Santa Cruz, you may have eaten at El Toro Bravo's sister restaurant in Capitola.

Asian

You won't find chow mein on the menu at Asian-influenced **Dragonfly** (10118 Donner Pass Rd., Truckee, 530/587-0557, www.dragonflycuisine.com, 11 A.M.–2:30 P.M. and 5:30–9:30 P.M. daily), but you will find Chinese five-spice pork tenderloin, Asian-style cioppino, and seared unagi. The menu may seem a bit trendy for downtown Truckee, but its fusion of Thai, Japanese, Vietnamese, and Indian cuisine is ingenious, and the Zen-like ambience of this place is sure to lower your blood pressure by a few points. Lots of diners favor the seafood noodle bowls, but if green curry is your thing, order it here. Lunch runs $8–10, dinner $20–28, appetizers $11–14. In summer, sit outside on the upstairs deck and watch the action on the street in downtown Truckee.

Don't think that just because you are 300 miles from the ocean, you can't get good sushi. All your raw favorites are available at **Mamasake** (the Village at Squaw Valley, 530/584-0110, www.mamasake.com, noon–9:30 P.M. daily, $5–12) and **Tsunami Sushi** (11429 Donner Pass Rd., Truckee, 530/587-2680, $5–12). True to its name, Mamasake has a sake bar (be sure to order a sake martini), plus lots of unusual roll combinations and tapas-style small plates that will keep non-fish-eaters happy. Truckee's Tsunami Sushi is also a smokehouse, so pulled pork, barbecue ribs, and smoked chicken and salmon are also on the menu.

DONNER LAKE AND SODA SPRINGS
Californian/Continental

Just 15 minutes west of Truckee off I-80 lies a special restaurant worthy of a special trip—the **Engadine Cafe** at Royal Gorge's Rainbow Lodge (50080 Hampshire Rocks Rd., Soda Springs, 530/426-3661, www.royalgorge.com, 7:30–11 A.M., 11:30 A.M.–2 P.M., and 5:30–8 P.M. daily, $19–27). Start off with a drink in the historic lodge's lounge, which is decorated with photographs of early-1900s life at Donner Summit. Then in summer, enjoy dinner on the patio overlooking the Yuba River; or in winter, by the river-rock fireplace in the dining room. Dinner entrees have a French country influence, and include grilled duck breast, artichoke chicken, steak Diane, venison medallions, and a vegetable cassoulet. Don't miss the wild mushroom streudel appetizer. You can also order from the bar menu, where burgers and bar food are in the $5–12 range.

Or, if a lake view appeals to you more than a river view, head over to the **Ice Lakes Lodge** at Serene Lakes (111 Soda Springs Rd., Soda Springs, 530/426-7660, www.icelakeslodge.com, 11:30 A.M.–8 P.M. daily, $17–24). This restaurant also has well-deserved bragging rights for lovely alpine scenery-its huge windows overlook Serena and Dulzura Lakes—and memorable meals. Dinner entrees include a layered vegetable napoleon, baby back ribs, grilled Alaskan halibut, and house-made chicken potpie.

Over at Donner Lake, dining choices are limited, but the open-in-summer-only **West End Bistro at the Lake** (15628 Donner Pass Rd., Truckee, 530/550-7770, www.westendbistro.com, $20–32) is a great option for dinner. By "at the lake" they mean across the road from Donner Lake, not on the lakeshore, so don't expect a view, but do expect great food. The menu changes constantly based on seasonal availability, but frequently seen items include wild salmon, grilled Kansas City steak, seared ahi, and seafood linguine. If you're on a budget, the bistro burger is only $13. Everything is as fresh as possible and memorably prepared.

American

If you've just come off the slopes at Sugar Bowl, Royal Gorge, or any of the Donner-area resorts, you probably want to eat ASAP. The **Summit Restaurant and Bar** (22002 Donner Pass Rd., Soda Springs, 530/426-3904, 9 A.M.–8 P.M. daily, $7–10) comes to the rescue, with a variety of sandwiches, including a half-pound sirloin burger or a big breast of chicken, plus a few salads and lots of calorie-replenishing foods like onion rings and ice cream. Think of it as a Denny's restaurant in the mountains. There's no ambience to speak of, but your belly will be full when you leave.

Practicalities

INFORMATION

The chamber of commerce visitors centers are particularly helpful if you are looking for lodging, restaurants, tours, or businesses of any kind: **The Truckee Donner Chamber of Commerce** (10065 Donner Pass Rd., Truckee, 530/587-2757, www.truckee.com) and **The North Lake Tahoe Chamber of Commerce** (245 N. Lake Blvd., Tahoe City, 530/581-6900, www.puretahoenorth.com).

The **U.S. Forest Service** has a visitors center near Truckee (10342 Hwy. 89, Truckee, 530/587-3558) and another at Big Bend (49685 Hampshire Rocks Rd., take the Big Bend or Rainbow Rd. exits off I-80, Soda Springs, 530/426-3609). Here you will find tons of information on hiking, biking, and other outdoor activities on Tahoe National Forest land. There are books on Tahoe's natural history for sale, as well as hiking maps and guides. Information on Tahoe National Forest can also be found on the web at www.fs.fed.us/r5/tahoe.

SERVICES
Medical Care

The North and West Shores are served by two hospitals under the same ownership: **Tahoe Forest Hospital** (10121 Pine Ave. at Donner Pass Rd., Truckee, 530/587-6011 or 800/733-9953, www.tfhd.com) and **Incline Village Community Hospital** (880 Alder Ave., Incline Village, 775/833-4100, www.tfhd.com).

Post Offices

Several post offices are conveniently located along the North and West Shores: the **Truckee Post Office** (10050 Bridge St. at Jibboom St., 800/275-8777); the **Tahoe City Post Office** (Lighthouse Shopping Center, 950 N. Lake Blvd., 800/275-8777); and the **West Shore** post office (5375 W. Lake Blvd., Homewood, 530/525-6777). Smaller post offices are located in Tahoma, Kings Beach, Carnelian Bay, Tahoe Vista, Olympic Valley, and Soda Springs.

Internet Access

Need to check your email or surf the Web? The North Shore's two public libraries have access: **Kings Beach Branch** (301 Secline St., Kings Beach, 530/546-2021) or **Tahoe City Branch** (740 N. Lake Blvd., Tahoe City, 530/583-3382). In Truckee, go to the Truckee Branch of the **Nevada County Library** (10031 Levon Ave., Truckee, 530/582-7846). You can also get Internet access at the **North Lake Tahoe Chamber of Commerce** office (245 N. Lake Blvd., Tahoe City, 530/581-6900).

If you are traveling with your laptop and it is enabled for wireless Internet, many businesses on the North Shore have wireless access. The Village at Squaw Valley, most of downtown Truckee, many Tahoe City establishments, and the Truckee-Tahoe airport are all Wi-Fi enabled.

GETTING THERE
By Air

The **Truckee-Tahoe Airport** (10356 Truckee Airport Rd, 530/587-4119 or 800/359-2875, www.truckeetahoeairport.com) is currently not operational for commercial flights. But visitors can fly into the **Reno/Tahoe International Airport** (2001 E. Plumb Lane, 775/328-6400, www.renoairport.com) and then rent a car, or take bus, shuttle, or limousine service. Several companies offer shuttle or limo service between the Reno-Tahoe International Airport and the North Shore/Truckee area: Airport Mini-Bus/Bell Limousine (800/235-5466), Executive Limousine (775/333-3300), Aladdin Limousine (800/546-6009), Sierra West Limousine (877/347-4789), North Tahoe Limousine (800/832-8213). North Tahoe Checker Cab (866/420-8294) also travels between the airport and North Shore/Truckee destinations.

Visitors could also fly into Sacramento, Oakland, San Francisco, or San Jose airports, then rent a car to drive to Lake Tahoe. Sacramento Airport is two hours from the North and West Shores, the three other airports are about 3.5 hours away.

By Car

From the San Francisco Bay Area or Sacramento, the primary driving route to the North and West Shores of Lake Tahoe is to take I-80 east to Truckee and then Highway 89 south to Tahoe City (about two hours or 100 miles from Sacramento and 3.5 hours or 200 miles from San Francisco).

From Reno/Tahoe International Airport, take I-80 west for 32 miles to Truckee. In Truckee, connect to Highway 267 to travel south to the lakeshore at Tahoe Vista or Kings Beach (12 miles), or Highway 89 to travel south to Tahoe City (15 miles).

By Bus

Visitors can access Truckee by two major bus lines: **Greyhound Bus Lines** (530/587-3822 or 800/231-2222, www.greyhound.com) or **Amtrak Bus** (800/872-7245, www.amtrak.com). Tahoe Area Regional Transit system buses connect with these bus lines at the Truckee Depot to take passengers to points along the West and North Shores.

By Train

The nearest Amtrak train depots are in Truckee or Reno. For schedules and information, contact **Amtrak** (800/872-7245, www.amtrak.com). Tahoe Area Regional Transit system buses connect with Amtrak at the Truckee Depot to take passengers to points along the West and North Shores.

GETTING AROUND
Shuttles and Buses

The **Tahoe Area Regional Transit** (TART) buses run a regular schedule from Meeks Bay north to Sugar Pine Point, Homewood, and Tahoe City. From Tahoe City, TART buses run north to Truckee and north and then

west to Squaw Valley. TART buses also run east from Tahoe City to Tahoe Vista, Kings Beach, and Incline Village. TART schedules and information are available at 800/736-6365 or www.laketahoetransit.com. One-way fares are $1.50 for adults, $0.75 for children 6–12, and free for children 5 and under. All-day passes are available.

TART also runs the Tahoe Trolley June 30–early September, with free service at night between Tahoe City and Squaw Valley, and Tahoe City and Incline Village. In the daytime, fares are charged ($1.50 one-way or $3.50 all-day pass).

The town of Truckee operates the Truckee Trolley, a year-round transit service between downtown Truckee and Donner Lake. During winter, the service is extended to include North-Star-at-Tahoe ski resort, the Donner Summit ski areas, and Kings Beach. For information, contact Aztec Transportation, 530/587-7451.

By Car

To get current updates on road conditions in California, phone 800/427-7623. To get current updates on Nevada road conditions, phone 877/687-6237.

For **car rentals,** contact Enterprise Rent-a-Car (11375 Deerfield Dr., Truckee, 530/550-1550) or Hertz (10266 Truckee Airport Rd., Truckee, 530/550-9191). Hertz also has a smaller location in downtown Truckee (10745 W. River St., Truckee, 530/587-5209). All the major car-rental agencies are also available at Reno/Tahoe International Airport.

By Taxi

North Tahoe Checker Cab (866/420-8294) operates throughout North Tahoe and Truckee. Other North Shore taxi services include Alpine Taxi (530/546-3232 or 775/833-4433), Ace High Taxi (530/412-3583), and Lake Tahoe Taxi (530/577-7000).

EAST SHORE

The sunny East Shore of Lake Tahoe has two decidedly differently personalities, embodied by the wealthy ski-and-golf town of Incline Village and the casino town of Crystal Bay to the north, and the miles of seemingly endless white sand that caresses the Nevada shoreline to the south. In Incline Village and Crystal Bay, you'll find some of the highest-income residents and most architecturally extravagant homes on the lake. Traveling southward, you'll find thousands of acres of undeveloped land—managed by the U.S. Forest Service and Lake Tahoe Nevada State Park—including the longest stretch of uninterrupted public shoreline on the entire lake.

The two biggest towns, Crystal Bay and Incline Village, are separated by a five-minute drive. Crystal Bay is marked by its four ca-sinos—Crystal Bay Club, Cal-Neva Resort, Tahoe Biltmore, and Jim Kelly's Nugget—which unlike their more modern South Shore counterparts, are a throwback to the gaming spirit of the 1950s and 1960s. The well-heeled town of Incline Village received its name not from its two nearby ski resorts but from the 1860s-era Incline Tramway, a 4,000-foot hydraulic tramway that hauled lumber 1,400 feet in elevation to the top of the ridge. The lumber then traveled in a water flume to the Virginia and Truckee Railroad yard near Carson City for use in the Virginia City silver mines.

By the late 1800s, Incline Village was completely deforested, and it remained a mere blip on the map until the late 1950s, when it was developed as a vacation resort as part of the Tahoe growth spurt instigated by the 1960 Winter

HIGHLIGHTS

(Memorial Point: This easy-access lake vista is located just a few miles south of Incline Village, and provides a scenic introduction to the boulder-lined beauty of the East Shore (page 162).

(Thunderbird Lodge: Sign up for a guided tour of Thunderbird Lodge and you can marvel at the eccentricities of fabulously wealthy real estate magnate George Whittell Jr., who built a 16,500-foot mansion on Tahoe's shoreline and kept exotic pets (page 162).

(Virginia City: A short drive from the lake into the interior of Nevada will bring you to Virginia City, the town made infamous by the Comstock silver-mining boom of 1857-1877 and at that time the second-biggest city in the West (page 163).

(Chimney Beach and Secret Harbor: This easy hike follows a wide trail that descends a little more than a half mile to Tahoe's east shoreline. From there, a path runs north and south to a series of rocky coves and secluded beaches, where there is plenty of room for swimmers and sunbathers to claim their own private stretch of sand (page 168).

(Flume Trail: If you're in good shape and have some experience on a mountain bike, don't miss the chance to ride one of the West's most famous trails, which runs high above the East Shore of Lake Tahoe, providing outstanding lake views and nerve-wracking drop-offs (page 172).

(Sand Harbor: One of the East Shore's most beautiful beaches, Sand Harbor is a long white stretch of sand dotted with rounded boulders. A fine place to while away a summer's day (page 174).

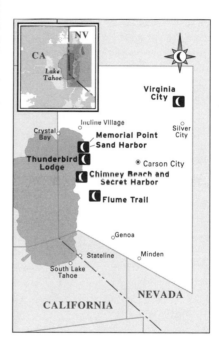

LOOK FOR **(** TO FIND RECOMMENDED SIGHTS, ACTIVITIES, DINING, AND LODGING.

Olympics at Squaw Valley. Even though the town is clearly well-to-do, its ambience is understated. The main landmark that defines the area is 10,778-foot Mount Rose, which offers some of Lake Tahoe's best skiing in winter and highest-elevation hiking in summer.

A drive along the East Shore in the 20-mile stretch from Incline Village south to Zephyr Cove is pure eye candy. Although much of Highway 28 is lined by densely forested slopes, where the groves of conifers part, stunning vistas of the boulder-strewn shoreline and cobalt blue waters are visible. You won't find any commercial enterprises here except for the Spooner Lake Outdoor Company, which in summer operates a shuttle for mountain bikers riding the famous Flume Trail, and in winter manages a cross-country ski area. Otherwise,

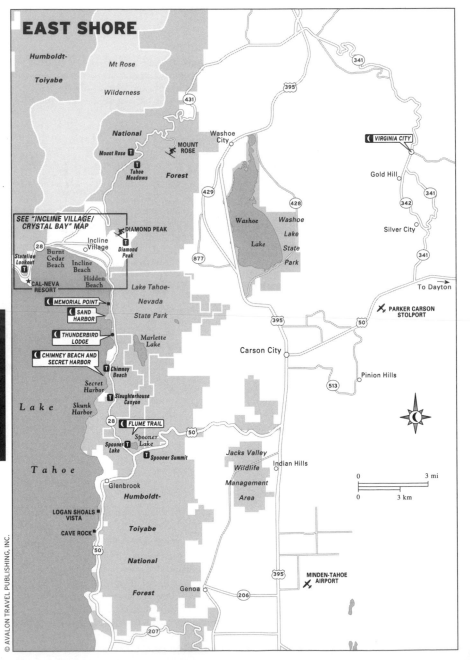

EAST SHORE

Humboldt-
Toiyabe

Mt Rose

Toiyabe

Wilderness

341

395

National

Washoe
City

431

MOUNT
ROSE

Mount Rose T

Forest

Tahoe
Meadows

429

428

Washoe

Washoe
Lake

Lake

Virginia City

Gold Hill

341

Silver City

342

SEE "INCLINE VILLAGE/
CRYSTAL BAY" MAP

DIAMOND PEAK

341

State
Park

Incline
Village

Diamond
Peak

28

Stateline
Lookout

Burnt
Cedar
Beach

Incline
Beach

877

CAL-NEVA
RESORT

Hidden
Beach

Lake Tahoe-

To Dayton

PARKER CARSON
STOLPORT

MEMORIAL POINT

Nevada

SAND
HARBOR

State Park

395

50

THUNDERBIRD
LODGE

Marlette
Lake

Carson City

CHIMNEY BEACH AND
SECRET HARBOR

Chimney
Beach

Pinion Hills

Secret
Harbor

513

Lake

Skunk
Harbor

Slaughterhouse
Canyon

28

FLUME TRAIL

50

Spooner
Lake

Spooner
Lake

Tahoe

Spooner Summit

Jacks Valley

Glenbrook

Wildlife

Indian Hills

Humboldt-

Management

LOGAN SHOALS
VISTA

Toiyabe

Area

CAVE ROCK

50

National

3 mi

3 km

MINDEN-TAHOE
AIRPORT

Forest

Genoa

395

206

207

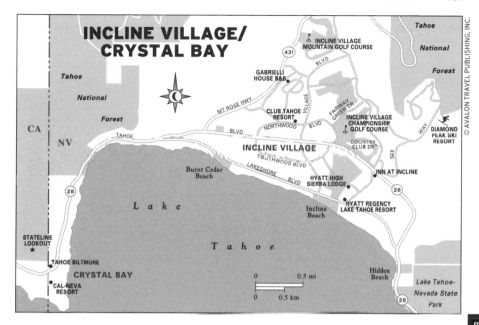

INCLINE VILLAGE/ CRYSTAL BAY

© AVALON TRAVEL PUBLISHING, INC.

there is nothing but public shoreline, and little for visitors to do except wander along the sand at one of a half dozen beaches with intriguing names, like Hidden, Sand Harbor, and Secret. More than anywhere else on Tahoe's shores, this is the place to go when you want to feel sand between your toes, wade into the lake, bask on warm granite boulders, and get lost in your own thoughts.

PLANNING YOUR TIME

Except for the towns of Incline Village and Crystal Bay, there is little in the way of visitor services on the East Shore. While mountain bikers and hikers could easily spend a week or more exploring the area's trails in summer, most visitors will be satisfied with two or three days here, whether for a skiing vacation in winter or a swimming and sunning vacation in summer. Be sure to allow enough time to drive the length of the East Shore and spend some time at one or more of its scenic beaches, such as **Sand Harbor.** In the summer months, a tour of the **Thunderbird Lodge** is a must, and year-round you'll want to spend a half day or longer at **Virginia City,**

Sights

CAL-NEVA RESORT

Even if you aren't a gambler, Cal-Neva Resort casino (2 Tahoe Blvd./Hwy. 28, Crystal Bay, 775/832-4000 or 800/225-6382, www.calneva-resort.com) is worth a look. The casino, which was once owned by crooner Frank Sinatra, has

a fascinating collection of photographs and artifacts of the Washoe Indian tribe housed in its Indian Room. The room's famous fireplace straddles the state line, as does the outdoor swimming pool. Like most casinos, this one is open 24 hours a day, so stop in any time.

◖ MEMORIAL POINT

Located just two miles south of Incline Village on Highway 28, Memorial Point Overlook features one of the best and easiest-to-access lake vistas. Short trails lead to the edge of the lake, and there are lots of big boulders to climb around on (but no sand). Pack along a picnic and you could easily while away an hour or two here, especially at sunset. Even in the winter months, when much of the lakeshore is covered with snow, this sunny spot is usually warm and accessible. Best of all, there's no fee.

SAND HARBOR

Part of the Lake Tahoe Nevada State Park system, Sand Harbor (2005 Hwy. 28, 775/831-0494, www.state.nv.us/stparks, 8 A.M.–6 P.M. daily in summer, parking $8 per car) offers a rocky shoreline for fishing, a cove for snorkeling and scuba diving, a boat launch, sandy beaches for swimming and sunning, a nature center and concession stand, and a self-guided nature trail along Sand Point. Sand Harbor's gentle turquoise coves backed by giant granite boulders are a favorite spot for sunbathers, swimmers, and photographers. The crescent-shaped beach has a fine-grained, soft white sand, not like the coarse gravelly stuff that is found on most of the East Shore's beaches. Every summer Sand Harbor hosts an annual Shakespeare Festival and other cultural events at its lakeside outdoor amphitheater. Sand Harbor is located three miles south of Incline Village. During July and August it is best to arrive before 11 A.M. or after 4 P.M., as the parking lot fills up during peak afternoon hours.

◖ THUNDERBIRD LODGE

Eight miles south of Incline Village is the Thunderbird Lodge (5000 Hwy. 28, 775/832-8750, www.thunderbirdlodge.org), an extravagant stone mansion that is Lake Tahoe's answer to Hearst Castle in San Simeon, California. The Thunderbird was built in the late 1930s by eccentric San Francisco real estate magnate George Whittell Jr., who kept a lion named Bill and a small elephant as pets, erected a lighthouse on his 140 acres of lake frontage,

and built a 600-foot-long underground tunnel to connect his boathouse (the largest one on Lake Tahoe) to the main house. The estate was later purchased and added to by financier Jack Dreyfus in the 1980s. Comprised of a 16,500-square-foot main lodge and a series of Tudor-revival cottages and outbuildings connected by winding pathways, bridges, staircases, and waterfall- and fountain-laden patios, the estate is a masterpiece of fine craftsmanship, with exquisite stone masonry and wrought-iron work. Docents lead 75-minute tours ($25 adults, $10 children) around the property, which will leave you with a whole new definition of "rich." Tours are available May–October by reservation only. Visitors must be shuttled by bus to the lodge from the Incline Village/Crystal Bay Visitor Center (969 Tahoe Blvd./Hwy. 28, Incline Village, 775/832-1606 or 800/468-2463). The property can also be toured by boat charter from the South Shore, aboard the 40-foot wooden yacht *Tahoe* (Woodwind Cruises, 888/867-6394, www.tahoeboatcruises.com), and from the Hyatt Regency in Incline Village aboard the 45-passenger catamaran *Sierra Cloud* (775/832-1234 or 800/553-3288).

LOGAN SHOALS VISTA

Located on the lake side of the highway, one mile north of the Cave Rock tunnels, this vista point (free) off Highway 28 is a fine spot to take a break from the highway and enjoy a view of Lake Tahoe and a banquet of peaks—Echo, Tallac, the twin Maggies, Rubicon, Ellis, Barker, Twin, Ward, Squaw, and Watson, among others. Directly across the lake is the broad U-shaped valley of Emerald Bay, which was carved out by receding glaciers. Peering through a cluster of pines, you also can get a fair view of Cave Rock to the south.

CAVE ROCK

Formed about three million years ago by a volcanic eruption, the rugged face of Cave Rock is the most notable geologic feature of the East Shore. The rock, which rises 360 feet above the lake's surface, was named not for the manufactured Highway 50 tunnels that pass through it, but the small caves on its southwest side that were cut by waves during the ice age when the lake was 200 feet higher than it is today. Cave Rock is actually not a rock at all, but an andesite plug that was the neck of an old volcano.

Washoe Indians, who lived at Lake Tahoe for more than 10,000 years, have always believed that Cave Rock is a sacred place. Only the Washoe shaman was allowed to enter its cave, to seek guidance for aiding the tribe. Today much of the cave has been altered by development, but Washoes still visit here to pay tribute to their past.

Also of great significance to white miners in the mid-1800s, Cave Rock was a major landmark on the Lake Bigler Toll Road, which the gold diggers used to travel back and forth to the Comstock mines in Nevada. The current tunnels in the rock were blasted for the construction of Highway 50—the first in 1931 and the second in 1958.

Just south of Cave Rock is a small Nevada state park with a boat launch and day-use area ($6 fee per vehicle). The park is popular with anglers. Picnickers will enjoy a spectacular view of the West Shore with a 12-mile-wide expanse of Tahoe in between.

◖ VIRGINIA CITY

If you are curious about the West's mining history, don't miss a chance to visit the "living ghost town" of Virginia City, about a 50-minute drive from the lake, just east of U.S. 395 in Nevada (25 miles southeast of Reno and 15 miles northeast of Carson City). This once-thriving metropolis was the centerpiece of the Comstock Lode silver strike in 1859, which served as the main catalyst for the early development of the Lake Tahoe basin. In a period of just under two decades, the Comstock Lode produced roughly $400 million in silver and gold, which made it the biggest ore-producing area in the nation during that time. Many men became millionaires in Virginia City. Money from the mines helped to finance the Civil War and paid to build old San Francisco. Partly because of these great riches, Nevada was granted statehood in 1864.

Today, Virginia City with its false-front buildings and wooden sidewalks looks much like the Old West towns featured in a multitude of Hollywood movies. A bit of a tourist trap but fascinating nonetheless, the nation's largest National Historic Landmark is visited by more than 1.5 million people per year. Visitors can ride an old steam train past abandoned mining sites, tour Victorian mansions, cruise through town on a horse-drawn stagecoach, drink sarsaparilla, gamble, or tour an underground mine inside the Ponderosa Saloon. Not surprisingly, T-shirts, candy, and assorted other souvenirs are available for purchase in almost every shop on C Street, the town's main drag.

A few highlights not to be missed include the Silver Queen Hotel and Wedding Chapel, which has a wall-sized painting made

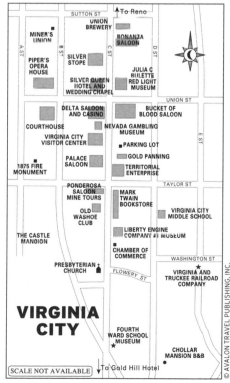

© ANN MARIE BROWN

Virginia City looks much the same as it did during the silver mining boom of 1857-1877.

EAST SHORE

up of more than 3,000 silver dollars; and the Delta Saloon and Casino, famous for its "Suicide Table," where three of the casino's previous owners reputedly killed themselves over debts incurred from lopsided poker games. The Fourth Ward School, erected in 1876, is now a museum. The historic Piper's Opera House was built in 1885 and is still used for concerts and performances. May–October, be sure to take a ride on the restored **Virginia and Truckee Railroad** (775/847-0380, www.steamtrain.org, $7 adults, $3.50 children 5–12) from Virginia City to Gold Hill. Passengers can sit in open-air cars or in an enclosed caboose. During the 35-minute ride, the conductor tells stories about the history of the area and the bonanza of the Comstock mines. Trains depart Virginia City eight times a day 10:30 A.M.–5 P.M.

Practicalities

Most visitors can see and do Virginia City in less than a day, but if you'd like to spend the night, several intriguing lodging options are available. At **Tyson's Seven Mile Canyon Ranch** (Seven Mile Canyon, 775/847-7223, www.nevadaduderanch.com, $125–175), a herd of longhorn cattle roam amid five deluxe guest cottages. The **Chollar Mansion** B&B (565 S. D St., 775/847-9777, $125–150) was the home of a silver mining baron in 1861. Nevada's oldest hotel, the 1859 **Gold Hill Hotel** (Hwy. 342, 775/847-0111, www.goldhillhotel.net, $80–225) is still in operation after nearly a century and a half. It offers 19 rooms and guesthouses, plus a bookstore, saloon, and wonderful restaurant. Most establishments are open for business 10 A.M.–5 P.M. daily year-round; the saloons stay open later.

From Spooner Summit, take Highway 50 east to Carson City, then continue east for another seven miles to the Highway 341 turnoff. Turn north and drive seven miles to Virginia City. For more information, contact the Virginia City Chamber of Commerce (775/847-0311) or Virginia City Convention and Tourism Authority (775/847-7500, www.virginiacity.org).

GENOA

Nevada's oldest permanent settlement, the town of Genoa was originally established in 1851 as the trading post Mormon Station. Today it is home to a wealth of antique shops and art galleries, Nevada's oldest bar (still in business), and the cemetery where Snowshoe Thompson, the man who carried the mail across the Sierra Nevada on skis, was laid to rest. A museum is housed in the historic Genoa Courthouse. From Spooner Summit, take Highway 50 east to Carson City, then turn right at the third stoplight on Jack's Valley Road.

Recreation

HIKING

One of the most popular activities at Lake Tahoe is going for a hike, as the spectacular Sierra scenery quite naturally inspires the urge to explore. Before you set out on the trail, make sure you are prepared with a few essentials, such as bottled water (or some sort of water-filtering device), food, and a trail map. Because many of Tahoe's trails have rocky, uneven surfaces, hiking boots are highly recommended. Sunscreen and/or a sun hat are musts at this high elevation, and you don't want to be without mosquito repellent if the bugs are biting. And keep in mind that weather in the Sierra can change dramatically in a short period of time, so it's always wise to carry a lightweight rain poncho or jacket, and other clothing for layering.

For more information on the trails described below, contact the Carson Ranger District of Humboldt-Toiyabe National Forest (1536 Carson St., Carson City, 775/882-2766, www.fs.fed.us/htnf). Or contact Lake Tahoe Nevada State Park (2005 Hwy. 28, Incline Village, 775/831-0494, www.parks.nv.gov).

The following hikes are listed from north to south along the east side of the lake.

Mount Rose

- Distance: 10 miles round-trip
- Duration: 3–4 hours
- Rating: Strenuous
- Elevation change: 2,300 feet
- Trailhead: Mount Rose
- Directions: From Incline Village, take Hwy.

431 (Mount Rose Hwy.) north for 8 miles to the highway summit and the large trailhead parking area on the left, signed as Mount Rose Summit Welcome Plaza. The trail begins behind the restrooms.

Hikers accustomed to exploring Yosemite and points farther south in the Sierra Nevada are always somewhat surprised at the lower elevations of the "big peaks" in the Tahoe area. Despite the magnitude of Lake Tahoe and its grand mountain scenery, only a few hikeable summits in the area top the 10,000-foot mark. Mount Rose is one of them, and at 10,778 feet, it is the undisputed monolith of Tahoe's northeast shore. A good trail leads all the way to the top, making it a must on every Tahoe hiker's itinerary. Mount Rose is a volcanic peak and much of the route to the summit is treeless, waterless, and exposed, so be sure to pack along lots of extra water and sunscreen.

The trail begins at the large parking area just below the summit of the Mount Rose Highway. Take the trail from behind the restrooms and begin a moderate ascent on a shadeless slope carpeted with sagebrush, lupine, and mule's ears. Views of Tahoe Meadows, far below, will inspire you to visit that spot on another day. After a mellow ascent of 1.5 miles, the trail descends through a hemlock forest, where evidence of long-ago logging operations can be seen, to a lush meadow highlighted by Galena Creek's waterfall coursing down to its edge. In peak season, this meadow is filled with larkspur, paintbrush, lupine, and many other colorful flowers.

© ANN MARIE BROWN

A hiker takes in the view of Lake Tahoe from atop 10,778-foot Mount Rose.

From the edge of the meadow, Mount Rose looks so close that you might assume you'll be on top in no time. However, the majority of this hike's 2,300 feet of elevation gain takes place in the next 2.6 miles, so the grade will surely rein in your ambitions. The trail makes its way steeply to a saddle west of the summit, where you go right for Mount Rose and another trail continues straight toward Big Meadows. You may be feeling a bit breathless but you still have another 1.5 miles to the top, skirting along the broad shoulder of the peak. At first, low-growing whitebark pines provide a modicum of shade, but soon these disappear. Keep your eyes on the ground alongside the trail and you may spot the wood-fruited evening primrose, a rare alpine plant with big yellow flowers on low-lying stems that grows only on the upper slopes of Mount Rose. The final half mile is a real butt-kicker, partly because of the high-elevation air and partly because the volcanic terrain is so open and exposed. But the view from the top is well worth the effort. On clear days, it is easy to pick out Mount Lassen nearly 100 miles to the north. The Sierra Buttes in Plumas National Forest can also be seen, as well as the desert lands surrounding Reno and Sparks, plus three major reservoirs—Prosser, Boca, and Stampede—and of course, mighty Lake Tahoe. Low rock walls have been built on the summit to give hikers shelter from the frequent wind.

Tahoe Meadows

- Distance: 1.3 miles round-trip
- Duration: 1 hour
- Rating: Easy
- Elevation change: 40 feet
- Trailhead: Tahoe Meadows/Tahoe Rim Trail
- Directions: From Incline Village, take Hwy. 431 (Mount Rose Hwy.) north for 7.5 miles to the large parking area on the right (southeast) side of the highway. The trail begins behind the visitors center.

The Tahoe Meadows Whole Access Trail was designed for wheelchair users, but hikers using two feet will find it equally enjoyable. This wide, high-desert meadow is set at 8,870 feet in elevation, with Mount Rose towering 2,000 feet above to the north. The loop trail's surface is smooth dirt, with nearly a dozen footbridges that were constructed to protect the multiple tiny creeks meandering through the wetlands. In early summer, wildflowers abound, including the pink tufts of pussypaws, bright yellow buttercups and marsh marigolds, and a variety of penstemon species. In August, pink and white elephant heads make an appearance. Although this trail is bordered by the busy Mount Rose Highway and the road noise never goes away, Tahoe Meadows somehow manages to retain a tranquil ambience that keeps visitors and locals alike coming back for more.

Ophir Creek

- Distance: 4 miles round-trip
- Duration: 2 hours
- Rating: Moderate
- Elevation change: 800 feet
- Trailhead: Tahoe Meadows/Tahoe Rim Trail
- Directions: From Incline Village, take Hwy. 431 (Mount Rose Hwy.) north for 7.5 miles to the large parking area on the right (southeast) side of the highway.

During the Tahoe wildflower season, which generally peaks in mid-July (although the timing varies greatly from year to year), there may be no better trail on the Nevada side of the lake than this one for admiring the blossoms. Some of the showiest flower species that thrive here are crimson columbine, mountain penstemon, and Sierra evening primrose. The Ophir Creek Trail begins at Tahoe Meadows just below the summit of the Mount Rose Highway, then descends over the course of six miles to Davis Creek Park. Most people don't travel the entire length of the trail, as it makes a daunting descent of 3,300 feet, requiring a strenuous return trip unless a car shuttle is arranged. Instead, a satisfying

walk can be had just by hiking out and back for a couple of miles each way. Begin by starting at the Tahoe Meadows Trailhead on the northeast end of Tahoe Meadows, hiking southwest across the meadow, then entering a lodgepole-pine forest. You'll pick up Ophir Creek Trail just beyond a crossing of Ophir Creek, 0.7 mile from the start. The Tahoe Rim Trail heads right; you'll go left. Once you are officially on the trail, which is the remains of an old road, you never stray far from the lovely creek's side. If you hike about two miles, you will be treated to a superb overlook of Wahoe Valley and its lake, thousands of feet below. On warm summer days, hikers will often spot paragliders and hang gliders riding the thermal breezes over the valley. Note that this trail is also popular with mountain bikers, although many only travel it in one direction—downhill.

Snowflake Lodge

- Distance: 2.6 miles round-trip
- Duration: 1.5 hours
- Rating: Moderate
- Elevation change: 700 feet
- Trailhead: Diamond Peak Ski Resort
- Directions: From Hwy. 28 at Incline Village, turn north on Country Club Dr. and drive 1 mile to Ski Way. Turn right and follow Ski Way to its end at Diamond Peak Ski Resort.

The mid-mountain Snowflake Lodge is the destination of this short, view-filled hike from the base of Diamond Peak Ski Resort (775/832-1177 or 800/468-2463, www.diamondpeak.com). Although the route to get there is on a ski-lift maintenance road, not a real hiking trail, it's worth suffering through the exposed, 700-foot climb to reach Snowflake Lodge's 4,000-square-foot sundeck and its horizon-stretching view of Lake Tahoe. The deck is covered with picnic tables, so don't forget to pack your lunch. The road/trail starts at the ski resort's base lodge and follows the dirt and gravel road alongside the Lodgepole Quad Chair.

EAST SHORE

Stateline Lookout

- Distance: 2 miles round-trip
- Duration: 1 hour
- Rating: Easy/moderate
- Elevation change: 500 feet
- Trailhead: Rd. 1601
- Directions: From Hwy. 28 at Crystal Bay, turn north on Reservoir Dr. (just east of the Tahoe Biltmore Casino). Drive 0.2 mile and turn right on Lakeview Dr. Continue 0.5 mile to the gated fire road on the left (Rd. 1601). If the gate is open, you can drive uphill 1 mile to the parking lot. Usually the gate is locked and you must park in pullouts alongside Lakeview Dr., then walk up the fire road.

You can't beat the Stateline Lookout Trail for an early-morning or sunset walk. Located at the site of an old fire-lookout tower, this half-mile interpretive loop trail sits smack on the California/Nevada border at an elevation of 7,017 feet, offering a bird's-eye view of Tahoe's North and East Shores. The fire road that leads to the lookout site and its trail is most often closed, so the road is usually part of the hike, making this 0.5-mile hike a 2-mile hike. But no matter; it's a pleasant walk up a fir- and pine-forested hillside. (Because the fire road is wide and exposed to the sun, you might want to avoid a midday walk in summer.) When you reach the parking area for the interpretive trail, located by a large signboard, head out in either direction and start enjoying gorgeous high lake views. A dozen interpretive panels explain about the North Shore's logging history, the 1870s conflict over where in Lake Tahoe to set the California/Nevada boundary line, and the onset of the gambling and resort era on the North Shore. At one time, a Forest Service lookout person was stationed up here to spot fires. The small lookout building was known as "Hotel de Chipmunk."

Chimney Beach and Secret Harbor

- Distance: 3 miles round-trip
- Duration: 1.5 hours
- Rating: Easy
- Elevation change: 300 feet
- Trailhead: Hwy. 28
- Directions: From Incline Village, drive 6 miles south on Hwy. 28 to a large paved parking lot on the right (lake) side of the highway (2.9 miles south of the San Harbor turnoff).

If you've become accustomed to all the private property that lines the North, West, and South Shores of Lake Tahoe, the amount of public land on Tahoe's East Shore comes as a welcome surprise. Much of the East Shore's sparkling shoreline and sandy beaches are accessible to anyone who is willing to walk, and no day-use or parking fees are required. From the large Forest Service–managed parking lot, a wide trail descends just over a half mile (dropping 350 feet in elevation) to just above the water's edge, then runs north and south

A short walk to Stateline Lookout leads to spectacular views of Crystal Bay and Lake Tahoe's north and east shores.

along the shoreline. Heading right will take you to Chimney Beach, where the remains of an old stone chimney can be seen. Heading left will take you to Secret Harbor, with its numerous rocky coves. Despite the fact that hordes of visitors descend to this shoreline on warm summer days, there is plenty of room for everyone to spread out and find their own stretch of sand. Don't forget your beach towel, and don't be shocked if you pass by an occasional nude sunbather. Bathing trunks are optional here.

Prey Meadows and Skunk Harbor

- Distance: 3 miles round-trip
- Duration: 1.5 hours
- Rating: Easy/moderate
- Elevation change: 600 feet
- Trailhead: Slaughterhouse Canyon
- Directions: From the junction of Hwy. 50 and Hwy. 28, drive 2.4 miles north on Hwy. 28 to a pullout by a green metal gate on the left (lake) side of the highway. Park safely off the highway in the pullout.

Since Skunk Harbor is one of Lake Tahoe's most picturesque coves, it's hard to understand why its trailhead isn't signed and visitor parking is so limited. But that's reality at the Slaughterhouse Canyon Trailhead along Highway 28, and those factors, combined with the fact that the beach is a 1.5-mile hike from the highway, keep the crowd factor to a minimum. The trail is an easy-to-follow dirt road that starts at the highway and heads downhill through a Jeffrey pine and fir forest. You'll reach a junction 0.7 mile down the trail; the left fork heads to wildflower-filled Prey Meadows in Slaughterhouse Canyon, a must-see during the peak of the bloom. The right fork continues to Skunk Harbor on the shore of Lake Tahoe, a secluded beach where George Newhall built a stone house in 1923 as a wedding gift for his wife, Caroline. The Newhall House was used not as an actual home, but as their private family picnic site. George and Caroline lived across the lake at Rubicon Bay and would cruise by boat to Skunk Harbor for afternoon outings. Later the house became the property of George Whittell, the eccentric owner of Thunderbird Lodge, who used it as a guesthouse. Although the house is now boarded up and in disrepair, it's a fascinating reminder of the glory days at Lake Tahoe. Meanwhile, just a few yards distant, the Skunk Harbor beach is a mix of coarse sand and rocks, and the shallow waters along the shore warm up quite nicely for swimming on summer days.

Spooner Lake Loop

- Distance: 2.1 miles round-trip
- Duration: 1 hour
- Rating: Easy
- Elevation change: 50 feet
- Trailhead: Spooner Lake
- Directions: From the junction of Hwy. 50 and Hwy. 28, drive 0.6 mile north on Hwy. 28 to the Spooner Lake/Lake Tahoe Nevada State Park entrance. A $6 day-use fee is charged.

Spooner Lake is an artificial water body on the Nevada side of the lake that played an important role in the Comstock gold- and silver-mining boom. The lake served as a mill-pond and was part of a system of reservoirs, flumes, and pipelines that supplied lumber and water to the Virginia City and Gold Hill mines. Interpretive displays at the parking area detail this fascinating period in Tahoe's history. At 7,000 feet in elevation, the 1.6-mile trail that circles Spooner Lake's perimeter is snow-free much of the year, and when it is snow-covered, it makes a fine track for snowshoeing or cross-country skiing. From the day-use parking area, follow the trail near the restrooms downhill to the tranquil lake's dam, 0.2 mile away. Cross the dam to start the loop and you'll wander amid aspens and Jeffrey pines. Watch for large granite boulders that are marked by Native American morteros, or grinding holes. As you curve around the lakeshore, keep on the lookout for osprey (often seen diving into the lake for fish),

© ANN MARIE BROWN

An easy stroll along the shores of Spooner Lake often leads to wildlife sightings.

killdeer, and even bald eagles. Binoculars are a handy accessory for this hike; several benches are conveniently placed in good spots for bird- and wildlife-watching. On the southeast side of the lake, a spur trail leads to the parking area at Spooner Summit. (Some people prefer to hike in 0.75 mile from this trailhead to avoid paying the state park day-use fee). Fishing is permitted in Spooner Lake but it is catch-and-release only. Because of the presence of leeches, swimming is a bad idea.

Marlette Lake

- Distance: 9 miles round-trip
- Duration: 5 hours
- Rating: Moderate
- Elevation change: 700 feet
- Trailhead: Spooner Lake
- Directions: From the junction of Hwy. 50 and Hwy. 28, drive 0.6 mile north on Hwy. 28 to the Spooner Lake/Lake Tahoe Nevada State Park entrance. A $6 day-use fee is charged.

The North Canyon Road to Marlette Lake is a favorite path of mountain bikers making their way to the start of the infamous Flume Trail, but now hikers have their own trail to the beautiful lake—the North Canyon Trail, completed in 2005, takes off from North Canyon Road and travels four miles to the lake. Bikers stay on one trail, hikers stay on another trail—everybody is happy. It's a toss-up whether it is better to hike this trail in early summer (for wildflowers) or mid-autumn (for the quaking aspen fall color show). Both seasons are winners. Begin the trip by following the wide path from near the parking lot restrooms toward Spooner Lake's dam. Before reaching the dam, you'll turn left (north) on North Canyon Road. Soon you'll pass the right turnoff for Spooner Lake cabin, which is available for overnight rental (see *Accommodations*), and the historic Spencer Cabin, which is sometimes used as a warming hut for skiers in the winter. At 0.7 mile from your start, you'll meet up with the new North Canyon Trail. Here you leave the dirt road and follow the narrower, hikers-only trail. The well-built path stays along the west bank of North Canyon Creek and is a gentle climb almost all the way until the last half mile, where it junctions with a trail coming up on the left from Chimney Beach, then drops steeply to the lake's southern shore. The closer you get to the lake, the denser the stands of aspens. Once you arrive, you can wander along the shoreline to find the best spots for picnicking and swimming. Those with extra energy to burn can take the 1.2-mile trail along the lake's East Shore to Marlette Overlook, which provides breathtaking views looking west over Marlette Lake and Lake Tahoe. Note that fishing is not permitted in the lake because it serves as a fish hatchery for the state of Nevada. Given that the lake also supplies drinking water via a flume to Carson City and Virginia City, it's surprising that swimming is permitted here, but it is.

South Camp Peak

- Distance: 10.6 miles round trip
- Duration: 5–6 hours
- Rating: Moderate/strenuous
- Elevation change: 2,200 feet
- Trailhead: Spooner Summit/Tahoe Rim Trail
- Directions: From the junction of Hwy. 50 and Hwy. 28, drive 0.8 mile east on Hwy. 50 to Spooner Summit and the parking area on the right (south) side.

This hike on a portion of the Tahoe Rim Trail takes you to one of the most view-filled peaks in the Carson Range. Before you go, remember that this trail is in dry Nevada, not the much wetter mountains on the California side of Lake Tahoe, so you need to carry plenty of water with you (there are no streams or springs along the trail). For early-season hikers, this is good news—South Camp Peak will be snow-free a month earlier than other summits around the lake. It is usually accessible by June.

The trail begins with an ascent over open slopes, then delves into a mixed conifer forest and delivers you to your first wide views

at 1.5 miles, where a short spur trail leads a high knoll. Snap a few pictures here, then continue onward. Much of the trail is smooth, hard-packed sand, making it a favorite area for mountain bikers. Two miles farther the trail crosses Genoa Peak Road amid a heavily logged area. Catch your breath here before attacking the final 1.5-mile, 800-foot ascent to the top of South Camp Peak, mostly over densely forested slopes. The 8,818-foot peak has a broad, flat summit that seems to go on forever. You'll arrive on the northwest edge of it; which spot you decide to call the tippy-top is up to you. Views are excellent from just about everywhere along the nearly level, open plateau. Dozens of landmarks are easy to spot, including nearby Genoa Peak with its telltale radio towers, Mount Rose, Fallen Leaf Lake, Emerald Bay, Pyramid Peak, Freel Peak, Mount Tallac, and the tall buildings of the Stateline casinos.

BIKING

Skinny-tire riders who want to rack up some road mileage have a wealth of routes to choose from in the Carson City/Carson Valley area, including a 50-mile loop tour that cruises through Virginia City. A great source for information on Nevada road biking is www.bicyclenevada.com.

Bike rentals and equipment are available in Incline Village at Porters Ski and Sports (885 Tahoe Blvd./Hwy. 28, 775/831-3500) and Village Ski Loft and Bicycles (800 Tahoe Blvd./Hwy. 28, 775/831-3537).

Lakeshore Bike Path

Those seeking an easy, scenic ride on the East Shore should head for the Lakeshore Bike Path in Incline Village. This mostly level, paved trail connects with Highway 28 on both ends, and its entire one-way length is only three miles. However, there are places to stop, including Burnt Cedar Beach and Incline Beach on Crystal Bay, and numerous mega-mansions to ogle along the way. Parking is easiest at the west end of the trail at the junction of Highway 28 and Lakeshore Drive (0.5 mile west of the Hwy. 431/Hwy. 28

EAST SHORE

PONDEROSA RANCH

For decades, one of the most popular tourist attractions at Lake Tahoe was the Ponderosa Ranch, a theme park based on the television show *Bonanza*, which depicted the life of the Cartwright family – Pa, Adam, Hoss, and Little Joe – and their fictional struggles on their magnificent Nevada ranch. The popular show, which aired 1959–1973, was partly filmed on a strip of land near Incline Village, including its famous opening scene.

In the 1960s Bill Anderson, one of the contractors who worked with the film crews building "fake" outbuildings and roads on location at Tahoe, got the idea to use the sets from the show to create a theme park. He even built an exact replica of the Cartwright house, which never existed at Lake Tahoe but rather was filmed on a Hollywood soundstage, at the Incline Village shooting location. The theme park operated 1968–2003 and featured hayrides, pony rides, staged gunfights, a petting zoo, vintage car and wagon exhibits, souvenir shops, and an entire false-front Western town, including the Silver Dollar Saloon and the re-created Cartwright ranch house.

When the owners of the 570-acre park put it up for sale at a price tag of $50 million, a consortium of government agencies struggled to come up with the money to buy the land and preserve it from commercial development. Their efforts failed, and in 2004 Incline Village resident David Duffield, founder of the technology company People-Soft, became the new owner of the Ponderosa Ranch. What will happen to the property is anybody's guess, but for now, Duffield says he doesn't plan to reopen the theme park or develop the land.

junction). The trail parallels Lakeshore Drive, crossing it only once, until its terminus where it meets Highway 28 again, near the old Ponderosa Ranch.

(Flume Trail

Proceeding directly from the mild to the wild, on the opposite end of the biking spectrum is the Flume Trail. Probably the most famous single mountain biking trail in the West, the Flume Trail can be ridden in different ways. The most common route is to start at Spooner Lake State Park, off Highway 28 just north of its junction with Highway 50. Follow the trail east from the parking area to just before Spooner Lake's dam, then turn left and follow the wide dirt road toward Marlette Lake. The road travels north alongside North Canyon Creek through increasingly dense aspen groves (gorgeous fall colors can be seen here in late September–early October). The grade gets progressively steeper during the first four miles, then in the last mile you drop steeply to the shore of Marlette Lake. Plenty of beginning and intermediate riders just turn around here for a 10-mile round-trip with about 1,100 feet of elevation gain. Those heading for the Flume Trail go left at a signed fork at the lakeshore, follow a dirt road along the water's edge for another mile, then are deposited on the Flume Trail's famous single-track. The trail is built on the grade of an old square-box logging flume, which carried water and timber from Lake Tahoe to the silver mines of Virginia City in the late 1800s. The flume's route was carved into the side of the precipitous slope above Lake Tahoe's East Shore. Good bike-handling skills are important here, as the east side of the trail is lined with car-sized boulders, and the west side has near vertical drop-offs of up to 1,600 feet. Because the trail follows the route of the old flume, it is almost level—it drops only 40 feet per mile—so your cardiovascular system won't be working hard, just your nervous system. If the trail gets too hairy for you, there is no crime in stopping for a minute, or getting off your bike and walking. Plenty of riders do so, especially since the lake views are so breathtaking that you don't want to spin by too fast.

After almost five miles of this adrenaline-pumping riding, the trail forks again and most riders bear left on Tunnel Creek Road and descend via the sandy, dusty fire road to Incline Village, dropping 1,600 feet in only 2.5 miles. Some riders who have made it through the entire Flume Trail without a mishap manage to lose control on this final descent, so use caution. If you haven't arranged shuttle transportation, it's a 10-mile ride back to Spooner Lake on a narrow stretch of Highway 28. If a shuttle is waiting for you, your one-way ride will be about 13 miles, with 1,100 feet of elevation gain and 2,000 feet of loss. Most people take about three to four hours to complete the one-way Flume trip from Spooner Lake to Incline Village.

For those who don't have patient friends who are willing to pick them up at the end of the ride, the **Spooner Lake Outdoor Company** (775/749-5349, www.theflumetrail.com or www.spoonerlake.com), located at the Spooner Lake parking lot, runs a mountain bike shuttle service seven days a week. The fee is $10 for a one-way shuttle, or $7.50 if you rent one of their bikes. Bike rentals are $39–55 per day. Or if you would prefer to tackle the Flume Trail with a knowledgeable guide, the Spooner Lake Outdoor Company will be happy to accommodate you.

There are two options for extending the Flume Trail ride into a longer loop, but both are intended for very strong and experienced riders only. For the first loop option, instead of descending via Tunnel Creek Road, stay right at the junction and keep riding along the ridge for 1.3 miles to another segment of the Flume Trail, called Red House Flume. A right turn on Red House Flume will connect you to a series of fire roads that will bring you back above Marlette Lake. All junctions along the route are well signed, and free maps are available at the Spooner Lake trailhead. From Marlette Lake, just retrace your tire treads back to Spooner Lake. The total loop ride is about 24 miles and very challenging, with a total 2,600-foot elevation gain. The second option is to loop back via the Tahoe Rim Trail. Go right on Tunnel Creek Road and follow it uphill for only 0.5 mile to the Twin Lakes junction, then follow the Rim Trail south for five miles to Hobart/Marlette Road, above Marlette Lake. A right turn here will bring you back to Marlette Lake and Spooner Lake. The total loop ride is 22 miles with 2,000 feet of elevation gain.

South Camp Peak

Another popular mountain-biking destination on the East Shore is the 8,818-foot summit of South Camp Peak, accessible from the Tahoe Rim Trail trailhead just east of Spooner Summit on Highway 50. Although the view of the Lake Tahoe basin at the summit is grand, getting there is half the fun, as you pedal past wildflower-covered slopes and through groves of quaking aspen. The trail is smooth, mostly hard-packed sand all the way, and the grade is fairly moderate for the first 3.8 miles until you near the top, where it steepens considerably. The last 1.5 miles are a serious challenge, with an 800-foot elevation gain. Total mileage out-and-back to South Camp Peak is 10.6 miles.

BOATING AND WATER SPORTS
Kayaking

The East Shore of Lake Tahoe is one of the loveliest areas for kayaking, with miles of pristine, development-free shoreline. Many kayakers put in at **Sand Harbor** (Lake Tahoe Nevada State Park, 2005 Hwy. 28, 775/831-0494, www.state.nv.us/stparks), then paddle south along a string of secluded coves and white sand and boulder-strewn beaches. There are abundant spots where you can pull up on shore for rest stops, swimming, and picnicking, but look carefully before you land—occasional East Shore beachgoers prefer to sunbathe au naturel. You may get an impromptu anatomy lesson. Another popular put-in spot is at **Cave Rock,** farther south at Lake Tahoe Nevada State Park.

For **kayak rentals,** go to Action Watersports (behind the Hyatt, 967 Lakeshore Blvd., Incline Village, 775/831-4386, www.action-watersports.com) or one of several kayak rental

© ANN MARIE BROWN

Those with their own boats can sail to Skunk Harbor; everyone else must walk.

EAST SHORE

companies on the North or South Shores. For guided tours or kayaking lessons, contact Tahoe Paddle & Oar (North Tahoe Beach Center, 7860 N. Lake Blvd., Kings Beach, 530/581-3029, www.tahoepaddle.com). In addition to renting kayaks, they also offer tours ($110 per person) along the boulder-lined shores of Sand Harbor.

Kayakers with bigger ambitions should check out the Lake Tahoe Water Trail map (530/542-5651, www.laketahoewatertrail.org), which shows available boat launches, campsites, lodging, dining, and more for all 72 miles of lake shoreline.

Water Sports Outfitters and Marinas
All types of powerboats and personal watercraft can be rented at **Action Watersports** (behind the Hyatt, 967 Lakeshore Blvd., Incline Village, 775/831-4386, www.action-watersports.com). They also offer parasailing rides from the Incline Village beaches.

If you brought your own boat or personal

watercraft to Lake Tahoe and just need a boat ramp where you can put it in the water, you can do so on the East Shore at Cave Rock (775/831-0494) or Sand Harbor (775/831-0494).

SWIMMING
The Nevada side of the lake is a favorite for swimmers and sunbathers, due to its abundance of undeveloped shoreline and shallow, relatively warm water. On the warmest days of July and August, Tahoe's water temperature within a few feet of the East Shore can be as high as the 70s—as much as 20 degrees warmer than at many other points in the lake. Beachgoers can choose between drive-in, fee-required beaches with picnic tables, restrooms, and other facilities, and secluded hike-in beaches, including some that are clothing-optional. Residents and visitors staying at the condominium resorts in Incline Village have guest access to two developed beaches, **Burnt Cedar** and **Incline Beach,** that are managed by the Incline Village General Improvement District (775/832-1310).

◖ Sand Harbor
Those who are staying elsewhere on the East Shore can head for the developed beach at Sand Harbor, three miles south of Incline Village (Lake Tahoe Nevada State Park, 2005 Hwy. 28, 775/831-0494, www.state.nv.us/stparks). This is one of Lake Tahoe's most scenic beaches, a white crescent of sand framed by giant rounded boulders. The beach has a concession stand, a nature trail, and a separate cove for snorkeling and scuba diving. Beach patrol lifeguards are on duty Memorial Day–Labor Day. Parking is $8 per car.

Free, Hike-in Beaches
A vast majority of beachgoers prefer the no-fee option of finding their own beach paradise in the stretch of shoreline immediately south of Incline Village, known as **Hidden Beach.** This land is part of Lake Tahoe Nevada State Park but there is no official parking area. Beachgoers must park in narrow pullouts alongside Highway 28 and then walk a short distance to the lake. Be

sure to obey all No Parking signs and carry out any trash with you. Because these beaches are state-owned, dogs are not permitted.

South of Sand Harbor and north of Spooner Summit are more no-fee, hike-in beaches. The best parking and access is at the Forest Service-run **Chimney Beach** parking lot, 2.9 miles south of Sand Harbor on Highway 28 (although many people also park in pullouts alongside the highway). From the large parking lot, a downhill walk of 0.6 mile is required to reach the lakeshore. From there you can follow trails to the north or south to find your special spot. Walking north about 0.25 mile will bring you to the namesake stone chimney at **Chimney Beach.** Walking south leads you to **Secret Cove** and **Secret Harbor.** At either beach, don't be surprised if you run into sunbathers wearing nothing but their birthday suits. Leashed dogs are permitted on these Forest Service beaches.

Farthest to the south is **Skunk Harbor** beach, which requires the longest hike to reach (1.2 miles one-way). The trailhead is located 2.4 miles north of Spooner Summit on Highway 28. The shoreline here is comprised of coarse gravel, compared to the sandier beaches to the north. Dogs are permitted on this beach, and visitors can take a look at the exterior of the **Newhall House,** a stone cottage perched on the shoreline that was built in 1923.

FISHING

The steep shoreline and rocky shoals at **Cave Rock** ($5 day-use fee per vehicle) create one of the few places in Lake Tahoe where shore anglers have half a chance of catching fish, especially rainbow trout and occasionally brown trout. Most shore fishermen try their luck with worms, spinners, marshmallows, or salmon eggs. Two launch ramps at the site lead to deep water close to shore. Another spot on the East Shore that is popular with shoreline anglers is the rocky shoreline at **Sand Harbor** ($8 day-use fee per vehicle). If you need to purchase a fishing license or buy tackle or equipment, try Ace Hardware (910 Tahoe Blvd./Hwy. 28, Incline Village, 775/831-2020). Both Sand Har-

bor and Cave Rock come under the jurisdiction of Lake Tahoe Nevada State Park (2005 Hwy. 28, 775/831-0494, www.state.nv.us/stparks).

If it's the big mackinaw you're after, you'll have much better chances going out in a boat. Avid Fisherman Professional Sport Fishing Charters (775/588-7675, www.avidfisherman.net) will take you out from Cave Rock or Zephyr Cove.

On the other end of the fishing spectrum, fly fishers enjoy catch-and-release fishing at **Spooner Lake** for rainbow, brown, and brook trout. Only artificial lures and single barbless hooks are permitted.

ROCK CLIMBING

Rock climbers were sorely disappointed when craggy, volcanic Cave Rock was closed to climbing in 2003 due to its importance as a Native American cultural site. To climbers, Cave Rock was revered as Tahoe's premier sport climbing crag, with a multitude of difficult routes and fantastic lake views. For now, Cave Rock is expected to be closed to climbers until at least 2008. Several other rocks on the East Shore are suitable for intermediate climbers, including **Shakespeare Rock** and **Trippy Rock.** Shakespeare Rock towers 400 feet above U.S. 50, a quarter mile north of the Glenbrook turnoff (on the east side of the highway). Trippy Rock is located five miles north of Incline Village on Highway 431. For more information on these sites, contact the Carson Ranger District of Humboldt-Toiyabe National Forest (775/882-2766).

GOLF

Incline Village has not one but two excellent golf courses—the **Championship Course** (955 Fairway Blvd., Incline Village, 775/832-1146 or 866/925-4653, www.golfincline.com) and the **Mountain Course** (690 Wilson Way, Incline Village, 775/832-1150 or 866/925-4653, www.golfincline.com). Designed by Robert Trent Jones Jr. and consistently ranked as one of the top 10 public courses in the country, the Mountain Course is an 18-hole, par-58 maze of boulders, pines, and meandering streams that demands accurate hitting. The mid-length course (3,500 yards) is completely natural with no artificial landscaping, and has been designated a certified Audubon Cooperative Sanctuary. The course usually plays quickly, but the lake views may slow you down. Rates are a reasonable $55 (twilight rates are $36).

The Championship Course is an 18-hole, par-72, lake-view beauty that was designed by the senior Robert Trent Jones. The course recently underwent a two-year, multimillion-dollar renovation orchestrated by architect Kyle Phillips. After being closed for two years, it reopened in 2005. Accuracy and distance are required for successful play, with fairways surrounded by ponderosa pines, strategically placed bunkers, meandering streams, and small greens. Course length is 7,100 yards from the back tees. Green fees are $155 (twilight rates are $100). The course clubhouse, The Chateau, was completely redesigned as well, and now features The Grille, a lunch spot for hungry golfers.

Farther from the lake, three more courses are found between Incline Village and Reno: **Lake Ridge Golf Course** (775/825-2200, www.lakeridgegolf.com), **Northgate Golf Club** (775/747-7577), and **Wolf Run Golf Club** (775/851-3301, www.wolfrungolfclub.com).

In the Carson Valley area of Nevada, about one hour from the lakeshore, are a consortium of courses known as the **Divine Nine** (www.divine9.com): The Golf Club at Genoa Lakes, Genoa Lakes Golf Resort, Silver Oak Golf Club, Sunridge Golf Club, Eagle Valley East, Eagle Valley West, Dayton Valley Golf Club, Carson Valley Golf Course, and Empire Ranch Golf Course. The Nine's total 171 holes of golf encompass 70,000 yards of terrain—enough to keep any golfer busy for more than a week. Golf packages and special discounts are available for golfers who want to play a majority of the courses.

WINTER SPORTS
Downhill Skiing and Snowboarding

The East Shore of the lake sports two major ski resorts: Mount Rose and Diamond Peak, both just a handful of miles from Incline Village. **Mount Rose Ski Area** (22222 Hwy. 431/ Mount Rose Hwy., 11 miles northeast of Incline Village, 775/849-0704 or 800/754-7673, www.skirose.com) has the highest base elevation of any resort at Lake Tahoe (8,260 feet), making its slopes the last place where the snow turns to slush on warm spring days. It's also known for having few, if any, lift lines. Total skiable acreage at the resort is 1,200 acres; the longest vertical drop is 1,800 feet. A total of 43 runs, the longest measuring in at 2.5 miles, are serviced by seven lifts. The views from the mountain's slopes take in not just Lake Tahoe to the south but also the Nevada desert to the east. Boarders have access to the entire mountain, and they can shred all day at five terrain parks and two half-pipes.

In 2004, Mount Rose added a new section to its skiable terrain, an area of steep, ungroomed powder called The Chutes, which for many years was out-of-bounds, illegal territory. Now The Chutes has its own chairlift and 16 official new double black-diamond runs. Another 200 acres on the back side of Mount Rose have also been made legal.

Despite the newfound popularity of the steep and deep Chutes, this resort is not just for envelope-pushers. Plenty of kids learn to ski or ride at **Rosebuds Ski and Snowboard Camp.** And adult beginners can choose from first-timer instruction, rookie classes, and intermediate lessons. With rental equipment and lift tickets, lesson packages cost only $49–69 for adults.

Lift ticket prices at Mount Rose are a little lower than at comparable Tahoe resorts (full-day tickets are $54 adult, $38 teens, $34 seniors 60–74, $12 children 6–12, free for seniors over 75 and children 5 and under), but many skiers take advantage of Mount Rose's regular weekly bargains, like "2 for Tuesday," when you can buy two adult tickets for the price of one, and "Ladies Day Thursdays," when women receive a full-day ticket for less than half price. Consecutive three-day tickets are only $99. If you are staying in Reno, you can take the **ski shuttle** to Mount Rose. The shuttle runs from major Reno hotels (Nugget, Hilton, Sands, Silver Legacy, Peppermill, Atlantis) twice each morning to Mount Rose Ski area (a 25-minute drive). Reservations are recommended (775/325-8813, www.tahoeskishuttle.com) The fare is $15 round-trip, but combined lift ticket and shuttle packages are available.

Nearby, the intimate and family-oriented **Diamond Peak Ski Resort** (1219 Ski Way, Incline Village, 775/832-1177 or 800/468-2463, www.diamondpeak.com) is located just 1.5 miles from downtown Incline Village. Its 30 runs access 655 skiable acres. The longest run is 2.5 miles with a vertical drop of 1,840 feet. The resort's summit elevation (8,540 feet) is about the same as the base elevation at Mount Rose. With average snowfall of only about 350 inches, they often have to make snow, but they are equipped for it. Like at Mount Rose, the vistas from the chairlifts and the slopes take in Lake Tahoe and a wide expanse of Nevada desert. Diamond Peak may not have the most varied and challenging slopes around, but they are among the most scenic.

Beginners will be happy here, as the resort has plenty of affordable lessons options. Kids as young as three can attend ski school (and kids as young as four can take snowboarding lessons). A total of six chairlifts service the resort, and three operate with a "Launch Pad" conveyor belt system to make loading and unloading easier. Boarders can bust air at Diamond Peak's freestyle terrain park (www.snowbomb .com) and superpipe, or if they want to improve their skills, sign up for two- or four-hour freestyle snowboarding clinics.

Lift tickets are some of the best bargains near the lake: All-day tickets for adults are $46, teens are $36, children 6–12 and seniors 60–79 are $17, children 5 and under are free. Discounted family packages for one or two adults and one or more children are also available. And, if you are not satisfied with the snow conditions within your first hour of skiing, you can return your ticket and receive a free voucher for another day. Free shuttle service to the slopes is available from

points in Kings Beach, Crystal Bay, and Incline Village.

If you want to rent your equipment before you arrive at the slopes, try one of these three rental shops in Incline Village: Village Ski Loft (800 Tahoe Blvd./Hwy. 28, 775/831-3537), Porter's Sports Shop (885 Tahoe Blvd./Hwy. 28, 775/831-3500), or Ski Rents USA (869 Tahoe Blvd./Hwy. 28, 775/831-4724).

Cross-Country Skiing

The best single place for cross-country skiing near Tahoe's blue shoreline is at **Spooner Lake Cross Country Ski Area** (Hwy. 28, Glenbrook, 775/749-5349, www.spoonerlake.com), which has more than 20 trails spanning 9,000 acres of terrain and 80 kilometers of groomed track. A variety of loops are possible, from the novice-level Spooner Lake Trail (about three miles in length) to The Big Loop, a challenging 20-mile trek on groomed trail. Whether you prefer easy paths or daylong glides into the backcountry, you'll be happy here. Trails are maintained and regroomed every evening. The ski area is located 0.5 mile north of the junction of Highway 28 and Highway 50 near Spooner Summit (12 miles north of Stateline and 12 miles south of Incline Village). A day lodge with a fireplace and snacks is at the trailhead, and there are two wilderness cabins for those who would like an overnight adventure (see *Accomodations*).

All-day trail passes are $21 for adults, $10 for teens, $16 for seniors ages 60–69, and free for children 12 and under and seniors 70 and older. But if you strategize a bit, you can take advantage of bargain deals. For example, if you are going to ski two days in a row, your second day is only $14. Every Tuesday, trail passes are only $10. Twilight passes, good 3–5 P.M. daily, are only $10. On Thursdays, lessons are free.

If you don't have your own equipment, you can rent it for $19 per day or $15 per half day (less for children and seniors). If you don't know how to cross-country ski, lesson packages with equipment rentals and a trail pass are only $45.

EAST SHORE

© ANN MARIE BROWN

Kids make the most of the white stuff at the roadside Spooner Summit Snow Play Area.

EAST SHORE

Cross-country skiers looking for a no-cost place to kick and glide can head to **Tahoe Meadows,** on the southeast side of Highway 431/Mount Rose Highway, just below Mount Rose Summit (7.5 miles from Incline Village). This is a great place for moonlight skiing.

Snowshoeing

Snowshoers can take their pick from the 20 groomed trails, spanning a distance of 80 kilometers, at **Spooner Lake Cross Country Ski Area** (Hwy. 28, Glenbrook, 775/749-5349, www.spoonerlake.com). You can rent snowshoes at the Spooner Lake day lodge; rentals are $12–17 for adults and $8 for teens. Trail passes are an additional $17–21 for adults, $9 for teens and seniors, so the best deal is the combined snowshoe rental/trail pass package, which is $26. For no-cost snowshoeing, head to Tahoe Meadows, 7.5 miles north of Incline Village on Highway 431/Mount Rose Highway.

Sledding and Tubing

On the East Shore, there are three places where you can bring your own sleds, tubes, saucers, or garbage-can lids and slide down snow-covered slopes. **Tahoe Meadows** (7.5 miles north of Incline Village on Highway 431/Mount Rose Highway) has a few mellow hills for young sledders, and abundant spots to build snowmen or make snow angels. **Incline Village Snow Play Area** (on Fairway Blvd. next to the Chateau Clubhouse, at the Championship Course driving range) has a gentle hill for sledding. The **Spooner Summit Snow Play Area** (junction of Hwy. 28 and Hwy. 50), 12 miles north of Stateline and 12 miles south of Incline Village, has a variety of hills ranging from mild to very steep.

If you'd rather take the kids to a place where there is organized snow play, head for Bee's Snow Play at **Diamond Peak Ski Resort** (1219 Ski Way, Incline Village, 775/832-1177 or 800/468-2463, www.diamondpeak.com).

Entertainment and Shopping

NIGHTLIFE

Unless your idea of nightlife is cross-country skiing under a full moon, the only place to find any late-evening action on the East Shore is at the Crystal Bay and Incline Village casinos. The king of them all is the **Cal-Neva Resort** (2 Tahoe Blvd./Hwy. 28, Crystal Bay, 775/832-4000 or 800/225-6382, www.cal-nevaresort.com), which straddles the California/Nevada state line. Once owned by singer Frank Sinatra, the Cal-Neva has a large indoor showroom for live entertainment, a wedding chapel, a European-style health spa, as well as all the usual casino and sports-book offerings. Right next door is the **Crystal Bay Casino** (14 Tahoe Blvd./Hwy. 28, Crystal Bay, 775/833-6333 or 775/831-0512, www.crystalbay-casino.com), remodeled in 2004, which offers live music, dancing, live entertainment at the Stage Lounge and the Crown Room, the Crystal Bay Steak and Lobster House, a full-service sports book, and 30 plasma TVs. In the summer months, Crystal Bay Club also showcases performers at its 1,900-seat rooftop stage.

Across the street, the **Tahoe Biltmore Casino** (5 Tahoe Blvd./Hwy. 28, Crystal Bay, 775/831-0660 or 800/245-8667, www.tahoebiltmore.com) has a sports book, dancing, and live entertainment in an old-fashioned nightclub atmosphere at the Breeze Nightclub. At **Jim Kelly's Nugget** (20 Tahoe Blvd./Hwy. 28, Crystal Bay, 775/831-0455), the beer bar is where the action is in summer. If you are diligent, you can taste all 101 beers on the menu and be inducted into the Nugget Beer Drinkers Hall of Fame. Whoopee, you get a T-shirt and a plaque.

Down the road in Incline Village, the Fantasy Forest casino and sports book at the four-diamond **Hyatt Regency Lake Tahoe** (Country Club Dr. at Lakeshore Dr., Incline Village, 775/832-1234 or 800/327-3910, www.hyatt.com) is somewhat more refined. If you get tired of playing keno or betting on football, you can get a massage at the resort's 20,000-square-foot Stillwater Spa, which was added in 2005.

If you are looking for more passive entertainment, check out the evening's offerings at **Incline Village Cinema** (901 Tahoe Blvd./Hwy. 28, Incline Village, 775/546-5951).

SHOPPING

Because of the general lack of commercial enterprises on the East Shore, except for the Incline Village area, shoppers won't have much browsing to do unless they head to Truckee, Tahoe City, Stateline, or South Lake Tahoe. However, Incline Village does have a small shopping center at **Christmas Tree Village** (on Hwy. 28 just west of Village Blvd.), which has a handful of interesting specialty shops: home design, jewelry, and art. A block away is the **Raley's Shopping Center** (on Hwy. 28 just east of Village Blvd.), where you can shop for practical items at a Radio Shack, Ace Hardware, Raley's Supermarket, and the like. **The Village Center** (Mays Blvd. at Southwood), has a half dozen shops of an equally pedestrian nature, including a post office.

FESTIVALS AND EVENTS

The East Shore's biggest and most famous annual event is the **Shakespeare at Sand Harbor Festival** (800/747-4697, www.laketahoeshakespeare.com, $22–67), which features two or more of Shakespeare's plays performed at Sand Harbor's natural outdoor amphitheater. Over the course of the month-long festival, about 30,000 ticket holders bring their own picnic dinner and a beach chair and wiggle their toes in the sand while watching a professional performance of one of the Bard's comedies or tragedies. The event, which has been taking place at Lake Tahoe for more than 30 years, has become so popular that in 2000 a new, $2 million stage was built at Sand Harbor. The festival runs mid-July–mid-August each year. Purchase tickets in advance.

Other events take place each summer at

EAST SHORE

Sand Harbor, including the **Lake Tahoe Chautauqua** (775/298-0068, www.tahoe-historyfestivals.com, $25–50), usually in late June, in which humanities scholars portray historical figures who share their life stories with the audience through anecdotal tales. Purchase tickets in advance. In September, Sand Harbor is one of several venues for the **Lake Tahoe Autumn Food and Wine Festival** (775/832-1038, free), a charity event that features West Coast wineries and food prepared by northern California's top culinary talent.

One event that spills over to Crystal Bay and Incline Village from the North Shore is the **Lake Tahoe Jazz Festival** (800/468-2463, www.laketahoejazzfestival.com, mid–late May, $22–60), featuring more than 20 bands, a parade, a gospel breakfast, and lots more. Concerts take place at multiple venues.

FAMILY FUN

Kids and adults alike will enjoy a trip to **Virginia City,** site of the 1860s Comstock gold- and silver-mining boom. The under-12 set will certainly want to take a ride on the Virginia and Truckee Railroad and tour the underground mine in the Ponderosa Saloon. Along the way, consider a stop at the **Children's Museum of Northern Nevada** (813 N. Carson St., 775/884-2226, 10 A.M.–

4:30 P.M. Tues.–Sun.) in Carson City, where kids are not just allowed to touch the exhibits, they are encouraged to do so. There's a walk-in kaleidoscope, a giant keyboard, and other fun stuff for ages 3–12.

Also in Carson City is the **Nevada State Railroad Museum** (2180 S. Carson St., 775/687-6953, www.nsrm-friends.org, 8:30 A.M.–4:30 P.M. daily, $2 adults, children 18 and under free), which houses a collection of restored historic Virginia and Truckee Railroad cars and locomotives. Steam-train rides are offered in summer.

If your kids are of the video age, they will probably prefer to spend a few hours at one of the East Shore's arcades. Not surprisingly, you'll find them at four Crystal Bay and Incline Village casinos—Cal-Neva, Crystal Bay, Hyatt Regency, and Tahoe Biltmore—giving the kids something to do while Mom and Dad gamble away their college funds.

For a more old-fashioned indoor game, consider knocking over a few pins at **Bowl Incline** (920 Southwood Blvd., Incline Village, 775/831-1900). In addition to the bowling lanes, there is a video arcade, billiards, video poker, darts, and the like. If you are concerned about the health of your kids' lungs in cigarette-happy Nevada, the bowling alley is smoke-free on Sundays.

Accommodations

INCLINE VILLAGE/ CRYSTAL BAY
Bed-and-Breakfasts

The only bed-and-breakfast in the Incline Village area is the **Gabrielli House** (593 N. Dyer Circle, Incline Village, 800/731-6222, www.gabriellihouse.com, $129–199). Five guest bedrooms each have their own private bath, balcony, and television, and the separate guest den is a good place to sit in a leather chair and read. A full breakfast is served each morning. In the summer months, guests have access to Incline Village's private beaches.

Casinos and Hotels

Straddling the California/Nevada border on the North Shore at Crystal Bay, **Cal-Neva Resort, Spa, and Casino** (2 Tahoe Blvd./Hwy. 28, Crystal Bay, 775/832-4000 or 800/225-6382, www.calnevaresort.com) enjoys a spectacular lakeside setting at Crystal Point and houses the oldest operating casino in the United States. The hotel was built in 1937 and was owned by Frank Sinatra in the 1960s. Old Blue Eyes and his cronies Sammy Davis Jr., Dean Martin, and Marilyn Monroe would pal around here when they wanted to flee the hectic L.A. celebrity lifestyle. Because of its stateline location, the Cal-Neva enjoys an odd twist of geography—guests can swim from California to Nevada, and back again, in its outdoor pool. All of its 210 guest rooms have lake views but the best vistas are seen from the pricier rooms on the seventh, eighth, and ninth floors ($99–199). A few of the "celebrity cabins" have nice views, too, and are reasonably priced ($99–149). Try to get Marilyn Monroe's cabin if it's available; the lake view is awesome. If you've won a small fortune at the casino, reserve a stay in one of the suites with living rooms and balconies, or chalets with fireplaces ($219–299). This is definitely a place where you should pay extra money for the better rooms. Stay-and-ski packages are superaffordable, especially midweek—as low as $79 per person for a ski ticket and lake-view room, based on double occupancy. Like most Tahoe casinos, this one has a restaurant, bar, and spa, so you can get all your entertainment in one building. *Condé Nast Traveler* called the Cal-Neva "Nevada's Best Getaway."

Located within a few miles of Mount Rose and Diamond Peak ski areas, and with a secure ski storage area and ski rental shop on the premises, the four-diamond **⟨ Hyatt Regency Lake Tahoe Resort** (111 Country Club Dr., Incline Village, 775/832-1234, www.hyatt.com) caters to the snow bunny crowd. The motto at this megaresort should be "but wait, there's more." The 1920s-era hotel features the Grand Lodge Casino, a heated pool (which they call a "year-round swimming oasis"), a fitness club, and the 20,000-square-foot Stillwater Spa—Tahoe's largest day spa offering all the latest feel-good treatments. Six restaurants feed the hungry, including the Lone Eagle Grille with its massive rock fireplaces, open-beamed ceiling, and enviable lake view. Forget skiing—you may never want to leave this place. The Hyatt's 449 rooms ($199–379) come with all the usual four-star hotel amenities, but the six suites on the upper floors of the 12-story tower are far superior, as you might expect. For the most privacy, book one of the 24 lakefront cottages with fireplaces

and private decks ($325 and up). Don't miss the wonderful breakfast buffet at the resort's Sierra Cafe.

For bargain lodging near Incline Village and Crystal Bay, book at stay at one of the 92 rooms at the **Tahoe Biltmore** (5 Tahoe Blvd./Hwy. 28, Crystal Bay, 775/831-0660 or 800/245-8667, www.tahoebiltmore.com, $39–99). The resort is showing its age, but it's clean and serviceable. Two accommodations are offered: rooms in the main hotel and "cottage" rooms. The cottage rooms are slightly lower priced and are grouped together with about six units per building. They are much larger than many of the hotel rooms, but unfortunately, they aren't soundproof. Light sleepers may hear people coming and going from the casino all night. Dogs are permitted in the cottages for an extra $10 per night. If you are planning a summer stay, be forewarned that the Biltmore has no air-conditioning, and the rooms can be stuffy. Rates include a huge, cholesterol-raising breakfast at the Biltmore Cafe. The Biltmore is far and away the best deal in town, but remember, you get what you pay for. In the winter months, check for stay-and-ski package deals.

Condominium-Style Resorts

Located near the Hyatt Regency Lake Tahoe Resort, the **⟨ Hyatt High Sierra Lodge** (989 Incline Way, Incline Village, 775/832-0220, www.hyatt.com) is an upscale time-share resort with 60 two-bedroom condominiums for rent. Like at the neighboring Hyatt, the lake views are incredible. The condos have private balconies, gas fireplaces, and master bedroom suites with king beds. Guests can take advantage of concierge service, babysitting referrals, and other typical resort perks, including use of a 500-foot private beach. Rates start at $349, but the condos can easily fit six people. Ask about stay-and-ski packages.

One mile outside downtown Incline Village, the unpretentious **Club Tahoe Resort** (914 Northwoods Blvd., Incline Village, 775/831-5750 or 800/527-5154, www.clubtahoe.com, $169–269) rents two-bedroom condos for a real bargain compared to other places in the area. Affordable stay-and-ski packages are available, too. The units are large—more than 1,000 square feet—and can easily sleep six people in a master bedroom, smaller second bedroom, and upstairs loft area. Rental units have a full kitchen, two bathrooms, fireplace, washer/dryer, two televisions, and everything else you'd expect. There's nothing terribly fancy about the place, but for an affordable family or small-group vacation, it works just fine.

Vacation Rentals

Since accommodations options in the Incline Village area are fairly limited, vacation home rentals take up the lodging slack. Whether you want a condo, a cabin, or a luxury home to rent, one of these three companies can find it for you, from the hundreds of vacation properties available in the area: Incline Vacation Rentals (901 Tahoe Blvd./Hwy. 28, Incline Village, 800/831-3304, www.inclinevacations. com), Vacation Station (110 Country Club Dr., Incline Village, 800/841-7443, www.vacation-station.com), and Incline at Tahoe Vacation Rentals (797 Southwood Blvd., Incline Village, 888/686-5253, www.inclineattahoe.com).

Motels and Lodges

The no-frills **Inn at Incline** (1003 Tahoe Blvd./ Hwy. 28, Incline Village, 775/831-0152 or 800/824-6391, www.innatincline.com, $69–169) is just the ticket for skiers who don't have stacks of extra cash under their mattresses. The 38 rooms are set in a two-story motel-style building, which looks fine from the outside but is aging somewhat gracelessly on the inside. Guests have access to an indoor pool, sauna, and hot tub. A continental breakfast is served on weekends only in the common room. Even though this is Nevada, the Inn at Incline is a completely nonsmoking property. Stay-and-ski packages are quite affordable. Diamond Peak Ski Resort is only a mile away.

Campgrounds and RV Parks

Located 7.5 miles north of Incline Village on Highway 431, the small, 24-site **Mount Rose Campground** (775/882-2766, $13–15) is run by the Forest Service and has restrooms, water, and a dump station. It can accommodate small trailers and RVs up to 16 feet long. If you are planning to climb to the summit of 10,778-foot Mount Rose, this is a great place to camp—the trailhead is right across the highway. A major trailhead for the Tahoe Rim Trail is nearby at Tahoe Meadows.

SPOONER LAKE

Many visitors complain that it's hard to find lodgings with real "nature appeal" around Lake Tahoe, since so much of the shoreline is a semiurban environment, with motels, hotels, and other businesses packed in right next to each other. That's what makes the **Spooner Lake Wilderness Cabins** (near Spooner Summit, 775/749-5349, www.spoonerlake.com, $95–160) so special. Set inside the boundary of Lake Tahoe Nevada State Park, the two Scandinavian-style cabins were constructed in 2002 with beautiful hand-hewn logs, and they are surrounded by nothing but parkland. It takes a little effort to get to the cabins—one is set on a knoll near Spooner Lake, a 0.75-mile walk from the parking lot; the other is a two-mile walk and has a great view of Lake Tahoe and Emerald Bay. The cabins can be accessed year-round, either on cross-country skis, snowshoes, or on foot or by bike in summer. They are equipped with a propane cooking stove and some kitchen supplies, a wood-burning stove for heat, propane lights, a queen-size bed, and a full-size futon. In place of a bathroom, guests use a composting toilet. (You said you wanted a nature experience, right?) Each cabin is provided with two gallons of water per day, so you don't have to haul that in, but you do need to bring your own food, or plan to hike/ski/snowshoe out for meals. For cross-country skiers who want to access the area's 80 kilometers of groomed trails, this is an ideal getaway. The same holds true for summer visitors who want to bike the famous Flume Trail (the trailhead is right here), or just sit on their own private deck and read a book in the warm Tahoe sun. Winter rates include trail passes, ski rentals, and lessons.

Food

INCLINE VILLAGE/ CRYSTAL BAY

Breakfast

The locals love **The Wildflower Cafe** (869 Tahoe Blvd./Hwy. 28, Incline Village, 775/831-8072, 7 A.M.–2:30 P.M. Mon.–Sat., 8 A.M.–2 P.M. Sun.), a 1950s-throwback breakfast joint that knows how to do justice to pigs in a blanket (two pancakes wrapped around link sausages), biscuits and gravy, and home fries. They do lunch, too—a variety of burgers and sandwiches including all the classics, like tuna melts and Reubens. Everything is under $10.

Seafood and Steak

Always dazzling diners with its drop-dead gorgeous lake view, the **(Lone Eagle Grille** at the Hyatt Regency Lake Tahoe Resort (111 Country Club Dr., Incline Village, 775/832-1234, www.hyatt.com) features a high, open-timbered ceiling, two massive rock fireplaces, and hearty American food (spit-roasted duck, braised lamb shank, and Black Angus steaks). This is not a restaurant for penny-pinchers; the two of you probably won't leave without dropping $100 and up on dinner. The resort has two other restaurants, both less expensive and more casual: Ciao Mein and Sierra Cafe. The latter is known for its extensive breakfast buffet, which includes lots of homemade muffins and pastries.

Sit back in one of the velvet-covered, highback booths and enjoy the first-class service at **Crystal Bay Steak and Lobster House** at Crystal Bay Casino (14 Tahoe Blvd./Hwy. 28, Crystal Bay, 775/833-6333, www.crystalbaycasino.com, 4:30–9 P.M. Tues.–Sun., $20–48). The casino came under new ownership in 2004, which led to a complete renovation of the restaurant. The new menu runs the gamut of quintessential American entrees—veal, duck, pork chop, scampi, and prime rib—but the namesake steak and lobster are prominently featured. In fact, you can add a lobster tail to

any other entree for an additional $24. Portions are huge. Top off your meal with a port or cognac from the extensive wine list.

American

Located across from the monolithic Hyatt, **Austin's** (120 Country Club Dr., Incline Village, 775/832-7778, 11 A.M.–2 P.M. Mon.–Fri., 5–9 P.M. daily, $8–20) is a cozy, home-style restaurant that is famous for its comfort food. If you are craving chicken-fried steak (or chicken-fried chicken, for that matter), you'll find it here, served with a side of mashed potatoes and gravy. Austin's buttermilk French fries with jalapeño dipping sauce are an Incline Village institution. Portion sizes are what you would expect; this is "mountain food."

At lunchtime, don't get in the way of the door at **T's Mesquite Rotisserie** (901 Tahoe Blvd./Hwy. 28, Incline Village, 775/831-2832, 11 A.M.–8 P.M. Mon.–Sat., 12–8 P.M. Sun.) or you are likely to get run over by a horde of hungry people. T's makes fast food the right way, with a large rotisserie oven that cooks whole chickens to perfection all day long. While you wait to order, the aroma can drive you crazy. Plenty of people order takeout; others find a spot in the crowded dining area or outside on a few picnic tables. In addition to the hormone-free chicken, there's corn-fed beef tri-tip, sandwiches, burritos, and tacos. *Sunset Magazine* rated T's tacos as "best in the West."

Californian/Continental

One of the most romantic dining experiences possible at Lake Tahoe can be had at **(The Soule Domain** (9983 Cove St., Crystal Bay, 775/833-0399 or 530/546-7529, www.souledomain.com, open from 6 P.M. nightly, $17–28). Dinner is the only meal served in this petit, 1930s-era log cabin located next door to the Tahoe Biltmore, and that's because it takes all day to prepare menu items as complex as fresh vegetables baked in pastry shells, grilled lamb chops with basil cashew pesto, and filet mignon pan-roasted with shiitake mushrooms, gorgonzola, and brandy. The meaning of the restaurant's name? This place is the "domain" of chef and owner Charles Edward Soule IV. He and his brother Steve have been successfully running The Soule Domain since 1985.

Now here's a distinction: the **(Big Water Grille** (341 Ski Way, Incline Village, 775/833-0606, www.bigwatergrille.com, 5:30–9 P.M. daily, $19–29) is the highest dining room on the North Shore at an elevation of 6,700 feet, located right below the entrance to Diamond Peak Ski Area. That great height means great lake views, which are coupled with an outstanding and creative menu that changes often. Current favorites include the lobster trio (lobster thermidor, lobster soufflé, and a lobster gazpacho) and heirloom tomato soup. The large bar is often bustling with Tahoe locals, who are known for their good taste.

No discussion of continental cuisine in Incline Village would be complete without mentioning **(Le Bistro** (120 Country Club Dr., Incline Village, 775/831-0800, 6–9:30 P.M. Tues.–Sat., $18–27). Located behind the Country Club Mall, Le Bistro's intimate provincial-style dining room is the perfect setting for entrees like quenelle of squab and beef tournedos. Can't decide what to order? Go for the five-course prix fixe menu ($40). Every item, from the baked escargot and romaine salad to the crème brûlée, is *très français*. Chef Jean-Pierre Doignon is a legend in the Lake Tahoe dining scene.

Most of us sold our fondue pots at garage sales sometime after the 1970s. But **La Fondue** (120 Country Club Dr., Incline Village, 775/831-6104, 5:30–8:30 P.M. Wed.–Mon., $15–24) delivers a much finer version of the sticky, melted stuff than we ever dreamed of in our avocado-green '70s kitchens. About a dozen different fondue dishes grace the menu, including the house specialty, a cheese fondue made of Swiss gruyere and emmentaler. Dip in some grapes, apple pieces, or French bread, and you're in fondue heaven. Meat eaters will prefer to try the filet mignon, lamb, meat-

ball, or jumbo prawn fondue, or order one of the schnitzels. Dessert is, of course, a sinful chocolate fondue.

Italian

Weekend brunches are very popular at **Bella Lago** (941 Tahoe Blvd./Hwy. 28, Incline Village, 775/831-9944, $13–25), but that might have something to do with the "bottomless glass" champagne service, or maybe it's the memorable eggs Benedict. The restaurant's extensive menu has a northern Italian slant to it, with plenty of chicken, veal, fish, shellfish, and beef dishes mixed in with classic pasta entrees. Owned by the same folks as nearby La Fondue, the restaurant features warmly painted walls decorated with Italian lake scenes. Bello Lago serves lunch and dinner daily; brunch on weekends only. Lunch on the outdoor deck is a winner in the summer months. Happy hour, 4–6 P.M., is popular, too, with bargains on appetizers and drinks.

For more than 20 years, **Azzarra's** (930 Tahoe Blvd./Hwy. 28, Incline Village, 775/831-0346, opens at 5 P.M. for dinner, closed Mon., $12–24) has been dishing out northern Italian meals to hungry Incline Village diners. It's hard to decide between the multiple pasta dishes and house specialties like *frutti de mare* and *melanzane,* but no matter what you order, save room for the unforgettable tiramisu. This is classic Italian food prepared just right.

Sometimes after a day of skiing, ordering a pizza to go or eat in sounds a lot more appealing than showering and dressing up for dinner. That's where **Mofo's Pizza** (in Christmas Tree Village, 868 Tahoe Blvd./Hwy. 28, Incline Village, 775/831-4999, 11:30 P.M.–2 P.M. and 5–8:30 P.M. Tues.–Sun., $10–20) comes in. They've been making pizzas for Incline Village residents and visitors since 1986, so they know how to do it right. Their calzones and homemade ravioli are rich and filling, and the 20-item salad bar gives you something to graze on while you wait for dinner. Another long running Incline Village pizza joint is the slot-machine-inspired **Bar Bar Bar Pizza** (760 Mays

Blvd., Incline Village, 775/831-2700, 10 A.M.–8 P.M. daily). Their "royal flush" pizza comes with five toppings plus cheese, for about $15.

If your pizza sensibilities are a little more gourmet, try the exotic toppings and whole-wheat pizza crust at **Tomaato's** (120 Country Club Dr., Incline Village, 775/833-2200, 5–9 P.M. Thur.–Tues., $10–20). Their calzones are great, too. Start your meal with a baked brie salad.

Mexican

The colorful **Hacienda de La Sierra** (931 Tahoe Blvd./Hwy. 28, Incline Village, 775/831-8300, 4–10 P.M. daily, $7–14) has everything you want in a Mexican cantina: great margaritas, large portions of fajitas, burritos, and all the classic Mexican dishes, plus unlimited bowls of chips and salsa. Adding to the festive atmosphere, Hacienda de La Sierra's dining area is spacious and bright-hued (tropical artwork and a parrot theme define the decor). In summer, diners can eat outside on the back patio.

Another traditional Mexican restaurant is found across the street at Raley's Incline Center. **La Esmeralda** (930 Tahoe Blvd./Hwy. 28, Incline Village, 775/831-3551, 11 A.M.–9:30 P.M. Mon.–Thurs., 11 A.M.–10 P.M. Fri.–Sat.,

11:30 A.M.–9:30 P.M. Sun., $10) has a full bar upstairs and restaurant downstairs, serving specialties like marinated chicken sautéed with onions and mushrooms, and the chef's special *parrillada* (marinated beef, chicken, shrimp, and sausage grilled with lots of veggies).

Asian

The soothing, purple-hued dining room at **Thai Recipe** (901 Tahoe Blvd./Hwy. 28, Incline Village, 775/831-4777, 11 A.M.–3 P.M. and 5–9 P.M. Tues.–Sun., $5–13) is the perfect setting for a meal of Thai egg rolls, lemongrass salad, and spinach curry, or any of your other Thai favorites. The restaurant's owner, a retired university professor from Bangkok, makes sure that everything is beautifully prepared and served with warm Thai hospitality.

If you're hoping to score some take-out food for an après-ski dinner at your condo, **China Village** (882 Tahoe Blvd./Hwy. 28, Incline Village, 775/831-9090, 11 A.M.–10 P.M. daily, $5–12) can make it happen. Barbecued spareribs, wonton soup, mu shui pork (or chicken or shrimp), Szechuan chicken, and dozens of seafood and beef concoctions make up the extensive traditional menu. Conveniently located in Christmas Tree Village, the restaurant works well for dining in, too.

EAST SHORE

Practicalities

INFORMATION

Visit the **Incline Village/Crystal Bay Visitors Bureau and Chamber of Commerce** (969 Tahoe Blvd./Hwy. 28 in Incline Village, 775/832-1606 or 800/468-2463, www.gotahoe.com). If you are traveling to or from Nevada to Lake Tahoe, you might also want to visit the Carson Valley Chamber of Commerce (1513 Hwy. 395, Gardnerville, 775/782-8144 or 800/727-7677, www.visitcarsonvalley.org) or Carson City Convention and Visitors Bureau (1900 S. Carson St., Carson City, 775/687-7410, www.visitcarsoncity.com).

SERVICES
Medical Care

Both of the following locations offer 24-hour emergency care: **Incline Village Community Hospital** (880 Alder Ave., Incline Village, 775/833-4100, www.tfhd.com) and **Incline Village Urgent Care** (995 Tahoe Blvd./Hwy. 28, Incline Village, 775/833-2929).

Post Offices

The largest post office on the East Shore is at The Village Center in **Incline Village** (770 Mays Blvd. at Southwood Blvd., 775/831-8994).

RENO'S HIGHLIGHTS

It's called the "Biggest Little City in the World," for reasons that are not entirely clear. It has always been the poor cousin to that other Nevada casino town – glamorous, infamous Las Vegas. Still, the northern Nevada city of Reno has its share of charms, and as a tourist destination it gets better every year. For an interesting day trip, take a 30-mile drive from Incline Village to Reno. Here are some of the highlights you will find:

Nevada Museum of Art: The permanent collection in this 55,000-square-foot architectural gem consists of nearly 2,000 works of art organized around the themes of land and environment. Don't miss the rooftop sculpture garden. After a look at the exhibits, take a walk past the lively restaurants, galleries, and shops on California Street. 160 West Liberty Street, 775/329-3333, www.nevadaart.org, noon–6 P.M. Tuesday–Sunday.

Truckee Riverwalk: This picturesque public plaza on the Truckee River in downtown Reno features wildlife art and unique fountains. A collection of trails, benches, parks, cafes, and small shops, Riverwalk mixes the best of Reno's urban and natural environments. Events are held throughout the year. 775/334-2417, www.renoriver.org.

Fleischmann Planetarium and Science Center: Check out a collection of meteorites, including four that were recovered in the state of Nevada, and enjoy a large-format feature film or a planetarium star show at the SkyDome. Kids will want to step on the scale and find out how much they weigh on the moon or Jupiter. 1650 North Virginia Street, University of Nevada at Reno, 775/784-4811, http://planetarium.unr.nevada.edu, 11 A.M.–7 P.M. weekdays, 11:30 A.M.–7 P.M. weekends, $8 adults, $4 seniors and children 12 and under.

National Automobile Museum: More than 200 fancy cars are housed here, including cars that have appeared in Hollywood films, cars that belonged to celebrities, and one-of-a-kind models that are like nothing you have ever seen on the road. 10 South Lake Street, 775/333-9300, www.automuseum.org, 9:30 A.M.–5:30 P.M. Monday–Saturday, 10 A.M.–4 P.M. Sunday, $8 adults, $7 seniors, $3 children.

Nevada Historical Society Museum: The state's oldest museum, founded in 1904, holds a wealth of exhibits, photographs, and research materials for history buffs, spanning the ages from prehistoric times to the Nevada mining boom of the 19th century. 1650 North Virginia Street, 775/688-1990, 10 A.M.–5 P.M. Monday–Saturday, $2 adults, free for children under 18.

Sierra Safari Zoo: Get up close and personal with over 200 animals of 40 different species at this open-air zoo. 10200 North Virginia Street, 775/677-1101, www.sierrasafarizoo.com, 10 A.M.–5 P.M. daily April–October, $7 adults, $6 seniors, $5 children.

Festivals and Events: Reno loves to party, and the town can think of plenty of excuses for a celebration. Every June, the **"Wildest, Richest Rodeo in the West"** features the world's best rodeo athletes competing in the fine arts of steer wrestling, bronc riding, bull riding, and more (www.renorodeo.com). Later in the summer, **Hot August Nights** is a weeklong celebration of 1950s music and cars (www.hotaugustnights.net). The country's top competitive aviation event takes place at the **National Championship Air Races** in September (www.airrace.org). Also in September, it's time for Reno's most colorful event: the **Great Reno Balloon Race** (www.renoballoon.com).

Crystal Bay also has a post office (26 Hwy. 28/Tahoe Blvd. at Crystal Bay Dr., 775/831-8994). Both are open 8:30 A.M.–5 P.M. Monday–Friday.

Internet Access

To check your email or surf the Web, go to the

Incline Village Public Library (one block off Hwy. 28 at 845 Alder Ave., 775/832-4130).

GETTING THERE
By Air

Visitors can fly into the **Reno/Tahoe International Airport** (2001 E. Plumb Lane,

775/328-6400, www.renoairport.com) and then rent a car, or take bus, shuttle, or limousine service. Several companies offer shuttle or limo service between the Reno-Tahoe International Airport and the Incline Village area: Airport Mini-Bus/Bell Limousine (800/235-5466), Executive Limousine (775/333-3300), Aladdin Limousine (800/546-6009), Sierra West Limousine (877/347-4789), North Tahoe Limousine (800/832-8213). North Tahoe Checker Cab (866/420-8294) also travels between the airport and Incline Village.

Visitors could also fly into Sacramento, Oakland, San Francisco, or San Jose airports, then rent a car to drive to Lake Tahoe. Sacramento Airport is about three hours from Incline Village, the three other airports are about 4.5 hours away.

By Car

From the San Francisco Bay Area or Sacramento, the primary driving route to Incline Village and the East Shore is to take I-80 east to Truckee and then Highway 267 south to Kings Beach. Incline Village is about five miles east of Kings Beach on Highway 28. Total driving distance is about 130 miles from Sacramento or 220 miles from San Francisco.

From Reno/Tahoe International Airport, take U.S. 395 south for seven miles to Highway 431 west. Drive southwest on Highway 431 for 20 miles to Incline Village.

By Bus

Visitors can access Truckee or Reno by two major bus lines: **Greyhound Bus Lines** (530/587-3822 or 800/231-2222, www.greyhound.com) or **Amtrak Bus** (800/872-7245, www.amtrak.com). Tahoe Area Regional Transit (TART) (800/736-6365, www.laketahoetransit.com) system buses connect with these bus lines at the Truckee Depot to take passengers to Incline Village.

By Train

The nearest Amtrak train depots are in Truckee or Reno. For schedules and information, con-

tact **Amtrak** (800/872-7245, www.amtrak .com). Tahoe Area Regional Transit system buses (800/736-6365, www.laketahoetransit.com) connect with Amtrak at the Truckee Depot to take passengers to Incline Village.

GETTING AROUND

Tahoe Area Regional Transit (TART, 800/736 6365, www.laketahoetransit.com) runs between Incline Village and Tahoma year-round, traveling along the North and West Shores and up to Alpine Meadows, Squaw Valley, and Truckee. TART also connects with the South Shore bus line at Meeks Bay in summer. There is currently no public transportation that runs south from Incline Village along the East Shore.

During the ski season, the major ski areas (Northstar, Squaw Valley, Alpine Meadows, Mount Rose, Diamond Peak) have shuttle service to and from designated stops along Highway 28. Contact the individual resorts for details.

In winter, the **Reno Ski Shuttle** (775/325-8813, www.tahoeskishuttle.com) runs from major Reno hotels (Nugget, Hilton, Sands, Silver Legacy, Peppermill, Atlantis) twice each morning to Mount Rose Ski area (a 25-minute drive). Reservations are recommended. The fare is $15 round-trip but combined lift ticket and shuttle packages are available.

By Car

All the major **car-rental** agencies are also available at Reno/Tahoe International Airport (775/328-6400, www.renoairport.com). To get current updates on road conditions in California, phone 800/427-7623. To get current updates on Nevada road conditions, phone 877/687-6237.

By Taxi

North Tahoe Checker Cab (775/833-0707 or 866/420-8294) operates throughout North Tahoe, including Incline Village. Other North Shore taxi services include Alpine Taxi (775/833-4433), Ace High Taxi (530/412-3583), and Lake Tahoe Taxi (530/577-7000).

CARSON PASS

Carson Pass may be less than an hour from bustling South Lake Tahoe, but psychologically, it's a world away. Named for the famous scout and explorer, Kit Carson, Carson Pass is as uncommercialized as the South Shore is commercialized. There isn't much in the way of visitor services except for a few scattered cabin resorts, a handful of restaurants, and one major ski area. The largest town, and county seat, Markleeville, has a population of only a few hundred people. In fact, all of Alpine County has only two residents per square mile. Private property is the exception rather than the rule; a remarkable 93 percent of the county's acreage is public land.

But this doesn't mean that Carson Pass is undiscovered. The region's population is boosted exponentially each year by the thousands of visitors who flock here in summer for hiking, mountain biking, and some of the best fishing anywhere in the Sierra; and in winter for an array of winter sports. Those who choose to visit come for the area's natural wonders. High volcanic peaks, alpine lakes, aspen groves, wildflower fields, and dramatic Sierra scenery wait to be explored. The home of Kirkwood Ski Resort, this area is well known for consistently receiving more snowfall than anywhere else in the Sierra—often as much as 700 inches per year. The remarkable volcanic landscape lends itself well to alpine and cross-country skiing, snowboarding, and snowshoeing. For the intrepid skier who prefers trackless snow, miles of backcountry terrain wait to be explored.

© ANN MARIE BROWN

HIGHLIGHTS

Markleeville: Turn back time with a walk along the streets of Markleeville, which are lined with 19th-century buildings, including the quaint Old Webster School at the Alpine County Museum (page 190).

Autumn Colors: Timing is everything if you want to witness one of California's best shows of fall colors along the roads of Hope Valley and Carson Pass. The prolific groves of quaking aspens generally attain their peak shades of gold, amber, and red somewhere between mid-September and mid-October (page 190).

Carson Pass Summit: Stop in at the visitors center located at Carson Pass Summit to learn about the journeys of the great scout Kit Carson and the thousands of emigrants who passed through this area (page 190).

Frog Lake: For a short, easy introduction to the scenic wonders of Carson Pass, take this 1.8-mile round-trip hike from Carson Pass Summit to Frog Lake. Most of the summer you'll be able to admire myriad wildflowers along the way (page 194).

Lake Margaret: This longer hike in the Carson Pass area is a great way to spend a half day. A nearly five-mile round-trip hike with relatively short uphill stretches brings you to the shores of lovely Lake Margaret, where swimming, fishing, and sunbathing are favored activities (page 197).

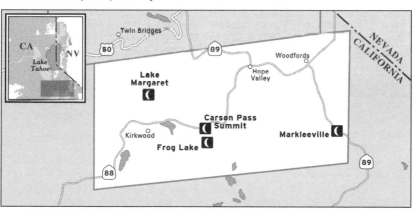

LOOK FOR **((** TO FIND THE BEST SIGHTS, ACTIVITIES, DINING AND LODGING YOU CAN'T MISS.

Anglers, too, consider Carson Pass to be a gold mine, with hungry trout lurking in more than 60 lakes, multiple streams, and the world-famous Carson River. Hikers swarm to the area in July to see one of California's best wildflower shows, and then return in late September for an incredible fall foliage display. Campers and hot-springs aficionados flock to Grover Hot Springs State Park, which in addition to its natural hot springs, has lovely meadows and pine-dotted woods. But the busiest weekend of the year occurs each July, when the annual Markleeville Death Ride takes place. One of California's premier cycling events, the Death Ride consists of a daunting 129-mile route with a total 16,000 feet of elevation change. Even if you'd never think of riding in a bike tour of this magnitude, it's worth showing up just to watch the spectacle.

PLANNING YOUR TIME

If you are a hiker, biker, angler, nature photographer, snowboarder, or skier, you'll easily find enough activities to keep you busy in the Carson Pass area for a week, a month, or more. Casual sightseers and those who prefer the city amenities of South Lake Tahoe will probably be content with a half-day drive through this area. Be sure to visit the quaint hamlet of **Markleeville,** where the main street is a throwback to the 19th century. And take the scenic drive up and over 8,573-foot **Carson Pass** itself, where you can stop in at the log-cabin visitors center and learn about the thousands of emigrants who passed this way before you, or take the short, flower-filled hike to **Frog Lake.**

Sights and Entertainment

◖ MARKLEEVILLE

The quaint town of Markleeville, with its 100-yard-long main street, is well worth a stop. Founded in 1861 during the Nevada silver rush, the town once boasted a population of nearly 3,000 people, but today it has only a few hundred. Most of the town's original 19th-century buildings still stand. Locals and visitors hang out on the front porch of the **Markleeville General Store** (14799 Hwy. 89); don't be surprised if you find a dog sleeping on the street. In summer and early fall, pay a visit to the **Alpine County Museum** (School St., Markleeville, 530/694-2317, 11 A.M.–4 P.M. Thurs.–Mon., Memorial Day–Oct., free). The museum consists of the Old Webster School, a one-room schoolhouse built in 1882, and an old log jail from the mid-1800s, constructed with seemingly impenetrable iron doors, two hand-riveted iron cells, vertical log walls, and a log foundation. Farming, mining, and lumbering tools are on display, as well as some Washoe Indian baskets and artifacts. Donations are accepted.

GROVER HOT SPRINGS STATE PARK

Located three miles from Markleeville, Grover Hot Springs State Park's (530/694-2248, www.parks.ca.gov) main attraction is its natural mineral springs, which were discovered by John C. Fremont, the explorer credited with the first sighting of Lake Tahoe. Unlike most hot springs, Grover's water contains little sulfur, so it doesn't have a strong "rotten-egg"

smell. The warmer of the park's two concrete pools is regulated between 102 and 104°F, although where the water springs from the ground it is a scalding 148°F. A cool-temperature pool is a more popular option in the summer months. The park also has a year-round campground and hiking and mountain-biking trails. The pools are open year-round except for Christmas, New Year's, and Thanksgiving, and a brief period in September for maintenance. A $6 fee per vehicle is charged to enter the park; pool fees are $5 adults, $2 children 16 and under.

◖ AUTUMN COLORS

The Carson Pass area is well known for its spectacular show of fall colors put on by the dense groves of quaking aspens that line both sides of the pass. Optimal viewing typically occurs mid-September–mid-October, but it's always wise to phone one of the area's resorts to get an update on current conditions. Some of the most popular spots for photographers and leaf-lovers are right along the road by Sorensen's Resort, on the north side of Highway 88 in the pastures of Hope Valley, near Red Lake, on the north side of Caples Lake, and on the road to Woods Lake Campground.

◖ CARSON PASS SUMMIT

At the top of Carson Pass, elevation 8,673 feet, is a log-cabin visitors center run by the U.S. Forest Service, a trailhead that leads into the Mokelumne Wilderness, and a monument to the great explorer and scout Kit Carson. The

© AVALON TRAVEL PUBLISHING, INC.

CARSON PASS

MARKLEEVILLE

Indian Creek Reservoir

Woodfords

Carson River

88

89

SPRINGS RD

Grover Hot Springs State Park

Grover Hot Springs State Park

HOT

Hope Valley

88 89

SORENSEN'S RESORT

Humboldt-

Toiyabe

National

Forest

Burnside Lake

Markleeville Peak 9,417ft

Humboldt-

Toiyabe

National

Park

Wilderness

Mokelumne

BLUE LAKES RD

Carson River

West Fork

Lost Lakes

Lower Blue Lake

Upper Blue Lake

Meadow Lake

Scotts Lake

88

89

Big Meadow

Dardanelles Lake

Round Lake

Upper Truckee River

Red Lake

CARSON PASS SUMMIT

Meiss

Carson Pass

FROG LAKE

Woods

Woods Lake

Round Top 10,380ft

Wilderness

Mokelumne

Summit City Creek

CAPLES LAKE RESORT

Caples Lake

Caples Lake Dam

Kirkwood

KIRKWOOD SKI RESORT

Squaw Ridge

Lake Margaret

LAKE MARGARET

Thunder Mountain

Eldorado

National

Forest

Camp Minkalo

Silver Lake

88

Shealor Lakes

Bear River

0   2 mi
0   2 km

CARSON PASS

Carson Pass Information Station (209/258-8606, summer and fall only) sells maps and guidebooks and provides free information to visitors. It's located at Carson Pass Summit on Highway 88, nine miles west of the junction of Highways 88 and 89 and five miles east of Caples Lake. Just east of Carson Pass, you can take a short walk to see large boulders painted with the names of gold-seeking pioneers who followed the route of the historic Emigrant Trail. If you have the time, be sure to take the short, one-mile walk to Frog Lake (see *Hiking*). A $3 parking fee is charged.

FESTIVALS AND EVENTS

The biggest event in the Carson Pass region is the **Markleeville Death Ride** (www.deathride.com) held each year in July (see *Biking*). The second most popular event is the **Kirkwood Wildflower Festival** (www.kirkwood.com), usually held in late July. The festival consists of guided flower hikes in the morning, and live music, arts and crafts, and food and wine in the afternoon.

FAMILY FUN

Ranger programs are available for children ages 7–12 at the campground at **Grover Hot Springs State Park** (530/694-2248 or 530/694-2249). Nighttime campfire programs, usually held on Saturday nights, cover topics such as bears, mountain lions, the forest ecosystem, and the history of Alpine County. Most programs are about one hour long.

Kirkwood Ski Area (209/258-6000 or 877/547-5966, www.kirkwood.com) has a multitude of activities that are suitable for kids, from scaling the Adventure Center's climbing wall in summer, to tubing and dog-sledding in winter.

Recreation

HIKING

The following hikes are listed from north to south along Highway 89 and from east to west along Highway 88. For more information on these trails, contact the Eldorado National Forest, Amador Ranger District (26820 Silver Dr., Pioneer, 209/295-4251, www.fs.fed.us/r5/eldorado).

Dardanelles and Round Lake

- Distance: 7.6 miles round-trip
- Duration: 4 hours
- Rating: Moderate
- Elevation change: 1,500 feet
- Trailhead: Big Meadow
- Directions: From the T-junction of Hwy. 50 and Hwy. 89 in Meyers, drive 5.3 miles south on Hwy. 89 to the Big Meadow parking area on the left (west) side of the highway. Park near the restrooms.

Nowhere is it more clear that the land around Lake Tahoe was shaped by diametrically opposed forces—fire (volcanic action) and ice (glaciers)—than on this pleasant day hike to Dardanelles and Round Lake. The trip begins at the large Tahoe Rim Trail parking lot at Big Meadow. Pick up the trail from the south side of the parking-lot loop and follow it to a crossing of Highway 89 in about 200 yards. On the far side of the highway, the trail ascends through red-fir and lodgepole-pine forest to expansive Big Meadow, a lovely place to visit at wildflower time, when it is covered with buttercups. After a too-brief level stroll through the meadow grasses, you head back into the trees for another mile of climbing. After a short, steep descent from a saddle, you'll reach a junction at two miles out and turn sharply right on the Meiss Meadow Trail toward Christmas Valley, leaving the Tahoe Rim Trail behind (you'll return to this junction to continue to Round Lake later). In about 200 yards, turn left at the next junction, cross a creek, and walk the final 1.2 miles to

Dardanelles Lake. This last level stretch is pure pleasure—it is lined with aspen and alder trees, which put on a colorful display in autumn, and odd-shaped volcanic outcrops. A highlight is a massive western juniper tree that appears to be the granddaddy of them all.

At 7,740 feet in elevation, Dardanelles Lake is a stunner, with a striking granite backdrop and plenty of spots for picnicking, swimming, or camping. This is a deservedly popular spot. Spend as long as you wish here, then backtrack to the Tahoe Rim Trail junction, turn right for Round Lake, and follow the trail 0.75 mile to its shores. Round Lake provides a stark contrast to Dardanelles Lake. It is about twice as large, brownish-green in color, and surrounded by dark volcanic rock, not granite. Although not as scenic as Dardanelles Lake, it, too, provides excellent swimming, plus good fishing for cutthroat trout.

Hot Springs Creek Waterfalls
* Distance: 3 miles round-trip
* Duration: 1.5 hours
* Rating: Easy
* Elevation change: 200 feet
* Trailhead: Grover Hot Springs State Park
* Directions: From the junction of Hwy. 89 and Hwy. 88 in Hope Valley, drive east on Hwy. 88/89 for 7 miles to Woodfords, then turn south on Hwy. 89 and drive 6 miles to Markleeville. Turn right (west) on Hot Springs Rd. and drive 3.5 miles to the Grover Hot Springs State Park entrance ($6 per vehicle fee). Continue past the entrance kiosk, then take the left fork past the campground to the signed trailhead, a gated dirt road.

A short and easy walk from the campground and hot-spring pool at Grover Hot Springs State Park leads to an early-summer waterfall along Hot Springs Creek. The route begins as a dirt road but in 0.6 mile, it veers off to the left onto a narrower trail. You'll hike through an open forest of Jeffrey and sugar pines with an understory of aromatic sagebrush. Odd-shaped volcanic formations can be seen be-

yond the trees. Soon the trail moves closer to Hot Springs Creek, and with the stream on your left, the canyon begins to narrow and the terrain gets increasingly rocky. When the waterfalls are running strong with spring runoff, you will hear them before you see them. The largest of three falls drops about 30 feet over a tower of volcanic rock. The pools below the big fall are filled with trout, and make great swimming holes later in summer when the creek flow slows and the water warms up.

Red Lake Peak
* Distance: 4.8 miles round-trip
* Duration: 2.5 hours
* Rating: Moderate
* Elevation change: 1,500 feet
* Trailhead: Meiss
* Directions: From the junction of Hwy. 89 and Hwy. 88 in Hope Valley, drive west on Hwy. 88 for 9 miles to Carson Pass summit. The Meiss Trailhead is on the right (north) side of the highway, across from and slightly west of the Carson Pass Information Station. A $3 parking fee is charged.

The hike to Red Lake Peak is a trek for history-lovers. When you stand on the 10,063-foot summit, you can imagine what it felt like when explorer John C. Fremont climbed this peak on February 14, 1844, after nearly perishing from weeks of struggling through the snow-covered Sierra, and became the first white man to lay eyes on Lake Tahoe. At the time, what was even better for Fremont and the men of his expedition was that from this high point, they could see the pass that would lead them out of the mountains and down to the Sacramento Valley.

There is no official trail to Red Lake Peak, but so many hikers have made the trip that there is a clearly beaten path to the summit, which is also a popular backcountry skiing and snowboarding destination in winter. From the Meiss Trailhead parking lot, follow the Pacific Crest Trail west and then north, switchbacking gently uphill through acres of mule's ears and

CARSON PASS

sagebrush. At a saddle above Meiss Meadow, 1.3 miles from your start, you'll see a cattle pond and just beyond an unmarked spur trail on the right that heads up the southwest slope of Red Lake Peak (although you can't see the summit from here). The spur trail leads very steeply up to a notch, from which you can see both Lake Tahoe and Red Lake Peak's volcanic summit block. The last stretch to the top has the worst gradient yet; the final few yards will require some hands-and-feet scrambling, but it's manageable for most. In addition to the view of Lake Tahoe, about 20 miles away, the summit also offers views of Hope Valley, Round Top Peak, Elephants Back, and the Mokelumne and Desolation wildernesses.

Showers and Meiss Lakes

* Distance: 10.2–11.4 miles round-trip
* Duration: 5–6 hours
* Rating: Moderate
* Elevation change: 1,500 feet
* Trailhead: Meiss
* Directions: From the junction of Hwy. 89 and Hwy. 88 in Hope Valley, drive west on Hwy. 88 for 9 miles to Carson Pass summit. The Meiss Trailhead is on the right (north) side of the highway, across from and slightly west of the Carson Pass Information Station. A $3 parking fee is charged.

Because is it located near an equestrian campground, Showers Lake is quite popular with the horsey set, but worth a look for two-legged visitors as well. Although the lake is pleasant enough for a quick swim, the hike to reach it is more of a highlight than the destination itself. That's because the trail departs the Meiss Trailhead at Carson Pass and wanders through some remarkable Sierra scenery, providing a brilliant wildflower display in midsummer and splendid ridgetop views year-round. The trail follows the same route as the path to Red Lake Peak to the saddle above Meiss Meadow, 1.3 miles from the trailhead, where the views spread wide. For many, this spot is a satisfying destination by itself. Where

the Red Lake Peak spur takes off to the right, you continue straight, heading steeply downhill into boggy but beautiful Meiss Meadow, the headwaters for the Upper Truckee River, and then bear left for Showers Lake. The trail meanders up open flower-covered slopes and into occasional groves of lodgepole pines, and crosses the Upper Truckee twice. After a moderate climb, the last half mile is a 350-foot descent to Showers Lake at 8,790 feet, the highest lake in the Upper Truckee River basin. If you still have energy on the way back, you might want to take the fork on the south side of Meiss Meadow that leads 0.6 mile gently downhill to Meiss Lake, a shallow and warm body of water. Fishing is not permitted in this lake, but swimming (or wading, for very tall people), is recommended. If you visit both lakes, your distance for the day will be 11.4 miles.

🌑 Frog Lake

* Distance: 1.8 miles round-trip
* Duration: 1 hour
* Rating: Easy
* Elevation change: 200 feet
* Trailhead: Carson Pass
* Directions: From the junction of Hwy. 89 and Hwy. 88 in Hope Valley, drive west on Hwy. 88 for 9 miles to Carson Pass summit. Park in the lot on the left (south) side of the highway, next to the Carson Pass Information Station. A $3 parking fee is charged.

Hikers seeking a brief introduction to the Carson Pass area will enjoy this easy, short stroll to Frog Lake. The trail starts alongside the Carson Pass Information Station and meanders just under a mile to the lakeshore. After an initial climb of about 0.5 mile, the grade levels out. Note the contorted shapes of the lodgepole pines that grow along this path, a result of the heavy snow load they face each winter. During the peak of the July flower season, the lupine bloom and the seemingly endless acres of mule's ears are spectacular. Turquoise-colored Frog Lake is just off the trail on the left; the distinct shape of Elephants Back, an old lava dome, rises behind it, and many choose to make the easy climb to its summit. Many hikers get inspired by the scenery here and continue another 1.4 miles to Winnemucca Lake, with a total elevation gain of only 500 feet from Carson Pass. You can also reach that lake by starting at Woods Lake Campground (see next listing).

Round Top Peak and Winnemucca Lake Loop

* Distance: 6.8 miles round-trip
* Duration: 4 hours
* Rating: Strenuous
* Elevation change: 2,200 feet
* Trailhead: Woods Lake
* Directions: From the junction of Hwy. 89 and Hwy. 88 in Hope Valley, drive west on Hwy. 88 for 10.5 miles to the Woods Lake Campground turnoff on the left (south) side of the highway, 1.5 miles west of Carson Pass. Turn left and drive 1 mile to the trailhead parking area, which is 0.5 mile before the campground. A $3 parking fee is charged.

As with most hikes in the Carson Pass area, this trail is incredibly popular all summer long, but especially during the peak of the wildflower bloom in July. As many as 300 people per day will hike to Winnemucca Lake on summer weekends. Although many people just walk out-and-back to the lake starting from either the Carson Pass or Woods Lake trailheads, you might as well pack the most you can into this trip by hiking the full loop to Winnemucca and Round Top Lakes, and taking the spur trail to the summit of 10,381-foot Round Top Peak, an ancient volcanic vent that is the highest peak in the Carson Pass area. The trip begins at the Woods Lake trailhead; campers can start right from their tents while everyone else has to start at the trailhead parking lot a half mile before the camp. The path wanders through the forest for a while, then breaks out onto open slopes with a straight-on view of Round Top Peak. The outlet creek

A strenuous ascent leads to the 10,381-foot summit of Round Top Peak, where a dramatic view awaits.

from Winnemucca Lake flows merrily on your right; the hillsides to your left are completely covered with flowers during the height of the season. In a mere 1.9 miles, you reach the shore of Winnemucca Lake, a gorgeous blue-green gem that is set directly below Round Top Peak and surrounded by mule's ears, scarlet gilia, Indian paintbrush, and a host of other colorful flowers. At the lake, you'll see plenty of other hikers who have arrived on the other trail from Carson Pass to the northeast, but your loop continues to the west for another mile of ascent to Round Top Lake. Heading there, you'll leave most of the crowds behind. Beautiful Round Top Lake is considerably smaller than Winnemucca, but its deeply carved glacial cirque is quite dramatic, and a few whitebark pines provide shade for picnickers.

At Round Top Lake, you've gained almost 1,200 feet from your start at Woods Lake, but Round Top Peak still towers imposingly 1,000 feet above you. Experienced, sure-footed hikers shouldn't miss the chance to climb it by

© ANN MARIE BROWN

CARSON PASS

following the obvious use trail from the lake's east end. The path struggles up, up, and up over the peak's volcanic slopes. You will need to use your hands as well as your feet as you near the top; most hikers are satisfied with attaining a false summit a few yards below the actual summit, as the going gets quite hairy in the last stretch. Truthfully, it doesn't matter how high you go; the views are dazzling from just about everywhere along Round Top's knife-thin ridge.

Rest on a high point—and your laurels—and take in the marvelous vista of the Dardanelles, Lake Tahoe, Caples Lake, Woods Lake, Round Top Lake, Winnemucca Lake, and Frog Lake—all to the north. Although this view is certainly captivating, perhaps more dramatic is the southward vista of deep and immense Summit City Canyon, which drops 3,000 feet below Round Top. On the clearest days, Mount Diablo in the East San Francisco Bay Area can be seen, 100 miles to the west.

After backtracking to the base of the peak, finish out your loop with a descent on the Lost Cabin Mine Trail alongside Round Top Lake's outlet creek, through more wildflower gardens, and past the structures of an old mine site, back to the campground at Winnemucca Lake. Walk through the camp and down the access road back to your car.

Fourth of July Lake

- Distance: 9.4 miles round-trip
- Duration: 5 hours
- Rating: Strenuous
- Elevation change: 2,200 feet
- Trailhead: Woods Lake
- Directions: From the junction of Hwy. 89 and Hwy. 88 in Hope Valley, drive west on Hwy. 88 for 10.5 miles to the Woods Lake Campground turnoff on the left (south) side of the highway, 1.5 miles west of Carson Pass. Turn left and drive 1 mile to the trailhead parking area, which is 0.5 mile before the campground. A $3 parking fee is charged.

One way to escape the crowds of wildflower aficionados and scenery-lovers at Winnemucca and Round Top Lakes is to take this hike to Fourth of July Lake, which leaves the most heavily visited areas of Carson Pass behind and descends 1,000 feet on a merciless grade to the lake. Several routes will get you there, but the most scenic is to follow the 2.8-mile path from Woods Lake Campground to Winnemucca and Round Top Lakes (see *Round Top Peak and Winnemucca Lake Loop*), then depart the loop trail and take the left fork near Round Top Lake that leads west and then south to Fourth of July Lake. The trail reaches a rocky divide in 0.6 mile, and from there you can look almost straight down 1,000 feet to the lake. With only 1.3 miles of trail remaining, the grade is brutally steep. This steep and rocky descent—and ensuing ascent—is what stops the crowds from flocking here, although the wildflowers along this stretch are often some of the best in Carson Pass. (When the flowers aren't blooming, you might want to skip Fourth of July Lake altogether and head for other destinations.) After stumbling through the precipitous descent to the lake, you'll reach its shoreline and find good fishing for brook and cutthroat trout. Late in summer, as the lake level drops, a sandy beach becomes exposed—a perfect spot for a well-earned swim.

Emigrant Lake

- Distance: 8.6 miles round-trip
- Duration: 4 hours
- Rating: Moderate
- Elevation change: 900 feet
- Trailhead: Caples Lake dam
- Directions: From the junction of Hwy. 89 and Hwy. 88 in Hope Valley, drive west on Hwy. 88 for 13.5 miles to the west side of Caples Lake and the trailhead parking area by the dam (5 miles west of Carson Pass).

Although the mileage is substantial along the trail to Emigrant Lake, the grade is so gentle you may wonder if you are still in the Sierra. In fact, the trail is basically flat for the first 2.5 miles, as it parallels the southwest shore of Caples Lake, traveling under the shady canopy of big conifers. You'll pass traces of the old emigrant trail along this route, but there is little evidence left of the multitudes who once traveled this way. But just when you get into cruising mode, you do have to do some work. Almost all of the elevation gain takes place in the last 1.8 miles, beginning soon after the trail reaches the end of Caples Lake. You'll ascend alongside Emigrant Creek, crossing it creek once, then march up a final few switchbacks to the lake at 8,600 feet. There's only one trail junction to worry about, 3.4 miles out, where you bear left. Emigrant Lake is a spectacular sight, set in a glacial cirque with steep granite walls rising up to Covered Wagon Peak and Thimble Peak. Swimming, sunbathing, and scenery-admiring are the preferred activities here.

🄲 Lake Margaret

- Distance: 4.8 miles round-trip
- Duration: 2.5 hours
- Rating: Easy/moderate
- Elevation change: 450 feet
- Trailhead: Lake Margaret
- Directions: From the junction of Hwy. 89 and Hwy. 88 in Hope Valley, drive west on Hwy. 88 for 13.7 miles to the Lake Margaret trailhead on the north side of the road (0.2 mile west of Caples Lake dam and 0.1 mile east of the Kirkwood Inn).

For an easy hike in the Carson Pass area, you just can't do better than this trail to Lake Margaret, which requires only gentle climbing and descending and reaches the lake in a mere 2.4 miles. Most children five and up will be very comfortable on this trail, and will certainly enjoy a swim in Lake Margaret. The path begins with a descent from the parking lot through a forest of red firs and lodgepole pines. It then meanders through an eclectic mix of terrain: across granite slabs, alongside meadows, across Caples Creek (a favorite area of fly fishers), past a couple of small ponds,

and through more dense forest. At two miles, after a second creek crossing, you'll find yourself in a lovely grove of aspens and, in season, knee-high wildflowers. The final stretch to the lake is the most strenuous ascent of the day, but still nothing to complain about. When you reach the top you get your first look at lovely Lake Margaret, elevation 7,500 feet. Surrounded by granite slabs, the intimate-sized lake provides just enough room for all comers to find their own spots for picnicking, fishing, or swimming. A few tiny islands and multiple shoreline boulders make for fine sunbathing. Although this trail is a great walk any time it is snow-free, plan your trip for the July wildflower bloom and you will be astonished at the beauty here.

Thunder Mountain

- Distance: 7.2 miles round-trip
- Duration: 4 hours
- Rating: Moderate
- Elevation change: 1,450 feet
- Trailhead: Thunder Mountain
- Directions: From the junction of Hwy. 89 and Hwy. 88 in Hope Valley, drive west on Hwy. 88 for 16 miles to the Thunder Mountain Trailhead on the south side of the road, 1.8 miles west of the Kirkwood Ski Area access road and 4 miles east of Silver Lake.

Although the Thunder Mountain Trail can be hiked as a 10-mile loop, the first leg offers such fine views and excellent scenery that the vast majority of hikers walk it out-and-back for a 7.2-mile round-trip. The trail begins with a moderate ascent through a lovely lodgepole-pine and red-fir forest, then emerges from the trees on a sagebrush- and mule's ear–covered ridge, just below the snow deflectors above the highway at Carson Spur. From here on you enjoy expansive views as you wander across an exposed landscape marked by strange volcanic mudflow formations, each one more odd-looking than the next. Lichens on their nubby surfaces give them an orange and greenish cast. The trail passes to the west of the Two Sentinels, elevation 8,780

Two hikers traverse dry volcanic slopes en route to Thunder Mountain.

feet, and follows the line of the ridge above Kirkwood Ski Resort. The only thing that mars the otherwise compelling scenery is the sight of the condominiums and development in Kirkwood Valley. Continuing along the ridgeline, the trail passes Martin Point and warning signs for out-of-bounds skiing at Kirkwood. A few switchbacks lead to a small saddle below a massive volcanic crag on the left and the high point of Amador County (9,410 feet) on the right, which is actually two feet higher than Thunder Mountain. Shortly beyond the saddle, a use trail leads northwest a few hundred feet to the top. The main trail continues around the back of this high ridge to a three-way junction, where you head right for Thunder's 9,408-foot summit. The peak is marked by a metal pole and superb views of Desolation Wilderness to the north, Round Top Peak to the east, Silver and Caples Lakes, and the Mokelumne and Emigrant wildernesses to the south. If you search around, you should be able to locate a summit register. Read the pithy remarks of others and then add a few of your own.

Minkalo Trail to Granite Lake

- Distance: 2 miles round-trip
- Duration: 1 hour
- Rating: Easy
- Elevation change: 300 feet
- Trailhead: Camp Minkalo at Silver Lake
- Directions: From the junction of Hwy. 89 and Hwy. 88 in Hope Valley, drive west on Hwy. 88 for 20 miles to the Kit Carson Lodge turnoff on the north side of the road, at Silver Lake. Turn north and drive past Kit Carson Lodge. Go left at the first fork and right at the second fork to reach the parking area for Minkalo Trail, 1.5 miles from Hwy. 88. Walk back on the road for about 150 feet to pick up the trail.

Silver Lake is owned and managed by the Eldorado Irrigation District, providing much-needed water for the folks "down the hill" in the Sierra foothills. The lake has numerous private homes and a few resorts and camps on its edges, making it seem somewhat less wild than nearby Caples Lake. Still, the big blue lake and its large, solitary Treasure Island is quite scenic, and this trail from its eastern shoreline leads to Granite Lake in only one mile—a walk of less than a half hour with a climb of only 300 feet. The path crosses Squaw Creek and meanders uphill through a granite landscape of big boulders and slabs (watch for trail cairns to keep you on the path). The trail leads right to Granite Lake's shoreline, which makes a fine destination for casual hikers and families. True to its name, the lake is lined with granite. A swim and a picnic here could get your kids hooked on the Sierra for life. Those who want more exercise can continue for another two miles to Hidden Lake, which is unfortunately not as scenic as Granite Lake, and loop back to the Minkalo trailhead by descending to Plasse's Resort, then following the trail along the east side of Silver Lake back to Minkalo Camp.

Shealor Lakes

- Distance: 3 miles round-trip
- Duration: 2 hours
- Rating: Moderate
- Elevation change: 800 feet
- Trailhead: Shealor Lakes
- Directions: From the junction of Hwy. 89 and Hwy. 88 in Hope Valley, drive west on Hwy. 88 for 21 miles to the Shealor Lakes trailhead on the north side of the road, 1.2 miles west of Silver Lake's dam and 0.5 mile east of the Plasse's Resort turnoff.

The best swimming in the Carson Pass region may well be at the granite-lined Shealor Lakes, and the lakes certainly win top honors in the scenery department as well. But aside from the tempting waters, the brief, rewarding trip to Shealor Lakes is all about polished granite. Even for the geologically challenged, it's not hard to picture the glaciers moving through here. The trail starts out in a red-fir and lodgepole-pine forest and climbs for a half mile up a granite-studded slope to a ridgetop. At the top, you are rewarded with an amazing view looking north toward the Desolation Wilderness; pointy Pyramid Peak is an obvious landmark. Once you've reach this high ridge, the next mile to the lakes is all downhill, traveling over exposed granite slopes into the basin that cradles the Shealor Lakes. Trail cairns mark the way, but as long as you are descending, you'll be heading for the lakes, which are in plain sight. This means that most of the work will be on your return, when you have to climb back up out of the lakes' basin, but no matter; the scenery is so gorgeous that it's worth every step. There are two Shealor lakes, but most people go no farther than the first, largest one. Surrounded by polished granite slabs, with a stand of trees on the south side that allows for a few camping spots, the lake is the perfect place to bring a book and spend a day.

BIKING

No discussion of biking in the Carson Pass area would be complete without singing the praises of the annual **Markleeville Death Ride** (www. deathride.com), which takes place in July. The Death Ride brings even expert riders to their knees with its staggering 129-mile length and 16,000 feet of elevation change. The route begins and ends in Markleeville and goes out-and-back across three Sierra passes—Carson, Ebbetts, and Monitor. Each year, hundreds of cyclists sign up for the chance to pedal all or part of the epic ride.

To prepare for the Death Ride, a challenging training ride is the out-and-back from **Woodfords to Lake Alpine** (80 miles). From Woodfords, take Highway 89 south past Markleeville to Highway 4, then turn west and crank up a strenuous seven-mile ascent over Ebbetts Pass. Beyond the summit, you'll descend to Hermit Valley, then climb up again through some nasty switchbacks to Mosquito Lake. From there, you have a big sigh of relief as you coast to Lake Alpine, where you can get some much-needed snacks at the store and cafe. Don't get too relaxed, however, as you have to turn around and retrace your tire marks for the ride back to Woodfords.

For those with more sensible biking aspirations, the Carson Pass area offers a multitude of trails. Mountain bikers looking for an easy cruise will enjoy the dirt road that leads to **Burnside Lake** from the junction of Highways 88 and 89 in Hope Valley (13 miles round-trip with 1,100 feet of elevation gain). The lake makes a fine swimming destination. More-experienced mountain bikers looking for some technical challenges will enjoy the 8.4-mile single-track ride on the Tahoe Rim Trail to **Round and Dardanelles Lakes.** The trail begins at the Big Meadow Trailhead on Highway 89 (5.3 miles south of Meyers and 5.7 miles north of Hope Valley), and follows the Tahoe Rim Trail south through Big Meadow and on to the lakes.

A variation on this route is to follow the Tahoe Rim Trail to a fork a half mile before Round Lake, then turn north (right) on the trail to **Christmas Valley.** This very technical downhill stretch will make you glad you have a full-suspension bike (or wish you had one if you don't). When the trail reaches pavement, turn right and follow the old road back to the trailhead. This makes a loop of about seven miles.

From the same Big Meadow trailhead, superadvanced mountain bikers take off on **Mr. Toad's Wild Ride,** otherwise known as the Saxon Creek Trail. This treacherous point-to-point ride travels from the Big Meadow Trailhead to Oneidas Street in South Lake Tahoe. Some claim that the route is so boulder-strewn and technical that it is simply not rideable. But that doesn't stop people from trying. For details, see *Biking* in the *South Shore* chapter.

At **Kirkwood Ski Resort** in summer, you can ride up Chairs 1 and 2 with your bike, then pedal around a network of 13.5 miles of dirt roads and trails across the ski area, and 25-plus miles of trails just outside the ski area. The most popular ride is to Caples Crest for a spectacular view of Caples Lake and the Mokelumne Wilderness. Lift access is available only on summer weekends 9 A.M.–4 P.M., but the rest of the week you can ride under your own power on Kirkwood's trails. Summer lift tickets are $20 adults, $15 children.

Bike rentals and route advice are available at Hope Valley Outdoor Center at Hope Valley

Resort (14655 Hwy. 88, Hope Valley, 530/694-2266, www.hopevalleyoutdoors.com), and at Kirkwood Adventure Center (1501 Kirkwood Meadows Dr., 209/258-7294 or 877/547-5966, www.kirkwood.com). Rentals are $30 per day, $20 per half day.

BOATING AND WATER SPORTS

Boat rentals are available at Caples Lake Resort and Silver Lake Resort. At **Caples Lake** (1111 Hwy. 88, one mile east of Kirkwood, 209/258-8888, www.capleslakeresort.com), the marina is open 7 or 8 A.M.–6 P.M. in summer and fall. Twelve- and 14-foot aluminum boats with 7.5 horsepower motors are available for fishing or just cruising the lake. Rates are $30–40 for two hours, $50–65 for four hours, $80–100 for eight hours. If you'd rather travel under your own power, kayak and canoe rentals are $20–25 for two hours, $30–35 for four hours, $50 for eight hours. If you have your own boat, the launch ramp is open 7 or 8 A.M.–8 P.M. Launch fees are $10–15. Over at **Kay's Silver Lake Resort** (48400 Kay's Rd. and Hwy. 88, 209/258-8598, www.kaysresort.com), you can rent 13-foot aluminum fishing boats with 7.5 horsepower motors ($15 first hour, $9 per hour thereafter). Or launch your own boat from their concrete launch ramp ($8).

Rafting and Whitewater Kayaking

In the early summer months (May–July), the **East Fork of the Carson River** provides exciting white-water action in its rugged, rock-walled canyon. Guided day trips are available from Tahoe Whitewater Tours (530/581-2441 or 800/442-7238, www.gowhitewater.com).

For calm-water kayaking on one of Carson Pass' many lakes, kayak rentals are available at Kirkwood Adventure Center located in the Red Cliffs Day Lodge at Kirkwood Mountain Resort, at Hope Valley Outdoor Center in Hope Valley Resort, or at Caples or Silver Lakes.

SWIMMING

The best place for swimming, aside from the multiple mountain lakes you can hike to, is at

© ANN MARIE BROWN

Motorboats await passengers at the Kit Carson Lodge beach on Silver Lake.

Grover Hot Springs State Park (530/694-2248, www.parks.ca.gov), where hot springs bubble up from the ground and the water is channeled into two concrete pools of varying temperature. The pools are open year-round except for Christmas, New Year's, and Thanksgiving, and a brief period in September for maintenance. A $6 fee per vehicle is charged to enter the park; pool fees are $5 adults and $2 children 16 and under.

FISHING

The Hope Valley and Carson Pass area is known as one of the greatest fishing regions in the Sierra Nevada. From April to October, the **West Fork Carson River,** which runs through Hope, Faith, and Charity valleys, offers excellent trout fishing. It flows alongside Highway 88 and Blue Lakes Road, providing easy access, and is regularly stocked with rainbow and cutthroat trout. A fishing access area is located on the northwest side of the T-junction of Highways 88 and 89 in Hope Valley. You're more

likely to find solitude if you access the river along Blue Lakes Road.

Fishing is also good in the Upper and Lower **Blue Lakes** themselves, 12 miles up Blue Lakes Road from Highway 88. The primary catch is rainbow trout, with occasional brook trout and cutthroat trout. Fish here early in summer before Pacific Gas and Electric Company drops the lake level.

The **East Fork Carson River** is a fly fisher's dream. From Hangman's Bridge (south of Markleeville) downstream to the Nevada state line, you must use artificial lures with single barbless hooks. The river has rainbows, Lahontan cutthroat, brown trout, and mountain whitefish. If you're not familiar with fly-fishing, or want to sharpen your skills, sign up for lessons with **Horse Feathers Fly Fishing School** (530/694-2399), which operates out of Sorensen's Resort.

Caples Lake and **Silver Lake** both have excellent fishing for rainbow, brown, and mackinaw trout. You can rent boats at either lake and try your luck at trolling, or fish from shore. For the intrepid angler who can't wait for the snow to melt, ice fishing is possible in both Caples and Silver Lakes.

Fishing licenses, flies, bait, and tackle are available at Woodfords Station, the Markleeville General Store, Carson River Resort, Hope Valley Outdoor Center, Kirkwood General Store, and Silver and Caples Lakes.

HORSEBACK RIDING

The handsome steeds at the **Kirkwood Corral** (1501 Kirkwood Meadows Dr. at Hwy. 88, Kirkwood, 209/265-2664, www.kirkwood.com) have been a picturesque fixture in Kirkwood's meadow for years. But in the summer of 2005, the meadow was sadly devoid of horses due to environmental concerns about the impact the animals have on the meadow's creek. Check with the corral to see if the horses will be returning in 2006; if so, they will be more than happy to take you trotting along trails in the Mokelumne Wilderness and Carson Pass area.

WINTER SPORTS
Downhill Skiing and Snowboarding

At **Kirkwood Ski Resort** (1501 Kirkwood Meadows Dr. at Hwy. 88, Kirkwood, 209/258-6000 or 877/547-5966 or, www.kirkwood.com), the operative word is "snow." From 2001–2006, the resort had the deepest snowpack of any ski area not just at Lake Tahoe, but anywhere in North America. Average annual snowfall is more than 500 inches—some years more than 700 inches—and this is quality stuff, typically the driest snow in the entire Sierra. Like Northstar-at-Tahoe, Kirkwood is in the process of building a $250 million Mountain Village, with shops, restaurants, condos, a swimming complex, and an ice-skating rink. Soon, sleepy little Kirkwood will be a destination resort with its own town, shopping, and nightlife.

The slopes at Kirkwood feature steep chutes, plenty of tree skiing, big cliffs, and powder-filled open bowls. Twelve lifts serve almost 70 runs, which are carved over 2,300 acres of skiable terrain. The longest vertical drop is a respectable 2,000 feet; the longest run is 2.5 miles. Kirkwood's base elevation is 7,800 feet, which is higher than all other Tahoe-area resorts except Mount Rose, and snow depths even at the bottom of the mountain are generally more than 20 feet. Its top elevation is 9,800 feet.

For those who prefer fresh tracks, Kirkwood also features some of the best backcountry skiing anywhere in the Tahoe basin, with great terrain and easy access. The resort capitalizes on this with Expedition Kirkwood, a school that teaches backcountry skills, including avalanche awareness and survival techniques, and provides snowmobile tours. Kirkwood is the only resort in California to offer such a program. A special area called Beacon Basin is reserved as an avalanche transceiver training area.

Snowboarders have plenty of cheer about at Kirkwood, too. It has several terrain parks, including at 350-foot-long superpipe with 18-foot walls. Beginning riders and skiers don't get left behind. The gentle terrain at Kirkwood's Timber Creek has been rated as one of the top learning areas in the country. The Mighty Mountain Children's School teaches kids ages 4–12 how to ski and ages 7–12 how to snowboard. All-day packages for kids including lessons, rentals, and lunch are $100. For kids too young to ski, day care is available. Learning programs for adults include three-day programs in which students are guaranteed to learn to ski or ride on the first day, and one-day packages for $59 that include rentals, lessons, and a limited lift ticket.

A day spent skiing or riding at Kirkwood will cost about the same as most of the Tahoe resorts. All-day lift tickets for adults are $62, teens 13–18 are $50, children 6–12 are $13, children 5 and under are $6, seniors 65–69 are $34, and seniors 70 and up are $13. On holidays, all ticket prices go up $3. To save a few bucks on Kirkwood lift tickets, buy them in advance at Kirkwood's website. Or if you plan to ski two days in a row on non-holidays, you can buy a discounted two day ticket. On Sundays, adults who buy a lift ticket can bring along one or two kids 12 and under and the kids ski free.

Cross-Country Skiing and Snowshoeing

More than 80 kilometers of groomed cross-country ski and snowshoe trails are available at **Kirkwood Cross Country and Snowshoe Center** (1501 Kirkwood Meadows Dr. at Hwy. 88, Kirkwood, 209/258-7248 or 877/547-5966, www.kirkwood.com), located across the highway from the downhill ski resort, next to the Kirkwood Inn. The trail system is divided into three interconnected sections, which cover more than 4,000 acres. Trailside warming huts and a day lodge are available for drinks, snacks, and a place to get warm by a blazing fire. Snowshoers are allowed to go everywhere skiers can go, and dogs are allowed on two trails in Kirkwood Meadow. All trails are machine groomed each morning and are double-tracked with skating lines. A special one-kilometer loop trail is set aside for young

SHOWSHOE THOMPSON

Sacramento farmer John A. Thompson, better known as Snowshoe Thompson, holds the title of Tahoe's first skier and the man who carried the mail across the Sierra in the winter months. A resident of Diamond Valley in Alpine County, he skied through the heart of winter in the mountains hundreds of times, beginning in 1856 and continuing for two decades. Had it not been for his weekly mail runs, there would have been no communication between the eastern and western slopes of the Sierra for a six-month period each year.

Thompson did not use any single route, but varied his path according to the weather and snow conditions. Most commonly, he traveled from Hangtown (Placerville) to Woodfords (near Markleeville), then followed the route of the Mormon Emigrant Trail (today the route of Highway 88) to Genoa, Nevada, then known as Mormon Station. He routinely passed through Kirkwood and the Carson Pass area on this three-day journey eastward. The return trip usually took only two days.

A Norwegian immigrant, Thompson was born Jon Torstein-Rue in 1827. He learned to ski in the Telemark region of Norway, then left his native country at the age of 10. His handmade, 10-foot-long skis were fashioned from green oak and lashed to his boots with leather straps. In the 19th century these heavy, unwieldy contraptions were known as "snowshoes"; Thompson's were said to weigh 25 pounds. In addition to the burden of the skis, Thompson carried as much as 60-100 pounds of mail on his back. The mail sack contained not just letters but also medicine, emergency supplies, clothing, books, and whatever else the people of Genoa needed.

Using one long pole for balance and support, Thompson skied 25-40 miles per day to keep his delivery on schedule. He wore a Mackinaw jacket, wide-brimmed hat, and covered his face with charcoal to prevent snow blindness. The isolated residents of Genoa were so thrilled at his arrival they would drop whatever they were doing to watch the tall blonde Norwegian ski down from Genoa Peak. He regularly boasted that he never got lost, and never got scared. When a storm became an "inconvenience," he would find a big boulder, clear its surface of snow, and dance Norwegian folk dances until the weather cleared.

In 1866, Thompson married an Englishwoman named Agnes Singleton. They farmsteaded in Diamond Valley in the warm months, and Agnes gave birth to a child in 1867. Thompson taught his only son and many other children to ski, and showed his neighbors how to make their own "snowshoes." He was famous for showing off his racing and jumping skills. In 1872, he was clocked skiing at 55 miles per hour, and successfully ski-jumped 180 feet.

Snowshoe Thompson died of appendicitis in 1876, and his grave can be seen in the town cemetery in Genoa, Nevada. Despite his great services to the people of Nevada, he was never paid a single cent for delivering the United States mail.

children. The trail circles around a meadow by the day lodge, and has life-sized outlines of forest animals and other fun interpretive signs. All skiing and snowshoeing equipment rentals are available. All-day trail passes are $21 for adults ages 19–64, $17 for teens 13–18 and seniors 65–69, $12 for seniors 70 and up, and $8 for children 7–12. Trail passes for dogs are $4. Beginners packages, which include cross-country skiing lessons, trail passes, and rentals are $46. Two-for-one beginners packages are available midweek. Beginning snowshoers can take part in daily lessons that take place every day at noon. For $42, you receive a trail pass and snowshoe rentals, and trek on the trails with a guide.

At the **Hope Valley Outdoor Center** (14655 Hwy. 88, Hope Valley, 530/694-2266, www. hopevalleyoutdoors.com) at Hope Valley Resort, just down the road from Sorensen's, you can rent cross-country and telemark skis ($10–18) and snowshoes ($16). Cross-country ski lessons for beginners are offered weekends at 11 A.M. ($45), or midweek by reservation.

Guided full-moon skiing and snowshoe tours are offered. Their cozy cafe serves hot and cold drinks, pies, and other calorie-replenishing treats. Sixty miles of trails are available nearby in the national forest.

For do-it-yourselfers, two Sno-Parks are found about 500 feet apart on Highway 88 at Carson Pass and Meiss Meadows. Both have parking for about 40 cars. As at all California Sno-Parks, you must purchase a Sno-Park permit ($5 per day or $25 per year; contact the Eldorado National Forest at 530/644-6048 for a list of places that sell them) in order to park your car and access the trails. From the **Carson Pass Sno-Park,** you can ski or snowshoe the intermediate Wilderness Boundary Trail, which connects with Woods Lake Road and the trail from Meiss Sno-Park. From **Meiss Sno-Park,** you can ski or snowshoe the easy route to Woods Lake (you have to cross the highway to access the trail) or head north to Meiss Meadows on an unmarked route that roughly follows the Pacific Crest Trail.

A third Sno-Park is located at Blue Lakes Road and Highway 88, three miles west of the T-junction of Highway 88 and 89, but because snowmobiles are allowed, this Sno-Park is not as popular for cross-country skiing and snowshoeing. For an easy cross-country glide, many skiers park along the road near the junction of Highways 88 and 89 in **Hope Valley,** then ski around the meadows near the junction, or along the Burnside Lake Road to **Burnside Lake** (13 miles round-trip). Two miles north of this junction on Highway 89 is the meadow at **Grass Lake,** another good place for easy skiing. A three-mile trail leads to Hope Valley. Both of these areas are great for moonlight skiing.

Sledding and Tubing

Kirkwood gets in on the tubing action with its **Slide Mountain Tube Park** (1501 Kirkwood Meadows Dr. at Hwy. 88, Kirkwood, 209/258-6000 or 877/547-5966, www.kirkwood.com, 10 A.M.–5 P.M. weekends), located near Red Cliffs Day Lodge. Tubing rates are $10 per hour, including the tube and a handle tow that carries you back up the slope.

Snowmobiling

Lake Tahoe Adventures (3071 Hwy. 50, South Lake Tahoe, 530/577-2940 or 800/865-4679, www.laketahoeadventures.com) specializes in introducing beginners to snowmobiling with a two-hour tour around Hope Valley and Charity Valley. Helmets, goggles, gloves, and boots are included in the price; tours cost $102 for single riders and $148 for two riders on one machine.

Ice-Skating

The outdoor **Village Ice Rink** (1501 Kirkwood Meadows Dr. at Hwy. 88, Kirkwood, 209/258-6000 or 877/547-5966, www.kirkwood.com, 10 A.M.–5 P.M. Fri.–Sun. in winter, weather permitting) is a fun place to practice your pirouettes. Skating fees for adults are $6 for two hours, or $9 with skate rental. Fees for children are $6 with or without rentals. On holidays, all rates go up by $3.

Dogsledding

At the entrance to Kirkwood Ski Resort, the Siberian huskies at **Running Creek Sled Dogs** (775/266-4720) mush their way through Kirkwood's snow-covered meadow. Rates are $110 plus $45 per child 60 pounds or less and $85 per adult. The sleds have a weight limit of 400 pounds, which usually will accommodate a family of three or four. Full-moon tours are available as well as day rides; all rides last about 40 minutes. Advance reservations are required.

Over in Hope Valley, 30-year veteran sled-dog musher Dotty Dennis and her pack of frisky pups at **Husky Express** (775/782-3047) will take you on a five-mile, hour-long ride. The dogsleds have a load limit of 375 pounds each, with room for two adults and one or two small children. Reservations are required. Rates are $100 per adult and child over 60 pounds; $50 per child under 60 pounds. There is a minimum charge of $185. If you get hooked on dog mushing, Dotty offers a comprehensive hands-on mushers course and a skijoring clinic.

Accommodations and Food

MARKLEEVILLE AND HOPE VALLEY

Motels and Lodges

The intimate, 11-room **Creekside Lodge** (14820 Hwy. 89, Markleeville, 530/694-2511 or 866/802-7335, www.markleevilleusa.com, $80–160) is located in downtown Markleeville right next to the historic Wolf Creek Restaurant. The recently renovated rooms are decorated in mountain-lodge style, with colorful quilts, historic photographs and prints, and wrought-iron lamps and headboards. Eight rooms have king beds, two have queen beds, and one suite is set up for families with a king bed, two twin beds, and a kitchenette. All rooms have telephones and satellite television.

For budget lodging in the Carson Pass Area, you won't find a better deal than the 20-room **Woodfords Inn** (20960 Hwy. 89, Woodfords, 530/694-2410, www.woodfordsinn.net, $79–84). Rooms have one queen bed or two doubles. Rates are low partly because it's a half-hour drive to Kirkwood and six miles to Markleeville. All rooms have cable television and VCRs, and there is a hot tub on the premises.

One more option in downtown Markleeville is the **J. Marklee Toll Station** (14856 Highway 89, Markleeville, 530/694-2507, www.tollstation.com, $70), which has five ultrabasic rooms.

Cabins

Located in a dense grove of quaking aspens in Hope Valley, **Sorensen's Resort** (14255 Hwy. 88, Hope Valley, 530/694-2203 or 800/423-9949, www.sorensensresort.com, $95–395) is a deservedly popular spot. Set on nearly 170 acres, the cabin resort was first developed in the 1920s by Danish sheepherders. Much of the architecture is Norwegian in style and each of the 30 cabins is unique. Some have gas fireplaces or woodstoves, and a few cabins are pet-friendly (rates vary based on cabin size). The resort is well suited to both serious outdoor recreationists and

romantics looking for a weekend getaway. An excellent restaurant is on the premises, and cross-country skiing is popular in winter. A wide variety of excursions and organized activities are available year-round, from history hikes to watercolor painting classes to bird-watching to astronomy lessons.

If you want to fish the world-class trout waters of the East Fork Carson River, book at stay at the cabins at the **Carson River Resort** (12399 Hwy. 89, Markleeville, 877/694-2229, www.carsonriverresort.com, $70–150), just 2.5 miles south of Markleeville. This no-frills resort is a perfect base for fly fishers, with a general store that can supply the wet or dry flies you forgot and the few groceries you'll need for basic sustenance. Pets are allowed in some cabins. The resort also has RV spaces, a campground, and gas and propane for sale.

Campgrounds and RV Parks

The campground at **Grover Hot Springs State Park** (530/694-2248, www.parks.ca.gov., $25) is a favorite of bathers and others who believe in, or at least enjoy, the healing power of mineral waters. Located three miles outside downtown Markleeville, the park has two pools—one hot and one cool—plus a 76-site campground for tents or RVs up to 24 feet long, which has showers, water, flush toilets, picnic tables, and fire pits. Reserve at 800/444-7275 or www.reserveamerica.com.

The Carson River Ranger District of Toiyabe National Forest runs five campgrounds (775/882-2766, $12) in the lands around Markleeville and Woodfords: **Crystal Springs, Snowshoe Springs, Kit Carson, Hope Valley** and **Markleeville Creek.** Each have only 10–20 sites. All campgrounds are first-come, first-serve except Hope Valley, which can be reserved in advance at 877/444-6777 or www.reserveusa.com.

Just outside Markleeville, **Turtle Rock County Park** (530/694-2140, $8) has 28 sites for tents or RVs up to 35 feet long set in an open pine forest. And a few miles off Highway 89 near Indian Creek Reservoir, the Bureau of Land Management runs the 29-site **Indian Creek Campground** (775/885-6000, $15–30), which can accommodate RVs up to 30 feet long and has a few luxuries, including showers and flush toilets. Boating, fishing, and swimming are popular here.

The private **Hope Valley Resort** (800/423-9949, sites $15–30, trailer $65–75), run by the folks at Sorensen's, has 25 sites alongside the West Fork Carson River for tents or RVs up to 36 feet long, with full hookups, flush toilets, and showers. If you are a tent camper, you'll love the three walk-in sites. If you don't care to rough it, rent their 1947 housekeeping trailer with a front deck that overlooks the river.

Additionally, the Pacific Gas and Electric utility company manages a large, 70-site campground at **Blue Lakes** (916/923-7124, $15), a popular fishing and boating spot on Blue Lakes Road near Hope Valley. Lastly, the **Carson River Resort** also has campsites and RV spaces for rent, as does **Sorensen's Resort** (see *Cabins*).

Food

Think of Markleeville and you probably don't think of fine Italian dining. **[Villa Gigli** (145 Hot Springs Rd., Markleeville, 530/694-2253, www.villagigli.com) will make you think again. Open summer weekends only, the restaurant features the art of Gina Gigli and the exemplary cooking of her husband, Ruggero Gigli. On Friday nights, the fare is usually homemade pizza. On Saturday and Sunday nights, Ruggero's homemade Tuscan-style bread sets the stage for lasagna, taglietelle with scampi or salmon, homemade cannelloni, or a prix fixe dinner made from whatever is ripe and fresh that day. All of this takes place in the Gigli home, so only a lucky 20 or so diners get to partake in the culinary magic each night. Make reservations far in advance. Perhaps most surprising, the prices are very reasonable—you'll dine very well for about $25 per person, and the entire experience will be one you'll long remember.

The center of all activity in Markleeville, **Wolf Creek Restaurant and Cutthroat Saloon** (14830 Hwy. 89, Markleeville, 530/694-2150, www.markleevilleusa.com, 11 A.M.–3 P.M. Mon.–Tues., 11 A.M.–8 P.M. Wed.–Fri., and 7 A.M.–8 P.M. Sat.–Sun., $7–24) serves three meals a day in its historic three-story building. The structure was moved to Markleeville in 1885 from its original site in Silver Mountain City, which was once the Alpine County seat (now it's a ghost town). The menu runs the gamut from simple hamburgers and an array of salads to Wolf Creek filet mignon, scampi Mediterranean, and calamari piccata. It's all good, and served up with a big dose of Markleeville atmosphere.

Another dependable bet for three meals a day year-round is the cafe at **[Sorensen's Resort** (14255 Hwy. 88, Hope Valley, 530/694-2203 or 800/423-9949, www.sorensensresort .com, cafe hours 7:30 A.M.–4 P.M. and 5–9 P.M. daily, $15–29). Homemade soups, beef burgundy stew, grilled salmon, barbecued chicken, seafood pasta, and New York steak round out the classically American menu. Don't miss the homemade berry cobbler.

For a quick stop for breakfast or lunch, or for the latest fishing advice or local gossip, stop in at the historic **Woodfords Station** (290 Hwy. 88 at Markleeville turnoff, Woodfords, 530/694-2930, www.woodfordsstation. com, 7 A.M.–6 P.M. daily, $4–8). Have a seat in the old Pony Express stop and try the McWoodford's egg, ham, and cheese sandwich for breakfast or a slice of Lynda's quiche. A variety of hot and cold sandwiches are served, plus chili or the soup of the day, and a passel of pies and milk shakes.

An equally casual menu is offered at the small cafe at **Hope Valley Outdoors** (14655 Hwy. 88, 530/694-2266, www.hopevalleyoutdoors.com, $5–9). Hamburgers, veggie burgers, and salmon burgers are served up with microbrews and imported beers on tap. Have a meal and rent a kayak, fishing pole, or mountain bike at the same time.

Groceries and supplies are available at the **Markleeville General Store** in downtown

Markleeville (14799 Hwy. 89, 530/694-2448, 9:30 A.M.–6 P.M. daily) and at the store at **Carson River Resort** (877/694-2229). If you need to do some serious stocking up, your best bet is to head to South Lake Tahoe, a 40-minute drive.

SILVER LAKE, CAPLES LAKE, AND KIRKWOOD
Cabins

The Highway 88 corridor has a handful of cabin resorts located right on the shores of Caples and Silver Lakes. Try **Caples Lake Resort** (1111 Hwy. 88, Kirkwood, 209/258-8888, www.capleslakeresort.com) for a convenient fishing or skiing getaway. Located just one mile from Kirkwood Ski Resort, the resort has eight cabins and six lodge rooms that are just a stone's throw from Caples Lake. The rustic cabins have kitchens, bathrooms, and gas fireplaces, and can accommodate two to six people ($90–210 in summer, $110–360 in winter). The lake-view lodge rooms ($80–100 in summer, $100–160 in winter) have private bathrooms but they are across the hall, so bring your bathrobe. A con-

tinental breakfast is included with the lodge rooms, but not the cabins. A sauna, small store, and boat rentals are available.

Over at Silver Lake, the cabins at **Kay's Silver Lake Resort** (48400 Kay's Rd., Pioneer, 209/258-8598, www.kaysresort.com, $75–185) are situated on a hill across Highway 88 from the lake, offering fine lake views from their decks. The eight cabins supply all the basics for a fishing or hiking vacation, with gas heat and fully equipped kitchens. The cabins range in size from studios to two bedrooms. Weekly rates are discounted. The resort is open year-round, but in winter you have to hike 100–200 yards through the snow to your cabin (snowshoes are often required). A small grocery store and boat rentals are available across the street at the lake. Silver Lake is an excellent fishery for rainbow, brown, and mackinaw trout. Kirkwood Ski Area is only a 10-minute drive away.

A more luxurious option on Silver Lake is the **C Kit Carson Lodge** (Hwy. 88, Silver Lake, 209/258-8500, www.kitcarsonlodge.com), situated on 12 acres on the eastern end

A cabin at Caples Lake is the perfect setting for a Carson Pass fishing and hiking vacation.

© ANN MARIE BROWN

CARSON PASS

of Silver Lake just out of sight of Highway 88. The resort is deservedly popular, with naturally landscaped grounds surrounding wood-and-stone cabins featuring decks, fireplaces, kitchens, and private baths located right on the shore of Silver Lake. Here "rustic elegance" is done right. In addition to 19 cabins priced at $795–1,780 per week (cabins are available by the week only June–Labor Day), eight bed-and-breakfast rooms are available in two fourplex units ($105–145 per night with a two-night minimum). After Labor Day and until the resort closes in mid-October, cabins can be rented on a two-night basis for $100–270 per night. Although the bed-and-breakfast rooms aren't quite as intimate and spacious as the standalone cabins, each has a private deck that looks out on to the lake. Breakfast and dinner are available in the resort's restaurant, which is adjacent to a small art gallery featuring paintings and sculptures of the Sierra. A swimming beach and boat rentals are also available. In winter, the resort keeps only a couple of cabins open for cross-country skiers.

Condominium-style Resorts

For skiers and riders, lodging is available right at Kirkwood Ski Resort. **Kirkwood Accommodations** (800/967-7500, www .kirkwood.com) rents privately owned ski-in/ski-out vacation homes, condos, and town houses at Kirkwood Towers, The Lodge at Kirkwood, Meadowstone Lodge, the Mountain Club, Snowcrest Lodge, and other Kirkwood properties. Typical lodging rates during ski season weekends and holidays are $175–295 per night for two people in a studio unit or hotel-style room. Two-bedroom units that can sleep six people go for $375–625 per night. "Stay and ski free" packages are the best deals, but these are only available in the first two weeks of December, midweek in January, and throughout April.

Campgrounds and RV Parks

The U.S. Forest Service runs four campgrounds near Silver and Caples Lakes: Woods Lake, Silver Lake East, Caples Lake, and Kirk-wood Lake (209/295-4251, www.fs.fed.us/r5/ eldorado, $10–12). Silver Lake East is the largest camp with 62 sites that can be reserved in advance at 877/444-6777 or www.reserveusa. com. The other three campgrounds are first-come, first-serve and each have 12–34 sites. A major trailhead into the Mokelumne Wilderness is located at scenic 【 **Woods Lake Campground,** which has a compelling view of Round Top Peak from several of its sites. The camp is suitable for tents only, as is Kirkwood Lake. The other two camps can accommodate RVs up to 40 feet long. Caples Lake Campground is right across the highway from Caples Lake.

The 35 sites at **Silver Lake West Campground** (530/644-2545, $16) are managed by the Eldorado Irrigation District. Reservations are not taken. The private **Plasse's Resort** (209/258-8814, www.plassesresort .com, $20) at Silver Lake has a 60-site campground for tents or RVs up to 32 feet long, plus flush toilets, showers, laundry, dump station, and a small store and restaurant. Canoe and kayak rentals are available.

Food

First opened in 1864 by Zachary Kirkwood, the 【 **Kirkwood Inn and Saloon** (Hwy. 88 across from Kirkwood, 209/258-7304, 11 A.M.– 8 P.M. Mon.–Fri., 8 A.M.–8 P.M. Sat.–Sun., $7–24) is a throwback to early times in the Carson Pass area. Housed in the original log cabin, the inn is a great place for a hearty meal after a day on Kirkwood's slopes or a long hike to an alpine lake. Even if you are just driving through Carson Pass, be sure to stop and have at least one meal here. Have a seat by the roaring fire or straddle a bar stool at the rustic bar and you'll swear you've been transported to the 19th century. The dinner menu consists of hearty salads, burgers, and hot sandwiches or heartier fare like New York strip steak, campfire chicken, pork tenderloin, or a variety of pastas. Barbecue ribs are a specialty. The inn is open for three meals a day most of the year. A breakfast here is the perfect way to fuel up for a day exploring Carson Pass.

The dining room at ⟨⟨ **Kit Carson Lodge** (Hwy. 88, Silver Lake, 209/258-8500, www .kitcarsonlodge.com, $20–35) is probably best known for its Sunday brunch, although its nightly dinners are exemplary as well. Entrees are on the expensive side, but the classic American cuisine (duck, salmon, filet mignon) is well prepared and graciously served, and the airy and bright dining room is a perfect setting for any meal.

If you are staying and playing at Kirkwood Ski Resort, you'll find several choices for casual meals (Timber Creek Bar and Cafeteria, Outback Grill, Monte Wolfe's, Bub's Sports Bar and Grill). Although an honorable mention goes to **Bub's Sports Bar and Grill** (209/258-7225, 3–8 p.m. Mon–Fri., 11 a.m.– 9 p.m. Sat.–Sun.) for its brick-oven-fired pizzas

and all-American food, the best of the resort's dining options is the **Off the Wall Bar and Grill** (209/258-7365, $15–28) in Kirkwood Village near the ice rink. Daily in winter you can grab a seat on the outdoor deck and chew on a prime rib sandwich while you watch the action on the slopes, or on winter weekends, enjoy an elegant dinner with entrees like fresh lobster ravioli with goat cheese and curry, scallops Rockefeller on a bed of wilted spinach, or filet mignon with wild mushroom bordelaise. Open daily during ski season for lunch; dinner on Friday and Saturday only.

Groceries and supplies are available at the Kirkwood General Store (1501 Kirkwood Meadows Dr., 209/258-7294), but for serious stocking up, the 40-minute drive to South Lake Tahoe is your best bet.

Practicalities

INFORMATION

The **Alpine County Chamber of Commerce and Visitors Center** (530/694-2475, www .alpinecounty.com) is located at 3 Webster Street, Markleeville. The best source of information on outdoor activities is the **Amador Ranger District** of Eldorado National Forest (26820 Silver Dr., Pioneer, 209/295-4251, www.fs.fed.us/r5/eldorado), which operates a visitors center just off Highway 88 in Pioneer. In summer and fall, the volunteers at the Carson Pass Information Station at Carson Pass summit on Hwy. 88 (209/258-8606) are a great source for information. Or contact the **Pacific Ranger District** in Pollock Pines (530/644-2349, www.fs.fed.us/r5/eldorado).

SERVICES

Medical Care

The nearest hospital is located in South Lake Tahoe, about a 40-minute drive from Carson Pass: **Barton Memorial Hospital** (2170 South Ave., South Lake Tahoe, 530/541-3420, www .bartonhealth.org). South Lake Tahoe also has

two 24-hour emergency-care centers: **Tahoe Urgent Care** (2130 Hwy. 50, South Lake Tahoe, 530/541-3277) and **Stateline Medical Center** (155 Hwy. 50, Stateline, 775/588-3561 or 530/543-5700).

Post Offices

A post office (14845 Hwy. 88, 530/694-2125) is located in downtown Markleeville. Kirkwood has its own post office located in the Kirkwood General Store (1501 Kirkwood Meadows Dr., 209/258-7294).

GETTING THERE
By Air

Visitors can fly into the **Reno/Tahoe International Airport** (2001 E. Plumb Ln., 775/328-6400, www.renoairport.com) and rent a car to drive to Carson Pass, about a 90-minute drive. Visitors could also fly into Sacramento, Oakland, San Francisco, or San Jose airports. Sacramento Airport is about two hours from Carson Pass; the other airports are about four hours away.

CARSON PASS

By Car

From South Lake Tahoe, take Highway 89 south to Meyers, then turn south (left) to stay on Highway 89. Drive 11 miles to Hope Valley, then turn east or west on Highway 88. East leads to Markleeville in 13 miles; west leads to Carson Pass in 9 miles and Caples and Silver Lake beyond. It takes about 40 minutes to drive from South Lake Tahoe to Carson Pass.

From Sacramento, Stockton, or the San Francisco Bay Area, the primary driving route to Carson Pass is to follow Highway 88 east through Jackson. From Sacramento, take Highway 16 east and then Highway 49 south to Jackson, then take Highway 88 east to Carson Pass. From the San Francisco Bay Area, take I-580 east to Tracy, then take I-205 east to I-5 north. In Stockton, take Highway 4 east to Highway 99 north to Highway 88 east.

From Reno, take U.S. 395 south to Garderville, Nevada, then take Highway 88 west to Carson Pass.

By Bus

The nearest bus terminal is in South Lake Tahoe at the South Y Transit Center on Highway 50. From there, you would have to rent a car to access Carson Pass.

GETTING AROUND

In winter, you will most certainly need chains for driving around the Carson Pass area. Chains are sometimes required even if you have a four-wheel-drive vehicle. To get current updates on road conditions in California, phone 800/427-7623. To get current updates on Nevada road conditions, phone 877/687-6237.

BACKGROUND

The Land

GEOLOGY

The tale of Lake Tahoe began about 400 million years ago when the land that is now the Sierra Nevada Mountains lay quietly beneath an ancient sea. This landmass was made up of thick layers of sediment that were piled thousands of feet deep. As the number of layers continued to build, pressure caused the bottom layers to be folded, twisted, and compressed into rock forms. Eventually these massive rocks were thrust upward above the sea's surface by movements of the Pacific and North American continental plates. In the process, a mountain range was formed—what would eventually become the **Sierra Nevada,**

the longest and highest single mountain range in the contiguous United States.

As the mountains rose, molten rock welled up from deep within the earth and cooled slowly beneath the layers of rock and sediment, forming the substance we know as **granite.** Over eons of time, erosion gradually wore away almost all the overlying sediment and exposed the granite underneath. Today, much of the rock seen around Lake Tahoe is granite. With its salt-and-pepper appearance, created by a random distribution of light- and dark-colored minerals, it is easy to distinguish from other types of rock.

Next, around 10 million years ago, the

© ANN MARIE BROWN

entire block of the mountain range was up-lifted and tilted to the west. A few million years later, two parallel **faults**—or fractures in the earth's crust—evolved in the block, and the landmasses on both sides of the faults continued to rise. On the west side, the Sierra Nevada was created, with upthrown fault blocks forming the South and West Shores' highest peaks, including Freel Peak, Monument Peak, Pyramid Peak, and Mount Tallac. On the east side, the equally dramatic Carson Range came into being. In between, the land between the two parallel faults sank and created the valley that would later hold the Lake Tahoe basin.

The major structure of the Tahoe Sierra was now formed, and only required a few finishing touches. About two million years ago, **lava** began to flow from Mount Pluto and other volcanoes on the north and east side of the basin. The lava formed a plug across the huge basin's northeastern outlet. Rivers, streams, and snowmelt that flowed into the dammed basin filled it with water to a depth several hundred feet higher than Lake Tahoe's current level. Eventually a new outlet was eroded through the lava dam, creating the present course of the Lower Truckee River, and stabilizing the lake level at its current depth. Today, the Lower Truckee River by Tahoe City remains Lake Tahoe's only outlet, although 63 separate tributaries and two hot springs pour into the lake.

Another series of geologic events put the final touches on the Lake Tahoe area. Several times during the past million years the planet cooled, one of a series of **ice ages** descended, and the entire Sierra Nevada mountain range was engulfed in snow and ice. **Glaciers,** or rivers of ice, went to work on the exposed granite, moving slowly down established river valleys on the western side of the lake and carving the broad U-shapes of Emerald Bay, Fallen Leaf Lake, and Cascade Lake. It is uncertain how many times glacial ice moved through the Tahoe area, advancing and then retreating, although there is evidence that at least three major glaciations occurred. Only the sturdiest chunks of granite withstood the glaciers' onslaught. Softer, weaker rock was chiseled

away and ground into rubble by the fierce power of the glaciers' grinding ice and rock. The gravel left behind by the melting glaciers formed hills that are known as lateral and terminal **moraines.** One such wall of rubble forms the basis for Highway 89 just south of Emerald Bay, where the road follows the line of a narrow moraine between Cascade Lake and Lake Tahoe. Emerald Bay is encircled by an incomplete moraine. Had the moraine been completed, Emerald Bay would be a separate lake, like nearby Cascade Lake, not a part of Lake Tahoe.

The sum total of these varied geologic events formed the Lake Tahoe we know today. The lake's statistics are laced with superlatives. With a deepest point of 1,645 feet near Crystal Bay, Tahoe is the third-deepest lake in North America (after Great Slave Lake in Canada and Crater Lake in Oregon) and the 10th deepest in the world. Its average depth is 989 feet, and with 193 square miles of surface area, the lake holds almost 39 trillion gallons of water. Lake Tahoe is 22 miles long and 12 miles wide, with approximately 72 miles of shoreline. It is the largest alpine (high-elevation) lake in North America. Several million tons of water evaporate from its surface every day, yet this decreases the lake level by only one-tenth of an inch. Still, it is estimated that because the lake surface is so vast, if the water that evaporates every 24 hours could be recovered, it would supply the daily requirements of a city the size of Los Angeles.

CLIMATE

Elevations in the Tahoe basin range from the lake's elevation of 6,223 feet to 10,881 feet at Freel Peak's summit on the South Shore. Given that range, the climate change can be dramatic. Summertime temperatures can reach 90°F at the lakeshore, but it can snow any month of the year on the highest peaks.

Generally, the climate at Tahoe is quite mild year-round, with daytime temperatures in the high 70s or low 80s (Fahrenheit) in summer and nighttime temperatures in the 40s or low 50s. Spring and fall are somewhat cooler. Win-

© ANN MARIE BROWN

Found along the Bayview Trail in Desolation Wilderness, this glacial erratic is a remnant of the ice age.

ter days average 36°F, and nights will often drop below 20°F. Lake Tahoe typically sees 275 days of sunshine per year. Precipitation is common in winter, with the average annual snowfall at lake level averaging 10–12 feet. At the higher elevations of Tahoe's ski areas, the annual snowfall averages 25–40 feet. Rain occurs occasionally from spring to fall, with average annual rainfall totaling just over eight inches. Typical rainfall in the months of July, August, and September is less than 0.5 inch, ensuring plentiful days of summer sunshine at the lake.

Because of the immense size of Lake Tahoe, its huge volume of water is in constant motion, with the cold water on the surface sinking while the warm water rises from the deep. Although Emerald Bay has frozen over a few times in recorded history, the main body of the lake never has. The water is notoriously cold, though. Even in the summer heat of August, when the air temperature might reach the high 80s, the lake's surface temperature to a depth of about 10 feet tops out at 68°F. In February

or March, the surface temperature is 40–50°F. Below a depth of about 600 feet, the water is a constant chilly 39°F year-round.

ENVIRONMENTAL ISSUES

Despite the impressive statistics of the massive lake, it is not the size or depth of Lake Tahoe that is its most prized feature, but rather the **clarity** of its water, which is considered to be 99.8 percent pure, about the same as distilled water. This is partly due to the fact that 40 percent of the precipitation that falls in the Lake Tahoe basin lands directly on the lake, so it has no opportunity to be contaminated. The remaining percentage drains through coarse granitic soil, which serves as an excellent filter.

John LeConte, the third president of the University of California at Berkeley, completed the first study of Tahoe's water quality in 1884. Using a technique developed by Pietro Secchi, LeConte attached a rope to a white disk, similar to a 10-inch-wide dinner plate, and lowered it into the water. The **Secchi disk** disappeared from view 103 feet below the lake's surface.

Continuous monitoring of the lake using a Secchi disk began in 1968 under the direction of renowned scientist Dr. Charles Goldman of the U.C. Davis Tahoe Research Group. This led to the alarming discovery of a decrease in the lake's clarity. The Secchi disk could be seen clearly at 102 feet deep in 1968. By 1996, it could only be seen 77 feet deep. In 2005, it is visible only 73.6 feet below the lake's surface.

The problem with maintaining Tahoe's clarity lies in the fact that there is little intake or outflow of fresh water, so pollution and sediment that enters the lake stays there for a very long time. Logging activities that occurred around the lakeshore 150 years ago still affect the water clarity today. Of the 63 tributaries that feed into the lake, only one watershed is large enough to be considered a river—the **Upper Truckee River,** which enters the lake in the city of South Lake Tahoe. The lake's only outflow is the Lower Truckee River in Tahoe City, by Fanny Bridge. (The river flows northwest to Truckee and then turns east and travels through downtown Reno and into Pyramid Lake.) It is estimated that about 25 percent of the lake's water comes from the Upper Truckee. Unfortunately, so does a lion's share of sediment. The Upper Truckee River was channeled and restricted to create room for the South Lake Tahoe airport, golf courses, and subdivisions. Where the river meets the lake, wetlands and marshes were permanently altered in order to construct the Tahoe Keys marina and townhouses. Moving and straightening a river leads to erosion of its banks, which leads to sedimentation. Removing a river's natural wetlands means there is no longer any filtering system in place before the water reaches the lake. The resulting sedimentation leads to the ideal conditions for algae to flourish, and that leads to a lake that is no longer blue but greenish in color, and no longer clear but obfuscated. Compounding the damage, we've added fertilizers and other pollutants to the lake—including runoff from farming in the Sacramento Valley and auto emissions from car traffic on the lake's highways.

Out-of-state visitors to California notice an abundance of cars on highways and roads bearing a familiar blue slogan: Keep Tahoe Blue. Created by the **League to Save Lake Tahoe,** the car tags were an ingenious marketing effort designed to raise money for and create awareness of the need to preserve Tahoe's famous water clarity. The nonprofit league was formed in 1957. Its numerous successes have included stopping plans to build a bridge over Emerald Bay and high-speed freeways around the lake, and a ban on carbureted two-stroke watercraft engines, such as those found on older personal watercraft and outboard motors. The league also hosted the 1997 Presidential Forum at Lake Tahoe, when President Bill Clinton and Vice-President Al Gore took a tour aboard the U.C. Davis lake-monitoring vessel with members of the Tahoe Research Group. The league manages an office and Environmental Education Center near the Y at South Lake Tahoe (955 Emerald Bay Rd., 530/541-5388, www.keeptahoeblue.org), where visitors can learn about ongoing efforts to preserve Tahoe's water clarity.

Several state-run agencies also work to protect Lake Tahoe. The **California Tahoe Conservancy** acquires sensitive lands around the lake and preserves them from development. The conservancy's major focus is on saving wetlands, meadows, and marshes, which are important filters for sediment and pollutants. Only an estimated 30 percent of the lake's wetlands and meadows still exist today. Where wetlands have already been altered by development, the conservancy attempts to return them to their natural state. The **Lahontan Water Quality Control Board** is responsible for water quality on the California side of the lake. The **Tahoe Regional Planning Agency** (www.trpa.org) regulates all types of development around the lake, from big issues such as public transportation, logging, and erosion control, to smaller matters like the size of private driveways and business signage. Its multiple projects fall under the umbrella of an Environmental Improvement Program (EIP), which is funded by the federal government and the California and Nevada state governments.

This gives Washington a say in the health of Lake Tahoe as well. Adding to the federal stake at the lake, the U.S. Forest Service owns nearly 80 percent of the land around Lake Tahoe.

All in all, the management of Lake Tahoe is a political pea soup, with several regulatory agencies performing frequently overlapping functions. But that's not surprising, considering the fact that the lake is a national treasure, and its shoreline lies in five separate counties, two states, one incorporated city (South Lake Tahoe), and several nonincorporated towns. The good news is that everyone seems to agree that preserving Tahoe's water quality is of utmost importance not just for the health of the lake, but also for the economic prosperity of the region. How that preservation takes place will be a subject of much controversy and debate as long as people choose to live in the Tahoe basin.

Flora

With elevations ranging from 6,200 feet at Tahoe's lake level to well over 10,000 feet on the basin's highest peaks, plus a combination of granitic and volcanic soils, the Tahoe region provides a wide mix of environments for a variety of flora, from giant conifers to the tiniest of alpine wildflowers. Tahoe supports four separate life zones for plants. The Yellow Pine Zone covers the lowest elevations, up to about 6,500 feet. The Red Fir Zone includes elevations from 6,500 feet to 9,000 feet. The Subalpine Zone covers elevations from 9,000 to 10,500 feet, and the Alpine Zone covers the few areas that are above 10,500 feet.

YELLOW PINE ZONE

The conifers of Yellow Pine Zone, the region nearest Tahoe's shoreline, can be identified by a few easy-to-remember characteristics. The three-needled **Jeffrey pine** is the most common tree in the Tahoe basin, growing at elevations from 6,000 feet to 10,000 feet. It is a favorite of many Sierra tree-lovers because of the unique scent of its bark, which smells sweet, like vanilla or butterscotch. Sometimes the odor is so strong that it wafts over you from several feet away; other times you must put your nose right up to the tree's bark crevices to smell it. The Jeffrey pine has distinct, jigsaw-puzzle bark (it's especially pronounced on older, wider trees), and its cones have spines that point downward, not outward, so they are easy to pick up and handle. This rugged tree is often seen growing on granite slabs seemingly without the aid of soil.

Similar to the Jeffrey pine is the **ponderosa pine,** a species that is also known by its clearly delineated, jigsaw puzzle–style bark and needles bundled in groups of three. The ponderosa's needles grow up to 10 inches long, and its cones are prickly to the touch. Generations of schoolchildren have been taught the mnemonic "prickly ponderosa and gentle Jeffrey" to remember how to distinguish the two pines' cones.

The **sugar pine** is the tallest and largest of more than 100 species of pine trees in the world. Old trees frequently reach 7 feet in diameter and 200 feet tall. This venerable pine has unmistakable cones, befitting a tree of its size: up to 20 inches in length, the longest of any conifer. The cones hang down like Christmas ornaments off the tips of the sugar pine's long branches. While they are still green, they weigh up to five pounds. Unlike the ponderosa and Jeffrey pine, the sugar pine's needles are bundled in groups of five.

Often seen in the company of Jeffrey, ponderosa, and sugar pines is the **incense-cedar,** which can be identified by its lacy foliage and thick, shaggy bark that is similar to that of a coastal redwood tree. The incense-cedar has unusual needles, which are completely flat at the ends, as if they have been ironed. The tree emits a slight spicy odor which some say is reminiscent of the scent of pencils. The incense-cedar's name is hyphenated because it is not a true cedar.

The second most common tree at Lake Tahoe is the **white fir.** Its sturdy, white-gray trunk commonly reaches a width of five feet. The white fir's needles grow in flat sprays that are distinctly two dimensional. Most people recognize white firs because the young ones look like little Christmas trees; indeed, this is a commonly marketed Christmas tree in California. Older trees easily attain heights of 150 feet.

A few deciduous trees also make an appearance around Tahoe's lakeshore, the most noticeable being the **quaking aspen.** This broad-leaved tree gets its name from its round leaves on flat leaf stems that flutter in the slightest breeze. Quaking aspens grow near streams and meadows or on moist slopes from 6,000 to 10,000 feet in elevation. In autumn, the aspen sports a spectacular coat of golden yellow. Especially noteworthy groves of quaking aspens can be seen along the shores of Fallen Leaf Lake on the South Shore and near Marlette Lake on the East Shore.

The aptly named, trunk-like blossoms of elephant head grow in wet, boggy meadows.

Other colorful deciduous trees that flourish near water are **willows** and **mountain alders.** Five separate species of willows grow alongside Tahoe's streams, most in the shape of small trees or large shrubs. The willow's leaves are long and narrow and turn bright red in autumn. Mountain alders, which often grow alongside willows, have rounder leaves with jagged edges and a dense network of veins. Alders form dense thickets that are almost impenetrable to humans. They have very small cones that look like tiny pinecones.

At areas around Lake Tahoe where the forests open up, wet mountain meadows are common, and within them bloom a variety of wildflowers in early summer: pink shooting stars, red and yellow western columbine, bright yellow coneflowers, red or orange paintbrush, and false hellebore (corn lilies), among many others.

RED FIR ZONE

As you hike uphill from the lake, you quickly leave the sugar and ponderosa pines behind and enter the Red Fir Zone, also called the Upper Montane Zone. Jeffrey pines from the Yellow Pine Zone grow well in these higher elevations, too, but the namesake red fir and lodgepole pine predominate. The deeply shaded forests in this zone also contain western white pines and western juniper. **Red firs** are easy to identify because of their reddish-brown, deeply furrowed bark. They can grow up to six feet in diameter and are often seen in pure groves made up of only their own kind. Depressions at the bases of the biggest trees are sometimes used by bears as winter dens (the same is also true for white firs). **Lodgepole pines** are the only two-needled pines in the Sierra. They earned their name because Native Americans used their dependably straight and slender trunks as poles for their tepees and lodges. Ironically, their Latin name is *pinus contorta*, or "contorted pine." Adding to the confusion, throughout history the tree has been mistakenly called a tamarack, which is actually a deciduous conifer that does not grow anywhere in the Sierra. (You'll find a

Tamarack Lake in Desolation Wilderness, bordered by lodepole pines, just off the Pacific Crest Trail a few miles from Echo Lakes.) The lodgepole's bark is thin and scaly and its needles are in bundles of two.

Finally, the **piñon pine** is a tree that grows only on the dry slopes of the Nevada side of the lake, often in fields or sagebrush and in the occasional company of western junipers. This hardy tree bears large meaty nuts that were a staple of the diet of the Washoe Indians, as well as a favorite food of many birds and animals.

Aside from the big conifers, one small plant common in the Red Fir life zone is worth a special mention. It is the **snow plant,** a red, thick, asparagus-like plant that has no green leaves. It is one of the first flora to make an appearance as the snow melts; early-season hikers will often see it protruding from the forest floor amid piles of melting snow. A member of the heath family, snow plant is so tough and determined to sprout that it can sometimes push up through asphalt.

SUBALPINE ZONE

Still higher, near timberline at 9,000–10,500 feet, only a few hardy trees survive: western white pines, western junipers, whitebark pines, and mountain hemlocks. The **western white pine** is a gray-barked pine with blue-green needles in bundles of five. The tree has eight-inch-long cones that are often slightly curved. Western white pines rarely exceed 100 feet tall, but their long limbs curve gracefully upward. **Western juniper** (also called Sierra juniper) is another distinctive tree of the Subalpine Zone, and easy to identify because of its bluish-green, scalelike needles and spiraling trunk, which makes it appear as if the tree twisted in circles as it grew. The roots of this hearty tree will tunnel through crevices in granite, so it often looks as if the western juniper is growing right out of rock. Western junipers in the Sierra can live as long as 2,000 years. As the juniper ages, its trunk becomes stripped of bark and bleached to a light blond. The juniper produces an abundance of blue-purple "berries" in the summer months, which are well loved

One of the Sierra's most majestic tree species, the western juniper can live for 2,000 years.

by birds, and were once used by humans for making gin. These are actually not berries at all but the juniper's cones. The western juniper is especially common around Carson Pass and Meiss Country. One huge specimen with a seven-foot-wide diameter can be seen on the trail to Dardanelles Lake.

The wind-battered and low-growing **whitebark pine** often looks more like a shrub with multiple small trunks than a single tree; at its tallest it grows to about 35 feet. Its cones are purple, egg shaped, and two inches long, with seeds that are highly coveted by Clark's nutcrackers, chickarees, and chipmunks. These trees, too, are common around Carson Pass.

The **mountain hemlock** is easily spotted by its uppermost branches, which droop downward or sideways, as if they are taking a bow. Naturalist John Muir was a great fan of the mountain hemlock and wrote a lengthy ode to them in his first book, *The Mountains of California.* The hemlock has greenish-blue foliage that is distinct when viewed close up; its needles are dense and completely cover the stems they grow on, like a soft coat of fur.

The dominant plants that grow in the high meadows of the Subalpine life zone are **sedges,** not the grasses found in lower-elevation meadows. Wildflowers at these elevations include many of the same species of the Red Fir life zone, although the higher the elevation, the more likely the plants will be of a smaller, more compact variety.

ALPINE ZONE

Finally, at 10,500 feet and above lies the region that only hardy Tahoe hikers will see: the Alpine life zone above the timberline, where trees are rare to nonexistent. Plants that grow here are typically very small, mainly because of harsh winds. The growing season is very short, making these alpine environments extremely fragile and easily disturbed by human presence. Cushions or mats of colorful flowers like penstemon and phlox brighten the generally stark landscape of gray, rocky slopes. Some of the loveliest of these mat-like plants are the mountain heaths or heathers, including John Muir's beloved cassiope, which can be seen along the shores of the lakes in the Crystal Basin of Desolation Wilderness.

Fauna

Many visitors to Lake Tahoe hope to catch a glimpse of some interesting wildlife. In this regard, Tahoe often delivers. The following is a brief guide to some of Tahoe's most commonly seen, or most notable, animal denizens.

LARGE MAMMALS
Black Bear
The only kind of bear that lives near Lake Tahoe, or anywhere in California, is the black bear. Although the fearsome grizzly once roamed here and is immortalized on the California flag, grizzlies have been extinct in the Golden State since 1924. Black bears have a somewhat misleading name—they are more commonly brown, blond, or cinnamon colored, only rarely pure black. Often they have a white patch on their chest. The smallest of all North American bears, they weigh as much as 450 pounds, can run up to 30 miles per hour, and are powerful swimmers and climbers. Despite the adult bear's enormous size, bear cubs weigh only a half pound at birth.

Black bears will eat just about anything, but their staple foods are berries, fruits, plants, insects, honeycomb, the inner layer of tree bark, and fish and small mammals. Contrary to popular belief, black bears do not hibernate. A pregnant female will "den up" in winter and usually give birth while she is sleeping, but this is not true hibernation. Male black bears are often seen roaming for food in winter.

Mule Deer
Frequently seen in the forests around Lake Tahoe, the mule deer is one of our largest American deer and can weigh up to 200 pounds. The deer gets its name from its ears, which are large and rounded. Mule deer in the Sierra have a white patch on their rumps and a black-tipped tail. The antlers on the bucks, which develop in summer, are usually an elegant, matched set of four points on each side. Tahoe's mule deer migrate downslope to the Carson Valley in winter, so visitors are more likely to see them around the lake in the summer months, when food is plentiful.

Mountain Lion
The most reclusive of all of Tahoe's creatures, the mountain lion is the largest cat in North America and is best distinguished from afar by its two- to three-foot-long tail. The adult cat's body minus its tail is often six feet long; a male cat typically weighs 250 pounds. The mountain lion is tawny except for its underside, which is white. It usually lives where deer, its main food source, are plentiful. Because

mountain lions have large territories, probably only two or three live in the entire Tahoe basin. There have been no mountain lion attacks on visitors to Lake Tahoe, although a few attacks have occurred elsewhere in California. Although you probably won't see a lion, you might be lucky enough to find its tracks. The large, cat-like footprints are easy to distinguish; they are four-toed prints that do not show claws.

Coyote

Many Tahoe visitors report seeing a wolf or a fox near the highway, but what they usually have seen is a coyote. (Wolves do not live in the Sierra; foxes are quite small and rarely seen during the day.) The coyote is a doglike animal with a grayish-brown coat; its back slopes downward toward its tail. An average-size coyote weighs about 30 pounds and stands about two feet tall. Coyotes can run as fast as 40 miles per hour, and make a series of "yip" cries, often followed by a howl. Across California, the coyote has acclimated well to the presence of humans, and is generally unafraid of them.

SMALL MAMMALS
Bobcat

A stocky feline about twice the size of a house cat, the bobcat is easily recognized by its short, "bobbed" tail, only four inches long. Bobcats are mostly nocturnal but are sometimes seen hunting during the day. Their coats are gray-brown in winter and reddish-brown in summer, and marked with black spots and bars. The bobcat's ears have short tufts above them.

Raccoon

This black-masked invader is sometimes seen scavenging around campgrounds, particularly in the evenings, or drinking and feeding at rivers or lakes. The raccoon has distinctive rings around its tail, and a large, gray-brown body that can weigh as much as 40 pounds. Despite its girth, the raccoon is a good swimmer and climber and can run as fast as 15 miles per hour. Its fingerlike toes are useful for washing its food.

Porcupine

Only the rare and fortunate Tahoe visitor gets to see the elusive porcupine, a mostly nocturnal mammal that is characterized by its body covering of thousands of quills, or sharp, hollow spines. The porcupine's quills lay flat when the animal is relaxed, but stand straight up when it is threatened. Porcupines spend most of their time high in trees, where they eat twigs and bark, but are sometimes seen waddling across meadows or forests in search of a new feeding tree. Porcupine tracks face forward and inward; the animal walks pigeon-toed. The most common sightings of porcupines at Lake Tahoe are on the South Shore near Fallen Leaf Lake and Camp Richardson.

Snowshoe Hare

Brown in summer and white in winter, this large member of the rabbit family is a master of disguise. The snowshoe hare derives its name from its huge hind feet, which act like snowshoes and allow the animal to "float" across the snow, without sinking in. The hare has distinctive, three-inch-long ears that stand upright and are marked by black tips.

Yellow-bellied Marmot

The largest and most curious member of the squirrel family, the yellow-bellied marmot, is frequently seen in Tahoe's high country. About seven inches tall and as long as two feet, the bold marmot has no enemies and is frequently seen sunning himself on high boulders. The marmot's coat is buff to brown and its belly is yellow. The animal is most often seen on talus-lined slopes or near rock piles at high elevations. If you see two or more marmots together, they are often wrestling or chasing each other. You may hear them make a high-pitched whistling sound. Some people refer to marmots as woodchucks or groundhogs.

Pine Marten

This large, slender member of the weasel family has a brown back, light head and underbelly, pointed nose, long bushy tail, and distinctive orange patch at its throat. Two to three feet long and with a sleek, acrobatic physique, the solitary pine marten is rarely seen by visitors, as it spends most of its time high in trees, hunting for squirrels and birds.

Beaver

First introduced to the Sierra by fur trappers, then later by the California Fish and Game Department, the nonnative beaver has prospered around Lake Tahoe because of the region's many waterways lined with aspen and willow groves. The trees' inner bark is the beaver's favorite food. The beaver has a flattened tail that makes a distinctive slapping sound on the water. Its webbed hind feet make it an agile swimmer. Adults are typically three feet long (including the tail) and weigh 50–60 pounds. Beavers mate for life, and if their mate dies, they never mate again.

Pika

A resident in alpine environments higher than 9,500 feet, the pika is a small relative of the rabbit that busily collects green grasses, then stacks them in the sun and dries them for winter food and insulation. The creature does not hibernate, so it needs to keep a full larder of dried grasses for its winter nourishment. The diminutive pika is most often seen on talus-lined slopes or rocky hillsides, and is easily recognized because of its small, rounded ears and absence of a tail.

Squirrels

The number and variety of squirrels and their close relations around Lake Tahoe can be quite daunting to the amateur naturalist trying to identify them. One of the easiest-to-spot species is the **golden-mantled ground squirrel,** a common sight at elevations above 6,000 feet. Frequently mistaken for large chipmunks, these cute squirrels can be correctly identified by their lack of the chipmunk's facial stripe. Otherwise, they look much the same, with one white stripe on each side of their brown bodies, bordered by a heavy black stripe. The golden-mantled ground squirrel must fatten himself up all summer to prepare for winter hibernation.

© ANN MARIE BROWN

The golden-mantled ground squirrel looks much like a chipmunk, but without a stripe on its face.

The **western gray squirrel** is the common gray-coated squirrel seen throughout California, with a long bushy tail and white belly. Western gray squirrels are great tree climbers and are mostly seen below 6,500 feet. The gray squirrel population around Lake Tahoe took a hit in the 1950s, when local residents set out poisons to stop the animals from damaging their houses. Their numbers are now increasing.

The hyperactive **Douglas squirrel** or **chickaree** is much smaller than the western gray, and colored a mix of brown and gray. This perky, constantly chattering squirrel remains active throughout the year, and is frequently seen both on the ground and in trees, where it cuts thousands of pinecones for its winter stash. The Douglas squirrel is easily excited and makes a high-pitched trilling sound that can be mistaken for the cry of a bird.

The **California ground squirrel** is best identified by a silver, V-shaped pattern on the shoulders of its grayish-brown coat. Its body is similar to that of the western gray squirrel, but it does not have a bushy tail. Although it can climb trees, the California ground squirrel is most often seen on the ground. The animals hibernate in winter, so you'll only spot them during the summer months.

Chipmunks

Not one but several kinds of chipmunks are found at Lake Tahoe. All are colored in various shades of golden brown and have a distinctive white stripe on both their body and face. Generally chipmunks at higher elevations hibernate and those at lower elevations do not. Like their cousins the squirrels, chipmunks eat nuts, seeds, and fungi, which they carry around in their fur-lined cheek pouches. Chipmunks hibernate in winter.

BIRDS
Steller's Jay

Nobody visits Lake Tahoe without seeing the Steller's jay, a bold and raucous bird who makes his presence known. The western cousin of the East Coast's blue jay, the Steller's jay has a distinctive black topknot of feathers that point backward, affording him a regal look. The jay's body is about 10 inches in length and a deep, pure blue. When on the ground, the Steller's jay hops, it does not walk. If you are eating a sandwich when one is near, keep a vigilant guard; the jay has no qualms about stealing food.

Clark's Nutcracker

Similar in size and behavior to the Steller's Jay (noisy and cantankerous, and often seen scouting at campgrounds and picnic areas for food), the Clark's nutcracker is light gray with white and black patches on its tail and wings. The birds are often spotted among the upper branches of whitebark pine trees, where they quarrel with each other as they collect pine nuts. The Clark's nutcracker stores nuts and seeds for winter in a massive granary, usually located on a south-facing slope. One pair can cache as many as 30,000 nuts and seeds in autumn. In spring, the birds can recall the placement of every single nut and will retrieve them to feed their young.

Raven

Frequently mistaken for the smaller crow, the common raven is a remarkably intelligent bird that is often seen scrounging for leftovers near campgrounds and picnic areas. Ravens are about two feet long, with glossy black feathers and a curved beak, and a strange call that sounds something like a croaking noise. While flying, they will also sometimes make a series of clicking sounds. In spring, the male raven performs a spectacular aerial dance for its mate—swooping, diving, and barrel-rolling, while making loud cries.

Woodpeckers

Plentiful around Lake Tahoe, a variety of woodpeckers are frequently seen and heard amid the conifer forest. With some variation, they are all black and white with a dash of flaming red on their heads or necks (although in some species only the males bear the red patch). Most common is the **hairy woodpecker,** which is often mistakenly identified as a downy woodpecker. The hairy is much larger than the downy—about the size of a robin—and has a much longer bill. The male has a bright-red neck patch. Both woodpeckers have a vertical white stripe on their black backs, and both drill into dead trees to find insects.

The **white-headed woodpecker** is seen mostly in pine forests, where it eats pine nuts and insects. White-headed woodpeckers do not drill like most woodpeckers; instead they look for food by pulling bark off trees with their beaks. The white-headed woodpecker is all black except for its white head and wing patch. The male has a small red patch on the back of its neck.

Also a member of the woodpecker family, the **red-breasted sapsucker** has a bright red "hood" that extends down below its throat. The rest of its body is speckled black and white, but it flashes a white rump and shoulder patches when it flies. Unlike many woodpeckers, the sapsucker feeds by drilling holes in live trees, then waits for the holes to fill with sap, which attracts insects. Hence the name "sapsucker." Both the male and female of the species look alike.

The **northern flicker** is another common woodpecker seen around Lake Tahoe. This foot-long bird is mostly brown and gray with some red under its wings, but it is most easily spotted by its bright-white rump, which is obvious in flight. The male has a dash of red on its cheeks. Flickers will drill into trees for insects, or feed on the ground, poking in the earth for ants. They have tongues as long as three inches that are particularly well adapted for sucking up ants.

Nuthatches

Three types of nuthatches commonly make an appearance in Tahoe's forests: the red-breasted, the white-breasted, and the pygmy. These compact birds have short necks and tails, and they travel down tree trunks headfirst looking for insects. Their upside-down stance makes them unmistakable. All three species are gray and white, and four to six inches long.

Mountain Chickadee

The most common bird in the Lake Tahoe basin, the small, gray mountain chickadee has a black cap, black stripe under its chin, and a white stripe above its eyes. It is often seen hanging upside down on branches, searching for insects and seeds. You'll know the call of a chickadee by its three-note whistle, which travels down the musical scale with each note.

Western Tanager

One of the most colorful birds of the forest, the male western tanager is a favorite of many bird-watchers. His orange-red head, bright-yellow body, and black wings and tail make him as bright hued as a pet-shop bird, and an unforgettable sight. The female's marking are much more subdued but still a colorful gold and olive. The orange on the male's head disappears in autumn when it is time to migrate.

American Dipper

One of naturalist John Muir's favorite birds, the dipper (also called the water ouzel) is an unusual songbird that is often seen amid the spray of waterfalls. Although it is colored a nondescript gray, the dipper lives an extraordinary life, diving underwater to feed on insects and larvae. The bird has a third eyelid that closes over its eyes to protect it from spray, a flap of skin that closes over its nostrils to keep out water, and an extra-large oil gland that waterproofs its plumage. It often builds its nest behind a waterfall, then flies back and forth through the torrent to feed its young. When searching for food in a stream, it can walk underwater.

California Gull

Many a first-time Tahoe visitor has been surprised to see gulls—a species associated with the seashore—hanging out on Tahoe's beaches. The California gull is well adapted to almost any environment where it can scavenge for garbage, insects, and fish. The ring-billed gull, which has a black stripe around its bill, also makes an appearance on Tahoe's shoreline.

Great Horned Owl

The only living creature that will prey on a skunk, the magnificent great horned owl can stand up to two feet high and calls out a haunting "hoo, hoo, hoo" at night. This owl is a terrific nocturnal hunter that can take down animals as large as the snowshoe hare. The bird's distinct ear tufts or "horns" are its namesake feature. When a great horned owl perches and flies, it appears to have no neck.

American Bald Eagle

Even if you've never seen one before, you'll have no trouble identifying our national bird. The bald eagle's white "bald" head and white tail on its otherwise dark brown body are dead giveaways, even from a distance. While soaring, the eagle's wings can expand to more than seven feet. Bald eagles are commonly seen around Emerald Bay, where a pair often nests near aptly named Eagle Point, and at Kiva Point, near the Forest Service's Taylor Creek Visitor Center. Seen from up close, the eagle has a huge, yellow hooked bill, which it uses for tearing up fish.

Osprey

This large raptor is a specialist in high-flying fishing. Dark brown (almost black) and white, the bird will hover above a lake, then plunge feet-first to capture fish. It is well known for its keen eyesight, which is more than 10 times that of a human. Occasionally the osprey is mistaken for a bald eagle, because it, too, has a white head, but the osprey is a much smaller bird, with a wingspan of only five feet. Also, ospreys display more white on the underside of their wings when they fly.

Canada Goose

The largest bird that most visitors will see at Lake Tahoe, the Canada goose feels comfortably at home on the lake's shoreline, as it does many places in North America. The goose can be as much as four feet in length and will stand three feet high with its long neck extended. Their bodies are brown and white, but their necks are glossy black with a wide stripe of white beneath their chins. Elevated platforms installed by the Forest Service at the marsh at Pope Beach have provided the birds with a safe place to nest.

FISH
Rainbow Trout

A favorite of fishermen throughout the Sierra, the rainbow trout is a colorful fish with a pink-to-red band along the centerline of its body, with darker green above and a lighter green below. The fish also has black spots on its back and fins. To a greater extent than any other trout species, they have vast variation in their coloration, particularly from one body of water to another. Rainbow trout will grow up to 24 inches in large lakes, but only half that size in streams.

Brown Trout

Brown trout are not as dark-colored as you might surmise from their name; they vary from golden to olive to cinnamon-colored, with light tan bellies. The fish is easily recognized by the large dark spots on its head and back, and red spots on its lower sides. It is the only trout in California that has both black and red spots, although it is not a California native. Brown trout in the Sierra originally came from a strain of fish in Germany or Scotland. The brown trout is generally very wary and more difficult to catch than the rainbow trout. Many fish will grow to old ages and trophy sizes, longer than two feet.

Mackinaw Trout

This monster of the deep is the coveted prize of many sport fishers. The fish has a gray, spotted body that varies from pale gray to almost black. The average size of a mackinaw in Lake Tahoe is 3–5 pounds, but fish as large as 10 pounds are fairly common. Occasionally a 20–30 pounder will be caught; the lake record was more than 37 pounds. Mackinaw are also found in Fallen Leaf Lake and Donner Lake; they prefer deep, cold water most of the year. The trout is not native to the Tahoe area and was first introduced for sportfishing in 1894. In other areas of the country, mackinaw are simply known as lake trout.

Kokanee Salmon

A distant cousin of the sockeye salmon, the foot-long kokanee is a landlocked salmon that is blue-green above and silvery white below, with a smattering of black spots. Most people know the kokanee in its spawning colors, when its body turns bright red and the male develops a protruding, hooked jaw. During the autumn spawn, they are easily seen in Taylor Creek near the Forest Service Visitor Center on the South Shore. Kokanee salmon are not native to Lake Tahoe; they were planted in the 1940s to serve as a sport fish and have thrived well. Despite their small size, they are strong fighters and provide exciting fishing.

History

TAHOE'S FIRST VISITORS

Three separate tribes of the Washoe Indians spent summers at the shores of Lake Tahoe for thousands of years. Every year, as the days lengthened and warmed, the Washoes would travel from their winter homes in the Carson Valley to the shores of the lake, where they would harvest piñon nuts, fish in the lake's bountiful waters, and hunt the abundant game. The women of the tribe made woven baskets of exceptional artistry from the lakeshore's willows and grasses.

The huge lake did not appear on the radar of European Americans until 1844, when explorer John C. Fremont first sighted it during a February snowstorm. Fremont had been traveling for several months with the legendary scout Kit Carson and an expedition of 34 men, attempting to locate and map a waterway described by earlier geographers as the Buenaventura River, which supposedly flowed through the Sierra Nevada and into the Gulf of Mexico or San Francisco Bay. They had also heard tales of a big lake located somewhere high in the Sierra. Although Fremont's Washoe Indian guides warned him against traveling through the mountains in winter, the explorer pushed on, facing fierce weather, extreme deprivation, and arduous treks through deep snow. Fremont's famous diary entry from the night before his sighting of Lake Tahoe read: "We had tonight an extraordinary meal—pea soup, mule, and dog."

In the morning, when the skies had partially cleared, Fremont and mapmaker Charles Preuss climbed to the 10,651-foot summit of Red Lake Peak, 20 miles southwest of Lake Tahoe near what is now Carson Pass. Hoping to locate a suitable route through the mountains and down to the Sacramento Valley, they spied not only the pass but a section of the legendary lake as well. Overjoyed at finding a way out of the snowy Sierra, the group set off immediately to the west and traveled down the South Fork of the American River to Sutter's Fort, a 16-day trek. Although Fremont did not lose a single man during the entire expedition, two of his party went mad from starvation and exhaustion. Only half of the party's 67 pack animals made it through the arduous trip; the rest had frozen or were eaten.

NAMING THE LAKE

After recovering from the journey, Fremont named the mystery lake "Bonpland" after a French botanist and explorer who had traveled with him on previous expeditions. The name never came into common usage, nor did Fremont's mapmaker's chosen name, the plain "Mountain Lake." By 1853, the official cartographers for the State of California had renamed Tahoe "Lake Bigler" in honor of the third governor of California, John Bigler. Bigler, to his credit, had led a rescue effort to the snowbound Donner party on the north shore of the lake in 1852. The lake's name stuck loosely for about a decade until 1862, when a federal cartographer for the Department of the Interior, William Henry Knight, began a crusade for the name Tahoe, which was believed to be Indian name for the lake, translating to "big water" or "high water." (Today we know that the Washoe Indians called the area "Da-ow-a-ga" for "edge of the lake," but early explorers heard the unfamiliar sounds as "Tahoe.") Knight argued that Governor Bigler had not distinguished himself enough for history to name such a remarkable lake after him. In fact, after the Civil War broke out, Bigler was accused of being a Southern sympathizer and fell into public disfavor. Knight's arguments were convincing, and "Tahoe" became the moniker with staying power. It did not become official, however, until 1945, when the California legislature put its seal on the name.

COMSTOCK LODE 1859 GOLD RUSH

Despite all the wrangling over what to call it, Tahoe remained little more than the peaceful gathering place of the Washoe Indians for

TAHOE'S PLACE NAMES

Al Tahoe: This street and neighborhood in South Lake Tahoe is named for a hotel which once stood in the area, built in 1907 by Almerin (Al) Sprague. He named it after himself: the Al Tahoe Hotel.

Carson Pass: The pass and the river were named for Christopher (Kit) Carson (1809-1868), the scout and guide who aided John C. Fremont in his early explorations of the Sierra Nevada. Although the famous mountain man was illiterate, he dictated his autobiography, which became a best seller.

Dicks Peak and Dicks Lake: This peak and lake in the Desolation Wilderness is named after Captain Richard "Dick" Barter, who was known as the Hermit of Emerald Bay. He lived alone on Fannette Island for many years, and spent his days drifting around the lake in a small rowboat.

Donner Lake, Pass, and Peak: Named for brothers George and Jacob Donner, who with James F. Reed led the Donner Party of emigrants across the Sierra Nevada. Caught by an early snowstorm in October 1846, the party was marooned for the winter near what is now Donner Pass. More than three dozen members lost their lives to starvation and exposure. The Donner Party is remembered most for the fact that some of its survivors resorted to eating the bodies of their dead companions.

Jobs Peak and Jobs Sister: These two peaks south of Heavenly Ski Resort were named for Moses Job, a storekeeper who lived in Carson Valley, Nevada, in the 1850s. Jobs Sister is the second-highest mountain in Tahoe at 10,873 feet, topped only by nearby Freel Peak at 10,881 feet.

Lola Montez Lake and Mount Lola: The lake and peak near Donner Summit were named for a mid-1800s European dancer and showgirl who eventually settled in Grass Valley, where she ran a saloon and kept a pet bear. Throughout Lola's extravagant life she made colorful news for a variety of reasons, but was perhaps most famous for her affairs with powerful men, including King Ludwig I of Bavaria, who made her a countess.

Markleeville: This small town in Carson Pass was named for settler Jacob Marklee in 1864, who lived at the site of what is now the Alpine County Courthouse. Marklee was killed in a gunfight a few years later.

Mount Pluto: The centerpiece of Northstar-at-Tahoe Ski Area, Mount Pluto was one of the last volcanoes in Tahoe to erupt. Pluto is the name of the Roman god of the underworld and is named for plutonic rock, evidence of volcanic activity.

Mount Tallac: One of only two place-names in the Tahoe Basin that are derived from Native American names, Tallac is from the Washoe Indian word "dala'ak," which means "big mountain" or "great mountain." The only other Tahoe place-name derived from the Washoe language is "tahoe" itself, which comes from "Da'ow," meaning "big water" or "lake."

Ophir Creek: This stream near Mount Rose bears a Biblical name referring to a "land of gold." A handful of towns throughout the Gold Country have also borne the name Ophir, but most of them no longer exist.

Truckee: The town and the river were named for a northern Paiute Indian chief, who guided a party of emigrants across the Sierra in 1844. His name meant "all right" in the Paiute language.

another 15 years after Fremont's sighting, although hundreds of emigrants traveling from the eastern United States to the goldfields and farmlands of California passes near its shores. None stayed long; they were bound by the hope of a prosperous future and single-mindedly sought their destination.

The quiet was shattered in 1859 with the discovery of the massive Comstock Lode of silver ore in Virginia City, Nevada, just east of Lake Tahoe. The timing of the strike was fortuitous, as the Union needed funds to finance the Civil War, and silver provided it. Miners and prospectors rushed in to Nevada from points west, where the California gold rush was already winding down. Whether they

© ANN MARIE BROWN

The naturally carbonated spring that inspired the development of Glen Alpine Springs Resort in the 1860s can still be seen today.

arrived from the north, at Donner Pass, or the south, at Carson Pass, they had to circle around Lake Tahoe to get to Virginia City. In a few short years, the Bonanza Road on the South Shore (now the route of Highway 50 and Pioneer Trail) was carved through the mountains, and it became the primary route to Nevada from San Francisco and Sacramento. Dozens of way stations, tollhouses, inns, stores, and livery stables sprung up along its path. Virginia City soon grew to be the second-largest city in the West, after San Francisco, and the road around Lake Tahoe was so busy that wagon drivers sometimes had to wait for hours before they could break into the nonstop stream of traffic. In 1860, one observer counted 350 wagons passing by in a single day.

The Comstock Lode provided silver ore, but the mines required massive quantities of lumber to shore up their tunnels, and the new boomtowns of Nevada required fuel for their boilers. With the densely wooded slopes of Lake Tahoe only 30 miles from the Comstock mines, the commerce of logging became as lucrative as mining. A timber empire was created, with an elaborate system of flumes, steamboats, barges, and incline railways utilized to transport lumber to Virginia City. The town of Glenbrook had four lumber mills by 1875, including the largest one run by lumber baron D. L. Bliss. Beginning on the east side of the lake and then spreading to most of its shoreline, thousands of pine trees that were hundreds of years old were felled to fuel the mines. The easy availability of these timber-rich forests led to their annihilation. Trees were felled, then transported by oxen or narrow-gauge railway to the lake, where they were floated in large rafts to the lumber mills. After a while, this system was deemed too inefficient, so lengthy wooden flumes were built along the East Shore hills, then filled with water in which the timber was floated to the Glenbrook mills. To transport the milled lumber, a rail system was constructed from Glenbrook over Spooner Summit to Carson City. Another railway, known as the Great Incline, was built at the Hobart mills on the North Shore. In Carson City, the Virginia and Truckee Railroad served as the connecting link to the mines.

The appetite of the Comstock Lode was insatiable. Between 1860 and 1885, the entire East Shore was denuded. If the Comstock ore hadn't eventually played out, not a single tree would have been left standing anywhere around the lake.

Sadly, the environmental damage from this massive logging effort still affects the lake today. Vast amounts of sediments, which negatively impact Tahoe's water quality, entered the lake from the indiscriminate logging. The second- and third-growth trees that have grown up in place of the original logged forests are mostly moisture-loving red and white firs, which are not as well adapted to the Tahoe environment as the original pines were. A drought that began in the late 1980s weakened many of these firs; since then many have been killed by disease and an infestation of bark beetles. Although to the casual observer Tahoe's tree-lined shores may look rich and healthy, the forests still suffer the aftereffects of greed from more than a century ago.

THE RESORT ERA

By the close of the 19th century, wealthy families throughout California and Nevada had gotten word of the wonders of Lake Tahoe. Despite the rape of its landscape by lumber barons and mining engineers, the lake's virtues had been extolled by popular writers of the day such as J. Ross Browne of *Harper's Weekly,* Horace Greeley of *The New York Times,* and humorist Mark Twain. The elite from San Francisco, Sacramento, and Nevada City flocked to the lakeshore, and luxurious hotels and resorts were constructed to accommodate them in fine style. Many marveled at the industrial wonders of the Glenbrook mills as much as the scenic beauty of the lake itself.

With the completion of the Central Pacific Railroad through Truckee in 1869, a critical link was made in the transcontinental rail line. Travel to the Tahoe area had become immensely easier than it was for the struggling emigrants who passed through here only two decades earlier. A passenger could board a train in San Francisco and be at the lakeshore in only nine hours. Tahoe-bound travelers disembarked at the Truckee depot, then took at 14-mile stagecoach ride to Tahoe City. Later, the stage was replaced by a narrow-gauge train, which traveled along the scenic Truckee River to the city (today the same route is a paved bike path). At Tahoe City, tourists could stay and play in the town's Grand Central Hotel, or board a steamship to cruise to Campbell's Hot Springs Resort on the North Shore, Tallac House on the South Shore, Glen Brook House on the East Shore, or a number of other lakeside resorts ranging from the rustic to the pretentious.

Until the 1920s, automobile use was not widespread and good roads had not yet been built, so steamships were the preferred mode of passenger travel at the lake. The steamers carried not just people but also mail, cargo, farm animals, groceries, and everything else that was needed by those who settled or vacationed at the lake. Vessels as large and grand as the 200-passenger SS *Tahoe* plied the waters, providing essential and nonessential services. The hour when the "mail boat" arrived was one of the high points of the day, when visitors would converge on the pier to see the "Graceful Lady" dock. When this ship and others like it outlived their usefulness, they were scuttled into the lake's depths.

The state of Nevada legalized gambling in 1931, and the resort era led to the onset of the casino era when Harvey's Gambling Wheel Saloon and Gambling Hall opened its doors. Gambling at Lake Tahoe proved to be so popular that by the 1940s, winter roads were regularly plowed to provide year-round access. By the 1950s, Tahoe had become both a summer and winter resort, and its fate as a major snow-sports destination was sealed by the success of the 1960 Winter Olympics, held at Squaw Valley USA.

ESSENTIALS

Getting There and Around

BY AIR

The closest major airport to Lake Tahoe is **Reno/ Tahoe International Airport** (www.reno-airport.com) in Nevada, a 30-minute drive from Incline Village on the northeast shore of the lake or a one-hour drive from South Lake Tahoe and Stateline on the south shore. The medium-sized airport has two main terminals that serve Alaska, America West, American, Continental, Delta, Frontier, National, Northwest, Skywest, Southwest, and United airlines. Scattered among the gates are the usual cabal of airport shops: a Starbucks, Pizza Hut, Taco Bell, Burger King, golf shop, yogurt shop, and several gift shops and newsstands.

Tahoe-bound travelers can also fly into **Sacramento International Airport** (www.sacairports.org), which is a 2.5-hour drive from Lake Tahoe. The airport is served by these airlines: Alaska, Aloha, America West, American, Continental, Delta, Frontier, Hawaiian, Horizon, Jet Blue, Mexicana, Northwest, Southwest, United, and United Express. A typical array of airport restaurants and shops can be found here: a Starbuck's, Cinnabon, Burger King, several bookstores and souvenir shops, and the like.

Visitors might also want to look into flights at **San Francisco International Airport (SFO)** (www.flysfo.com), or the San Francisco

Bay Area's two other major airports in Oakland (www.oaklandairport.com) and San Jose (www.sjc.org). It is a 4.5-hour drive from San Francisco or San Jose to Lake Tahoe; Oakland is about a half hour closer.

Smaller airports are located at South Lake Tahoe and Truckee, but they do not offer commercial passenger service.

Airport Shuttles/Limousines

Several companies offer shuttle or limo service between the Reno-Tahoe International Airport and various points at Lake Tahoe: Airport Mini-Bus/Bell Limousine (800/235-5466), Aladdin Limousine (800/546-6009), Executive Limousine (775/333-3300), North Tahoe Limousine (800/832-8213), No Stress Express (800/426-5644 or www.nostress-express.com), Sierra West Limousine (877/347-4789), South Tahoe Express (866/898-2463 or www.southtahoeexpress.com), and Tahoe Casino Express (800/446-6128).

CAR RENTALS

Several major car-rental companies are located at Reno/Tahoe International Airport: Advantage (800/777-5500, www.arac.com), Alamo (800/462-5266, www.alamo.com), Avis (800/984-8840), Budget (800/527-0700, www.budget.com), Dollar (800/800-4000, www.dollar.com), Hertz (800/654-3131, www.hertz.com), National (800/227-7368, www.nationalcar.com), and Thrifty (800/367-2277, www.thrifty.com). Additionally, Enterprise Rental Car (3002 Mill St., Reno, 775/329-3773, www.enterprise.com) is located near the airport.

Travelers flying into Sacramento or the San Francisco Bay Area airports also have their pick of all the major car-rental companies.

Suggested Driving Routes

Visitors to Lake Tahoe coming from the west (Sacramento or the San Francisco Bay Area) should use Highway 50 to access the South Shore and I-80 to access the North Shore. Highway 50 splits off I-80 in downtown Sacramento, and travels east through Placerville and over Echo Summit to South Lake Tahoe (about two hours or 100 miles from Sacramento and 3.5 hours or 200 miles from San Francisco). For visitors heading to the North Shore, I-80 continues east from Sacramento for another 90 miles to Truckee. At Truckee, take Highway 89 south for 15 miles to Tahoe City.

Visitors traveling to Lake Tahoe from the east (Reno) can take U.S. 395 south for seven miles to Highway 431 west. Drive southwest on Highway 431 for 20 miles to Incline Village on the northeast shore of the lake. Or, to reach the South Shore directly, take U.S. 395 south from Reno through Carson City, then take Highway 50 west to South Lake Tahoe (about one hour or 60 miles). Or, to reach points near Tahoe City or the West Shore, take I-80 west from Reno for 32 miles to Truckee. In Truckee, connect to Highway 267 and travel south to the lakeshore at Tahoe Vista or Kings Beach (12 miles), or connect to Highway 89 and travel south to Tahoe City (15 miles).

To get current updates on road conditions on the California side of Lake Tahoe, phone 800/427-7623. To get current updates on Nevada road conditions, phone 877/687-6237.

One note: When crossing into California by automobile, all visitors are subject to agricultural inspections. These inspections are run by the California Department of Food and Agriculture (CDFA). The inspection may be as simple as an officer stopping your car momentarily to ask you where you have been traveling and if you are carrying any fruits, vegetables, or plants from other states. Be sure to declare anything you are carrying. In very rare cases, vehicles are searched. As a general rule, most out of state produce and plants should be kept out of California, unless they have been properly inspected by the CDFA. For more information on current regulations, phone the CDFA consumer help line at 800/675-2427.

RV RENTALS

The biggest and oldest RV rental company in Reno is Sierra RV (9125 S. Virginia St., Reno, 775/324-0522 or 800/972-8760, www.sierrarv.com). It rents RVs of all shapes and sizes, from 20-foot Class B motor homes that sleep only two to 35-foot motor homes that sleep eight. All are fully contained models with kitchen, bath, color TV, CD player, generator, and microwave. Pets and smoking are not permitted. The daily rate for three to six days is $120–195 (depending on the size of the rig); the weekly rate is $700–1,260. Keep in mind that as with most RV rental companies, you get only 100 free miles per day; you'll pay $0.29 per mile for the first 2,000 extra miles. Also, plan to spend a small fortune on gasoline—most RVs get 6–10 miles to the gallon. The smallest rigs may get a whopping 14 miles per gallon.

Another RV rental company is Reno-Tahoe RV Rentals and Sales (1565 Vassar St., Reno, 775/324-7368). If you'd rather go with a national chain, try Reno's Cruise America (85 Gentry Way, Reno, 775/824-0576 or 800/327-7799, www.cruiseamerica.com).

In Sacramento, RV rentals are available at Cruise America (located at B&L RV Parts and Service, 11 Quinta Court, 800/671-7839, www.cruiseamerica.com). Expect to pay about $500 for three nights in the low season (Oct.–May) or $650 in the high season (June–Sept.) for an RV that can sleep six people. You can save a little money by renting an RV for a week. Seven nights' rental will run about $1,000 during the low season, $1,400 during the high season. But don't forget to tack on the mileage fee—any mileage above 100 per day is charged at $0.29 per mile.

GETTING AROUND
By Car

Except on the most crowded summer days, driving a car around Lake Tahoe is quite easy. Parking, on the other hand, is another matter, especially at some of the top sightseeing destinations. If you are visiting the South Shore in summer, consider leaving your car at your lodging and taking the Nifty Fifty Trolley (530/541-7149, www.bluego.org). On the North Shore, public transportation is readily available through Tahoe Area Regional Transit (TART).

When visiting Tahoe from November to April, know that chains may be required on any road at any time. Always carry chains in your car and know how to put them on your drive wheels. To get current updates on road conditions on the California side of Lake Tahoe, phone 800/427-7623. To get current updates on Nevada road conditions, phone 877/687-6237.

Maps

For visitors to the South Shore, a street map of South Lake Tahoe, Stateline, and its environs is available for a small fee from South Shore visitors centers. Hikers, mountain bikers, and others who want to explore beyond the highways will want a detailed trail map, such as the Lake Tahoe Recreation Map or Desolation Wilderness Trail Map published by Tom Harrison Maps (415/456-7940 or 800/265-9090, www.tomharrisonmaps.com). These are available for a fee at most Tahoe outdoor stores and visitors centers or by ordering direct. Another good map for outdoor recreationists is the Lake Tahoe Trail Map by Adventure Maps (800/849-6589, www.adventuremaps.net), also available for a fee from Tahoe outdoor stores and visitors centers or by ordering direct.

Tours and Shuttle Buses

Discover Lake Tahoe Tours (530/542-1080, www.demotours.com, $35–40 adults, $25–30 children) offers narrated shuttle bus tours around the lake and to Virginia City most of the year. They also offer tours from the South Shore to Yosemite National Park and San Francisco.

In the summer months, the Nifty Fifty Trolley provides narrated tours combined with shuttle service along the length of the South Shore. The trolleys are open-sided buses—replicas of 19th-century streetcars with polished oak seats and brass poles—that allow riders to enjoy the fresh mountain air while they travel. Riders can get on and off as often as they like with a $3 all-day pass. Also in summer months, the Tahoe Trolley (800/736-6365, www.laketahoetransit.com) travels along much of the North and West shores.

The South Shore casinos offer their own free shuttles to and from most lodgings along the Highway 50 corridor. Most major ski resorts on both the North and South Shores also offer free winter ski shuttles from various locations to the slopes. Contact the individual resorts, or see the specific chapters in this book, for more information.

Numerous boat tours and cruises on the lake are available from both the North and South Shores; see the specific chapters for each region for more information.

Tips for Travelers

FOREIGN TRAVELERS
Entering the United States and California

Generally, citizens of foreign countries who wish to visit the United States must first obtain a visa. To apply for a visa, applicants must prove that the purpose of their trip to the United States is for business, pleasure, or medical treatment; that they plan to remain for a limited period of time; and that they have a residence outside the United States as well as other binding ties that will guarantee their return abroad.

However, under the Visa Waiver Program, citizens of 28 foreign countries do not need a visa for travel to the United States, provided they are staying no more than 90 days. The countries are: Andorra, Australia, Austria, Belgium, Brunei, Denmark, Finland, France, Germany, Iceland, Ireland, Italy, Japan, Liechtenstein, Luxembourg, Monaco, The Netherlands, New Zealand, Norway, Portugal, San Marino, Singapore, Slovenia, Spain, Sweden, Switzerland, the United Kingdom, and Uruguay.

As part of the customs process, the United States Department of Agriculture screens all foreign visitors at their first point of arrival in the United States (usually, at the airport). Foreigners must declare, in writing, all fruits, vegetables, fruit and vegetable products, meat, meat products, and dairy products that they have brought from another country. Failure to declare an apple or orange, or a leftover sandwich containing meat, can lead to a major delay in getting through customs.

Once a foreign visitor is inside the United States, he or she may travel freely from state to state. However, all visitors (foreign or not) are subject to additional agricultural inspections when entering California by automobile from bordering states. A California Department of Food and Agriculture (CDFA) officer may stop your car momentarily to ask you where you've been traveling and if you are carrying any fruits, vegetables, or plants from other states. In rare cases, vehicles are searched. Most out-of-state produce and plants should be kept out of California. For more information on current regulations, phone the CDFA consumer help line at 800/675-2427.

Finally, there is no compulsory or government insurance plan in the United States. Foreign travelers are advised to purchase travel and health insurance in case of an emergency.

Money and Currency Exchange

Most large banks in the United States exchange major foreign currencies. Several major American banks (Wells Fargo, Bank of America, and the like) are found in the cities of South Lake Tahoe and Tahoe City. Large international airports such as Reno/Tahoe also have currency exchange offices in their terminals.

While traveling in California, your best bet is to use traveler's checks and credit cards for purchases (both are accepted widely), and use an ATM (automated teller machine) to get cash. ATMs are found at numerous locations around the lake.

Electricity

Electrical current in the United States is 110 volts. A hair dryer or electric shaver from England

FUN WITH FIDO

There's only one place your dog wants to be, and that's with you. Why leave him or her at home when you go on vacation, when Lake Tahoe offers so much for a doggie to do?

First you need to choose a **pet-friendly lodging,** and this should always be done in advance of your trip, so you can be sure there is a space reserved for you and your dog. When making a reservation, always state clearly that you want to bring your dog, and inquire about the establishment's current rules and fees for pets. Lodgings can and do change their pet policies from time to time, so make sure you know what you are signing up for before forking over your credit card number. Some excellent dog-friendly accommodations on the South Shore are the Inn at Heavenly, Fireside Lodge, Motel 6, Best Western Timber Cove Lodge, Ambassador Motor Lodge, Super 8 Motel, 3 Peaks Resort and Beach Club, and Inn by the Lake. On the North Shore, a favorite spot for canine travelers is the cabins at Tahoma Lodge, although gam-

bling dogs prefer the Tahoe Biltmore, while rafting dogs prefer the River Ranch Lodge. Some lodgings charge a per night fee for your dog; some require a deposit; some don't require anything.

Budget-minded dogs will prefer to save money by **camping,** rather than enjoying a roof over their heads and HBO each night. Most campgrounds around the lake allow leashed dogs, except for a few private ones, like Camp Richardson. Advance reservations are a necessity at almost every Tahoe campground in the summer months, so be sure to plan ahead.

With your lodging secured, you and your pooch are ready to have fun at Lake Tahoe. If you have a swimming dog, take him or her for a **dog paddle** in some of the calmer waters around the lake. A few of the best beaches where dogs are permitted are at Fallen Leaf Lake on the South Shore, Kiva Beach on the southwest shore, Chimney and Secret beaches on the East Shore, and Lake Forest Beach on

or Germany won't work here without an adapter, which is available at most travel stores.

Foreign Language Assistance

Within the United States, you may phone 888/US1-INFO (888/871-4636) for free access to emergency services and travel assistance in more than 140 languages.

California and Nevada Laws

You must be 21 years of age to purchase and/or drink alcohol in California or Nevada. Drinking and driving is a serious crime in both states; the simple act of having an open container of alcohol in your car, even if it is empty, is punishable by law. If you are arrested for driving under the influence of alcohol, you must submit to a chemical test to determine blood alcohol content.

Smoking is prohibited on public transportation and in all public buildings in California. Most restaurants and bars have no-smoking

policies. For the most part, you aren't allowed to light up unless you are in a private space, or outside in an open area. In Nevada, the opposite is true—smoking is allowed almost everywhere, unless a business has its own individual policy about smoking. You must be 18 years of age to purchase tobacco products in California or Nevada.

Gambling is legal in the state of Nevada for persons over the age of 21.

Taxes and Tipping

The Nevada state sales tax is 6.5 percent but local taxes as high as 1.0 percent are usually added on top of that. The California state sales tax is 7.25 percent, but local taxes as high as 1.25 percent may be tacked on, adding a total 8.5 percent to almost everything you buy.

At sit-down restaurants in either state, it is customary to tip 15 percent on top of the bill. The tip is your payment to your food server for the North Shore. If your dog is a retriever, don't forget the tennis balls.

Seafaring dogs have a couple of options at Lake Tahoe. If your dog has good balance and won't tip the boat over, you can take him or her **kayaking** along the Tahoe lakeshore. A company called Kayak Tahoe leads guided kayak tours along the East Shore and Emerald Bay, and yes, good dogs are permitted. Or just rent a kayak and go out on your own (but if you have a big dog, make sure you rent a double kayak). Dogs are also permitted on the inflatable **rafts** that float down the Truckee River from Tahoe City to River Ranch. And dogs and their people can ride as passengers on the **boat taxi** at Echo Lake ($3 for dogs, more for humans). Take the boat to the far side of the upper lake, then hike back along the shoreline; or, if you have a lazy dog, ride the boat both ways.

Of course, some dogs simply aren't seaworthy. If your dog is a landlubber through and through, take him or her for a romp in the woods instead. Dogs are allowed on all **trails** in Tahoe National Forest and Desolation Wilderness, but not on trails in state parks like D. L. Bliss and Emerald Bay. For an experience your dog can brag about when he gets back home, take him for a ride on the **cable car** at Squaw Valley USA (there is no charge for leashed, well-behaved dogs), then hike back downhill through beautiful Shirley Canyon.

When it's time for **dinner,** there are a few outdoor spots where your dog may be able to join you, but always check with the restaurant management beforehand. One spot where hip, friendly dogs are often spotted is at the lakeside patio at the Watermark Cafe and Wine Bar in Ski Run Marina. Don't let your dog sample any of the wine flights, though. Another popular dog-friendly spot is at the picnic tables outside of Sprouts Cafe in South Lake Tahoe. On the North Shore, dogs have been known to sample the gourmet cuisine on the back deck of the Black Bear Tavern.

good service. Most servers count on your tip as part of their day's pay.

TRAVELING BY RV

Recreational vehicles (RVs) are welcome at Lake Tahoe, although some drivers may find it difficult to negotiate them on mountain roads and through the lakeshore traffic. If you are planning to camp in your RV, check the *Accommodations* sections of this book to see which campgrounds have sites specifically for RVs, including hookups and dump stations.

TRAVELING WITH CHILDREN

Families and Lake Tahoe are a perfect match. Tahoe is an ideal place to teach kids about nature and the environment. Kids invariably have fun in the outdoors, and with all the kid-friendly activities around the lake, parents are never left wondering what to do with their charges. At Tahoe, kids can go for hikes, climb on rocks, help with camp chores, learn about the local flora and fauna, ride bikes, toast marshmallows, go rafting, ride horses, go skiing or sledding or snowboarding, or just hang out in a meadow and be kids. The list of possible activities for kids at Lake Tahoe is endless—just as it is for adults.

TRAVELING WITH PETS

Traveling with your pet to Lake Tahoe is a reasonable proposition. Some (but not many) lodgings allow pets, and most campgrounds do as well. Always contact lodgings in advance to make sure they permit pets, and to let them know that you plan to bring yours. Where pets are allowed, there is often an additional fee or deposit charged. Remember that if you choose to camp with your pet, he or she should be in your tent, RV, or car at night, or you risk having your pet tangle with a bear or other wild animal. Pets should never be left unattended at any time.

HEALTH AND SAFETY

If you should happen to have a medical problem while you are visiting Lake Tahoe, you'll be in good hands. Several hospitals and 24-hour emergency medical centers are located around the lake. On the South Shore, there is Barton Memorial Hospital (2170 South Ave., South Lake Tahoe, 530/541-3420, www.bartonhealth.org) as well as two 24-hour emergency-care centers: Tahoe Urgent Care (2130 Hwy. 50, South Lake Tahoe, 530/541-3277) and Stateline Medical Center (155 Hwy. 50, Stateline, 775/588-3561 or 530/543-5700).

On the North and East Shores, there is Tahoe Forest Hospital (10121 Pine Ave. at Donner Pass Rd., Truckee, 530/587-6011 or 800/733-9953, www.tfhd.com), Incline Village Community Hospital (880 Alder Ave., Incline Village, 775/833-4100, www.tfhd.com), or Incline Village Urgent Care (995 Tahoe Blvd./Hwy. 28, Incline Village, 775/833-2929).

By far the biggest dangers to be faced at Lake Tahoe are those created by visitors who don't follow posted rules and regulations. If a sign says "Stay Back from the Edge," obey it. Be wary of waterfalls, slick hiking trails, and cliffs and ledges with steep drop-offs. Remain on the trails to avoid getting lost or getting yourself into a hazardous situation. Always carry a good trail map. If you are heading out for a hike, tell someone where you are going and when you will be back. Carry a pack filled with the essentials for a day out, and a few emergency items.

A few more rules to live by: Don't drink water from streams and lakes without purifying it; carry and use a filter for purifying water from natural sources, or pack along bottled water. While you're at it, take along extra water and food; if you don't need it, you can give it to someone else who does.

While hiking, be aware of your surroundings: Pay attention to the direction you've traveled and landmarks you've passed. Keep an eye out for approaching storms, and stay off exposed ridges and peaks if a thunderstorm is threatening. Watch yourself and your companions for symptoms of altitude sickness and problems encountered from high elevation.

INFORMATION AND SERVICES

If you've just arrived in town, the best sources for all-around information, maps, and brochures are the South Lake Tahoe Chamber of Commerce (3066 Hwy. 50, South Lake Tahoe, 530/541-5255, www.tahoeinfo.com), the North Lake Tahoe Chamber of Commerce (245 N. Lake Blvd., Tahoe City, 530/581-6900, www.tahoefun.org), the Tahoe-Douglas Chamber and Visitor Center (195 Hwy. 50, Zephyr Cove, 775/588-4591, www.tahoechamber.org), and the Incline Village/Crystal Bay Visitors Bureau (969 Hwy. 28, Incline Village, 775/832-1606, 800/GO-TAHOE, or 800/468-2463, www.gotahoe.com). For information about Truckee and nearby areas, try the Truckee Donner Visitors Center (10065 Donner Pass Rd., Truckee, 530/587-2757, www.truckee.com).

RESOURCES
Suggested Reading

GEOLOGY

Hill, Mary. *Geology of the Sierra Nevada.* University of California Press, 1975. Even though it is more than 30 years old, this useful book is still of great interest to Tahoe hikers and travelers with inquiring minds who marvel at glacially sculpted wonders such as Emerald Bay, and the granitic and volcanic peaks surrounding Lake Tahoe. Multiple illustrations and photos help to explain the results of the forces of geology in action.

Königsmark, Ted. *Geologic Trips: Sierra Nevada.* Bored Feet Press, 2003. Written for the layman, this book interprets more than 100 of the most famous geologic landmarks in the Sierra Nevada, from Half Dome in Yosemite to Emerald Bay and Cave Rock at Lake Tahoe. It's a fun read even for those who are geologically challenged.

HUMAN HISTORY

Calabro, Marian. *The Perilous Journey of the Donner Party.* Clarion Books/Houghton Mifflin, 1999. For children who want to learn more about the tragedy of the Donner Party, this book tells the tale from the perspective of 13-year-old Donner Party survivor Virginia Reed. The author includes an epilogue on many of the party's survivors, and reprints in its entirety a letter written by Virginia after she was rescued. The book won a California Library Association Beatty Award for a young-adult book that promotes awareness of California history.

Dixon, Kelly J. *Boomtown Saloons: Archaeology and History in Virginia City.* University of Nevada Press, 2005. This scholarly but approachable account of the excavation of four historic saloon sites in Virginia City presents scientific evidence of what life was truly like in the great silver-mining era. Using historical photographs and maps and modern-day technology such as DNA analysis, the author's research supports the theory that Western saloons were not as wild as legend leads us to believe, but rather that they served an important and complex social role in their communities.

Donner, Houghton, Eliza P. *The Expedition of the Donner Party and Its Tragic Fate.* University of Nebraska Press, 1997. Originally published in 1911, this book was written by George Donner's youngest daughter, Eliza, who was only four years old at the time of the Donner Party's ill-fated journey. Her recollections were later substantiated by her older siblings and other survivors. She also recounts parts of her life story after the party's rescue, detailing the difficulties of being known as a member of the infamous Donner family.

Frohlich, Robert. *Mountain Dreamers: Visionaries of Sierra Nevada Skiing.* Coldstream Press, 1997. Ski aficionados will enjoy this account of the development and promotion of ski resorts at Lake Tahoe, Yosemite, and elsewhere around the Sierra. The story begins with the original 12-foot-long wooden skis, the first rope tows, and the introduction of the American public to skiing, and leads up to today's high-tech equipment and megaresorts.

Frohlich, Robert, and Humphries, S. E. *Skiing with Style: Sugar Bowl 60 Years.* Coldstream Press, 1999. The story of one of the oldest and grandest ski resorts in the West is told in detail, complete with more than 100 black-and-white photographs and quotes from Sugar Bowl's first investors, ski instructors, and managers. The focus of the book is on Hannes Schroll, the man who in the 1930s envisioned and created a European-style resort similar to those from his native Austria, but many other characters who played a part in Sugar Bowl's history also are featured.

Landauer, Lyndall Baker. *The Mountain Sea: A History of Lake Tahoe.* Flying Cloud Press, 1996. Written by a respected historian and past editor of the Lake Tahoe Historical Society's newsletter, this is the most complete version of Lake Tahoe's history in print. For readers who wish to learn more about Tahoe's resort era, the Comstock boom and subsequent development of roads around the lake, the grand steamships of the late 19th century, or the beginning of the gambling era, this hard-to-find book is the ultimate reference.

Lavender, David. *Snowbound: The Tragic Story of the Donner Party.* Holiday House, 1996. A kid-friendly book covering the chronicles of the ill-fated Donner Party, featuring dozens of black-and-white photographs and illustrations. Unlike many Donner Party books, this one focuses more on the overall dangers and hardships of emigrant travel than on the infamous Donner cannibalism, providing a more general description of the suffering endured by the pioneer wagon trains that crossed the Sierra Nevada in the mid-19th century.

Lekisch, Barbara. *Embracing Scenes About Lakes Tahoe and Donner: Painters, Illustrators, and Sketch Artists, 1855–1915.* Great West Books, 2003. Providing an unusual take on Tahoe history, this book contains brief biographies, diary entries, and letters of more than 150 artists who drew their inspiration from the Tahoe region, including reproductions of their paintings, illustrations, and sketches.

Lekisch, Barbara. *Tahoe Place Names: The Origin and History of Names in the Lake Tahoe Basin.* Great West Books, 1988. This is the book you need if you find yourself wondering what "Tallac" means (it is "Great Mountain," and it's the only mountain at Lake Tahoe that has a Washoe name) or pondering the origin of the moniker "Heavenly Valley" (it was a purely commercial invention, thought up by the ski resort's marketing team). The book also serves as a great introduction to Tahoe's long and varied history; for example, descriptions of Snowshoe Thompson's remarkable feats are listed under the Thompson Peak entry. The January–February 1844 diary of Charles Preuss, who with explorer John Fremont was one of the first white men to see Lake Tahoe, is reprinted as an appendix.

McLaughlin, Mark. *Sierra Stories: True Tales of Tahoe,* and *Sierra Stories: True Tales of Tahoe Volume Two.* Mic Mac Publishing, 1997 and 1998. A series of short and fascinating biographies of some of Tahoe's most interesting characters, including "Lucky" Baldwin, Nelly Bly, Mark Twain, D. L. Bliss, a ragtag assortment of miners, and the bold pioneer women of the West.

Mullen, Frank Jr. *The Donner Party Chronicles: A Day-to-Day Account of a Doomed Wagon Train, 1846–1847.* Nevada Humanities Committee, 1997. Of the dozens of books available on the Donner Party tragedy, this one also serves as a guide to present-day evidence of the Emigrant Trail, including color photographs of still-existing wagon ruts and landmarks. The author provides a day-by-day chronicle of the Donner Party's travels from the Midwest to California, following the misleading route advice of an enterprising land speculator.

Oberding, Janice. *Legends and Ghosts of the Lake Tahoe Area.* Thunder Mountain Productions Press, 2004. Written by an expert on ghosts and paranormal activity, this volume tells the ghostly stories of Tahoe travelers and visitors from the Donner Party to Marilyn Monroe. If you ever suspected that the Cal-Neva Resort or the Thunderbird Lodge might be haunted, this book is for you.

Scott, Edward B. *The Saga of Lake Tahoe: A Complete Documentation of Lake Tahoe's Development Over the Last 100 Years.* Sierra-Tahoe Publishing Company, 1957. Part history book and part photo collection, this volume documents Lake Tahoe's history from 1857 to 1957, with nearly 300 photographs and a large foldout map of the lake. It includes authentic images of the Bonanza Trail, Tahoe lumber industry, and the steamships and wooden vessels that once sailed Tahoe's waters.

Stewart, George R. *Ordeal by Hunger: The Story of the Donner Party.* Mariner Books, 1992. Written by a noted historian who taught for more than 50 years at the University of California, Berkeley, this book is considered to be the definitive history of the Donner Party's trials. Stewart incorporates the survivors' diaries and other historical documents in his account.

Strong, Douglas Hillman. *Tahoe: An Environmental History.* University of Nebraska Press, 1984. The only book available that details Tahoe's complex environmental problems and their historical origins, this book is a fascinating account of the damage done by 19th century logging and farming and 20th-century urbanization, and the difficult political and scientific processes required to preserve the lake today.

Wheeler, Sessions, and Bliss, William W. *Tahoe Heritage: The Bliss Family of Glenbrook, Nevada.* University of Nevada Press, 1997. More than a century ago, Duane L. Bliss, the namesake of the West Shore's D. L. Bliss State Park, built a lumber empire on the shores of Lake Tahoe. This story tells Bliss's enterprising story, including his transition from lumber baron to railway builder to owner of the renowned Glenbrook Inn.

NATURAL HISTORY

Arno, Stephen F. *Discovering Sierra Trees.* Yosemite Association and Sequoia Natural History Association, 1973. Beautifully illustrated, this brief, 89-page tree guide gives thorough and easily digestible descriptions of 19 conifers and 17 broad-leaved trees of the Sierra. The author's lyrical writing is a pleasure, even if you are far from the nearest Jeffrey pine or mountain hemlock.

Blackwell, Laird R. *Wildflowers of the Tahoe Sierra: From Forest Deep to Mountain Peak.* Lone Pine Publishing, 1997. This compact and indispensable wildflower guide, written by a Sierra Nevada College professor, details the common colorful blooms of the Tahoe Basin. High-quality color photographs and descriptive text make it easy to identify more than 100 flowers.

Carville, Julie Stauffer. *Hiking Tahoe's Wildflower Trails.* Lone Pine Publishing, 1989. A longtime resident of Tahoe, author Julie Carville shares her local knowledge about where to see the best wildflower displays. A combination hiking-trail book and wildflower field guide, this book describes in detail a variety of hikes for all ability levels and nearly 300 wildflowers that you may see along the trails. Featuring more than 100 illustrations and some color photos, this book was previously published by Mountain Gypsy Press and titled *Lingering in Tahoe's Wild Gardens: A Guide to Hundreds of the Most Beautiful Wildflower Gardens of the Tahoe Region.*

Graf, Michael. *Plants of the Tahoe Basin: Flowering Plants, Trees, and Ferns.* University of California Press, 1999. Filled with hundreds of beautiful full-color photographs, this comprehensive guide covers more than 600 species of flowering plants, the majority being wildflowers. The book is organized taxonomically (alphabetized by scientific classification) rather than by flower color, which may prove challenging to beginners, yet is a great way learn about plant families, genera, and species. For each flower, identification clues are provided, as well as notes on where in the Tahoe Basin to find it.

Haulenbeek, Rod. *Tree Adventures at Tahoe.* Wide Eyed Publications, 1995. In this small self-published volume, the author takes readers on an intimate tour of Tahoe's most interesting trees. The book serves as a personal travel companion, pointing out not just interesting facts about the trees but also the highways, towns, geology, and wildlife around them.

Horn, Elizabeth L. *Sierra Nevada Wildflowers.* Mountain Press Publishing Company, 1998. Good photographs accompany descriptions of more than 300 species of flowering plants and shrubs. Unlike most flower identification guides, this one is organized alphabetically by scientific classification (not by color of flower), which could prove problematic for novices. Still, the photographs and descriptions are useful, and the information is solid.

Paruk, Jim. *Sierra Nevada Tree Identifier.* Yosemite Association, 1997. This practical guide to the Sierra's 20 conifers and 24 broad-leaved trees provides useful tips on tree identification as well as an interesting natural history of each species.

Stokes, Donald and Lillian. *Field Guide to Birds: Western Region.* Little, Brown, and Company, 1996. Utilizing more than 900 full color photographs, the Stokes have created a nonintimidating bird guidebook that is respected by novice and expert birders alike. General identification information is provided for each species, as well as feeding, nesting, and other characteristic behaviors.

Tekiela, Stan. *Birds of California Field Guide.* Adventure Publications, 2003. This pocket-sized guide is easy to carry along the trail and includes gorgeous close-up photos of each bird. Although it is not as comprehensive as the Stokes guide, it's a better choice for hikers and backpackers.

Wiese, Karen. *Sierra Nevada Wildflowers.* Falcon Publishing, 2000. This wildflower guide is loaded with clear, easy-to-see photographs of more than 230 wildflowers specific to the Sierra Nevada Mountains. In addition to the expected descriptive information, each listing includes an explanation of the flower's genus or species name and other interesting facts.

OUTDOOR RECREATION

Bonser, Carol, and Miskimins, R. W. *Mountain Biking South Lake Tahoe's Best Trails* and *Mountain Biking North Lake Tahoe's Best Trails.* Mountain Biking Press/Fine Edge Productions, 1997 and 1998. These two slim volumes feature about 40 rides apiece in the South and North Shore areas. Although some of information is outdated, the books serve as a good general guide to trail rides around the lake, and both include useful appendices on mountain-biking skills, bike maintenance, and roadside repairs.

Carville, Mike. *Rock Climbing Lake Tahoe.* Falcon Publishing, 1999. More than 1,000 routes at a dozen major climbing areas around Lake Tahoe are described, including Donner Pass, the Truckee River Canyon, Christmas Valley, Echo Pass, Lover's Leap, Phantom Spires, Eagle Creek Canyon, East Shore Crags, Sugarloaf, Pie Shop, and Indian Springs. Due to the 1999 publication date, some of the information is outdated (access roads have closed; regulations have changed), but the maps and cliff drawings are excellent. Bouldering, top roping, and ice climbing are also briefly covered.

Haggard, Stephen Rider. *Fly Fishing the Tahoe Region.* Aquabonita Books, 2002. Everything a fly-fishing angler needs to know to fish 77 streams and 97 lakes in the Desolation Wilderness, Truckee and Carson River drainages, and other Tahoe regions. Includes information on hatches, directions and access, nearby lodging and services, and angling regulations.

Hauserman, Tim. *The Tahoe Rim Trail: A Complete Guide for Hikers, Mountain Bikers, and Equestrians.* Wilderness Press, 2002. Written with an enjoyable dose of humor, this book divides the 165-mile Rim Trail into eight segments, each described in detail, with attention paid to the needs of the trail's three user groups: hikers, bikers, and horseback riders. Worthwhile side trips off the trail are also described. The author is a member of the Tahoe Rim Trail Board of Directors and has walked every inch of the trail.

Jeneid, Michael. *Adventure Kayaking from the Russian River to Monterey, Including Lake Tahoe, Mono Lake, and Pyramid Lake.* Wilderness Press, 1998. Although this book includes only two kayak tours in the Lake Tahoe area, it features accurate instructions on put-in sites, suggested paddle routes and campsites, notes on the presence of powerboats or picnickers, information on local birds and wildlife, and a detailed map for each route. Armchair readers will enjoy the author's first-person kayaking anecdotes.

Jeneid, Michael. *Cross-Country Skiing California.* Wilderness Press, 2000. Covering 22 cross country ski resorts, including a half dozen near Lake Tahoe, this book has driving directions, a description of each resort's offerings, information on trail passes and rental fees, and suggestions on accommodations. A general introduction to cross-country skiing and a wealth of how-to advice is included. The author is a certified cross-country ski instructor.

Libkind, Marcus. *Ski Tours in the Sierra Nevada: Lake Tahoe,* and *Ski Tours in the Sierra Nevada: Carson Pass, Bear Valley, and Pinecrest.* Bittersweet Publishing Company, 1995. With tours for every level of cross country skier, from beginner to expert, these two books provide useful information for those who wish to kick and glide across dozens of routes around Lake Tahoe and Carson Pass. Each ski trail description includes clear directions to the starting and ending points, a topographic map, and ratings for overall difficulty, trail length, and elevation change.

McNamara, Chris. *South Lake Tahoe Climb-*

ing. Supertopo, 2004. This comprehensive rock-climbing guide to various sites near the South Shore (Christmas Valley, Echo Pass, Lover's Leap, Phantom Spires, Wrights Lake) includes lots of interesting climbing history, as well as practical where-to and how-to information and gorgeous climbing photos.

Pike, Charlie. *Paddling Northern California.* Falcon Publishing, 2001. This kayaking guide contains only a smattering of Lake Tahoe tours, but offers detailed maps with put-in information and trip landmarks, plus a useful introduction on how to prepare for a kayaking trip, and appendices of local paddling organizations and information resources.

White, Michael. *Snowshoe Trails of Tahoe.* Wilderness Press, 1998. Nearly 50 snowshoe trips around Lake Tahoe are described, complete with topographic maps of the routes. Each trip includes a difficulty rating, directions to the trailhead, and a detailed description of the route. The same Tahoe trails are covered in White's *Snowshoe Trails of California,* which also has 40 additional routes around Mount Shasta, Lassen Volcanic National Park, Yosemite, and the Eastern Sierra.

Yesavage, Jerome. *Desolation Wilderness: Fishing Guide.* Frank Amato Publications, 1994. Hikers and backpackers who want to catch golden, rainbow, brook, and brown trout in the Desolation Wilderness will be pleased with this diminutive, 64-page guide, which details more than 60 lakes. The book includes tips on what types of trout are found where and how to fish for them, plus where to find backpacking campsites (take the camping info with a grain of salt, however; the book is quite old and many regulations have changed). The author is active in CalTrout (a non-profit organization dedicated to preserving trout habitat) and an avid fly fisher.

PHOTO COLLECTIONS

Cameron, Robert, and Lerude. Warren, *Above Tahoe and Reno: A New Collection of Historical and Original Aerial Photographs.* Cameron and Company, 1995. One in a series of aerial photography books by Robert Cameron, this coffee-table book focuses not just on the natural beauty of Lake Tahoe and its environs but also the manufactured marvels of bustling Reno, Nevada.

Goin, Peter. *Lake Tahoe: Images of America.* Arcadia Publishing, 2005. This black-and-white photo collection is filled with historical images from Lake Tahoe's past, with accompanying commentary on each image.

Goin, Peter, and Raymond, C. Elizabeth. *Stopping Time: A Rephotographic Survey of Lake Tahoe.* University of New Mexico Press, 1992. This book puts Tahoe history in perspective. Photographer Peter Goin juxtaposes more than 100 of his modern-day photographs of the lake and its surrounding landscape with 19th-century archived photographs, creating a visual record of Tahoe's evolution. Writer Elizabeth Raymond supplies the historical text and photo captions.

Pesetski, Larry. *A Journey to Lake Tahoe and Beyond.* Sierra Vista Publications, 2005. This coffee-table book of stunning color images shows Tahoe in all four seasons and at all hours of the day. Many close-ups of plants and animals are also included.

Scott, E. B. *The Saga of Lake Tahoe, Volumes I and II.* Sierra-Tahoe Publishing, 1957 and 1973. These two volumes combine to create a detailed pictorial history of Lake Tahoe, featuring hundreds of Scott's black-and-white photographs.

Internet Resources

About Lake Tahoe
www.aboutlaketahoe.com

One of the few not-blatantly commercial Lake Tahoe tourism websites, this one focuses mostly on outdoor activities (skiing, golf, hiking, fishing, beaches, and the like) and less so on casinos, shopping, and nightlife. Accommodations and events are also included.

Classic Yacht
www.classicyacht.org
www.tahoeclassicyacht.org

This is the primary source for news and stories about the classic yachts in and around Lake Tahoe that are restored or currently undergoing restoration.

Dream Lake Tahoe
www.dreamlaketahoe.com

This highly commercial Tahoe website features a hodgepodge of links to vacation rentals, hotels, restaurants, and other vacation-related businesses.

Go Tahoe
www.gotahoe.com
www.laketahoechamber.com

The Incline Village/Crystal Bay Chamber of Commerce and Visitors Bureau sponsors these two websites, which include helpful visitor information (dining, recreation, attractions, and regional transportation) plus current events and local news for the Incline Village area.

Keep Tahoe Blue
www.keeptahoeblue.org

The website of the League to Save Lake Tahoe, this well-designed site includes background on the nonprofit organization, information on how visitors can help preserve Tahoe's water quality, current environmental issues at the lake, and interesting facts and news tidbits.

Lake Tahoe Concierge
www.laketahoeconcierge.com

This site's owners, Alpine Marketing, are the same people who manage the racks filled with color minibrochures advertising Tahoe businesses that are seen in every major hotel and motel lobby, and at visitors centers around the lake. Just like those wooden racks, this website has a wealth of listings and ads for ski resorts, accommodations, boat rentals, water sports, and almost every other commercial enterprise at Tahoe.

Lake Tahoe Hotels Online
www.laketahoehotelsonline.com

The domain name says it all. Magellan Vacations operates this website, which offers amenity details and reservation information for about two dozen of Lake Tahoe's biggest hotels, including the large casino properties and Squaw Valley's condo resorts.

Lake Tahoe Recreation
www.laketahoerecreation.com

Navigating through this eclectic site isn't easy, but if you click your way through the maze, you'll find an abundance of information on everything related to Tahoe, from bowling to the Flume Trail to ski area phone numbers. In addition to the usual commercial service listings, the site offers a rather random selection of useful articles on subjects as diverse as "Gasoline Prices at Reno and Lake Tahoe" and "Where to Kayak."

Lake Tahoe Reservation Bureau
www.tahoevacationguide.com

Managed by the Lake Tahoe Reservation Bureau, this website has information on 200-plus vacation rental properties on the South Shore—condos, town houses, and private homes—plus advice on skiing, casinos, lake cruises, and other vacation activities.

Lake Tahoe VIP
www.laketahoevip.com

This is yet another tourism-oriented Tahoe website that features ads and links to commercial enterprises such as golf courses, ski resorts, restaurants, lodgings, shops, and the like.

Lake Tahoe Visitors Authority
www.bluelaketahoe.com

The wellorganized website of the Lake Tahoe Visitors Authority, this site has web cams with live images of Lake Tahoe, historical informa-

tion, and a wealth of Tahoe visitor information, including where to stay, what to do, and climate and weather facts.

Nevada Commission on Tourism
www.travelnevada.com

The official site of the Nevada Commission on Tourism, this website has lots of travel-planning information for the Nevada side of Lake Tahoe, including outdoor recreation and accommodations.

North Lake Tahoe Resort Association/Tahoe City Chamber of Commerce
www.tahoefun.org
www.mytahoevacation.com
www.puretahoenorth.com

These three web addresses all lead to a site sponsored by the North Lake Tahoe Resort Association and Tahoe City Chamber of Commerce. This is the premier online reference for lodging and visitor information on the North Shore.

Reno-Sparks Convention and Visitors Authority
www.visitrenotahoe.com

The website of the Reno-Sparks Convention and Visitors Authority, this site will be of interest to people who are planning a stay in Reno or elsewhere in Nevada, with perhaps only a side trip to Lake Tahoe. Most everything you could ever want to know about Reno can be found here.

Ski Lake Tahoe
www.skilaketahoe.com

For the latest lowdown on Tahoe's biggest downhill ski areas, this one site can spare you a lot of extra surfing. Of particular interest is the "Hot Deals" page, where visitors can compare and contrast the current deals being offered at the big resorts.

South Lake Tahoe Chamber of Commerce
www.tahoeinfo.com

The website of the South Lake Tahoe Chamber

of Commerce includes visitor information (lodgings, restaurants, weddings, and activities) as well as background on living and working at Lake Tahoe.

Tahoe Activities
www.tahoeactivities.com

A potpourri of information is available at this site, not just on Tahoe activities as the name suggests, but also on lodging, real estate, casinos, nightlife, wedding planning, events, and almost anything else that's for sale at Lake Tahoe.

Tahoe Boating
www.tahoeboating.com

If you are a boater looking for information on piers, marinas, launching, charters, rentals, or fishing, or just want to know where you can tie up your boat and have lunch, this is your site.

Tahoe.com
www.tahoe.com

Because this all-encompassing website is the joint venture of several Tahoe area newspapers (*Tahoe Daily Tribune, North Lake Tahoe Bonanza, Tahoe World, Record-Courier, Sierra Sun, Nevada Appeal*), it's a great source for the latest intelligence on what's happening now at the lake. The site is updated daily and includes plentiful visitor information (lodging, dining, casinos, nightlife, outdoor recreation, travel tips) as well as news, feature stories, business directories, classified ads, and the like.

Tahoe-Douglas Chamber of Commerce
www.tahoechamber.org

The Tahoe-Douglas Chamber of Commerce sponsors this website, which is a useful reference for information on lodging, dining, shopping, events, outdoor and indoor recreation, and Tahoe history.

Tahoe Heritage Foundation
www.tahoeheritage.org

The Tahoe Heritage Foundation, which strives to preserve and protect the cultural and natural history of the Tahoe basin, manages this

website, which is chock-full of facts about the Tallac Historic Site, Taylor Creek Visitor Center, and Stream Profile Chamber, and events such as the Great Gatsby Festival. There is also an online bookstore where you can purchase Tahoe-related books.

Tahoe Integrated Information Management System
www.tiims.org

For current information on environmental planning and programs in the Tahoe Basin, the Tahoe Integrated Information Management System (TIIMS) website has the latest facts on complex issues such as transportation, fisheries, air quality, water quality, and restoration programs.

Tahoe Rim Trail
www.tahoerimtrail.org

The official website of the 165-mile Tahoe Rim Trail has useful tips on the trail itself, such as recommended short day hikes and how to plan for a circumnavigation of the entire loop. There is also a calendar of events including guided hikes and mountain bike rides, and information on how to become of member of the Tahoe Rim Trail Association, or take part in its Adopt-a-Mile or Adopt-a-Vista programs.

Tahoe's Best
www.tahoesbest.com
www.virtualtahoe.com
www.tahoereservations.com

As long as all the ads and pop-ups don't drive you insane, this site offers a wealth of information on all things Tahoe, from nightlife to weddings to real estate. Among many other possibilities, you can make lodging reservations online, check out current pictures from the Tahoe Sky Cam, or find out who is headlining at the casinos.

The Crag
www.thecrag.com

This site is a great source for online rock-climbing beta, not just at Lake Tahoe but at many other famous climbing sites around the world.

Index

HIKING

Internet access: 88-89, 156, 186
Internet resources: 240-242
Kahle Park: 31
kayaking: 54-55, 122, 173-174, 200
Kirkwood Wildflower Festival: 192
Knight, William Henry: 224
Kokanee Salmon Festival: 69
Lake Tahoe Autumn Food and Wine Festival: 180
Lake Tahoe Chautauqua: 180
Lake Tahoe Jazz Festival: 136-137, 180
Lake Tahoe Summer Music Festival: 137
laws and legal restrictions: 232
Logan Shoals Vista: 162
logging: 226-227

M
marinas: 55-56, 122-123, 174
Markleeville: 190
Markleeville Death Ride: 192
marmots: 219
Martis Peak Lookout: 101-102
medical care: general discussion 234; Carson Pass 209; East Shore 185; North and West Shores 156; South Shore 88
Memorial Point: 162
mining: 225-226
money: 231
mountain lions: 210-219
movie filming locations: 136
movie theaters: 68, 135, 179
Mr. Toad's Wild Ride: 54, 200
mule deer: 218
museums: Alpine County Museum 190; Children's Museum of Northern Nevada 180; Emigrant Trail Museum 99, 101; Fourth Ward School 164; Gatekeeper's Cabin Museum 97; Genoa Courthouse 165; Marion Steinbach Indian Basket Museum 97; National Automobile Museum 186; Nevada Historical Society Museum 186; Nevada Museum of Art 186; Nevada State Railroad Museum 180; 1960 VIII Olympic Winter Games Museum 99; Old Truckee Jail Museum 101; Pope Estate/Tahoe Classic Yacht Museum 32-33; Sierra Nevada Children's Museum 137; South Lake Tahoe Historical Society Museum 31-32; Tahoe Maritime Museum 99; Tallac Museum 32; Watson Cabin 98-99

NOP
National Championship Air Races: 186
nightlife: see specific place
North and West Shores: 12, 92-157; accommodations 138-147; entertainment and shopping 135-137; food 147-155; practicalities 156-157; recreation 102-135; sights 96-102
packing: 14-15
parks: see specific park; place
pets, traveling with: 232-233
pikas: 220
pine martens: 219-220
Pioneer Monument: 101
place names, origins of: 225
plants: 215-218
Ponderosa Ranch: 172
Pope-Baldwin Bike Path: 52
Pope Estate: 32
porcupines: 219
post offices: 88, 156, 185-186, 209

QR
raccoons: 219
rafting: 121-122, 200
railroad building: 226, 227
recreation: general discussion 17-24; see also specific activity; place
Red Fir Zone: 216-217
Reno: 186
Reno/Tahoe International Airport: 89, 156, 186-187, 209, 228
restaurants: see specific place
rock climbing: 59, 125-126, 175
RV travel and rentals: 229-230, 233; see also campgrounds/RV parks

S
safety precautions: 234
sailing: 55
Sand Harbor: 162, 174
seasons: 14
Shakespeare at Sand Harbor Festival: 179
shopping: see specific place
Sierra Safari Zoo: 186
skiing/snowboarding: 60-62, 127-131, 176-177, 202; see also Ski Resorts
sleigh rides: 66, 135
smoking: 232
Snow Festival: 137
snowboarding: see skiing/snowboarding
snowmobiling: 65, 133-134, 204
snowshoe hares: 219
snowshoeing: 63, 64, 132, 178, 202-204
South Lake Tahoe: see South Shore
South Lake Tahoe Airport: 89

MAP SYMBOLS

═══	Expressway	**C**	Highlight	✗	Airfield	≤	Beach
⋯⋯	Primary Road	○	City/Town	✈	Airport	⋙	Dive Site
⋯⋯	Secondary Road	⊛	State Capital	▲	Mountain	⚓	Anchorage
▭ ▭ ▭	Unpaved Road	⊛	National Capital	✦	Unique Natural Feature	**P**	Parking Area
– – –	Trail	★	Point of Interest			⚲	Church
⋯⋯⋯	Ferry	•	Accommodation	⇟	Waterfall	⚑	Gas Station
┼┼┼	Railroad	▾	Restaurant/Bar	⚑	Park	🗺	Mangrove
═══	Pedestrian Walkway	▪	Other Location	⊡	Trailhead	▱	Reef
▥▥▥	Stairs	▲	Campground	⚑	Golf Course	▱	Swamp

CONVERSION TABLES

°C = (°F - 32) / 1.8
°F = (°C x 1.8) + 32
1 inch = 2.54 centimeters (cm)
1 foot = 0.304 meters (m)
1 yard = 0.914 meters
1 mile = 1.6093 kilometers (km)
1 km = 0.6214 miles
1 fathom = 1.8288 m
1 chain = 20.1168 m
1 furlong = 201.168 m
1 acre = 0.4047 hectares
1 sq km = 100 hectares
1 sq mile = 2.59 square km
1 ounce = 28.35 grams
1 pound = 0.4536 kilograms
1 short ton = 0.90718 metric ton
1 short ton = 2,000 pounds
1 long ton = 1.016 metric tons
1 long ton = 2,240 pounds
1 metric ton = 1,000 kilograms
1 quart = 0.94635 liters
1 US gallon = 3.7854 liters
1 Imperial gallon = 4.5459 liters
1 nautical mile = 1.852 km

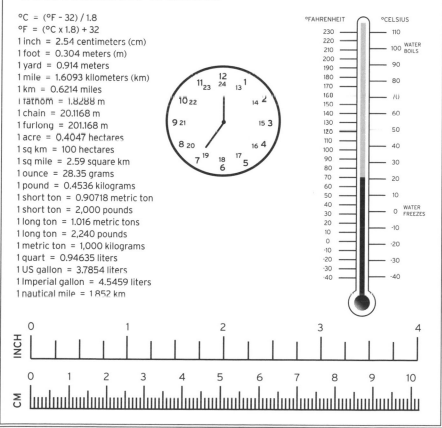

www.moon.com

For helpful advice on planning a trip, visit www.moon.com for the **TRAVEL PLANNER** and get access to useful travel strategies and valuable information about great places to visit. When you travel with Moon, expect an experience that is uncommon and truly unique.

MOON TAHOE

Avalon Travel Publishing
An Imprint of
Avalon Publishing Group, Inc.

AVALON
publishing group incorporated

1400 65th Street, Suite 250
Emeryville, CA 94608, USA
www.moon.com

Editor: Sabrina Young
Series Manager: Kathryn Ettinger
Acquisitions Manager: Rebecca K. Browning
Copy Editor: Gerardyne Madigan
Graphics and Production Coordinator:
  Domini Dragoone
Cover & Interior Designer: Gerilyn Attebery
Map Editor: Kevin Anglin
Cartographer: Suzanne Service
Cartography Manager: Mike Morgenfeld
Indexer: Greg Jewett

ISBN-10: 1-56691-933-9
ISBN-13: 978-1-56691-933-3
ISSN: 1542-5975

Printing History
1st Edition – 2000
3rd Edition – September 2006
5 4 3 2 1

KEEPING CURRENT

If you have a favorite gem you'd like to see included in the next edition, or see anything
that needs updating, clarification, or correction, please drop us a line. Send your
comments via email to feedback@moon.com, or use the address above.